736

PowerPoint 2000
Professional Results

D1249389

PowerPoint 2000
Professional Results

Ellen Finkelstein

Osborne/McGraw-Hill

Berkeley New York St. Louis San Francisco Auckland Bogotá
Hamburg London Madrid Mexico City Milan Montreal New Delhi
Panama City Paris São Paulo Singapore Sydney Tokyo Toronto

Osborne/**McGraw-Hill**
2600 Tenth Street
Berkeley, California 94710
U.S.A.

For information on translations or book distributors outside the U.S.A., or to arrange bulk purchase discounts for sales promotions, premiums, or fund-raisers, please contact Osborne/**McGraw-Hill** at the above address.

PowerPoint 2000 Professional Results

1234567890 DOC DOC 90198765432109

ISBN 0-07-211993-4

Publisher
Brandon A. Nordin

Associate Publisher andEditor-in-Chief
Scott Rogers

Acquisitions Editor
Joanne Cuthbertson

Project Editor
Emily Rader

Editorial Assistant
Stephane Thomas

Technical Editor
Ken Daley

Copy Editor
Nancy Crumpton

Proofreader
Karen Mead

Indexer
Rebecca Plunkett

Computer Designers
Gary Corrigan and Michelle Galicia

Illustrators
Brian Wells, Beth Young, and Robert Hansen

Series Designer
Peter F. Hancik

Cover Designer
Dodie Shoemaker

Cover Illustrator
Valerie Sinclair

This book was composed with Corel VENTURA.

To MMY, who taught me that enlightenment grows from within—and how to get there

About the Author

Ellen Finkelstein has written several computer books, including *AutoCAD 14 Answers! Certified Tech Support*. She is also a PowerPoint, Word, Excel, and AutoCAD trainer.

Contents at a Glance

Contents

Part III
Effectively Managing and Conveying Your Presentation

Acknowledgments

The creation of any book is a group enterprise, and this book is no exception. You would not be reading this without the contributions of many people. Some of the important contributions, such as the design, layout, production, and printing of the book, were made by people whose names I don't know, but I thank them anyway.

First, I'd like to thank Joanne Cuthbertson, Acquisitions Editor, who offered me the great opportunity of writing this book. Joanne came up with great ideas for the design and content of it, shaping it from beginning to end. Stephane Thomas, Editorial Assistant, coordinated every aspect of the book, always right on top of things and always cheerful. Stephane, you made it a pleasure!

Heidi Poulin and Emily Rader coordinated the production of the book, including keeping track of zillions of figures and illustrations (and the difference between them), copyediting schedules, and production schedules. I don't know how you do it, but I'm glad you do.

Ken Daley, thoroughly versed in both PowerPoint and the Internet, was my cheerful and competent technical editor. He came up with all sorts of good advice, most of which was incorporated into the book. Thanks, Ken!

I'm especially beholden to the professionals who freely (yes, freely) gave of their time and knowledge to write the "Advice from a Pro" essays throughout the book. You will find in these essays the expertise and experience of today's top experts in PowerPoint. Thanks to Claudyne Wilder, Stuart Friedman, Jon Hanke, Jennifer Rotondo, David Fine, Jim Endicott, Brian Reilly, William Bohannon, and George Torok. Brian Reilly also contributed Visual Basic for Applications code for Chapter 16.

Last, but certainly not least, I must thank my family for supporting me while I wrote. My husband, Evan, shopped, did countless washes, put the kids to bed, and dragged me away from the computer when I needed a break. My kids, Yeshayah and Eliyah, managed to put up with me being endlessly in front of the computer, except for Little League games, which I wasn't allowed to miss. I love you!

Introduction

Microsoft PowerPoint 2000 is a presentation program, which means that you create presentations that you develop and show on your computer. Presentations are like slide shows, but no physical slides are necessary. While almost all computer users are familiar with word-processing programs and many know what a spreadsheet is all about, many computer users have never used a presentation program.

All that is changing. The use of presentation programs is increasing geometrically. While design professionals once created most presentations, presentation programs such as PowerPoint have now made it easy for anyone to create an attractive, effective presentation in a few minutes. There are enough special features—such as clip art, sound files, and animation effects—to help you create a professional-looking presentation if you want to invest a little more time.

PowerPoint is the most popular presentation program available. PowerPoint 2000, an integral part of the Microsoft Office 2000 suite, has been updated to provide greater ease of use and a number of new features:

- New design templates
- A new view called *normal view*
- Graphical bullets
- Numbered lists
- HTML format as a second native format
- Broadcasting presentations in real time
- Placeholder text that automatically resizes to fit the placeholder
- Tables created within PowerPoint
- The Projector Wizard for setting appropriate screen resolution

Whether you're a new PowerPoint user or are trying to hone your existing skills, you'll find plenty about all of PowerPoint's features and how to use them to get professional results.

What's Special About This Book

PowerPoint 2000 Professional Results covers all the features you need to make using PowerPoint easy and productive and then goes further to explain how to make your presentations truly professional. In includes tips, pointers, and essays to give you the extra edge you need to create presentations that *communicate*.

I have designed this book to include not only the specific features of PowerPoint 2000 but also a great deal of information about designing and presenting slide shows that deliver the message effectively. This knowledge is contained in several features:

- **"Advice from a Pro" sections** contain, well, advice from a professional. They contain essays about such topics as using color, laying out a slide, creating clear charts, buying a projector, and so on.

- **Numbered steps** explain clearly how to accomplish complex tasks.

- **Annotated figures** lay out the steps needed to accomplish various tasks in PowerPoint.

- **"Tips"** offer you useful shortcuts or techniques. I give you some of my best advice here!

- **"Professional Pointers"** guide you to the wisdom of professionals.

- **"New in 2000" notes** let you know what features are new for PowerPoint 2000. If you already know PowerPoint, you can leaf through the book looking for New in 2000 elements to find just the material you need.

- **"Cross-Reference" notes** help you to quickly find related material elsewhere in the book.

Perhaps the most exciting feature of this book is the Slide Gallery. In full-color, the Slide Gallery helps you clearly visualize the effects used in the examples in the book. Most of the examples are real-life presentations created by users like you. Not only do you learn how to create the effects in the examples, but you can mine them for ideas and inspiration as well.

Who Needs This Book

I have designed this book for beginning and intermediate users who are familiar with Microsoft Windows (95, 98, or NT). For readers who are just starting to use PowerPoint, *PowerPoint2000 Professional Results* explains the basics of presentation programs and brings you through the creation of your first complete presentation by Chapter 2. For those of you who have already used PowerPoint but want to expand your skills, this book provides you with everything you need to know about PowerPoint and about creating presentations.

This book starts out with the basics and then presents the rest of PowerPoint's features systematically and comprehensively. If you read it from cover to cover, it will bring you to an intermediate-to-advanced level of knowledge and skill.

How This Book Is Organized

The overall organization of *PowerPoint2000 Professional Results* is from simple to complex, from wholeness to specifics, and from start to finish.

Part I, "Creating a Presentation," provides you with the basics you need to use PowerPoint. By Chapter 2, you know how to create a complete presentation using the AutoContent Wizard. Chapter 2 also demonstrates how to choose a background design and start a presentation from scratch. The rest of Part I details how to edit a presentation as well as format bullets and paragraphs.

Part II, "Adding Dazzle to a Presentation," describes how to add graphics, tables, and charts to a slide and explains how to work with colors, borders, fills, and 3-D effects. It then shows you how to include repeating elements and how to make sure that all the slides in a presentation have a unified appearance. Finally, it teaches you about animation, slide transition effects, and multimedia (the use of sound and video).

Part III, "Effectively Managing and Conveying Your Presentation," brings your presentation out of PowerPoint and into the rest of the world where it must inevitably go. I explain how to incorporate data from other applications, how to develop a presentation collaboratively, how to display a presentation on the Internet, and how to customize PowerPoint. I end the book with two chapters detailing the actual presentation process, including how to time and rehearse your presentation, use projection equipment, and actually present the slide show.

How to Use This Book

If you are a beginner, you should start from the beginning and read until you have enough information to create your presentation. Try out the features as you read. If you need to create a specific presentation, start creating it from the very first chapter. As you continue reading, you can improve and refine your presentation, using the chapters that cover the features you need.

If you have used PowerPoint before but want to improve your skills and increase your knowledge, scan Part I for "New in 2000" notes before going on to Part II. You can then start reading from Part II or go directly to the chapters that contain the topics you need.

Have Fun!

PowerPoint is great fun to use! However you use this book, enjoy the process and the satisfaction you will get from creating effective, professional presentations.

Part I

Creating a Presentation

Chapter 1: Getting Started for Professional Results

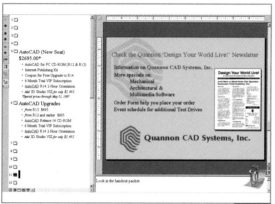

SLIDE 1

Normal view is the most flexible way to work; it shows you one slide, speaker's notes, and the text outline together on one screen. For more information, see "Using Normal View" and Figure 1-6.

SLIDE 3

Slide show view shows you only the slide so you can see how it will look when you present. You rehearse the presentation in this view. See "Using Slide Show View" and Figure 1-10.

Thanks to Jeff Walton at Quannon CAD Systems for this presentation. You can contact Quannon at 800-467-3467.

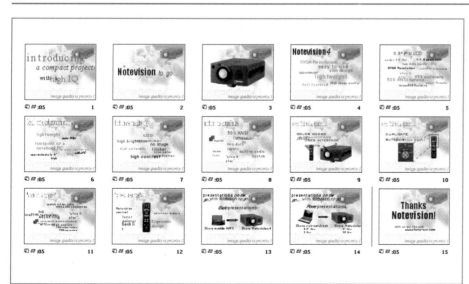

SLIDE 2

Slide sorter view lets you see all (or most of) your slides at once. It's the best view for deleting and reordering slides. See "Using Slide Sorter View" and Figure 1-9. You can also work with animation and timing in this view.

Thanks to Sharp Electronics for this presentation. You can contact Sharp about its projectors at 888-LCD-SHARP or visit the Web site at www.sharp-usa.com.

Engage your audience. Don't spend too long with the small talk, but this is your ice breaker to meeting with folks after the show.

The total time for this closing presentation is about 5-6 minutes. They have already been sitting for an hour and will not be excited about staying much longer.

SLIDE 4

Notes page view shows you your slide plus any notes you have written to yourself. You can use the notes to create speaker's notes, for supporting data, or for reminders. See "Using Notes Page View" and Figure 1-11.

Chapter 2: **Creating a Great First Presentation**

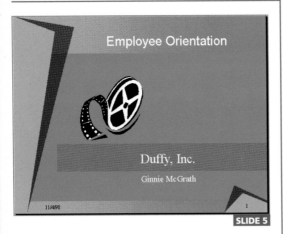

SLIDE 5

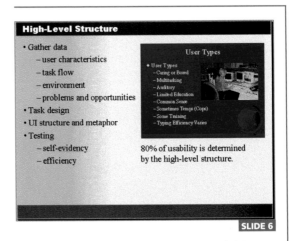

SLIDE 6

The AutoContent Wizard creates an instant, canned presentation. Use it when you need help organizing your content and need the presentation yesterday. See "Organizing Your Presentation with the AutoContent Wizard" and Figure 2-1.

The bulleted text was created using the text placeholder from the Text & Clip Art layout. It's easy to do and creates perfectly aligned and formatted text instantly. For details on text placeholders, see "Text Placeholders for Instant, Impressive Text" and Figure 2-5.

Thanks to Human Factors International (HFI) for this slide. HFI specializes in applying software ergonomics and human factors principles to software applications, Web sites, intranets, and graphical user interfaces to make them more usable. You can contact HFI at 800-242-4480 or visit the Web site at www.humanfactors.com.

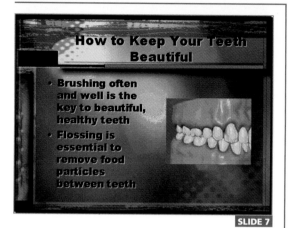

SLIDE 7

The label text in this slide was created using the text placeholder from the Text & Media Clip layout. The media clip contains a movie file. The text explains the concept and the movie plays to bring home the point in full-color animation. See "Text Placeholders for Instant, Impressive Text" and Figure 2-6.

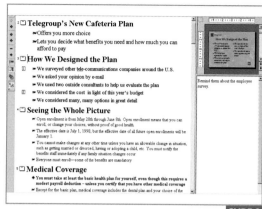

SLIDE 8

Working in outline view makes it easy to quickly create a complete presentation. You can easily view the flow of ideas from slide to slide. See "Creating Your Presentation from an Outline" and Figure 2-7.

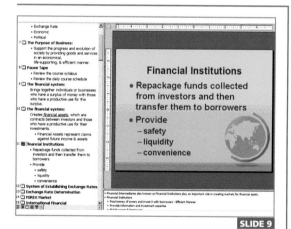

SLIDE 9

The outline is the key to organizing and developing most presentations. You can structure your entire presentation using the outline pane, then go back and add graphics and effects. See "Understanding Outlines" and Figure 2-8.

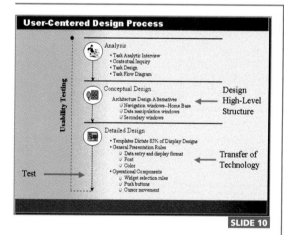

SLIDE 10

The label text was created using a text box. The text points out a section of the text at the center of the slide. The border and fill color were made invisible so that the text looks like it has been entered directly on the slide. See "Text Boxes for Flexibility" and Figure 2-11.

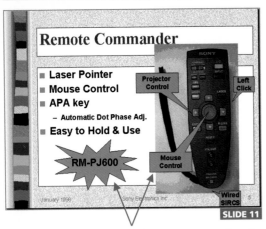

These AutoShapes contain text that is meant to stand out from the rest of the slide. See "Shapely Text in AutoShapes" and Figure 2-12.

This slide uses one of PowerPoint's standard design templates for a unified, attractive look throughout your presentation. To learn how to choose a design template, see "Choosing a Great-Looking Background Design."

Thanks to SONY Electronics for this slide, part of a presentation used for internal marketing purposes. You can contact SONY at www.sony.com.

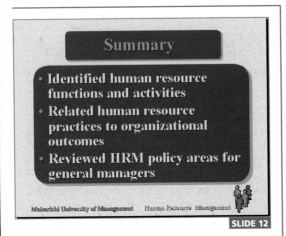

You can use AutoShapes instead of text placeholders for a bold appearance. The AutoShape uses an unusual orange shadow that matches the color scheme of the presentation. For information on AutoShapes, see "Shapely Text in AutoShapes" and Figure 2-13.

This text was created using WordArt, which creates fancy text effects. Use it for text that should jump out at the audience. See "WordArt for Razzle Dazzle" and Figure 2-14.

To edit text in a placeholder, you select both the placeholder and the text within the placeholder. The entire placeholder has a selection border and handles. Selected text is highlighted. You can now type the replacement text. Easy! See "Editing Placeholder Text" and Figure 3-1.

Thanks to Ruth Rabin and Lee Cohen of Trendlines International, and David Dodron of Hararit for this and the next two slides.

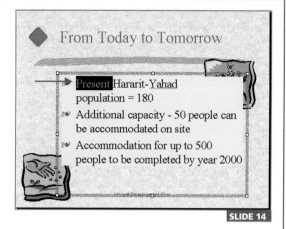

Pay attention to the case (capitalization) of your titles and body text. Titles usually have initial caps, but certain small words should be left lowercase.

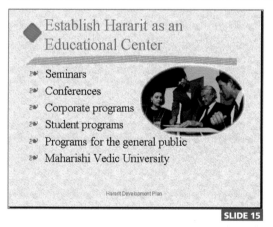

When you use PowerPoint's Change Case command, you still need to review the results.

Learn what to watch out for under "Changing Text Case" and Figure 3-3.

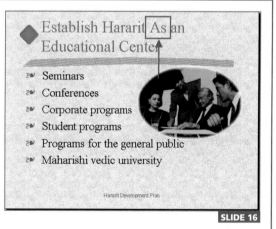

SLIDE 17

There's an art to choosing the right fonts. You should use only two or three fonts on a slide, and they should always be easily readable.

SLIDE 18

Don't use several fonts or hard-to-read fonts on a slide. It distracts from your message. For guidelines, see "Using the Right Font for the Message" and Figure 3-9.

SLIDE 19

Once you get the look you want, you can quickly copy it to other text, using the Format Painter. See "Copying That Great Look with the Format Painter" and Figure 3-12.

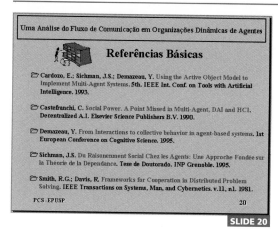

SLIDE 20

This slide, a bibliography, uses open file folders for bullets. The files represent holders of information and suit the topic perfectly. For details, see "Choosing Bullets" and Figure 4-2.

Thanks to Marcia Ito of Brazil for this slide.

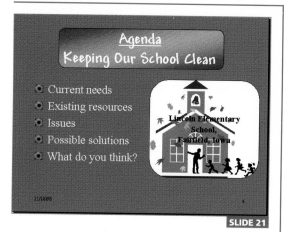

SLIDE 21

The bullets were created using a graphic file of a flower. Custom bullets are great fun, but learn the do's and don'ts under "Creating Custom Bullets."

The bullets were created using a GIF file of a rose. Bullets that relate to your topic can enliven a presentation and give a customized look. See "Creating Custom Bullets" and Figure 4-5.

SLIDE 22

Interbank Foreign Exchange Market

- Correspondent banks
- CHIPS - Clearing House Interbank Payments System
- SWIFT - International funds transfer system

SLIDE 23

Interbank Foreign Exchange Market

- Correspondent banks
- CHIPS - Clearing House Interbank Payments System
- SWIFT - International funds transfer system

SLIDE 24

You can control the distance between bullets and text using the markers on the ruler.

Don't move the text too far from the bullet or your audience will not see the visual connection between the two. For a step-by-step explanation, see "Indenting Paragraph Text."

Foreign Exchange Transaction

AmCorp, a U.S. corporation, purchases a product from BritCorp, a corporation in Great Britian. AmCorp agrees to pay BritCorp in British Pound Sterling £

SLIDE 25

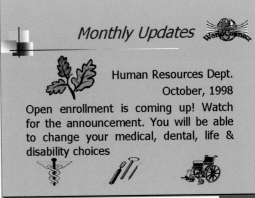

SLIDE 26

If you don't want any bulleted text in a placeholder, you should remove the hanging indent and create a blocked paragraph. The procedure is not intuitive, so see "Creating Paragraphs with No Hanging Indent" for the complete story.

While left-aligned text is most common, you can also center, right align, and justify text, as shown in this slide. It's easy to do: see "Aligning Text" and Figure 4-12.

Getting Started for Professional Results

Microsoft PowerPoint is all about effective communication. PowerPoint gives you the tools you need to create a professional-quality presentation. No longer do you need to spend big bucks for a graphic artist or a slide bureau to create presentations for you. You *can* do it yourself. This book explains how.

Microsoft PowerPoint 2000 is a *presentation* program. If you're a new user, you may not even be sure what that means. A presentation program creates slide shows, which you can then show on a screen or monitor directly from your computer. A PowerPoint file is called a *presentation*, and the individual unit of a presentation is a *slide*. Each slide is equivalent to a page, as shown in the slide show pictured in Figure 1-1.

PowerPoint 2000 is light years ahead of the traditional individual 35mm slides or overhead transparencies of yesteryear. For example you can:

- Add graphics, sound, music, and short video clips to maximize your impact
- Instantly make changes (similar to any computer document)
- Animate text or other objects to emphasize your point
- Create transition effects from one slide to another
- Instantly change the color scheme or background for an entire presentation or for a single slide

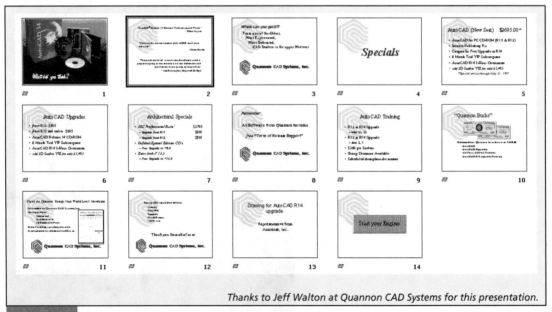

Thanks to Jeff Walton at Quannon CAD Systems for this presentation.

FIGURE 1-1 A presentation consists of a series of slides

- Add graphs and tables to make your point visually and clearly
- Create interactive and automatically looping slide shows—ideal when presenting at conventions and or using a kiosk
- Save your presentation in HTML format and publish it on the Internet or an intranet

Getting Your Message Across

As I indicated earlier, the purpose of a presentation is to communicate. Of course, you also communicate with your word processing documents. Even your spreadsheets communicate something from their numbers. But in a presentation, the process of conveying the message is the point. You use words, art, shapes, color, sound, and special effects to maximize the effectiveness of your message. It's called *multimedia*, and it's a hot, growing field. You may have never used multimedia tools before, but with PowerPoint, you easily get professional results. And with a little practice, you will soon be creating exciting, compelling presentations.

Why use multimedia anyway? A great deal of scientific research shows that visual aids and the use of color significantly increase the amount of material your audience understands and remembers. Moreover, presentations including visual aids and other multimedia effects have been shown more effective in convincing an audience to take the course of action suggested by the presenter.

Because it is now so easy to create great presentations, the number of PowerPoint users has skyrocketed in the last five years. PowerPoint presentations are everywhere, but customers, managers, and peers expect an ever-higher level of professionalism in the quality of the presentations they see. Come join the crowd (which includes your competitors), and start communicating professionally—this book will show you how.

Getting Started

If you have used PowerPoint before, you'll find that PowerPoint 2000 offers several new options for opening presentations. While the topic of opening a presentation may seem boring, the new options actually offer shortcuts to organizing your materials the way the pros do. The skills you learn here don't show up on your slides, but they will make your life a lot easier—and creating your presentation a lot smoother.

Well Begun Is Half Done

 The first step is to open PowerPoint. If you bought PowerPoint as part of Microsoft Office, the easiest way to open PowerPoint is to click its icon on the Office Shortcut bar.

If you don't have or use the Office Shortcut bar, the quickest way to open PowerPoint is with a shortcut that you create on your desktop. Here's how:

1. Use Windows Explorer to locate powerpnt.exe, which by default is in C:\Program Files\Microsoft Office\Office.

2. Right-click the file listing, and choose Create Shortcut.

3. Drag the shortcut, named "Shortcut to powerpnt.exe" to your desktop.

4. Click the shortcut name once, and then click it again (without double-clicking).

5. Type a simpler name, such as **PowerPoint**, for the shortcut.

6. Double-click the shortcut to open PowerPoint.

Of course, if you don't like shortcuts, you can open the PowerPoint icon by choosing Start | Programs | Microsoft PowerPoint 2000.

> **Tip:** You can set both Windows 95 and 98 to require only a single click. Choose Start | Settings | Control Panel | Mouse. On the Step Savers tab, check the ClickSaver check box.

Using the PowerPoint dialog box

Once you have opened PowerPoint, you see the dialog box shown in Figure 1-2, which segues you to the world of PowerPoint.

The top half of the dialog box gives you three options for starting a new presentation.

- The AutoContent Wizard offers you assistance organizing the content, that is, the text of your presentation.

- Choose Design Template to select one of PowerPoint's many backgrounds. You can then start creating your presentation.

- Choose Blank Presentation to start from scratch.

> **Tip:** If you want to open a recently used presentation, you can choose Start | Documents, and click your presentation.

Cross Reference: All these options are covered in Chapter 2, where you learn how to create a new presentation.

Using the Open dialog box

The bottom half of the dialog box lets you open an existing presentation. PowerPoint lists the presentations you opened most recently. Choose one, and click OK to open it. Your presentation opens displaying the last saved slide and view so you can go to work right where you left off.

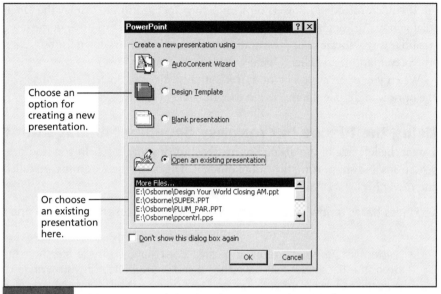

Choose an option for creating a new presentation.

Or choose an existing presentation here.

FIGURE 1-2   The PowerPoint dialog box that appears when you first open PowerPoint

If your presentation is not listed, choose More Files and click OK. PowerPoint opens the Open dialog box, shown in Figure 1-3.

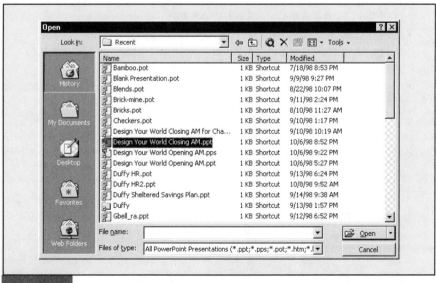

FIGURE 1-3   The Open dialog box lets you open a presentation from anywhere on your computer or network

If you are already in PowerPoint, click the Open button to display the Open dialog box. Although this dialog box has new features, you can use it in the same familiar way—locate your presentation in the Look In drop-down list box, click the presentation, and click Open.

When you open a presentation, if it contains macros, PowerPoint offers you the option to disable the macros in case they may contain a virus.

Using the Places bar for easy document management

Down the left side of the dialog box are five buttons that can help you find presentations and supporting files more quickly. Together, these buttons are called the *Places bar.*

New in 2000: The Places bar is a new option for organizing your presentation files and finding them quickly.

- *History* lists the most recently opened presentations. These are shortcuts from the Recent subfolder which is a sub-sub-subfolder in your Windows folder. If you keep presentations and supporting files all over your hard drive, the History button can be a savior when you're trying to find a file fast. Don't forget that the PowerPoint dialog box lists your most recently used presentations, too. It doesn't show as many, but if you can find a presentation there, you can skip the entire step of using the Open dialog box.

- *My Documents* shows you the contents of the My Documents folder. You can collect the documents you are currently using in this folder for easy access. When you first open PowerPoint, Documents is the default folder for opening and saving presentations. Unlike the Recent folder, you have to purposefully save and place files in My Documents.

- *Desktop* displays shortcuts and files you have placed on your desktop. Some users keep shortcuts to their current projects on their desktop so they can open them immediately with a double-click.

- *Favorites* lists the contents of the C:\Windows\Favorites folder. You can use the Favorites folder to place shortcuts to presentations (or other files) you use often. The files can be anywhere on your hard drive or network, but placing shortcuts all in one folder lets you find your files without having to navigate through drives and folders. Later in this chapter, I explain how to place a shortcut in your Favorites folder. This folder also includes shortcuts to Web sites that you have added to your Favorites list in your Web browser.

- *Web Folders* shows you the contents of the Web Folders folder, where you can organize Web-related documents in folders you create. The purpose of this folder is to store files you plan to publish on the Web.

Of course, you may organize your presentations in other locations. In that case, click the arrow to the right of the *Look In* drop-down list box, and navigate to your presentation. Click the desired presentation, and choose Open (or double-click the desired presentation).

Understanding the new Open options

You have some hidden options for opening a presentation. Two of them are especially useful if you are working on a networked computer.

New in 2000: The new drop-down arrow next to the Open button offers three new ways to open a presentation.

To use the new Open options, click the drop-down arrow next to the Open button, shown in Figure 1-3. You have the following options:

- *Open Read-Only* opens a presentation but doesn't allow you to make any changes. However, you can choose File | Save As to save the presentation under another name or in another location. Use this option when you are working on a network and someone else is currently working on the presentation you want to open.

- *Open as Copy* creates a duplicate of the presentation you choose in the same folder as the original and opens the duplicate. You can then make any changes you need.

- *Open in Browser* lets you open a presentation saved in HTML in your Web browser.

Tip: To open one of your four most recently opened presentations, you can skip the Open dialog box completely. Instead choose File, and choose the presentation from the bottom of the File menu as shown here.

Customizing the default file location

If you often work from one folder, you may wish to make it the default folder for the Open and Save dialog boxes. No longer will you have to navigate to your presentations and other files on your hard drive or network. Whenever you want to open or save a presentation, your preferred folder will be active in the dialog box.

To set the default folder, choose Tools | Options, and click the Save tab, shown in Figure 1-4. In the Default File Location text box, type the path for the default folder you want. For example, type **c:\presentations**. As you can see in Figure 1-4, the default is C:\My Documents. Click OK.

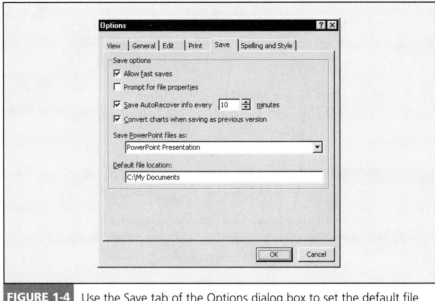

Use the Save tab of the Options dialog box to set the default file location

Using a presentation from the Osborne/McGraw-Hill Web site

If you would like to practice the skills in this chapter but don't have a presentation to work with, you can download two sample presentations from Osborne/McGraw-Hill's Web site. Cafeteria Plan is a simple presentation that you can easily work with. Note 4 is more complex because of its special effects. Go to **www.osborne.com/download/index.htm**.

Viewing a Presentation

PowerPoint professionals know all the tricks of the trade when it comes to using the PowerPoint window's features—the menus, toolbars, and buttons. They know the best way to view a presentation and how to move through a presentation like greased lightning. Here's how you can do the same.

Looking at the Screen

When you open a presentation, it appears exactly as it did when you last saved it. Figure 1-5 shows the PowerPoint screen and its elements. To understand the elements in Figure 1-5, refer to the numbered list that follows the figure.

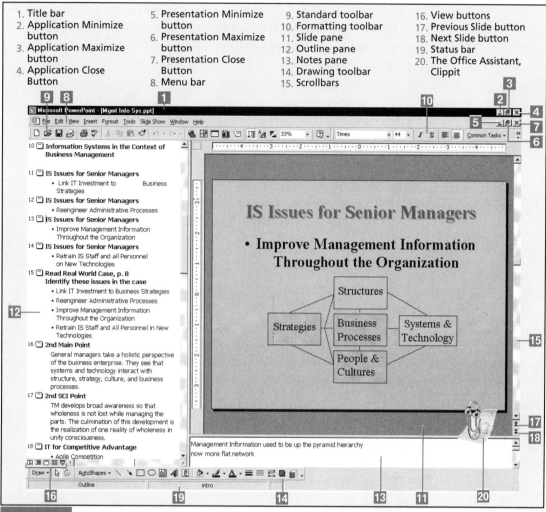

1. Title bar
2. Application Minimize button
3. Application Maximize button
4. Application Close Button
5. Presentation Minimize button
6. Presentation Maximize button
7. Presentation Close Button
8. Menu bar
9. Standard toolbar
10. Formatting toolbar
11. Slide pane
12. Outline pane
13. Notes pane
14. Drawing toolbar
15. Scrollbars
16. View buttons
17. Previous Slide button
18. Next Slide button
19. Status bar
20. The Office Assistant, Clippit

FIGURE 1-5 The PowerPoint screen

1. The title bar shows the name of your presentation.

2. Click the application Minimize button to reduce the application window to a button on the Windows taskbar.

3. Click the application Maximize button to make the application window smaller. Click it again to make the application window fill the entire screen. When you are working with more than one application or file at a time, making the window smaller lets you drag elements from one file to another. Chapter 11 explains this concept more fully.

4. Click the application Close button to close both the presentation and PowerPoint.

5. The presentation Minimize button collapses your presentation to a button on the Windows taskbar. The PowerPoint window remains unchanged.

6. Click the presentation Maximize button to display your presentation in a smaller window. Click it again to display your presentation full size.

7. The presentation Close button closes the presentation.

8. The menu bar contains the commands you give PowerPoint.

9. The Standard toolbar contains many of the most often used commands.

10. The Formatting toolbar mostly contains common commands for formatting text.

11. The slide pane shows the current slide.

12. The outline pane shows your bulleted text.

13. The notes pane shows speaker notes that you have created.

14. The Drawing toolbar contains commands for creating and editing graphics.

15. The scrollbars let you move backward and forward through your presentation.

16. View buttons let you change views. Views are covered later in this chapter.

17. Use the Previous Slide button to move to the previous slide.

18. Use the Next Slide button to move to the next slide.

19. The status bar tells you what pane you are in. If you are in a slide pane, the status bar tells you which number slide is displayed as well as the total number of slides, such as Slide 24 of 31. The status bar also displays the name of the *design template*, or background.

20. The Office Assistant, Clippit, provides help on PowerPoint. You'll hear more about Clippit and his friends in the section "Getting Help When You Need It," later in this chapter.

Getting the Most out of the Toolbars and Menus

As with all Windows programs, you use the toolbars and menus to tell PowerPoint what you want to do with your presentation.

New in 2000: The toolbars and menus have been updated for PowerPoint 2000. There are fewer toolbar buttons, but it is easier to add or remove buttons. PowerPoint automatically personalizes both the toolbars and menus as you work.

- Whenever you move a toolbar or resize the PowerPoint window, the toolbars may be reconfigured to show only the toolbar buttons you use. To view the other buttons for a toolbar, click the down arrow at its right end.

- Whenever you open a menu, only certain basic commands and the commands you have used are visible. To get back the rest of the commands, just place the mouse cursor over the down arrows at the bottom of the menu. You don't need to click—the rest of the commands magically appear.

Here you see the Tools menu in both its contracted and expanded states.

You can customize the toolbars any way you like. For further options, see Chapter 14.

All of the buttons in the toolbars are discussed elsewhere in this book, in their appropriate chapters. For now, you just need to know these two simple features that will make you a toolbar pro.

- Adding or removing toolbar buttons
- Displaying toolbars

Adding or Removing Toolbar Buttons

Follow these steps to add or remove toolbar buttons. To add other buttons or create your own toolbars, see Chapter 14.

1. Click the down arrow at the right side of the toolbar. The ToolTip says "More Buttons."
2. Move the mouse cursor over the Add or Remove Buttons command. A list of possible buttons drops down. Buttons currently displayed are checked. At the bottom of the list are other common buttons for that toolbar.
3. Click the button you want to add or remove.
4. Click anywhere off the toolbar to close the button list.

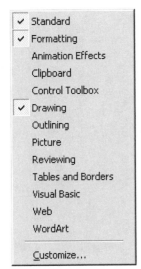

Displaying Toolbars

PowerPoint has ten additional toolbars that you can use. To display one of these toolbars, right-click any displayed toolbar to open the list of toolbars.

To display a toolbar, click any unchecked toolbar on the list. To hide a toolbar, click any checked toolbar. These toolbars will be discussed throughout the book where they apply.

Which Views to Use to Get the Job Done

PowerPoint offers six ways to view a presentation. You choose a view based on what you are doing. Using the right view provides the frictionless flow you need to get your work done.

Most commonly, you change views using the buttons at the bottom left corner of your screen, just above the Drawing toolbar and the status bar. The view buttons are shown here:

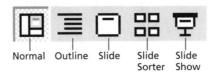

Normal   Outline   Slide   Slide Sorter   Slide Show

New in 2000: The normal view is new for PowerPoint 2000. It combines slide view, outline view, and notes view to let you work comfortably without having to change views often. The outline and slide views have also been enhanced to give you more information about your presentation.

If you wish, you can choose a view from the View menu.

Using normal view

Normal view, shown in Figure 1-6 (and number 1 in the Slide Gallery), combines a large view of an individual slide, speaker notes beneath the slide, and an outline of the text of the presentation along the left side of the screen. Each section of the view is called a *pane*. Each pane has a scrollbar if it cannot display all the material so you can scroll to any part of the presentation.

Note that text created in a text box is not included in the text outline. It is treated as a graphic object. See the next chapter for details.

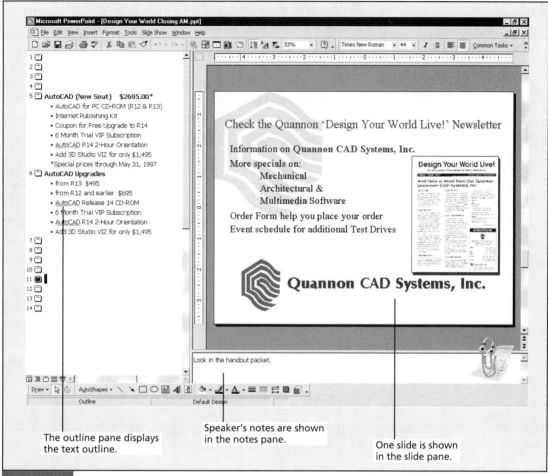

FIGURE 1-6   Normal view

You can use the normal view when you are creating or editing a slide, organizing and writing text, or creating notes for the presenter to refer to when showing the presentation. That's most of the time! The new normal view has made outline and slide views almost obsolete.

Tip: All the panes
are adjustable to your
preference. Place the
mouse cursor over the
dividing bar, and drag in
the desired direction. In
fact, normal view is so
flexible that you can make
it look like outline view or
slide view.

Quick navigation through a presentation is always the hallmark of a
pro. Here are some techniques:

- Use the scrollbar in the pane that you want to use. For example, to
  scroll through slides, use the slide pane scrollbar. As you drag the
  scrollbar, a ToolTip tells you which slide you're up to. Stop when you
  reach the one you want.
- Use the previous slide and next slide buttons.
- Click on the slide you want in the outline pane.

Press CTRL-HOME to move to the beginning of the presentation
and CTRL-END to move to the end of the presentation. When you move to a new
slide, PowerPoint automatically adjusts the outline pane if the new slide's text is
not visible. Similarly, if you scroll to the text of a different slide, PowerPoint automatically displays that slide.

Using outline view

Outline view, shown in Figure 1-7, has the same three elements as normal view,
but the proportions have changed. The pane containing the outline of the text is
largest. The view of the slide is much smaller, but the notes pane is larger than in
normal view. The emphasis is on text.

Use outline view when you are working on your text—and when the display
of the text in normal view is too cramped for you. You can make bulleted text
larger or smaller, move text around, change slide titles, work on speaker notes,
and so on.

You navigate through your presentation in outline view as described earlier for
normal view.

Tip: Because you
can adjust the panes in
outline view, you can
make it look just like
normal view. On the other
hand, if you are in normal
view and want to see
more text, you can drag
the divider between the
outline and the slide until
it looks like outline view.

Using slide view

In slide view you see a large pane showing an individual slide and a
narrow pane at the left showing slide numbers and an icon representing each slide, as shown in Figure 1-8.

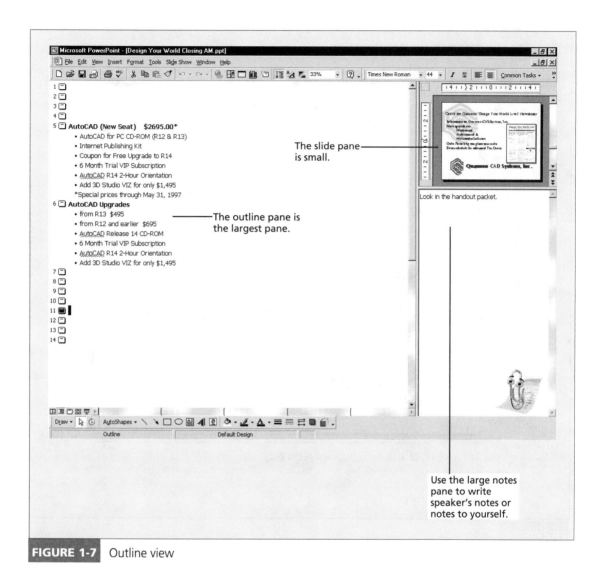

FIGURE 1-7 Outline view

Use slide view when you want the largest possible view of your slides. When you want to make precise adjustments to graphics on your slide, you may need a larger view of the slide.

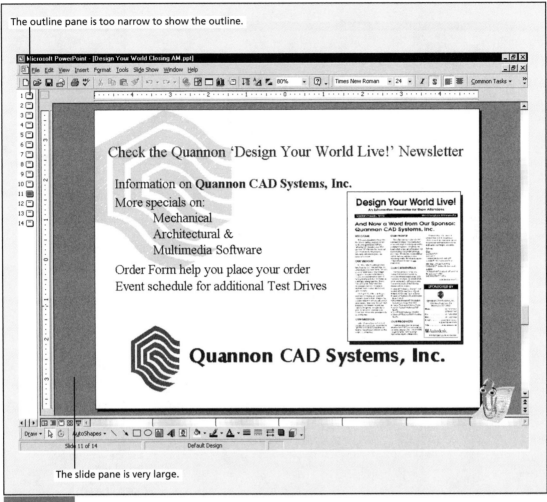

The outline pane is too narrow to show the outline.

The slide pane is very large.

FIGURE 1-8 Slide view

Interestingly enough, you can make this view look like normal view as well! While the notes pane is hidden, you can drag the bottom divider up to display it. And by dragging the left divider to the right, you display more of the notes. The opposite is true as well—you can make normal view (as well as outline view) look like slide view.

You navigate through your presentation in slide view as described earlier for normal view.

Using slide sorter view

Slide sorter view is quite different from the three views discussed previously. In slide sorter view, shown in Figure 1-9, you see a miniature view of all the slides at once. To view this presentation in color, refer to number 2 in the Slide Gallery.

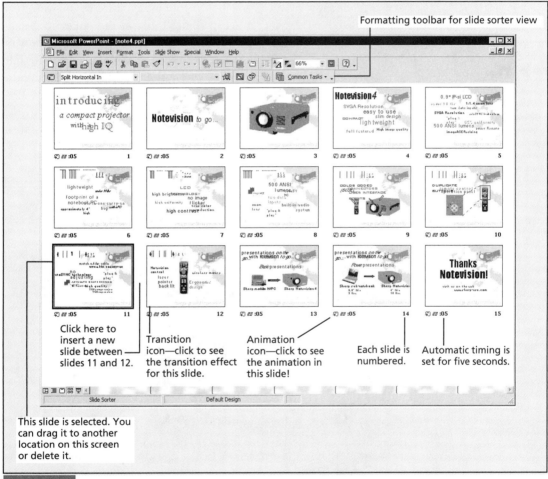

FIGURE 1-9 Slide sorter view

Slide sorter view is great when adding, deleting, and changing the order of your slides. You can also add timing and transition effects from one slide to the next. For this reason, when you switch to slide sorter view, PowerPoint displays a different Formatting toolbar, showing slide transitions, animation effects, etc.

Cross Reference: For details on adding, deleting, and moving slides, see Chapter 3. Transitions and animation are covered in Chapter 9, and timing is explained in Chapter 15.

Using slide show view

The last view, slide show view, lets you look at your presentation as you would see it during an actual show. As you can see in Figure 1-10, the slide takes up the entire screen. To view this slide in color, refer to number 3 in the Slide Gallery.

Tip: Double-click any slide in slide sorter view to switch to slide view for that slide.

Here's where you get to see the results of all your labor! Use slide show view to prepare for your presentation, including evaluating the results of your work and rehearsing what you are going to say. Preparing for a presentation is the subject of Chapter 15, but here are the basic techniques for moving around in slide show view. It is

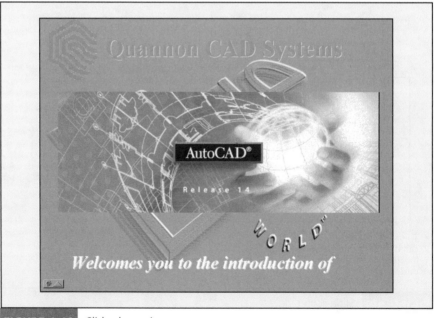

FIGURE 1-10 Slide show view

important to know these techniques because there are no menus, toolbars, or other obvious navigation tools.

Tip: Another way to open the pop-up menu is to move the mouse a little for two to three seconds until the icon shown here appears. Then click the icon.

- Press ESC to leave slide show view and return to your last view.
- Click the mouse to move to the next slide (or the next animation effect). When you click on the last slide, you automatically return to your last view.
- Right-click to open the pop-up menu. This menu lets you navigate to other slides, take notes or minutes, mark on the slide (temporarily) with an electronic pen as you present, change how the pointer looks and works, black out the slide, and end the show.

Using notes page view

Notes page view has no button, unlike the other view options; you can find it only on the View menu. It's helpful to print out notes pages to use for reference while presenting. Chapter 16 gives details on printing notes and handouts. Each page contains one slide and the speaker's notes for that slide. Figure 1-11 shows a notes page. To view this slide in color, refer to number 4 in the Slide Gallery.

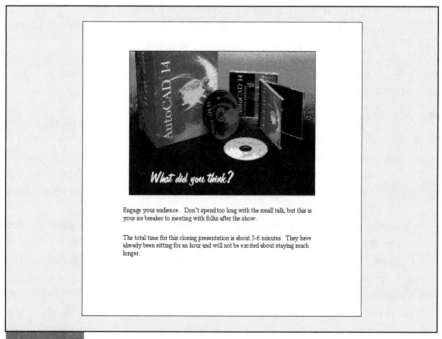

FIGURE 1-11 Notes page view

Notes are designed to support you as you present. However, you can also use them to write notes to yourself as you create your presentation or to include comments on the presentation for your boss or colleagues. Use your imagination, and you'll find many uses for notes in your presentations.

Getting Help When You Need It

No matter how familiar you are with PowerPoint, you will use the Help feature at some time or other. There are several ways to get help while you work. You can use the Office Assistant, a cute—or annoying (depending on your point of view)—animated character that answers your questions and offers unsolicited tips as you work. You can also try the three familiar forms of help—the Table of Contents, the Index, and the Answer Wizard.

Making the Office Assistant Serve You

The Office Assistant is a substitute for the Answer Wizard. It displays a lighted bulb when it thinks you could use a tip on how to work more effectively. To ask a question, click the Office Assistant to open the dialog box.

New in 2000: The Office Assistant now comes without a window and has new animation. Some new assistants are available as well.

Tip: If the Office Assistant obscures the help text you need, just drag it to another location

Sometimes several topics will be offered as suggestions, depending on what you are doing at the time. You can pick one of the topics or type a question or some keywords in the text box. When you have finished typing, press ENTER or click Search. Then pick one of the suggested topics. Long lists include a See More arrow to lead you to More topics.

Once you choose a topic, the help text opens up. To close Help, click its Close button at the top right corner of the Help window.

The last topic in the Office Assistant balloon is "None of the above, look for more help on the Web." If you click this topic, PowerPoint opens a separate Finding Help Topics window that offers search tips to help you phrase your question more effectively. You can also click Send and go to the Web to start your Web browser and go to Microsoft's Web site where you can ask your question online.

Managing the Office Assistant

The available assistants are shown here. OK, so your choice of office assistant makes no difference in your presentation—this is an issue of fun and sanity only.

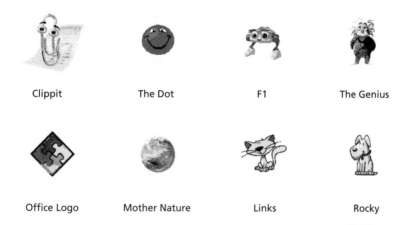

Clippit	The Dot	F1	The Genius
Office Logo	Mother Nature	Links	Rocky

To select a new office assistant, right-click the current one, and select Choose Assistant. Click Back or Next on the Gallery tab until you find the assistant you want. Then click OK.

One way to manage the Office Assistant is to get rid of it. But wait! Before you do that, you may want to try some other options.

- While all the Office Assistants provide the same information, you may find the movement of your Office Assistant annoying. Try choosing a different Office Assistant. Some assistants are less active. (The Office Logo, if you can stand it, is the least active.)
- Don't forget that you can drag the assistant to anywhere on your screen.
- If you find the assistant's noises distracting (I did), turn them off! Click the assistant, then click Options. Uncheck the Make Sounds check box.
- To hide the assistant until you need it, choose Help | Hide the Office Assistant. To get help, just press the F1 key, and the assistant appears as usual.

To customize how the assistant works, click it, and click Options. The Options tab of the Office Assistant dialog box, shown in Figure 1-12, has the following options:

- Uncheck Use the Office Assistant to turn off the assistant. Check the same box to turn the assistant back on.

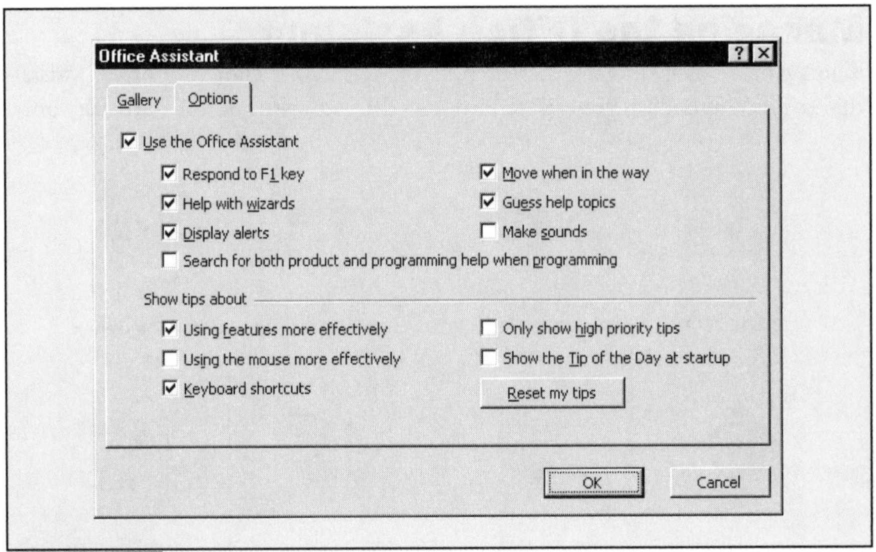

FIGURE 1-12 The Options tab of the Office Assistant

- If Respond to F1 Key is checked, the Office Assistant opens when you press the F1 key.
- If Help with Wizards is checked, the Office Assistant opens and provides help with wizards such as the AutoContent Wizard.
- If Display Alerts is checked, the Office Assistant automatically opens when it thinks (if that is the right word) that you need to be alerted to a situation.
- Check Search for Both Product and Programming Help When Programming if you want the Office Assistant to help you with Visual Basic for Applications or other programming tasks.
- If Move When in the Way is checked, the Assistant moves when it blocks a dialog box.
- If Guess Help Topics is checked, the Office Assistant provides you with suggested help topics when you open it, based on what you were just doing. If you uncheck this box, the assistant suggests help topics only when you ask for them.
- Uncheck Make Sounds to silence the assistant.

At the bottom of the dialog box you can customize the content of the assistant's tips. For example, by default, the Using the Mouse More Effectively check box is checked. However, if you don't need tips about using the mouse and like using keyboard shortcuts, uncheck this box, and check the Keyboard Shortcuts box instead.

The Reset My Tips button applies to the Tip of the Day message that appears if Show the Tip of the Day at startup is checked. Click this button so you can see again tips that have already appeared.

Of course, the Office Assistant is only one way to get help. Read further for more options.

Using the Help Menu to Get Answers Fast

You can also use the Help menu to get help. Choose Help | Microsoft PowerPoint Help, which is equivalent to pressing F1. If the assistant is on, it appears. If the assistant is off, the Help window opens as shown in Figure 1-13.

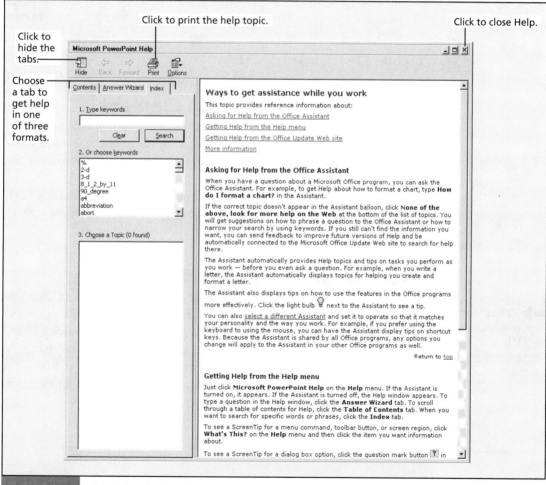

FIGURE 1-13 The Help window that opens when the assistant is turned off

Notice the three tabs—Contents, Answer Wizard, and Index. Each tab offers you a slightly different way to access Help.

New in 2000: Contents is now organized alphabetically.

- *Contents* lets you find help by topic. Look through the alphabetical list to find the topic you need. Click the plus sign to its left to open all the subtopics. Click the subtopic you want, and it appears in the pane to the right. A subtopic may contain several sections, which are listed at the top of the pane. You can click one to go to it immediately.

- *Answer Wizard* lets you type in a question or some keywords.

- *Index* lets you type or choose a keyword. The keywords are listed alphabetically. If you type a keyword, then click Search. If you choose a keyword from the listing, double-click it. Either way, you then double-click one of the topics listed at the bottom of the pane. The topic appears at the right. To start a new search, click Clear first.

Click the Close button to close Help.

Getting Help for a Screen Element

Suppose you want to know what a toolbar button, menu command, or screen region is for. Choose Help | What's This? Then click the item you want to know about. A brief explanation pops up. Click anywhere on the screen to close the explanation.

In any dialog box, you can click the question mark button (in the dialog box), and then click any option in the dialog box. Another box usually opens with an explanation of the option.

Finding Help on Microsoft's Web Site

Tip: For dialog boxes without a question mark button, select the option and then press SHIFT-F1.

Choose Help | Office on the Web to connect to Microsoft's Office Update Web site. Here you can access resources for technical support and download free PowerPoint updates, if there are any. Choosing Help | Office on the Web is equivalent to going to **http://officeupdate.microsoft.com/welcome/powerpoint.htm**. To go to PowerPoint's Web page, point your Web browser to **www.microsoft.com/office/powerpoint/default.htm**.

Saving a Presentation

You should save your presentation often as you work. As you have no doubt experienced, your computer system can crash or freeze—often destroying your most recent work. You should be especially careful to save before you print, switch to another application, or leave your computer to take a break.

The first time you save a new presentation, PowerPoint opens the Save As dialog box so you can name your presentation. Until then, your presentation is called Presentation1 (or a higher number if you have created more than one new presentation in a session). The Save As dialog box is shown in Figure 1-14.

Remember that taking care to organize your presentations and related files such as graphic files, sounds, and so on makes it a lot easier later on when you need to find them. Here are steps for saving a presentation for the first time using the Save As dialog box:

1. Use the Places bar to save your presentation in one of the standard locations. If you don't use the Places bar, click the Save In drop-down list to navigate to the desired folder.

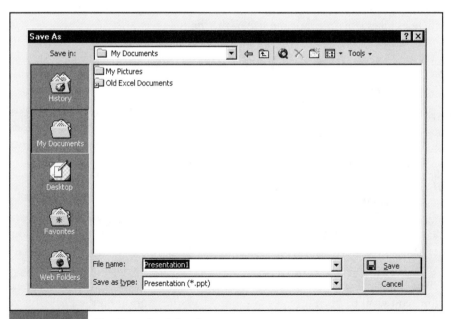

FIGURE 1-14 The Save As dialog box

2. Type the presentation's name in the File Name text box.

3. To save your presentation in another format, click the Save as Type drop-down box to choose the preferred type of document.

4. Click Save.

For a discussion of the Places bar, see "Using the Places Bar for Easy Document Management," earlier in this chapter.

PowerPoint 2000 (as well as all of Office 2000 except for Microsoft Access) uses the same file format as the previous version, PowerPoint 97. As a result, you will find it easy to share presentations with colleagues who are still using PowerPoint 97.

The Save as Type drop-down list offers a number of options for saving presentations, as explained in Table 1-1.

You also use the Save As dialog box (File | Save As) anytime you want to save a copy of a presentation under a new name or in a new location. If your presentation is a read-only file, meaning that you cannot make changes to it, you also use Save As to save the file under a new name.

After the first save, click Save on Standard toolbar to save your presentation. PowerPoint saves only the changes you made since your last save. Saving only the changes takes less time, but the size of the file is larger.

Tip: If storage space is a problem, you can decrease the size of your presentations by choosing Tools | Options and clicking the Save tab. Uncheck Allow Fast Saves, and click OK. If you like fast saves, uncheck this option only when you finish your presentation, just before the last save.

Saving So You Can Find It Fast the Next Time

As I mentioned earlier, good file organization is definitely an advantage when you need to find your presentations, graphic files, text files, sounds, etc. The following tips provide efficient ways to find your presentations.

Adding a presentation to the Favorites folder

As explained earlier in this chapter, the Favorites folder contains shortcuts to files you use often. (For example, you might use your company's logo for every presentation you create.) Once you have saved your presentation, you may want to add it to the Favorites folder. Doing so saves a shortcut to your presentation in the Windows\Favorites folder. The next time you want to open it, you can use the Favorites button on the Places bar to find it quickly.

Saving shortcuts in the Favorites folder originated with Microsoft Internet Explorer. For example, while you're browsing on the Web, you can save the address of a Web site you use often as a favorite. For this reason, you use the Web toolbar to add a presentation to the Favorites folder.

Type Option	Description
Presentation (95, 97–2000, and 4.0) (*.ppt)	The default.
Web page (*.htm or *.html)	Lets you display your presentation on the Internet. HTML documents can be read by an Internet browser. Drawing objects are converted to GIF files.
Design template (*.pot)	Saves the presentation as a template.
PowerPoint show (*.pps)	When a presentation is saved as a show and you open it from your desktop, PowerPoint opens, runs, and closes the show, and returns you to the desktop. If you open the file from within PowerPoint, it opens normally.
PowerPoint add-in (*.ppa)	A third-party supplemental program.
GIF Graphics Interchange Format (*.gif)	Saves the displayed slide as a GIF file—a common graphics format used on Web pages.
JPEG File Interchange Format (*.jpg)	Saves the slide as a JPG file. JPG (also called JPEG) is a graphics format used on Web pages. This format is best when using a photograph on a Web page because JPEG renders a truer image for photographs than GIF.
PNG Portable Network Graphics Format (*.png)	Saves the displayed slide as a PNG file. PNG is a graphics format used on Web pages. It compresses and downloads well but is not widely used.
Device Independent Bitmap (*.bmp)	Turns the displayed slide into a bitmap graphic that you can import into other applications. BMP is a pixel-based format.
Windows Metafile (*.wmf)	Turns the displayed slide into a graphic that you can import into other applications. WMF is a vector format and resizes well.
Outline/RTF (*.rtf)	Saves just the text of your presentation with most of its formatting so you can import it into a word processing (or other) application.
Tag Image File Format (*.tif; *.tiff)	Turns the displayed slide into a graphic that you can import into other applications. TIFF is a bitmap format, accepted by almost all applications that accept graphic files. Scanned images are typically in TIFF format.

TABLE 1-1   Presentation Type Options

Customizing where and how a presentation is saved

By default, when you first save a presentation, the Save As dialog box opens with the My Documents folder displayed in the Save In box. If you change the location, the presentation is, of course, saved in your chosen location each time you click the Save button. However, the next time you start a new presentation in the same session (without closing PowerPoint), the Save As dialog box displays the last location you chose.

L ▶ Tip: The Favorites folder can get so overpopulated that you can't find anything any more. That defeats the whole purpose. Go through the folder periodically, and delete shortcuts that you don't need any longer. From PowerPoint, choose Favorites from the Web toolbar, and choose Open Favorites. Then choose any shortcut, and press DEL.

If you want the Save As dialog box to open with another folder of your choice, you can change the default file location, as explained in the section "Customizing the Default File Location," earlier in this chapter.

You can also specify a default file format for saving presentations. By default, PowerPoint saves your files as PowerPoint 2000 presentations. However, if you're the only one you know with PowerPoint 2000 and you need to share your presentations with others, you may want to save your presentations in PowerPoint 97 format. Choose Tools | Options, and click the Save tab. In the Save PowerPoint Files As drop-down list, choose the file format you want. As long as the presentation isn't already saved in PowerPoint 2000 format, PowerPoint will prompt you to save your presentation in the file format you chose.

Backing Up Your Presentations

No discussion of saving would be complete without explaining the importance of backing up, or *archiving*, your work. If you care about your work, back it up. While most computer users are accustomed to backing up files to floppy diskettes, many presentations are too large to fit on a diskette, which holds a maximum of 1.44MB. There are many other options. Here are a few:

- Tape drives are fairly inexpensive and are large enough to back up an entire hard disk.
- Disk cartridge drives, such as those sold by Iomega, offer the convenience of a diskette but have more capacity.
- If you have a lot of presentations, a read/write CD-ROM drive lets you save your presentations to a CD-ROM.
- Optical drives have a long life and resist accidental erasure. Use them for long-term archiving, perhaps off-site.

The main point is not to walk away from your computer at the end of a day without backing up your day's work.

Professional Skills Summary

In this chapter, you learned the basics of PowerPoint: how to open PowerPoint presentation, organize/find your presentations, view presentations most effectively, and use the Office Assistant. In the next chapter, you get started actually creating PowerPoint presentations.

Creating a Great First Presentation

After learning the basics of PowerPoint in Chapter 1, you are now ready to create a great presentation. You can choose from three methods, depending on how independently you want to work:

- Use the AutoContent Wizard for professional help creating your text outline. This option provides the most support and structure. However, as you'll see, this method is often not the way to get the most professional results.
- Choose a design template to create a background. (PowerPoint comes with some great-looking backgrounds.) Other than that, you're on your own.
- Start with a blank presentation when you want to work from scratch and create both the text and the background yourself.

When you open PowerPoint, the PowerPoint dialog box (also called the Startup dialog box) opens, offering a choice of these three methods of starting a presentation. Refer back to Figure 1-2 in Chapter 1 for an explanation of this dialog box.

Getting Help for Your Content

If you need help organizing your thoughts and want the quickest way to a complete presentation, you can use the AutoContent Wizard. The AutoContent Wizard leads you to professionally designed presentation packages, complete with background and suggested content.

Organizing Your Presentation with the AutoContent Wizard

The AutoContent Wizard cannot divine exactly what you need to say. Rather, it provides a general structure and suggested topics. Most professionals ignore it because, in most cases, a presentation needs to be designed individually, rather than from canned content. Rarely can the AutoContent presentations even come close to fulfilling your needs.

Then when should you use the AutoContent Wizard? The answer is when your needs loosely match one of the presentations and/or you need a presentation on very short notice. Or you may be the type of person who needs help organizing your ideas. Finally, you can use it as a learning tool, a training exercise to help you ask the right questions and clarify how to unfold a mature PowerPoint presentation. The complete presentations included with PowerPoint's AutoContent Wizard have been created by professionals to thoroughly cover a topic. You just need to replace the text with the specifics applicable to your situation. Here are the topics PowerPoint offers:

- **General**   Includes Recommending a Strategy, Communicating Bad News, and Training

- **Corporate**   Offers presentations for a company meeting, a corporate home Web page, a financial overview, a business plan, a company handbook, and an orientation for new employees

- **Projects**   Includes Reporting Progress or Status, Project Overview, and Project Post-Mortem

- **Sales/Marketing**   Includes presentations for selling a product or service, a marketing plan, and an overview of a product or service

- **Carnegie Coach**   Includes Facilitating a Meeting, Introducing a Speaker, Managing Organizational Change, Motivating a Team, Presenting a Technical Report, and Selling Your Ideas

To start, click AutoContent Wizard in the PowerPoint dialog box to open the first step of the wizard, shown here:

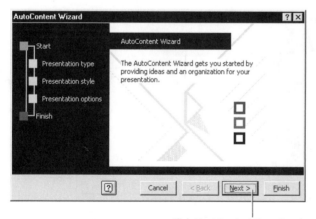

Click Next to start the wizard.

Tip: To start the AutoContent Wizard from within PowerPoint, choose File | New and click the General tab. Then double-click AutoContent Wizard.

The next step is to choose a presentation type and a specific topic. Here you see the topics available for the Corporate type of presentation.

1. Choose a presentation type from one of these buttons.

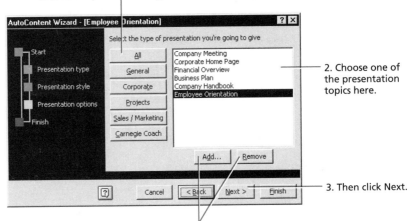

2. Choose one of the presentation topics here.

3. Then click Next.

You can also click Add or Remove to add a presentation to or remove a presentation from the wizard.

The next screen asks you for the type of output, as you see here.

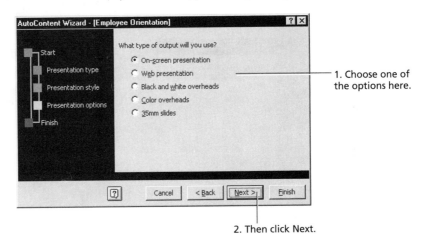

1. Choose one of the options here.

2. Then click Next.

This screen offers you some specific options for creating the presentation, as shown here. You can change any of these options at a later time.

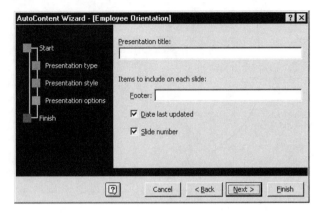

Here are the steps:

1. Type a presentation title. This title will appear as the heading on the first slide, called the title slide.

2. If you want a footer, type it in the text box—your name or department, for example.

3. Uncheck the Date Last Updated and Slide Number boxes if you don't want to-day's date and the slide number on each slide.

4. When you're done, click Finish. (If you click Next, the next screen just tells you to click Finish.)

PowerPoint creates an entire presentation once you click Finish. In Figure 2-1 you see a complete presentation created with the AutoContent Wizard. The title slide has been customized to suit the company's individual needs. To view this slide in color, refer to number 5 in the Slide Gallery.

Look at the outline in the outline pane in Figure 2-1. It covers all the topics most companies need for an employee orientation but includes no specifics. Once you have created a presentation with the AutoContent Wizard, you need to edit the text for your specific situation and needs. (Editing text is covered in the next chapter.) Nevertheless, it is a complete slide show with text and background, and may include other features such as footnotes, animation, etc. The slide show in Figure 2-1 includes today's date and the slide number at the bottom of each slide. In addition, transitions and animation have been added to the slides. (Transitions and animation are covered in Chapter 9.) You can use the information in the rest of this book to finalize the presentation.

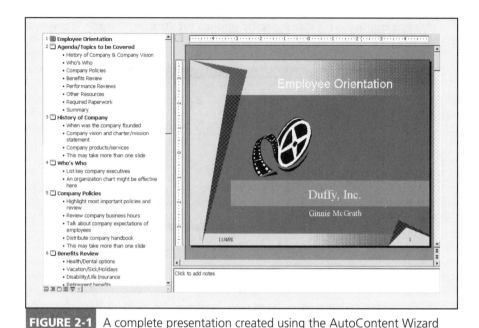

FIGURE 2-1 A complete presentation created using the AutoContent Wizard

For creating a complete presentation quickly, there's nothing like the AutoContent Wizard. However, you will almost certainly want to customize your content.

Choosing a Great-Looking Background Design

Let's say that you don't need any help with the text. You know exactly what you want to say and may already have prepared an outline. In this case, choose Design Templates from the Startup dialog box when you open PowerPoint and click OK. You see the New Presentation dialog box with the Design Templates tab on top, as shown in Figure 2-2.

To choose a design template, click one of the design templates to look at it in the preview box. Continue to preview design templates until you find one you like, then click OK.

Tip: If you are already in PowerPoint, choose File | New and click the Design Templates tab.

Design templates are backgrounds for your slides. A background comprises both a colored background and design elements that automatically appear on every slide. The template also includes other features such as bullet design, specific fonts, and font sizes. Using a

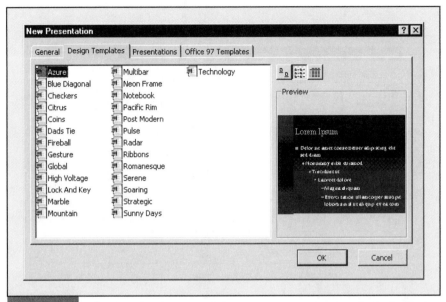

FIGURE 2-2 The Design Templates tab of the New Presentation dialog box

design template creates a unified look for your entire presentation; PowerPoint's design templates are designed by professional graphic designers.

The truth is that if you hire outside professionals to create a slide show for you, they will always create a background design from scratch. In many cases, this is appropriate, but sometimes they're just trying to make an impression! You can usually find an appropriate design template that will give your presentation a professional look. For an example, refer to number 11 in the Slide Gallery, which uses the Dad's Tie template. Your choice of design template will have a powerful effect on the impact of your presentation.

Tip: The conventional wisdom is to use a light background color for overhead transparencies and a dark one for 35mm slides or on-screen presentations. However, in some cases you'll find that medium backgrounds also work well for 35mm slides and on-screen presentations.

Cross-Reference: Chapters 5, 6, and 7 are packed with helpful information and tips on graphic layout, color, and visual effects that can help you decide which is the best design template to use. Refer to Chapter 7 for details on creating your own design template.

The Right Layout with AutoLayouts

Once you choose a design template, PowerPoint opens the New Slide dialog box, shown in Figure 2-3.

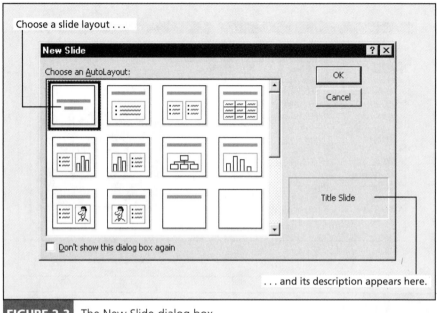

Choose a slide layout . . .

. . . and its description appears here.

FIGURE 2-3 The New Slide dialog box

This dialog box lets you choose a layout—also called an AutoLayout—for a new slide. These layouts are extremely helpful for creating slides. Picking the right one is essential for a legible slide that communicates instantly. You have the following choices:

- **Title Slide**   Use this for the first slide of your presentation. It includes a heading and a subheading.

- **Bulleted List**   Use this when you have only a few items and the items need the full width of the slide. There is a heading at the top of the slide. A *bullet* is a small dot or other shape that appears before each item in a list. Look ahead to Figure 2-4, which shows this AutoLayout before any additions have been made.

- **2 Column Text**   Use this when you have at least four items and each item is short. There is a heading at the top of the slide.

- **Table**   This slide lets you insert a table under a heading. A dialog box pops up letting you specify the number of columns and rows. Use a table when you need to communicate complex data and when a graph is not appropriate. Tables are covered in Chapter 8.

New in 2000:   PowerPoint 2000 now creates its own tables. Previously, you had to insert a table from a word processor as an embedded object.

- **Text & Chart**   Includes bulleted text on the left and a chart (graph) on the right. There is a heading at the top of the slide. Use this layout when you will discuss the text first and then the chart, because it is natural for the audience to look from left to right. A *datasheet*, which looks like a small spreadsheet, pops up with canned data. Insert your own data, and reformat the datasheet for your needs. The menu and toolbars change, to accommodate the commands useful for working with charts. Use a chart when communicating trends or patterns in numerical data—such as annual sales over the last three years. Adding charts to slides is discussed in Chapter 8.

- **Chart & Text**   This layout is just like Text & Chart, but the chart is on the left and the text is on the right. Use this layout when you will discuss the chart before the text.

- **Organization Chart**   Inserts an organization chart under a heading. PowerPoint opens Microsoft Organization Chart, an *applet* (small application) that creates organization charts. Chapter 8 explains how to create organization charts on slides.

- **Chart**   Just a chart under a heading. Use this layout when you want the chart to be as large as possible and you don't need any supplemental text. If your chart is well designed, you often do not need any text beside it.

- **Text & Clip Art**   Puts bulleted text on the left and a place for clip art or any other graphic (that you provide) at the right. There is a heading at the top of the slide. Professionals suggest that at least 50 percent of your slides should include some kind of graphic.

Cross-Reference: Chapter 5 explains how to add clip art and graphics to your slides.

- **Clip Art & Text**   Just like the previous layout, but the text is on the right and the clip art is on the left. There is a heading at the top of the slide.

- **Title Only**   As its name says, there is only a heading. Title Only is best when you want to create your own layout. For example, this layout is great for a large photograph of your product.

- **Blank**   For those who like to work from scratch.

- **Text & Object**   Like Text & Clip Art, but double-clicking the object placeholder opens the Insert Object dialog box so you can insert any type of object available on your computer system. You need to scroll down to display this option and those following it.

- **Object & Text**   The object is on the left; the text is on the right.

- **Large Object**   Just an object placeholder.

- **Object**   An object placeholder under a title.

- **Text & Media Clip**   Bulleted text on the left and a media clip placeholder on the right. A media clip includes various types of digital sound and movie files.

- **Media Clip & Text** The media clip is on the left and the text is on the right.
- **Object over Text** Includes a slide title, with an object placeholder below it and a text placeholder at the bottom.
- **Text over Object** Includes a slide title, with a text placeholder below it and an object placeholder at the bottom.
- **Text & 2 Objects** A text placeholder on the left and two small object placeholders on the right.
- **2 Objects & Text** Two small object placeholders on the left and a text placeholder on the right.
- **2 Objects over Text** Includes a title, then two objects side by side, and text at the bottom.
- **4 Objects** A title with four object placeholders.

Figure 2-4 shows a slide after choosing the Bulleted List AutoLayout. Notice the two dotted rectangles. These are called *placeholders*, and they hold the place for objects on your slide—in this case, text. Other placeholders are used for clip art, charts, and so on. Later in this chapter, I discuss how to use the placeholders to add text.

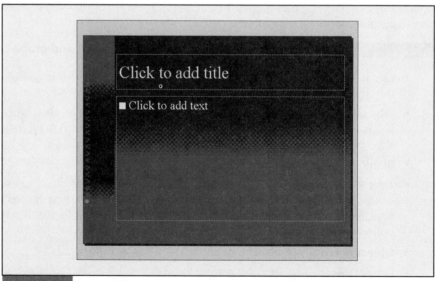

FIGURE 2-4 A new slide created using the Bulleted List AutoLayout

Completing the Presentation Structure

Once you have chosen a design template and an AutoLayout for your first slide, you can complete the structure of the entire presentation in one of two ways:

- Work in the slide pane and enter text in the text placeholder(s), if any. Then choose Common Tasks | New Slide to add a new slide. The New Slide dialog box opens again to let you choose an AutoLayout. Then add text in the text placeholder(s) for the new slide. Continue in this way until you have completed your presentation. You can add graphics and animation as you work or complete the text first and go back to work on the artistic parts.

- Work in the outline pane and create a text outline for the entire presentation. PowerPoint automatically creates new slides for you. Continue until you have completed your presentation. You can adjust the layout later. Of course, you will want to add graphics, animation, and so on.

The next few sections explain how to enter text in placeholders as well as to create outlines in the outline pane.

The Text Techniques of the Pros

Don't ignore your text in favor of razzle-dazzle graphics. While graphics are very important, they mostly serve to help your audience focus on the text. Text needs to be very clear—both visually and in content. In this section, you learn how to create professional-looking text. Later in the chapter you'll get some professional advice on the content.

Before you start to write, you must decide what kind of presentation you want to create. Is your main goal to provide information, to tell a story? In that case, your text is very important, and you'll probably want to use bulleted text in text placeholders. Or suppose you really want to create an impression, a mood. Perhaps you want to excite sales reps about a new product feature but will follow up with all the details on paper or your company's intranet. In this case, text is less important than graphics, color, and animation. You may not use any bulleted text at all. Instead, you may use text boxes, AutoShapes, and WordArt. You will see both types of presentations in this book, which will help you feel comfortable with both types. Once you know the goal of your presentation, you can choose the type of text you want.

Text Placeholders for Instant, Impressive Text

The easiest way to add text is to click a text placeholder. When you click a text placeholder, an I-beam cursor appears, showing where the text will appear; and a text box is displayed, showing the boundary for the text, as you can see in the following illustration. All you need to do is start typing. The dotted border changes to a thick selection border and displays *handles,* which you can drag to resize the text box. You can also move the entire text box by pointing to the border and dragging.

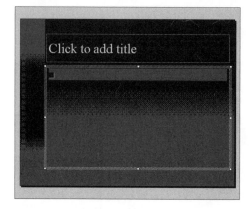

The beauty of text placeholders is that PowerPoint formats the text appropriately for the placeholder. For example, a title is usually centered and uses a larger font. Bulleted text is properly aligned to the right of the bullet and uses a smaller font. The design template controls this formatting although you can change it. As a result, you get perfectly formatted text every time, for professional results.

To start a new paragraph in the bulleted text area, press ENTER. PowerPoint automatically creates a new bullet so you can just continue typing. Remember that only text that you type in a text placeholder is displayed in the outline pane.

Note that the text in the text placeholder telling you to click to add text never appears on the slide during a presentation, even if you never add any text. The same is true of the dotted placeholder border. Therefore, if you insert a slide with a text placeholder and never place any text in it, at presentation you will have a blank slide that includes only the design template. Of course, if you don't need the text placeholder, you should probably delete it.

Chapters 3 and 4 explain how to customize your text to look any way you want. Chapter 7 covers slide masters, the part of the design template that controls text formatting for the entire presentation.

Figure 2-5 shows a slide that uses the Text & Clip Art layout. To view this slide in color, refer to number 6 in the Slide Gallery. Using the text placeholder makes it very easy to create a slide like this.

Figure 2-6 shows a slide that uses the Text & Media Clip layout. This layout places bulleted text on the left and a media clip, usually an AVI movie file, on the right. To view this slide in color, refer to number 7 in the Slide Gallery.

Creating Your Presentation from an Outline

It would be nice to create a presentation without having to type the text in text placeholders on each individual slide. You can. In fact, the quickest way to create a complete presentation is to type an outline of your text in the outline pane. Working with the outline pane is ideal for creating the text of your presentation because you can see most of the text at a glance. This lets you view the flow of ideas from slide to slide. You can easily rearrange text later by moving it from one slide to another.

When you type your outline, PowerPoint automatically creates new slides for you as you work. You immediately see the results in the slide pane at the right of your screen. When you have finished typing your outline, you have a complete presentation. All you need to do is refine it.

Click Show Formatting on the Outline toolbar to see the text formatting in the outline pane as you work. Bulleted text that you type in the outline pane is placed in text placeholders. By default, PowerPoint uses the Bulleted List layout.

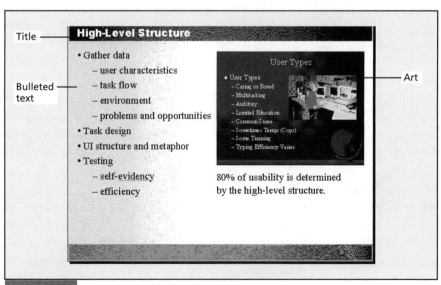

FIGURE 2-5	A slide using the Text and Clip Art layout

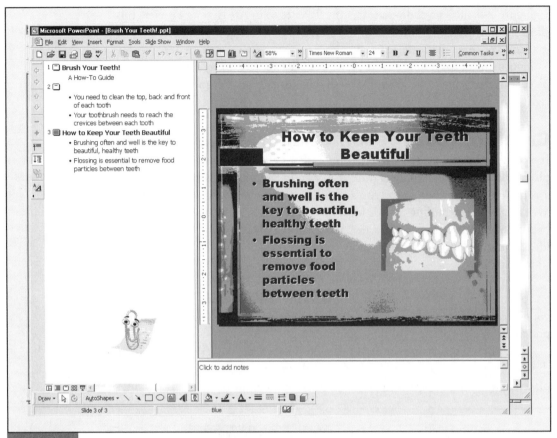

FIGURE 2-6 A slide using the Text & Media Clip layout

Tip: Before you start a new slide, choose Common Tasks | Slide Layout from the Formatting toolbar to choose another layout.

Figure 2-7 shows an outline in outline view. The outline helps you to organize and structure your entire presentation. To view this outline and its slide in color, refer to number 8 in the Slide Gallery.

Understanding outlines

An outline has *levels* of text, as shown in Figure 2-8. (To view this slide and outline in color, refer to number 9 in the Slide Gallery.) The level determines whether text becomes the title of a slide or a bulleted item (also called *body text,* because it makes up the body of the text on a slide). You can also create

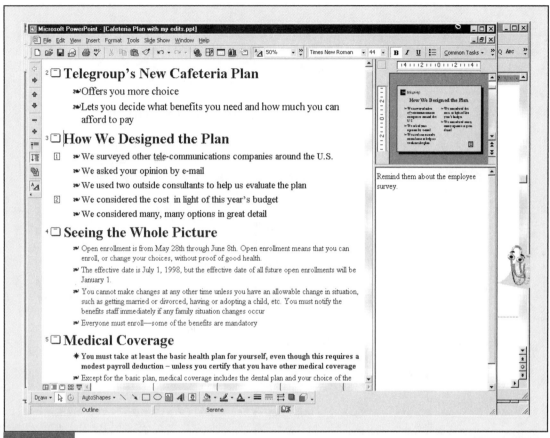

The outline of a presentation in outline view

up to five levels of bulleted items. Each level of bulleted text is indented more than the previous one and generally uses a smaller type size.

Once you know the special terms that apply to the outlining function, you will feel right at home working with outlines. They are listed and explained here:

- **Promote**   To make text one level higher. For example, second-level bulleted text becomes first-level bulleted text; first-level bulleted text becomes a slide title.

- **Demote**   To make text one level lower. For example, a slide title becomes first-level bulleted text, and first-level bulleted text becomes second-level bulleted text.

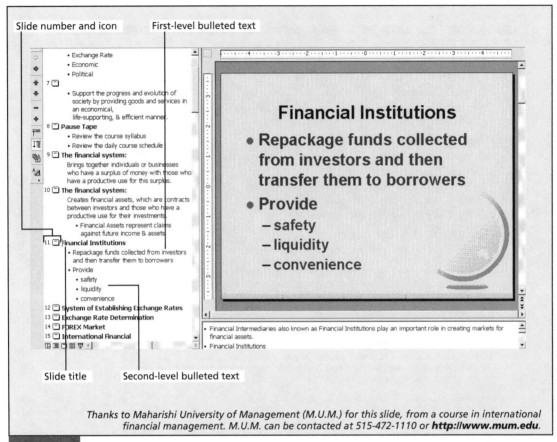

Slide number and icon   **First-level bulleted text**

- Exchange Rate
- Economic
- Political

7
- Support the progress and evolution of society by providing goods and services in an economical, life-supporting, & efficient manner.

8 Pause Tape
- Review the course syllabus
- Review the daily course schedule

9 The financial system:
Brings together individuals or businesses who have a surplus of money with those who have a productive use for this surplus.

10 The financial system:
Creates financial assets, which are contracts between investors and those who have a productive use for their investments.
- Financial Assets represent claims against future income & assets

11 Financial Institutions
- Repackage funds collected from investors and then transfer them to borrowers
- Provide
  - safety
  - liquidity
  - convenience

12 System of Establishing Exchange Rates
13 Exchange Rate Determination
14 FOREX Market
15 International Financial

Slide title   **Second-level bulleted text**

Financial Institutions
- Repackage funds collected from investors and then transfer them to borrowers
- Provide
  - safety
  - liquidity
  - convenience

- Financial Intermediaries also known as Financial Institutions play an important role in creating markets for financial assets.
- Financial Institutions

*Thanks to Maharishi University of Management (M.U.M.) for this slide, from a course in international financial management. M.U.M. can be contacted at 515-472-1110 or **http://www.mum.edu**.*

FIGURE 2-8   A text outline with its accompanying slide

Tip: The Promote and Demote buttons are also on the Formatting toolbar. You can also press the TAB key to demote a paragraph or SHIFT-TAB to promote it. Another way to promote or demote an item is to drag its bullet to the left

- **Collapse**   To hide all text lower than the slide title, for one slide only. Collapsing text lets you see more of your presentation so you can assess the overall structure of your presentation.

- **Expand**   To display all the levels of text, for one slide only.

- **Summary slide**   A slide that contains the titles of your other slides

The Outlining toolbar contains all the tools you need to create an outline quickly. To display the Outlining toolbar, right-click any toolbar and choose Outlining. The Outlining toolbar is shown in Figure 2-9.

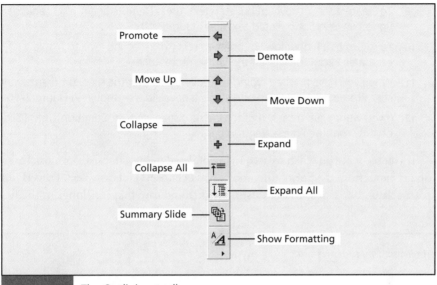

FIGURE 2-9   The Outlining toolbar

Creating an outline in PowerPoint

Here are the steps for creating a presentation by typing an outline:

1. Start a new presentation using either the Design Template or Blank Presentation option.

2. If you use the Design Template option, choose the design template you want and click OK.

3. If you would like a slide layout for the entire presentation other than Bulleted Text, choose the AutoLayout you want.

4. In normal or outline view, click the outline pane.

5. Type the title of the first slide and press ENTER. PowerPoint creates a second slide automatically (see Figure 2-10).

6. If you want bulleted text on a slide, press ENTER after typing the slide's title. Then click Demote on the Outlining toolbar (see Figure 2-10). Note that on a title slide only, if you click Demote you create a subtitle.

7. Type the bulleted text and press ENTER. PowerPoint starts a new line of bulleted text (see Figure 2-10).

8. Continue to type bulleted text.

9. To create a second level of bulleted text, press Demote again. You can create up to five levels of bulleted text (see Figure 2-10).

10. To return to a higher level of bulleted text (from second level to first level, for example), click Promote on the Outlining toolbar.

11. When you have finished typing the bulleted text for the slide, press ENTER and click Promote until PowerPoint starts a new slide, as shown in Figure 2-10.

12. If you want a different layout for the next slide, choose Common Tasks | Slide Layout from the Formatting toolbar.

If you see that you will have two many bulleted items, choose Common Tasks | Slide Layout from the Formatting toolbar and choose 2 Column Text. PowerPoint places a number 1 next to the existing text to indicate that it belongs in the first

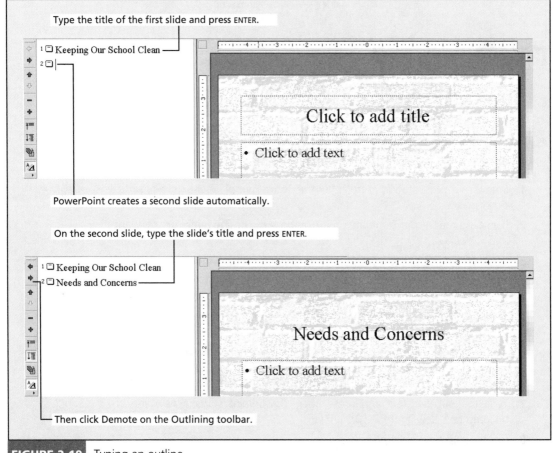

FIGURE 2-10 Typing an outline

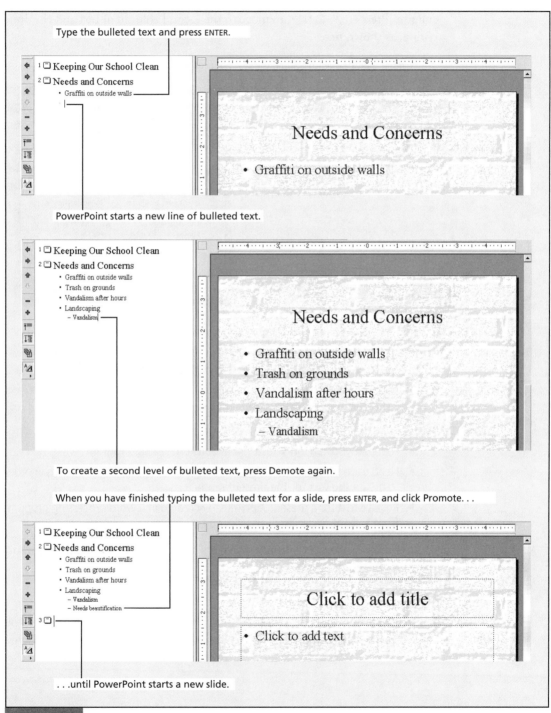

FIGURE 2-10 Typing an outline *(continued)*

column. Press CTRL-ENTER to move to the second column of text and continue typing, as shown here:

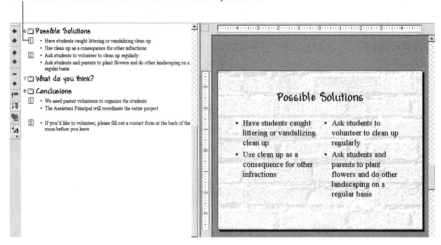

In Chapter 3, I cover techniques for editing existing outline text.

Instant Presentation! Importing an Outline

You may prefer importing an outline created in a word processing program over creating the outline in PowerPoint. You may choose this option for several reasons. Perhaps you:

- Feel that you can work faster in a word processing program
- Need to collaborate with others who don't have or know PowerPoint in order to create the text for the presentation
- Receive text for a presentation already created in a word processing program from a client, supervisor, or colleague

Anytime you have text already saved as a word processing document, import the text. There's no need to duplicate the effort of typing it.

Preparing the outline

Before importing the text, you should review it so that you get the results you want. Most word processing programs have a feature called *styles*. Styles help you organize the formatting of your paragraphs. For example, in Microsoft Word heading styles are used for headings. The Normal style is often used for the body of a paragraph. PowerPoint uses these styles, if they exist in your outline, to organize your text into a complete presentation. By creating the appropriate styles, you can determine exactly how your text will be organized on the slides of your presentation. Here's how it works:

- Heading 1 style becomes the slide title,
- Heading 2 style becomes first-level bulleted text,
- Heading 3 style becomes second-level bulleted text,
- . . . and so on.

You can also organize your document by indenting the paragraphs. Paragraphs with no indentation become slide titles, and indented paragraphs become first-level bulleted text. Be sure that there are no blank lines because they are imported as blank slides.

If you need to import a plain text (ASCII) file, you can use tabs at the beginning of paragraphs to create your outline.

Chapter 3 explains how to insert all or part of an outline into an existing presentation.

> **Tip:** You can use Outline view in Microsoft Word to create your outline. In Outline view, choose all the text and promote it to Heading 1. Then place the cursor in any text that you want to become first-level bulleted text, and click Demote. Word assigns Heading 2 to that text. Click Demote twice to create Heading 3 text, and so on.

Creating the presentation from your outline

Once you have created and formatted your outline, you can create the presentation. Here are the steps:

1. From PowerPoint, choose File | Open.
2. In the Open dialog box, choose All Outlines from the Files of Type drop-down list.
3. Navigate to your outline and double-click the document that contains your outline.

PowerPoint creates the presentation. The next step will probably be to assign a design template. After that, you can add clip art, charts, and other design features.

> **Tip:** From within Microsoft Word, you can automatically create a PowerPoint presentation from your Word outline. With the outline open on your screen, choose File | Send To and choose Microsoft PowerPoint.

Strategies for Creating Your Presentation Outline

by Claudyne Wilder

A defined objective saves you time, helps you choose which information to include, and focuses and narrows your research so that you do not spend extra time gathering superfluous information. Write down your objective in one sentence. Once you have clearly identified the objective, choose a format that will help you organize your information in a logical sequence and flow. The following are two format examples and how they should be organized:

- **Recommend a strategy.** This format is useful when you are presenting ways to accomplish a particular project, goal, or task. It allows you to systematically present potential strategies that the group needs to consider. Here is the structure:

  1. State the objective.
  2. State the present situation.
  3. State the desired outcome.
  4. State the potential strategies.
  5. List the advantages and disadvantages of each strategy.
  6. Recommend one or more strategies and what to do next.

- **Identify potential problems.** This format should be considered when you have made a decision to implement something new or when you are redirecting your efforts to a new orientation. You want to ferret out what could go wrong and suggest remedial action. Here is the structure:

  1. State the goal.
  2. List anticipated issues that may block achieving the goal.
  3. Rate the seriousness of the issues.
  4. State preventive and/or contingent actions.
  5. Identify a prime mover and deadlines.

No matter which format you use or how you combine them, always have these ingredients in your presentation:

- **Opening**   Tell your audience the subject and, if appropriate, the objective of your talk.

- **Agenda**   These are the key areas you plan on covering. Don't list more than five items on your visual. If your audience sees a long list, they will feel overwhelmed.

- **Examples and anecdotes**   Share anecdotes, show pictures, and use video clips to add human interest.

- **Conclusion**   Repeat the key areas you covered.

- **Next steps**   Explain the steps you want yourself or your audience to take.

Write the outline. Use level-1 headings for main topics: remember that these start new slides. Use level-2 headings for subtopics: these are your main bullets. Keep the bulleted text short so your audience can easily understand your message. Bulleted text is generally not complete sentences, yet must convey a complete thought.

Review your talk with someone not familiar with your subject and have that person tell you which words, acronyms, and charts just don't make sense. Practice speaking from the outline to see if it flows and adjust it as necessary.

Cut out unnecessary details. Many times you will be talking to an audience not that familiar with your subject. Also, ask yourself if you need to include all of the details in the body of the talk. Perhaps you can hide some slides and then if someone asks you a question you can answer by explaining the details using a hidden slide. (Hiding slides is covered in Chapter 15.) It is better to say and show less and have the audience wanting more. When using analogies, use ones familiar to your audience. The most important point to keep in mind is to organize your information around your objective. Include only relevant information. Resist the urge to put everything you know about the subject in an hour-long talk. By being brief and to the point, your audience will ask you to come back.

Consider placing text in a text box if it doesn't fit into the outline structure or to give that particular point more emphasis. Think about graphics as you work.

Remember that you can always change your text later.

Claudyne Wilder is a trainer, professional speaker, and author of several books, including Point, Click and Wow! A Quick Guide to Brilliant Laptop Presentations *and* The Presentations Kit: 10 Steps to Selling Your Ideas. *She is also one of the two authors of the "Before and After" column in* Presentations *magazine. You can contact her at 617-524-7172 or at claudyne@quik.com.*

Text Boxes for Flexibility

A common way to add text to a slide is to create a text box. Use a text box when you want to place text anywhere on the slide. For example, you can use a text box to create a caption for a graphic or to emphasize an important message. A text box is an *object,* which means that when you click it, you can move and resize it. You can format the text in a text box in whatever way you wish, but this text does not appear in the outline pane.

Figure 2-11 shows an example of text in a text box. This slide uses text boxes to create *callouts,* or labels, that point to the graphic at the center of the slide. To view it in color, refer to number 10 in the Slide Gallery.

A text box consists of a border, a background color or fill effect, and the text. The text boxes shown in Figure 2-11 do not have a visible border. A visible border is useful when you want to emphasize text; but on this slide, it would distract from the message. The fill has been eliminated so that the text looks like it has been written directly on the slide. Chapter 6 explains how to format borders and fills.

Professional Pointer

In this slide, the graphic contains most of the text. If you have a document or a brochure that contains the text you need, you can scan it and insert it as a graphic. See Chapter 5 for more about graphics.

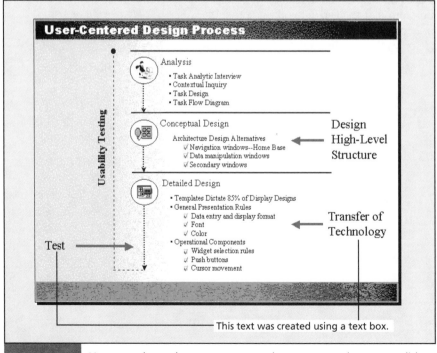

FIGURE 2-11   Use a text box when you want to place text anywhere on a slide

To create a text box, follow these steps:

1. Click the Text Box button on the Drawing toolbar. (You can also choose Insert | Text Box from the menu.)

2. Click and drag to create the text box. PowerPoint only pays attention to the width of the box you specify, not its length. Don't worry! The box now looks like a text placeholder.

3. Start Typing to add the text. When you type enough text to get to the right side of the text box, PowerPoint automatically wraps the text to the next line. The box's length expands as you add text.

4. Click anywhere else on the slide to remove the selection border and handles.

To create the effect shown in Figure 2-11, create the text box using the steps just explained. To remove the border and fill, right-click the text box and choose Format Text Box. On the Colors and Lines tab, click the drop-down arrow in the Fill section and choose No Fill. Click the drop-down arrow in the Line section and choose No Line.

Shapely Text in AutoShapes

PowerPoint includes a large number of shapes that you can add to a slide. These are called *AutoShapes*. You can use these shapes in many ways, but one way is for text. To insert an AutoShape, choose AutoShapes from the Drawing toolbar and use the menu that pops up to choose an AutoShape. Then drag the shape onto a slide. To place text in an AutoShape, click the shape (if it isn't already selected) and start typing. Click outside the AutoShape to remove the selection border and handles. Figure 2-12 shows an example of text in an AutoShape. To view this slide in color, refer to number 11 in the Slide Gallery. Here, Sony uses the text in AutoShapes for two purposes—to draw attention to a model number and to point to features of the remote commander.

Cross-Reference: For more thorough information on AutoShapes, go to Chapter 5.

Text that you type in an AutoShape is attached to that shape. You can move or rotate the AutoShape, and the text follows suit. Like text boxes, AutoShapes have a border and a fill color or effect. However, you rarely eliminate the border since the shape is then not apparent. As you can see on the slide, the distinctive shape and contrasting background color of the AutoShape help to make the text jump out from the rest of the slide.

To create the star-shaped AutoShape, choose AutoShapes | Stars and Banners on the Drawing toolbar and choose the top-left shape. On the slide, drag out the shape so that it is slightly wider than it is tall. To change the border, choose Line Color on the Drawing toolbar and then choose black. To change the fill, choose

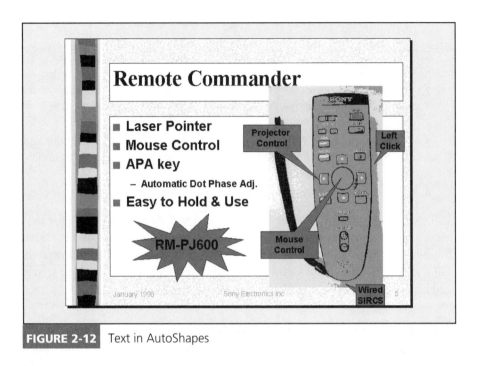

FIGURE 2-12 Text in AutoShapes

Fill Color, then More Fill Colors, and then whatever color you want. With the AutoShape still selected, type the text. The text will appear in the default font and size. The next chapter explains how to change the font and font size.

You can find the AutoShape callouts that point to the remote control in Figure 2-12 by choosing AutoShapes | Callouts on the Drawing toolbar. (This option may not appear on your menu at first. If necessary, point to the double down arrows on the menu.) Choose the top-left shape, called Rectangular Callout, and drag it to the desired size on your slide. As described in the previous paragraph, change the fill color as desired and type the text. To pull out the pointer part, look for the yellow diamond. If you don't see it at first, click elsewhere on your slide, and then click the AutoShape again on its border. Drag the yellow diamond until the pointer points just where you want it. Voila!

AutoShapes can be used instead of text placeholders. In Figure 2-13, all the text is in AutoShapes. The AutoShapes use an unusual orange shadow color that matches the color scheme of the slide. The formatting of the AutoShapes you see

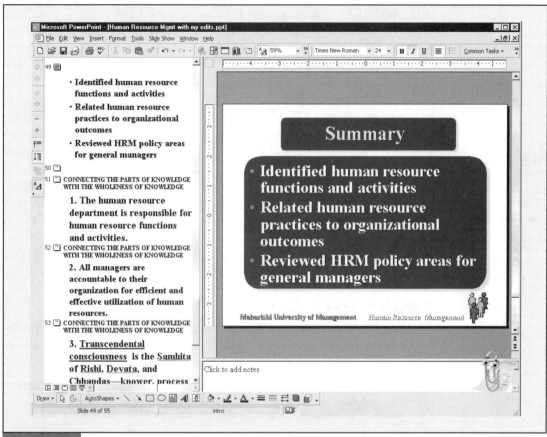

FIGURE 2-13 For a bolder appearance, you can use AutoShapes as a replacement for text placeholders

here is repeated often throughout the presentation for a unified appearance. To view this slide in color, refer to number 12 in the Slide Gallery.

Cross-Reference: See Chapter 6 for information on creating shadow effects.

WordArt for Razzle Dazzle

WordArt creates fancy text effects. It is ideal for text that you want to stand out. WordArt gives you much more control over the appearance of text than any other method of adding text to a slide. Figure 2-14 shows an example of WordArt text. To view this slide in color, refer to number 13 in the Slide Gallery. Although WordArt is a powerful tool and adds a new dimension to your presentation, use it sparingly for maximum effect (as the professionals do) and be careful that the words are still legible!

To create WordArt text, click Insert WordArt on the Drawing toolbar (or choose Insert | Picture | WordArt). WordArt opens its WordArt Gallery dialog box, shown in Figure 2-15. To choose a style, choose one of the boxes and click OK. Notice that the right column contains all the vertical text styles.

Tip: As explained later in this chapter, you can format WordArt to create many effects besides those shown in the gallery. Start by choosing a style that approximates what you want, and then refine it.

WordArt now opens the Edit WordArt Text dialog box, as shown in Figure 2-16. Start typing to replace "Your Text Here." Press ENTER whenever you want to start a new line. When you're done, click OK to close the dialog box.

WordArt now places your WordArt on your slide. Move and resize the WordArt object as needed.

Editing WordArt text

When the WordArt object is placed, the WordArt toolbar appears. The WordArt object remains selected so you can immediately use the buttons on this toolbar to

FIGURE 2-14 Use WordArt to create a powerful impression

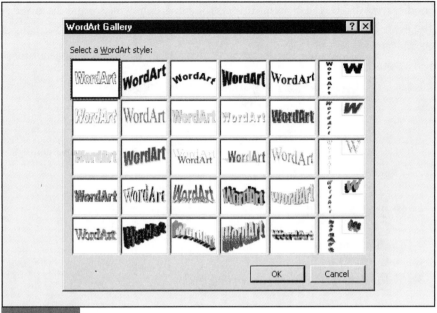

FIGURE 2-15 The WordArt Gallery dialog box

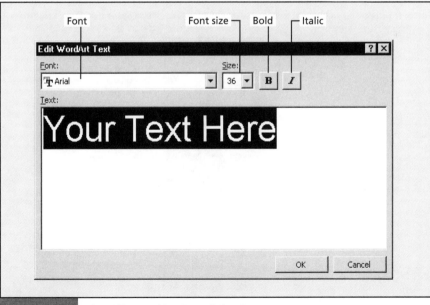

FIGURE 2-16 The Edit WordArt Text dialog box

modify the WordArt. The items on this toolbar are shown here and discussed in the next several sections of this chapter.

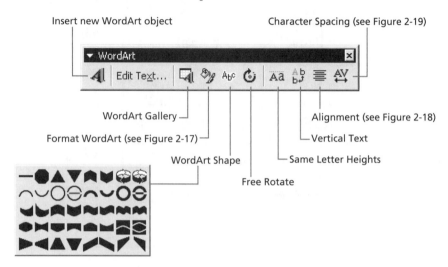

To edit another WordArt object, click to select it. The WordArt toolbar appears. (If it doesn't, right-click any toolbar and choose WordArt.)

Many WordArt objects also display one or more yellow diamonds when selected. Point and drag on the diamond to change the special characteristics of the WordArt's shape. A boundary appears to help you see the changes as you drag, as shown here. Each diamond does something different, so you need to experiment!

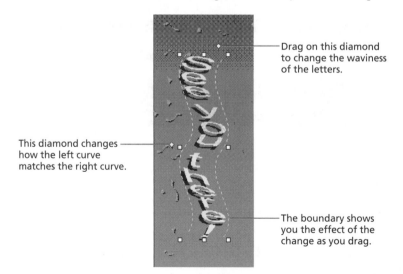

The WordArt Gallery makes it easy to choose a predesigned text effect. However, you have total control of all these effects, using the WordArt toolbar. A WordArt effect is made up of these properties:

- Text shape
- Line color, type (continuous, dashed, etc.), and weight (thickness); the line is actually the outline around the edges of the letters
- Fill color and fill effects
- Alignment
- Character spacing

To choose a text shape, click WordArt Shape and choose one of the options.

Formatting WordArt lines and colors

When you click Format WordArt on the WordArt toolbar, PowerPoint opens the Format WordArt dialog box with the Colors and Lines tab on top, as shown in Figure 2-17. The dialog box shows the settings for the selected WordArt object, also shown in Figure 2-17.

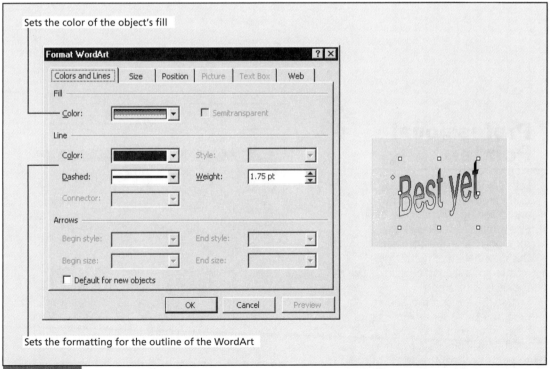

FIGURE 2-17 The Colors and Lines tab of the Format WordArt dialog box shows the settings for the selected WordArt object

Choose Fill Effects from the Color drop-down list to open the Fill Effects dialog box. Here you can create a two-color gradient to fill in your WordArt, as in the example in Figure 2-17. Refer to Chapter 6, which covers borders, colors, fills, and 3-D effects in detail. All of the effects explained there can be used for your WordArt objects.

Formatting WordArt size and position

Click the Size tab of the Format WordArt dialog box, shown here, to set the WordArt object's size, rotation, and scale. You can resize the object by dragging on the handles and rotate it with the Free Rotate button on the WordArt toolbar, but you should use this tab when you need precise settings.

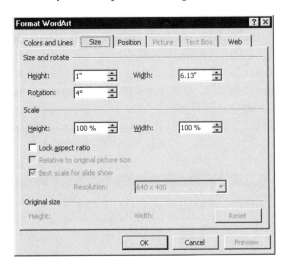

Professional Pointer

Let's say you rotate an object by using the Free Rotate button and dragging. You can use the Size tab to see the resulting rotation. You might then use this information to match the rotation of a second object to the first, for example.

Use the Position tab, shown here, to exactly set the object's position on your slide. You can set the position relative to the top-left corner or the center of the slide.

The Web tab lets you insert alternative text that is displayed while your slide is loading on a Web site. Use this option if you are going to use the presentation as a Web page.

Aligning WordArt text

When you click WordArt Alignment on the WordArt toolbar, you can choose from one of the six options shown in Figure 2-18.

All three Justify options spread out all lines of text so that they line up on both the left and right margins. However, note the difference between these options:

- Word Justify spreads out the words, without changing the height or width of the letters.
- Letter Justify spreads out the letters, without changing their proportion.
- Stretch Justify stretches and expands the letters, making them larger or smaller as necessary.

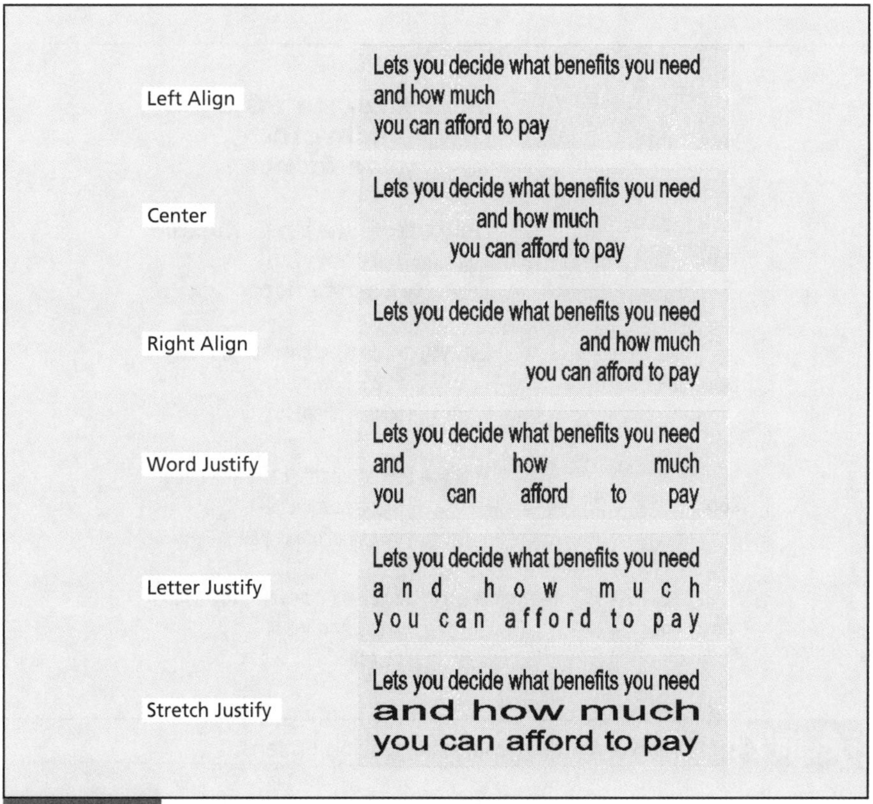

FIGURE 2-18   The six WordArt alignment options

Setting WordArt character spacing

Click WordArt Character Spacing on the WordArt toolbar to specify the spacing between characters. The results of the options are shown in Figure 2-19.

You can also type in a percentage in the Custom text box to set any spacing you want. Very tight sets the spacing at 80 percent, normal is 100 percent, and very loose is 150 percent.

Other WordArt formatting options

You can also edit WordArt using the Drawing toolbar, which is covered in Chapters 5 and 6. For example, you can add shadows and 3-D effects to your WordArt objects.

Look again at number 13 in the Slide Gallery. The WordArt has a gradient fill of two colors, yellow and orange, with horizontal shading using the top-left variant, which places the yellow on top. Lighter colors on top create an uplifting impression. To create this fill, choose Format WordArt on the WordArt toolbar,

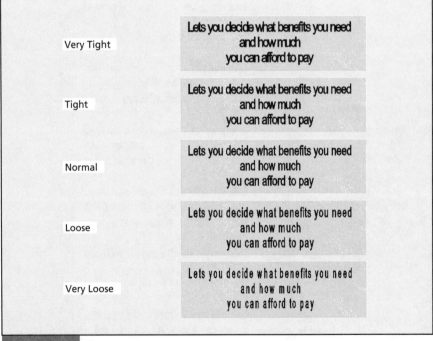

FIGURE 2-19   The five WordArt character spacing options

then click the Colors and Lines tab. In the Color section, click the drop-down box and choose Fill Effects. Then choose the Gradient tab where you can select the colors, type of shading, and type of variant.

The alignment for the WordArt on this slide is Center, and the Character Spacing is Normal. The shape is the second shape from the right in the bottom row of the WordArt Shape options on the WordArt toolbar. The only additional formatting is the 3-D effect (see Chapter 6).

Starting from Scratch

The third method of creating a new presentation is to start with a blank presentation. Choose the Blank Presentation option in the PowerPoint (Startup) dialog box. From within PowerPoint, choose File | New and double-click Blank Presentation on the General tab of the New Presentation dialog box. PowerPoint displays the New Slide dialog box so you can choose a layout for your first slide.

The main reason to start with a blank presentation is to create your own background design rather than use one of PowerPoint's design templates. Once you have created a design, creating a presentation from scratch is no different from using a design template. However, you can attach one of PowerPoint's design templates to your presentation at any time. The easiest way is to click Common Tasks on the Formatting toolbar and choose Apply Design Template.

Cross-Reference: You can find the steps for creating your own design template in Chapter 7.

The blank presentation comes with a number of default settings, such as the size of the title text, the type of bullets, and the color scheme. You can change these settings if you want so that the blank presentation uses your own. You might also want to add actual content, such as your company's logo. Here's how:

1. Create any presentation with the settings and/or content that you want.
2. Choose File | Save As.
3. In the Save as Type drop-down list, choose Design Template.
4. In the File Name box, type **Blank Presentation**.
5. Click Save.
6. Click Yes in the message box that PowerPoint displays to confirm.

Use a blank presentation when you're ready to start out on your own and customize the entire presentation.

Eliminating Unprofessional Spelling and Style Errors

Nothing screams "UNPROFESSIONAL!" more loudly than spelling errors in a presentation. PowerPoint not only lets you check your spelling but also adds a *style checker* that checks for consistency and style.

Checking Spelling

When you type a word that is not in PowerPoint's dictionary, you see a wavy line beneath it, appearing both in the outline and on the slide. To correct the word, right-click it to open the shortcut menu, as shown here.

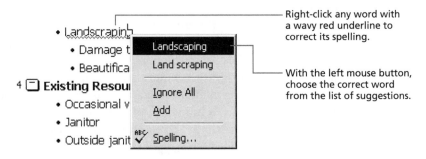

Right-click any word with a wavy red underline to correct its spelling.

With the left mouse button, choose the correct word from the list of suggestions.

Tip: If the wavy lines distract you, you can turn them off. Choose Tools | Options and click the Spelling and Style tab. Check Hide Spelling Errors in this Document to temporarily hide the wavy lines. When you are ready to spell check, you can go back, check this box, and the wavy lines will appear. If you uncheck Check Spelling as You Type (on the same tab), PowerPoint doesn't keep track of misspelled words as you type. When you have finished your presentation, choose Tools | Spelling to check your spelling.

Words are often underlined inappropriately. For example, many names of people and companies are underlined because they are not in the dictionary, which can be most annoying. If you use these words frequently, you can add them to the dictionary, and they will never appear underlined again. If the words appear only in this presentation, click Ignore All, and they will no longer be underlined in the presentation.

The shortcut menu is enough for most needs, but if you want more detail click Spelling to open the Spelling dialog box, shown in Figure 2-20.

PowerPoint doesn't check the spelling of WordArt text or text in charts, documents, tables, and other elements that have been brought in from other applications. You should therefore proofread this text carefully.

If your misspelled word is actually a word, but not the one you want, the spell checker will not find it. You may have seen examples, usually humorous, of text that passes a spell check with flying colors. Here's a slide with many errors, but the spell checker will not catch

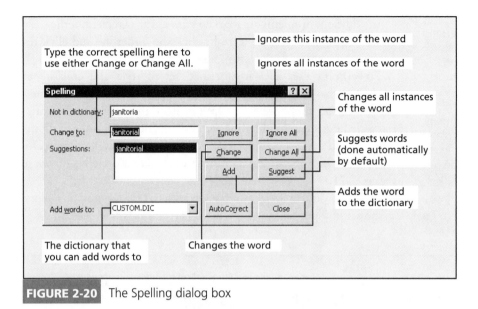

FIGURE 2-20 The Spelling dialog box

one of them! Therefore, always proofread your presentation carefully and never depend on the spell checker to catch all your errors.

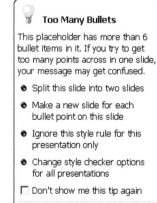

Too Many Bullets

This placeholder has more than 6 bullet items in it. If you try to get too many points across in one slide, your message may get confused.

- Split this slide into two slides
- Make a new slide for each bullet point on this slide
- Ignore this style rule for this presentation only
- Change style checker options for all presentations

☐ Don't show me this tip again

[OK]

Using the Style Checker

One of the hallmarks of a professional presentation is consistency. The Style Checker ensures consistency of style throughout your presentation. PowerPoint 2000 automatically checks your presentation for consistency and style. Consequently, PowerPoint 2000 no longer has a Style Checker dialog box. If you have the Office Assistant on, a message will often appear, reminding you of the style guidelines, as shown here.

Tip: Style checking can get very annoying while you are creating a presentation. To turn off style checking, uncheck the Check Style box on the Spelling and Style tab. When you have completed your presentation, you can turn style checking on again and run through your presentation to review PowerPoint's suggestions.

In addition, problems are marked with a wavy green underline. To check the potential problem, right-click the underline and click the option you want with the left mouse button.

PowerPoint uses a clearly defined set of style and consistency guidelines that you can change whenever you want. To access these guidelines, either choose Style Options from the shortcut menu after right-clicking a green underline, or choose Tools | Options, click the Spelling and Style tab, and then click Style Options. The Style Options dialog box opens. Its Case and End Punctuation tab is shown in Figure 2-21.

Click the Visual Clarity tab to set parameters for fonts and legibility, as shown in Figure 2-22.

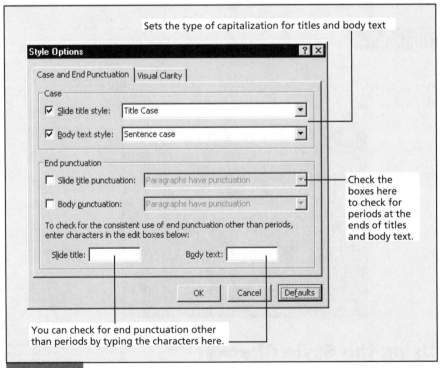

FIGURE 2-21 The Case and End Punctuation tab of the Style Options dialog box

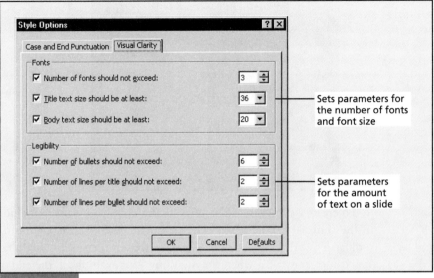

FIGURE 2-22 The Visual Clarity tab of the Style Options dialog box

The options on this tab are self-explanatory. They ensure that your text is large enough to be read by your audience and that there is not so much text as to be confusing.

Professional Pointer

You may want to change these parameters often, as your needs change. You can always click Defaults to return the settings to their original values.

Creating a Summary Slide

Audiences understand and remember a presentation better if they can grasp the wholeness of the message. For example, you may want to have an agenda slide near the beginning of your presentation so that your viewers know in advance all the topics that will be covered. A summary at the end of a presentation helps audiences to integrate all the material they have seen throughout. Both types of slides do the same thing—they summarize the topics covered in the presentation.

You can automatically create a *summary slide* in PowerPoint. A summary slide contains the titles of all the other slides, as shown next.

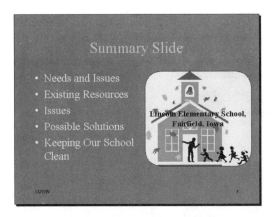

Tip: In outline view, you can select a group of consecutive slides by clicking the icon of the first slide you want to select, then pressing SHIFT, and then selecting the icon of the last slide you want to select. To select nonconsecutive slides, you need to switch to make the summary slide in slide sorter view. See Chapter 3 for more information.

To create a summary slide, select all the slides you want to include in the summary slide. Then click Summary Slide on the Outlining toolbar. PowerPoint places the new slide in front of the selected slides. You can then move it wherever you want—for example, at the end of the presentation.

PowerPoint names the new slide Summary Slide. Don't forget to change this title to something more meaningful! Even just Summary is better.

Don't let the term *summary slide* fool you. You can use this feature however you wish. For example, you could change the title to Agenda, or Tonight's Topics, and use the slide at the beginning of the presentation—perhaps just after the first slide.

Professional Skills Summary

In this chapter, you learned how to create a presentation with the AutoContent Wizard, by choosing a design template, and by starting with a blank presentation. You saw how to add text to a text placeholder, a text box, and an AutoShape. In addition, I explained how to create special text effects with WordArt. This chapter covered creating a text outline from within PowerPoint as well importing an outline. Once you have created an initial draft of a presentation, you should check both the spelling and the style—this chapter explained how.

In the next chapter, I explain the next step: how to edit a presentation.

Editing Text for Just the Right Look

In this chapter, you:

- Move and copy text with ease

- Copy multiple items to the clipboard

- Find and replace text like a veteran

- Add exotic symbols to your text

- Choose the right font, font size, and font style for the message

- Add special font effects

- Add, delete, and rearrange slides in a presentation

- Steal slides from other presentations

- Create two slides from one

- Change the margins around text in an object

- Duplicate text placeholders

Once you have created your presentation, you will find that it needs to be edited, just like any other document. Editing a presentation is somewhat different than editing a word processing document, although there are many common elements as well. The differences occur because of the graphical nature of a slide. In this chapter, you learn about editing text as well as your presentation as a whole.

Editing for Clarity

Your main concern when editing text is clarity. Text on a slide is quite different from text in a word processing document. Bulleted text is often not in full sentences, yet it needs to be clear, nonetheless. Try reading the text on each slide aloud to see if it makes sense.

A second reason to edit text is aesthetic. If you created your presentation using an outline, you need to run through each slide to see how the text fits on the slide. Text may need to be cut. You may even want to add text for a balanced look.

The basic techniques for editing text are the same in all Windows programs. To add text, you place the cursor where you want the new text to appear and start typing. To edit text, you select the text you want to change and type the new text that you want. To delete text, you select it and press DEL.

I cover changing fonts later in this chapter. Formatting bullets and paragraphs is covered in the next chapter.

Getting Text From Here to There: Moving and Copying Text

Within a presentation, you can often move selected text by dragging it to the new location in the outline pane. Hold CTRL to copy the text instead of moving it. However, if you can't fit both the source and destination locations on the screen at one time, you should use the clipboard. Use CTRL-X to move text and CTRL-C to copy text. Then place the cursor in the desired location, and use CTRL-V to paste the text. You can also use the Cut, Copy, and Paste commands on the Edit menu or the buttons on the Standard toolbar.

To copy text from another presentation or document, you can use the clipboard as well. Follow these steps:

1. Open the file that contains the source text.
2. Select the text.
3. Copy the text to the clipboard.
4. Move to the desired destination in the presentation, and place the cursor where you want the text to appear.
5. Paste the text from the clipboard.

Editing for Clarity **73**

You also use drag-and-drop to move or copy text from one file to another. It's more fun but requires more dexterity than using the clipboard. Here's how:

1. Open both files. (It may help to close other, unnecessary files.)
2. Choose Window | Arrange All. You see both your presentation and the other document on your screen. Make sure you can see both the source and destination locations in each window.
3. Click in the source document, and select the text you want to move or copy.
4. To move the text, point to it, and drag it to the desired location in your presentation. To copy the text, hold CTRL as you drag.

Later in this chapter, I explain how to copy slides from other presentations.

Using the Office 2000 Clipboard

Office 2000 now includes its own Office clipboard that lets you place up to 12 items on the clipboard at once.

Displaying the Clipboard toolbar

By default, when you copy or cut an item to the clipboard in any Microsoft Office program, the Clipboard toolbar appears. However, if you close the Clipboard toolbar three times without using it, Office assumes you don't want to see it automatically any more. In that case, you can manually display the Clipboard toolbar by right-clicking any toolbar and choosing Clipboard. You can also copy the same item twice in a row to the clipboard and Office will display the Clipboard toolbar. If you then use the Clipboard toolbar, Office will start to display it automatically again.

Using the Office 2000 clipboard

Once the Clipboard toolbar, shown here, is displayed, you simply copy a second item to the clipboard in the usual manner. You can then paste either item into your presentation. Each additional piece of data that you copy to the clipboard (up to 12) is added as a separate item.

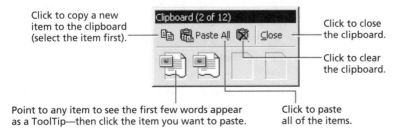

Click to copy a new item to the clipboard (select the item first).

Clipboard (2 of 12)

Click to close the clipboard.

Click to clear the clipboard.

Point to any item to see the first few words appear as a ToolTip—then click the item you want to paste.

Click to paste all of the items.

You can use the Paste All button to collect text from several places and paste it all in a new location.

Editing Placeholder Text

Because placeholder text also appears in the outline, you can edit it either in the outline or directly on the slide. Editing placeholder text on the outline may be more familiar to you because it is quite similar to editing text in a word processor. If all you want to do is simple text editing, do it in the outline pane.

However, for several reasons you may want to edit text directly on the slide. For example:

- The text is larger and therefore easier to see.
- The slide may contain a graphic, and you may need to see how the text fits with the graphic. For example, you may want to edit your text because it covers the graphic.
- You may be doing several editing functions at once, such as changing the placeholder's background color along with editing the text. Since you must change the placeholder's background color directly on the slide, it is easy to continue your work right on the slide.

When you edit placeholder text on the slide, two objects are involved—the placeholder and the text inside the placeholder. When you click on any text in the placeholder, PowerPoint places the cursor where you clicked. The placeholder gets a selection border and handles to show you that it is selected. You can also drag to select the text you want to edit, which automatically selects the placeholder as well. You also see a block in a different color than the background that shows the overall boundaries of the text. You are now in Edit Text mode, shown in Figure 3-1. (To view this slide in color, refer to number 14 in the Slide Gallery.) Although the placeholder is selected, your changes affect only the text within it.

To delete an entire bulleted item, place the cursor over the bullet. The cursor changes to a cross with arrows, as shown here. This works only when the placeholder is already selected. Then click to select the entire bulleted item, and press DEL.

If you backspace to delete the text in a bulleted item, or select only the words in an item, you may be left with just the bullet. With the cursor next to the bullet, press BACKSPACE twice to delete the bullet and the empty line. To add a bulleted item, place the cursor after the previous item, and press ENTER. You can then type the text.

To move a bulleted item above or below another item, place the cursor over the bullet, and drag to the desired location. A long cursor line appears, showing

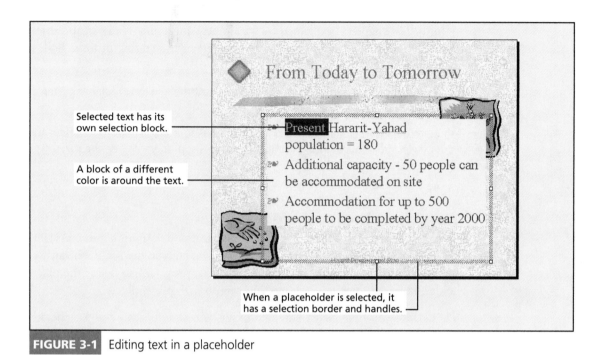

Selected text has its own selection block.

A block of a different color is around the text.

When a placeholder is selected, it has a selection border and handles.

FIGURE 3-1   Editing text in a placeholder

you where your bulleted text will appear, as shown here. Just release the mouse button to move the text. These techniques work in the outline pane as well.

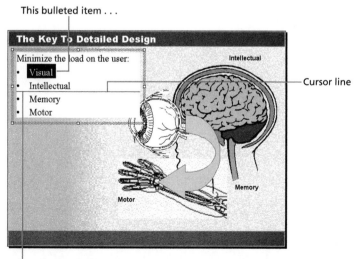

This bulleted item . . .

Cursor line

. . . will move here when you release the mouse button.

In the last chapter, I explained how to import an outline. You can also insert an outline into an existing presentation as part of the editing process. Follow these steps:

1. In the outline pane, click the slide you want the new text to appear after.
2. Choose Insert | Slides from Outline.
3. In the Insert Outline dialog box, shown in Figure 3-2, locate your outline and select it. Notice that the Files of Type drop-down list is already set to All Outlines.
4. Click Insert.

Working with placeholders

Once you click a placeholder, you enter Edit Text mode. Anytime you press DEL, text is deleted. In this case, how do you delete the placeholder itself? The answer is to click ESC to exit Edit Text mode and then press DEL to delete the placeholder. Here are some other things you can do with placeholders:

- Once you have exited Edit Text mode, you can duplicate the placeholder. Open the Edit menu, place the cursor over the down arrows until the menu expands (if necessary), and choose Duplicate. You now have twin placeholders. Move the new placeholder so it doesn't overlap the first one.

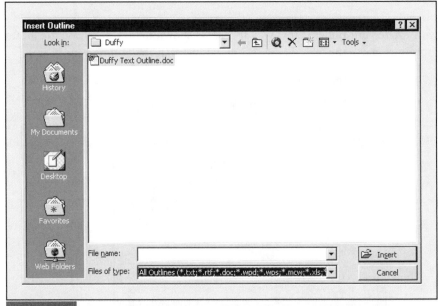

FIGURE 3-2 The Insert Outline dialog box lets you insert an outline in an existing presentation

- You can cut (or copy) and paste a placeholder to a new slide. Again, you need to exit Edit Text mode. Then press CTRL-X to cut or CTRL-C to copy. Move to the new slide and press CTRL-V to paste the placeholder.

- To move a placeholder, select it and place the cursor anywhere over the selection border until you see the crossed arrows cursor. Then click and drag the placeholder to its new position.

- To resize a placeholder, drag one of its handles. The placeholder grows or shrinks in the direction you drag.

Finding and replacing text like a veteran

You can search for text throughout the entire presentation. You can also specify replacement text. You are probably already familiar with the find and replace function in your word processor. To find text, choose Edit | Find (or press CTRL-F). The Find dialog box shown here is displayed.

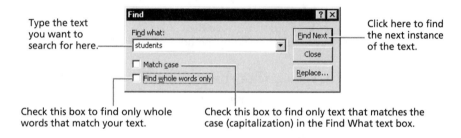

Type the text you want to search for here.

Check this box to find only whole words that match your text.

Click here to find the next instance of the text.

Check this box to find only text that matches the case (capitalization) in the Find What text box.

Use Match Case to find *Governor* but not *governor*, for example. Use Find whole words only to find *and* but not *sand*. PowerPoint highlights the text it finds in the outline pane only but displays the equivalent slide so that you can work on either the outline or the slide.

You can go directly to the Replace dialog box, shown here, by clicking Replace in the Find dialog box. Otherwise, choose Edit | Replace. Note that the Replace command is not initially on the menu. Place the cursor over the down arrows at the bottom of the menu, and it appears. You can also press CTRL-H.

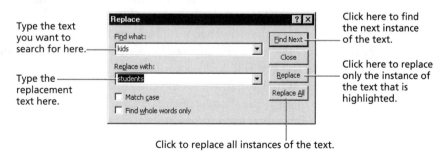

Type the text you want to search for here.

Type the replacement text here.

Click here to find the next instance of the text.

Click here to replace only the instance of the text that is highlighted.

Click to replace all instances of the text.

After PowerPoint has searched all the text in the placeholders—text that appears in the outline—you see the message shown here. Click OK to search for text in text boxes and AutoShapes. PowerPoint highlights this text on the slide, since it doesn't appear in the outline.

The Find and Replace commands cannot find WordArt text.

Changing text case

For a professional look, pay attention to proper use and consistency of *case*, that is, capitalization. PowerPoint's style checker (covered in Chapter 2) looks for case automatically. For example, the slide title usually uses title case and bulleted text uses sentence case. When you want to make changes, the Change Case command can help you quickly change the case of text. Just select the text, and choose Format | Change Case. Here are your options:

- *Sentence case* starts with an uppercase letter. All the rest of the letters are lowercase, and the sentence ends with a period. Be careful—PowerPoint often changes proper nouns to all lowercase, as shown in Figure 3-3, where the words that make up the title of the university should have initial capital letters.
- *lowercase* contains all lowercase letters.
- *UPPERCASE* contains all uppercase letters.
- *Title Case* capitalizes the first letter of each word. But you'll still need to review the results—if you don't want short words such as *with* capitalized, as shown in Figure 3-3. (To view these slides in color, refer to numbers 15 and 16 in the Slide Gallery.)
- *tOGGLE cASE* reverses the case of each letter.

When you have made your choice of case, click OK to close the dialog box.

Editing Text in AutoShapes and Text Boxes

Editing text in AutoShapes and text boxes is very similar to editing placeholder text. When you select the text, you are also selecting the object that contains the text, and a selection border and handles appear around the object.

As I mentioned in the last chapter, when you place text in a text box, the text box expands as you type. The text box similarly adjusts when you edit text. If you delete enough text, the text box will shrink accordingly.

If you add text to an AutoShape, it will overflow the boundaries of the shape. Right-click the shape to open the shortcut menu. Choose Format AutoShape. Then choose the Text Box tab to open the dialog box shown in Figure 3-4.

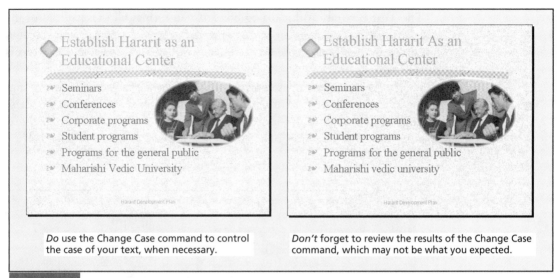

Do use the Change Case command to control the case of your text, when necessary.

Don't forget to review the results of the Change Case command, which may not be what you expected.

FIGURE 3-3 The Change Case command lets you control the case of your text, but you need to review the results

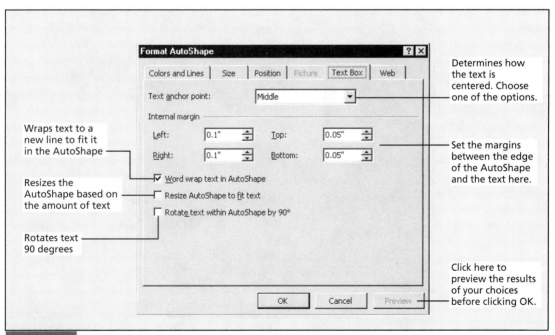

FIGURE 3-4 Use the Text Box tab of the Format AutoShape dialog box to specify how text in an AutoShape is formatted

The Text Box tab of this dialog box lets you format all the qualities of the AutoShape that pertain to text, as described in Figure 3-4. You can format text in a text box in exactly the same way—the only difference is that the dialog box is called Format Text Box.

Figure 3-5 shows examples of text in an AutoShape using some of the settings of the Text Box tab of the Format AutoShape dialog box. As you can see, these settings are very important for obtaining professional results. For example, text that overflows the boundary of an AutoShape looks sloppy, to say the least!

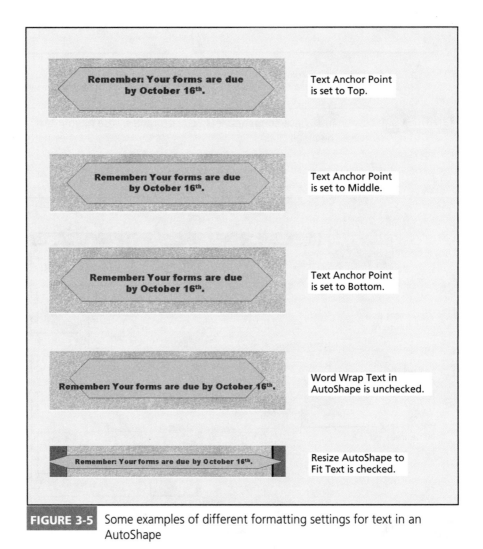

FIGURE 3-5   Some examples of different formatting settings for text in an AutoShape

Editing WordArt Text

To edit WordArt text, double-click the WordArt object. The Edit WordArt Text dialog box opens, shown here. You can also select the WordArt object (by clicking it once) and choose Edit WordArt on the WordArt toolbar.

As you can see, the text is already selected in the window. You can replace the entire text by typing new text. Otherwise, click to place the cursor or select part of the text to edit. When you have finished editing the text, click OK.

You can use the WordArt toolbar to edit any feature of the WordArt in the same way you created it.

Adding Exotic Symbols

To insert a symbol into new or existing text, choose Insert | Symbol. The Symbol command is only on the expanded menu, so you need to point to the down arrows (or wait). PowerPoint opens the Symbol dialog box, shown here:

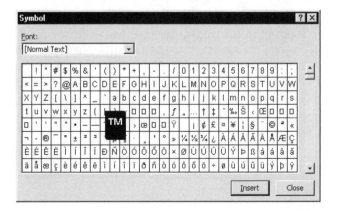

Tip: You cannot access the Symbol command while the Edit WordArt dialog box is open. To insert a symbol into WordArt, insert the symbol first into a text box or placeholder. Select the symbol and copy it to the clipboard. Then, with the Edit WordArt dialog box open, paste the symbol into the desired location.

First, choose a font from the Font drop-down list. The default is Normal Text. To view a symbol more clearly, click it. Then click Insert to insert the symbol. The dialog box stays open so you can insert other symbols. Click Close to close the dialog box.

Besides choosing technical symbols such as ° (the degree symbol), ø (the diameter symbol), and ± (the plus-minus symbol), you can find arrows, check marks, stars, and other more whimsical symbols. You may especially want to check the Wingdings and Monotype Sorts fonts.

Setting Editing Options for Consistent Results

PowerPoint lets you customize how PowerPoint's editing features function. Many users ignore these features, but a little time spent up front will speed up your work forever after—and ensure the precise results you want.

Using the Options dialog box

The Edit tab of the Options dialog box, shown in Figure 3-6, lets you set some of PowerPoint's text-editing features. You can use this dialog box to make PowerPoint's text editing suit your style better. Choose Tools | Options and click the Edit tab. By default, all of the check boxes are checked. Here is what each option does:

- *Replace Straight Quotes with Smart Quotes* automatically changes a double quotation mark to a curved quotation mark. If you type a pair of quotation marks (around a word or phrase), the quotation marks automatically face each other. The same goes for apostrophes. Uncheck this box if you need to use apostrophes and quotation marks as primes and double primes (to indicate feet and inches measurement).

- *When Selecting, Automatically Select Entire Word* selects an entire word even if you only dragged over part of a word. I recommend unchecking this box, which makes it hard to select part of a word. You can always double-click a word to quickly select the entire word.

- *Use Smart Cut and Paste* automatically adds or deletes a space before or after text when you insert or delete text so that each word has only one space before and after.

- *Drag-and-Drop Text Editing* lets you move text by selecting and dragging it. First select the text keeping the cursor over the selection until it changes to a left-pointing arrow. Then press the mouse button and drag the cursor to the desired location to move the text. Hold down the CTRL key while dragging to copy the text.

- *Auto-fit Text to Text Placeholder* automatically changes the size of place-holder text to fit the text placeholder. If you type more text than can fit in the placeholder, PowerPoint makes the text smaller. If you then delete some text, PowerPoint enlarges the text again. Uncheck this box if you want all your text to be the same size and prefer instead to move some text to another slide or shorten your text.

- *AutoFormat as You Type* automatically makes certain changes to your text as you type. For example, it changes 1/2 to ½ and automatically starts a num-bered list if you type a number, a period, a space, and some text.

In the Charts section of the dialog box, you can set whether or not new charts take on the current PowerPoint font. Finally, in the Undo section, you can set how many undos PowerPoint remembers. The default is 20. A higher number uses more memory and storage space because PowerPoint has to remember more actions.

When you have finished setting the features in the dialog box, click OK.

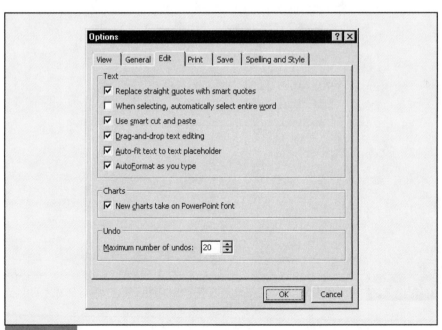

FIGURE 3-6 Use the Edit tab of the Options dialog box to specify how PowerPoint's text-editing features work

Using AutoCorrect

AutoCorrect is a feature that automatically corrects misspelled words. You can also use AutoCorrect as a shortcut for typing long, difficult words or phrases. To set up AutoCorrect, choose Tools | AutoCorrect to open the AutoCorrect dialog box, shown in Figure 3-7. The top four check box items correct common typing errors:

- *Correct TWo INitial CApitals* changes the second uppercase letter to lowercase.

- *Capitalize First Letter of Sentence* changes a lowercase letter to uppercase when PowerPoint thinks you have started a new sentence, usually after a period. See the following discussion regarding exceptions for this setting.

- *Capitalize Names of Days* automatically capitalizes the first letter of the days.

- *Correct Accidental Use of cAPS LOCK Key* reverses the case of letters when PowerPoint notices one lowercase letter followed by several uppercase letters.

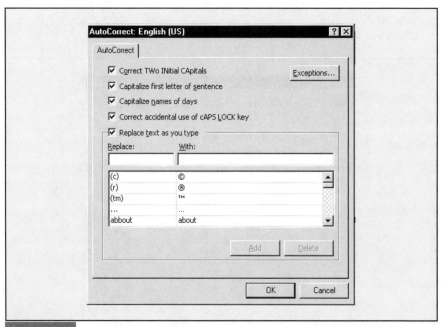

FIGURE 3-7   The AutoCorrect dialog box settings determine how PowerPoint corrects text as you type

The last item lets you add your own AutoCorrections. Type the incorrect spelling in the Replace box, type the correct spelling in the With box, and click Add. To delete an item, choose it and click DELETE.

You can use AutoCorrect to help you type long or difficult phrases. For example, you could put "hrd" in the Replace box and "Human Resources Department" in the With box. Then, every time you type **hrd**, PowerPoint will replace it with the full version. Make sure that you use a shortcut that you won't type in any other situation.

Click Exceptions to open the AutoCorrect Exceptions dialog box, shown in Figure 3-8. The First Letter tab specifies exceptions to the Capitalize First Letter of Sentence setting. Because PowerPoint bases its concept of a sentence as anything after a period, you may find that it incorrectly capitalizes words after an abbreviation that you follow with a period. By adding abbreviations that you commonly use, you can avoid this problem.

The INitial CAps tab fine-tunes the Correct TWo INitial CApitals setting. It comes with only one item, YNote. If you type similar words, where the first two letters should be capitalized, add them to this list.

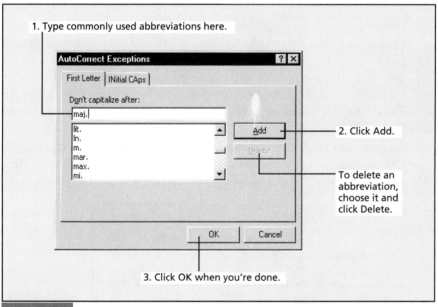

FIGURE 3-8 The AutoCorrect Exceptions dialog box lets you fine-tune the AutoCorrect feature

Choosing Text with Style

Part of editing text is formatting it. Fonts are an important feature of text formatting. The font type determines the shape of the letters in a font. You can also change the font size of any font. You can apply a font *style*, such as bold or italic. Finally, you can add certain effects to your text—underlining, a shadow, or embossing.

Using the Right Font for the Message

PowerPoint offers you a wide choice of fonts. Your choice of font affects the impact of your message on the audience. Here are some simple guidelines for choosing the right font:

- Don't use more than three fonts on a slide. The effect is chaotic and therefore distracting. A better choice is to limit yourself to one or two fonts. Figure 3-9 shows how a slide looks better when it uses fewer fonts. To view these examples in color, refer to numbers 17 and 18 in the Slide Gallery.

- Associate a font with a type of element. For example, make all your slide titles the same font.

- Keep the font type fairly simple for legibility.

The slides in Figure 3-9 use Mead Bold for the title. In this case, it is meant to look like white chalk on a chalkboard. An AutoShape was placed behind the title text and filled with a one-color gradient using one of the *diagonal up* shading styles. The body text of the slide on the left uses all Times New Roman font. See the next chapter for details on creating numbered lists. A stock clip art graphic was added.

Sans serif fonts have no extraneous lines and are good for titles and text that you want to stand out. The most common sans serif font in Windows is Arial, which comes in several variants. Some examples of sans serif fonts are shown here:

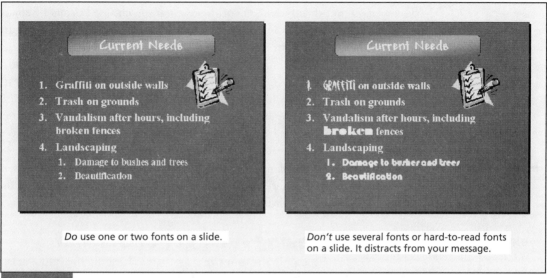

Do use one or two fonts on a slide.

Don't use several fonts or hard-to-read fonts on a slide. It distracts from your message.

FIGURE 3-9   Use one or two fonts for a more professional look

Serif fonts have small extra lines at the ends of letters. They are considered most readable for paragraph text. Times New Roman is the most common serif font in Windows. Some examples of serif fonts are shown here:

When you select text, its font appears in the Font drop-down list on the Formatting toolbar. To change a text's font, select the text and choose a new font from the drop-down list. A very helpful feature of this drop-down list is that fonts are displayed as they will appear, as shown to the right.

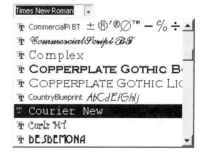

To replace a font throughout an entire presentation, choose Format | Replace Fonts. (This command is available only on the expanded Format menu.) Figure 3-10 shows the Replace Font dialog box that opens.

Remember that design templates come with preset fonts for all placeholder text. Therefore, even if you replace all the fonts in your presentation, if you create a new slide it will revert to the font that comes with the design template. These fonts are stored on the *slide master*, which is the topic of Chapter 7. By changing the slide master, you can change even the font that will be used for new slides.

To change the font for WordArt text, double-click the text and choose a new font from the Font drop-down list in the Edit WordArt dialog box.

Making It Bigger or Smaller

Changing the font size is as easy as changing the font—select the text and choose a new size from the Font Size drop-down list on the Formatting toolbar. (The Edit WordArt dialog box has its own Font Size drop-down list.)

Professional Pointer

If you aren't satisfied with the list of font sizes, you can type in another size. (This doesn't work in WordArt.) However, because of the extra calculations required, nonstandard sizes may look jagged, especially in slide show view.

Increase Font Size

Decrease Font Size

If you don't know exactly what size you want but just want to make your text a little bigger or smaller, use the Increase Font Size and Decrease Font Size buttons on the Formatting toolbar, shown here. Your text quickly goes to the next setting on the Font Size drop-down list, either smaller or larger, according to which button you have chosen.

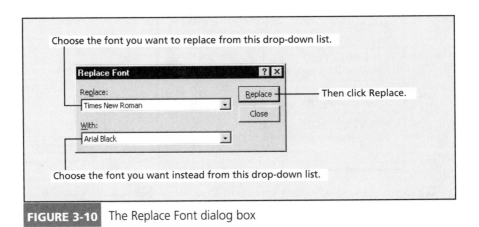

Choose the font you want to replace from this drop-down list.

Then click Replace.

Choose the font you want instead from this drop-down list.

FIGURE 3-10 The Replace Font dialog box

As you have no doubt discovered, typical font sizes are much larger on slides than in word-processing documents. Fonts are usually measured in *points*. A point is 1/72 of an inch. Here you see some samples of text in different font sizes:

12 pt = 1/6 inch —— • Graffiti on outside walls

18 pt = 1/4 inch —— • Trash on grounds

24 pt = 1/3 inch —— • Vandalism after hours

36 pt = 1/2 inch —— • Landscaping

While 12-point text is typical in a word-processing document, it is much too small for a slide. In general, you should not use text that is less than 18 points—and then only in a pinch. You will find that 24-point text is appropriate for most bulleted text, and your slide title should be larger than that.

As mentioned earlier in the discussion on font types, the default font size is stored in the master slide that comes with the design template. However, if you type more text than can fit in a placeholder, by default PowerPoint resizes your text to fit into the placeholder. You can turn this feature off by choosing Tools | Options and then the Edit tab. Uncheck Auto-Fit Text to Text Placeholder.

The Office Assistant's light bulb usually appears when you type too much text in a placeholder. Click it to display the tip shown here. You can choose to split the text onto two slides or make a separate slide from each paragraph.

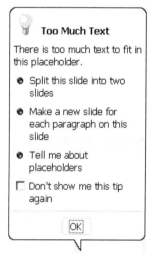

Too Much Text

There is too much text to fit in this placeholder.

- Split this slide into two slides
- Make a new slide for each paragraph on this slide
- Tell me about placeholders

☐ Don't show me this tip again

[OK]

Adding font effects

Add a font style to your text to emphasize it. To format text with a font style, select it and choose Bold or Italic from the Formatting toolbar. You can also add underlining or a shadow effect from the Formatting toolbar. Next you see some text using these font styles and effects.

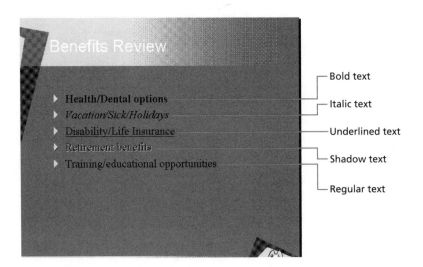

Note that you can also create shadows for objects. In general, you should use the Text Shadow button on the Formatting toolbar for text and the Shadow button on the Drawing toolbar for objects. For example, if you change the shadow settings from the Drawing toolbar while placeholder text is selected, PowerPoint applies the settings to all the text in the placeholder because the placeholder is one object.

By default, the shadow for text is gray. It does not show up well on a gray background.

Cross-Reference: Shadows for objects are covered in Chapter 6.

Using the Format | Font dialog box

Until now, I have described the easiest and most common ways of formatting text. However there is another way—the Font dialog box. The Font dialog box puts most of the settings for formatting text in one place and is shown in Figure 3-11.

To change existing text, select it and choose Format | Font to open the Font dialog box. Choose a font, font style, and font size from the drop-down lists. From the Effects section, you can choose Underline, Shadow, Emboss,

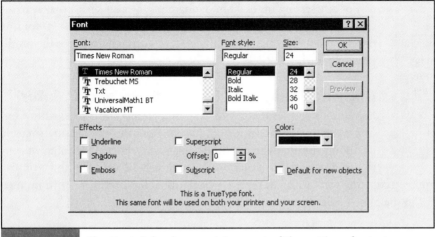

FIGURE 3-11 The Font dialog box contains most of the settings for text formatting

Superscript, or Subscript. Embossed text looks three-dimensional, as if it has been carved or stamped. Here you see some examples of text using effects:

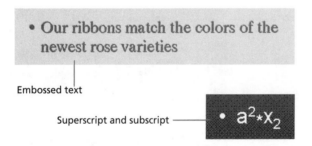

To change the text's color, click the Color drop-down list and choose a color. To choose from a full range of colors, choose More Colors from the drop-down list.

You can also change the default settings for new text. Follow these steps:

1. Format some text the way you want it.
2. Select the text.
3. Choose Format | Font to open the Font dialog box.
4. Choose Default for New Objects.
5. Click OK.

Tip: After you make several changes to some text in the Font dialog box and close the dialog box, you can make the same set of changes to another selection of text immediately by pressing CTRL-Y, which repeats the last action.

For any setting in the Font dialog box, you can click Preview to see the results before you click OK. However, since you are often working on selected text, which is highlighted, it is often hard to see the results precisely until you click OK and deselect the text.

Copying that great look with Format Painter

Sometimes you see text formatting that you like and you want to format other text in the same way. Figuring out the exact formatting and changing the text can be time-consuming. Format Painter was designed for just this situation. In Figure 3-12 you see how you can quickly copy the formatting of text. To view this slide in color, refer to number 19 in the Slide Gallery.

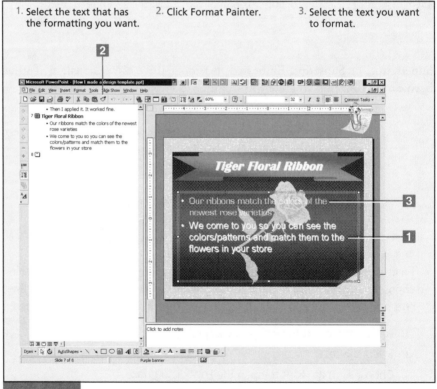

FIGURE 3-12 You can change the first bulleted item to look like the second bulleted item using Format Painter

The text shown on the slide (after the second bullet) was created using Arial 32-point text with embossing added. (Select the text, choose Format | Font, choose Emboss, and click OK.) This text has no other special formatting. Embossed text has no color; instead, it takes on the color of the slide background. This looks beautiful on rich, deep colors but is generally hard to read, because there is so little contrast. The trick is to place an AutoShape behind the text with a contrasting color. If the text is in a text placeholder, the only way to place an AutoShape behind the text is to place it on the slide master, as was done for this slide. Slide masters are fully explained in Chapter 7. To place an AutoShape behind a text box, insert it at the desired location, select the AutoShape, choose Draw | Order on the Drawing toolbar, and choose the appropriate option, such as Send Backward.

Tip: Remember that you can select an entire bulleted item by clicking its bullet.

Expanding One Slide into Two

If you just can't make the text fit properly on a slide, try splitting the text onto two slides. If the text is in a text placeholder, you can accomplish this easily in the outline pane, as follows:

1. Position the insertion point at the end of the last bulleted item that you want to appear on the first slide.

2. Press ENTER.

3. On the Outline toolbar, click Promote until a new slide icon appears.

4. Type a title for the new slide. You may have to adjust the bulleted text to get it to the proper level.

Making Text Count

The first rule for making text count is readability. Here are some pointers that will help you ensure your text is legible:

- Shadowed text can make text stand out, but make sure it looks good on your background color.

- When you place text over a full-color graphic, be sure that the text is readable everywhere on your slide. If the graphic has many colors, some of its areas may blend in too well with your text.

- Be careful about rotated and vertical text.

- To get text to stand out, concentrate on the right font, the right size, the right color, and a contrasting background instead of using all capital letters or a very fancy text effect. One of the text styles (bold, italics) or effects (shadow, embossed) can also work wonders.

Use text in conjunction with meaningful AutoShapes to make your point. For example, to show that sales went up 15 percent, put the text **15%** on an AutoShape of an arrow

pointing diagonally upward about 15 degrees. On the other hand, don't put too many AutoShapes with text on a slide. Sometimes simple bulleted text is easier to follow. When you place text in AutoShapes and text boxes, make sure these objects are aligned with each other to avoid a chaotic effect. You can use *guides*, discussed in Chapter 5, to align objects.

Have someone else read your presentation, on paper or on-screen, to make sure the flow of ideas is clear. For example, if you set up two columns and three rows of text, in which direction are readers supposed to look first—down the first column or across the first row? If necessary, you can place AutoShapes behind your text that unite groups of text that you want readers to consider all at once.

WordArt is great fun, but use it sparingly. Too many effects make your text less readable. Use WordArt for short phrases that are separate from the rest of the text, such as "See you there!" or "Don't forget!"

In Chapter 9, I explain how to animate text—a good way to emphasize it. You can make text appear when you want it to, as well as have lines you've already presented lines dim or disappear.

Adding, Deleting, and Rearranging Slides

Another aspect of editing a presentation involves adding, deleting, and rearranging slides. As I explained in Chapter 1, you do this editing in slide sorter view, where you can see most or all of your slides at once. In slide sorter view, you look at the wholeness and flow of your presentation, rather than the details on each slide.

Working in Slide Sorter View

In slide sorter view, you select a slide by clicking it. The selected slide has a black border. You can drag that slide to any new location. To copy the slide, press CTRL as you drag. You can also move a slide by cutting and pasting:

1. Select the slide.
2. Press CTRL-X to cut the slide and place it on the clipboard.
3. Click where you want the slide to go, between two other slides. PowerPoint uses a long vertical line to indicate the cursor between the slides.
4. Press CTRL-V to paste the slide.

You can delete a selected slide by pressing DEL. Whenever you move or delete a slide, PowerPoint automatically renumbers all the slides.

To add a new slide, click between two slides. Choose New Slide from the Common Tasks button on the Formatting toolbar. You can then choose a slide layout. The new slide automatically takes on the design template of the rest of the presentation.

Stealing Slides from Other Presentations

You may want to use a slide (or slides) from another presentation. You may even be able to build most of your presentation from slides in other presentations. Because the design template is attached to the presentation, not the slide, when you import a slide, it takes on the current template and fits seamlessly into your presentation.

Using the Clipboard to import slides

The most common technique for importing a slide is to use the clipboard. Here's how it works:

1. Open the presentation containing the slide or slides you want to use.
2. If you want only one slide, click its icon in the outline pane. If you want a series of slides, click the first slide's icon, hold down SHIFT, and then click the last slide's icon.
3. Press CTRL-C or click Copy on the Standard toolbar to copy the slides to the clipboard.
4. Open your current presentation. If it is already open, click its button on the Windows taskbar to display it. In the outline pane, click the icon of the slide you want the other slides to follow.
5. Press CTRL-V or click Paste on the Standard toolbar. PowerPoint places the new slide (or slides) after the selected slide.

This method of copying slides from one presentation to another is the easiest because you are usually in one of the tri-pane views, but what if you want to copy several slides that are not together? You can do this easily in slide sorter view, as shown in Figure 3-13.

You may also find it easier to paste slides in slide sorter view because the long vertical cursor between the slides makes it clear where your slides will appear. Click between two slides and paste. You can also click before the first slide or after the last one.

Using drag-and-drop to import slides

You can also use drag-and-drop to copy slides, as shown in Figure 3-14.

Using the Slide Finder

PowerPoint offers yet another way to import slides—the Slide Finder. Use the Slide Finder when you're not sure which presentation contains the slides you want to import. First select the slide that you want to insert the other slide(s) after. Then open the Slide Finder dialog box, shown in Figure 3-15, by choosing Insert | Slide from Files. (It's on the expanded menu.)

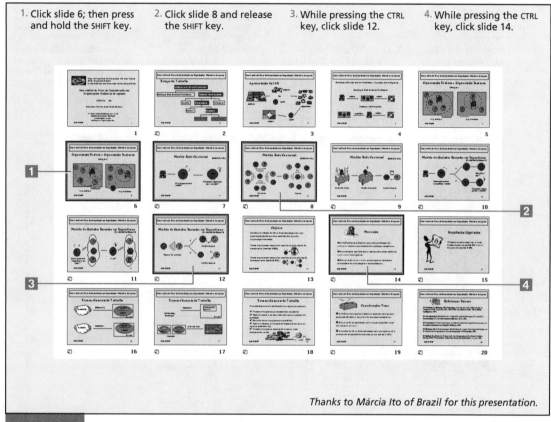

1. Click slide 6; then press and hold the SHIFT key.

2. Click slide 8 and release the SHIFT key.

3. While pressing the CTRL key, click slide 12.

4. While pressing the CTRL key, click slide 14.

Thanks to Márcia Ito of Brazil for this presentation.

FIGURE 3-13 To copy slides 6 through 8, 12, and 14 to the clipboard . . .

If you don't find the slide you want, choose another presentation. The Slide Finder makes it easy to browse presentations on your hard drive or network.

Making adjustments to imported slides

Although your new slides take on the design template of the current presentation, you may have to make other adjustments. Templates come with a color scheme that includes colors for the slide background, the text, bullets, and fill

1. Open both presentations. Make sure no other presentations are open.
2. Choose Window | Arrange All. (Arrange All is on the expanded menu, so you may not see it at first.)

3. In the active window, change to slide sorter view.
4. Click the inactive window. (The title bar is gray.)

5. Change to slide sorter view.
6. Select the slide(s) you want to copy.

7. Press CTRL and click any of the selected slides. Drag them to the desired location in the destination presentation using the vertical line cursor as a guide.

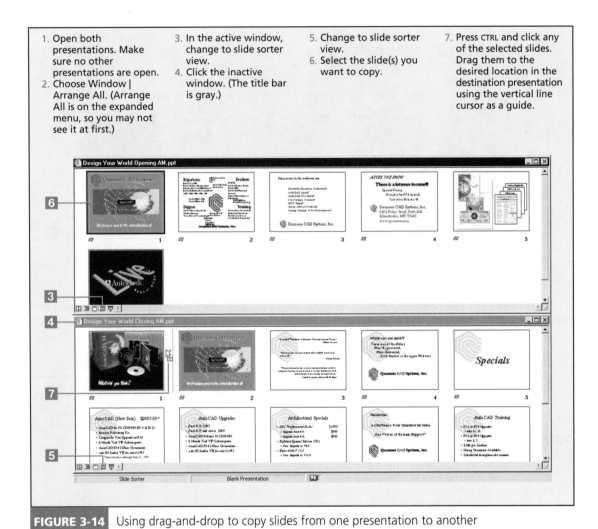

FIGURE 3-14   Using drag-and-drop to copy slides from one presentation to another

colors. If you have changed the color of any item in the source slide, such as the text color, the result in the destination slide may not be what you want. You can even find that the text disappears because it is the same color as the background! You can solve this problem by clicking a few times where you expect the text to be until you see handles and a selection border. Whew! You can now select the text and use the Font dialog box (choose Format | Font) to change its color.

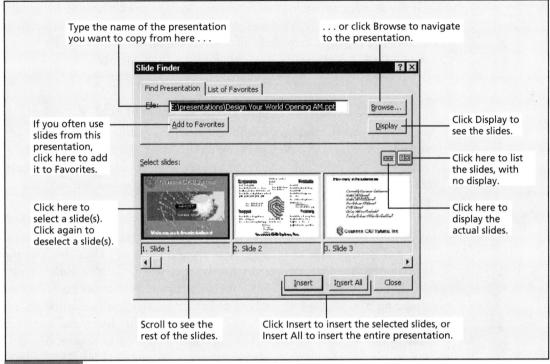

FIGURE 3-15 The Slide Finder lets you preview slides from other presentations so you can decide which ones you want to import

Keeping a Slide Library

Ever wonder how professionals find all the neat stuff they put into presentations? One secret is organization. If you reuse slides a lot, you can create a slide library. Here are a few techniques:

- Add presentations that contain slides you use a lot to the List of Favorites in the Slide Finder, as described in Figure 3-15.

- Create a special presentation that contains only slides that you use a lot. Give it a name that identifies its purpose, such as Source Slides or Reusable Slides. You can then add that presentation to the List of Favorites in the Slide Finder.

- For each slide that you want to reuse, create a presentation containing that slide alone. Place all such presentations in a folder, perhaps called Source Presentations. Name each presentation in a way that describes the slide it contains.

If you wish, print handouts of these presentations (see Chapter 16 for details) and keep them in a book. Mark the name of the presentations and their locations on the printouts and keep them in a folder or three-ring binder. By leafing through the handouts, you can quickly find the slides you need.

Professional Skills Summary

This chapter showed you how to edit text in a presentation, including moving, copying, changing, and deleting text. It discussed techniques for editing place-holder text, text in AutoShapes and text boxes, and WordArt text. Some special techniques included finding and replacing text, changing text case, and adding symbols.

You learned how to set PowerPoint's editing options to meet your needs and to use AutoCorrect to correct errors as you type, including certain spelling errors.

This chapter covered all the ways to work with fonts, including changing the font type, size, and style. PowerPoint has two special text effects, shadow and embossed, that you can also use. The Font dialog box gives you more control over formatting. You saw how to use Format Painter to copy text formatting.

The second part of the chapter discussed how to add, delete, and rearrange slides, usually in slide sorter view. You can also import slides from other presentations, using the clipboard, drag-and-drop, or the Slide Finder. This chapter ended with some techniques for creating a slide library of slides that you use regularly.

In the next chapter, I explain how to format paragraphs and bullets.

chapter 4

Formatting Bullets and Paragraphs

In this chapter, you:

- Choose and change the bullet type
- Format a bullet's size and color
- Use a picture as a bullet
- Create custom bullets
- Create numbered lists
- Use the ruler to align and indent text
- Remove hanging indents
- Work with tabs
- Align paragraph text
- Adjust line spacing

In many presentations, the majority of text is placeholder text. By default, this text comes with bullets. The purpose of bullets is to create a list of items. Each item is a paragraph of text. You can change the formatting of bulleted text to make it more readable or emphasize certain items. You can create bullets from pictures if you want to get really flashy. On the other hand, sometimes you might want to eliminate the bullets and work with regular paragraphs. Knowing how to format bullets and paragraphs is essential to creating a professionally designed presentation.

Using Bullets

When you stand up in front of an audience, you talk to the audience. Why do you need text on a slide? The purpose of bulleted text is to create a visual confirmation of your message. As mentioned in Chapter 3, bulleted text should be short and to the point. The more quickly the audience grasps the text, the sooner the audience will turn its attention to what you are saying.

If your text is not bulleted, you can add bullets by selecting the text and clicking Bullets on the Formatting toolbar. Click Bullets again to remove the bullets.

Choosing Bullets

Each design template comes with a default style of bullets for each level of heading (except for heading 1 text, which creates the title of the slide). Here you see a sample of five levels of bulleted text.

> ### Keeping Our School Clean
>
> - Needs and Issues
>   - Existing Resources
>   - Issues
>   - Possible Solutions
>   - What do you think?

In this illustration, the template uses three different styles of bullets and varies their sizes as well. Another template might use varying colors to distinguish between the heading levels. You can change every feature about any bullet to suit your taste and needs.

Of course, you don't want your bullets to distract from your text. Use those flashy bullets only when they have a meaningful purpose. For example, if you are selling floral ribbon to florists, you might want to use a picture of a rose as a bullet. In that case, use the rose bullets throughout the presentation. They make the point that you know the floral business, but they don't distract because they're on every slide and your audience soon knows to ignore them and pay attention to the text. Another good use of an unusual bullet is for occasional use—to draw attention to one or two items only.

Tip: To see the types of bullets in the outline pane, click Show Formatting on either the Outlining or the Standard toolbar.

To choose a bullet for an item of text, select the text and choose Format | Bullets and Numbering to open the Bullets and Numbering dialog box, shown in Figure 4-1. Any change you make applies to all of the selected text.

In Figure 4-2, you see a slide at the end of a presentation used for a graduate class in artificial intelligence. This slide is the bibliography, and the student used file folders as bullets, to represent containers of information. To view this slide in color, refer to number 20 in the Slide Gallery.

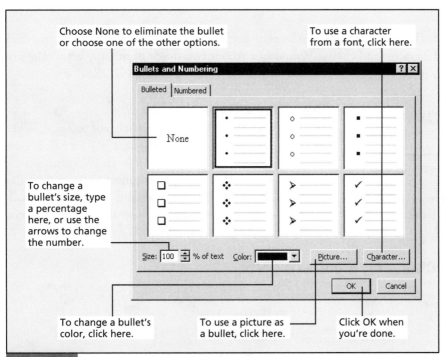

FIGURE 4-1 Use the Bulleted tab of the Bullets and Numbering dialog box to choose a bullet for your text

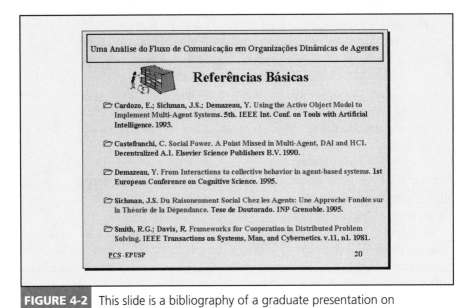

FIGURE 4-2   This slide is a bibliography of a graduate presentation on artificial intelligence

To create this effect, select the text and choose Format | Bullets. Then click Character and choose Wingdings. About two-thirds of the way across the first row of Wingdings, find the open folder, select it, and click OK.

Professional Pointer

If you make a bullet larger, make room for it by moving the text farther away from the bullet. I explain how to do so later in this chapter.

Changing a bullet's size

You change a bullet's size as a percentage of text size. When you change a bullet's size, let consistency be your guide. Generally, a higher-level item, such as a level-2 heading, should not have a smaller bullet than a less important item, such as a level-3 heading. Also, items of the same level should usually have the same size bullet, unless you are making an exception for emphasis.

Changing a bullet's color

When you click the Color drop-down list box, you see the choices shown here:

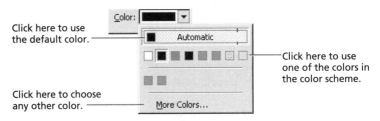

Like a bullet's size, a bullet's color should generally be consistent within a level heading unless you are using color for special emphasis.

Cross-Reference: Color schemes are covered in Chapter 6.

Using an image as a bullet

What if you want a bullet that is more exciting, one that specifically relates to the topic of the text that follows it? Are you selling to florists? Why not use flowers for bullets? To use an image as a bullet, click Picture in the Bullets and Numbering dialog box. PowerPoint opens the Picture Bullet window, shown in Figure 4-3.

New in 2000: Image bullets are a new feature in PowerPoint 2000.

To use one of the bullets displayed, choose it. The toolbar shown here pops up:

When you're done, click OK to close the window and return to your presenta-

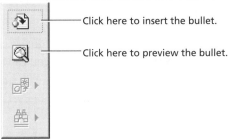

Click here to insert the bullet.

Click here to preview the bullet.

tion. Your new bullet is now in place.

Creating Custom Bullets

Did you find PowerPoint's choice of picture bullets boring? You can create your own bullets from any bitmap file. Examples of bitmap file types are .bmp, .tif, .gif, and .jpg files. Windows metafiles (.wmf) work as well.

To use your own bitmap as a bullet, click Import Clips at the top of the Picture Bullet window (see Figure 4-3). The Add Clip to Clip Gallery dialog box opens, shown in Figure 4-4.

The files shown in Figure 4-4 were found in C:\Program Files\MSOffice\Clipart\Bullets. If you have PowerPoint as part of Microsoft Office, you too probably have them, or similar files. Of course, don't have a field day and use every bullet you can find. On the

Tip: To find bitmaps on your computer system, choose Start on the Windows taskbar and then choose Find | Files or Folders. In the Find dialog box, specify the desired location in the Look In box. You can look anywhere on your hard drive, a network, or a CD-ROM drive. Then type ***.gif** in the Named box and click Find Now. You can do the same with .jpg, .bmp, and .wmf files. You'll probably be surprised how many images you have available. You can also look for images on the Web. If you have a scanner, you can scan photographs to create bitmap files (but watch out for copyrights).

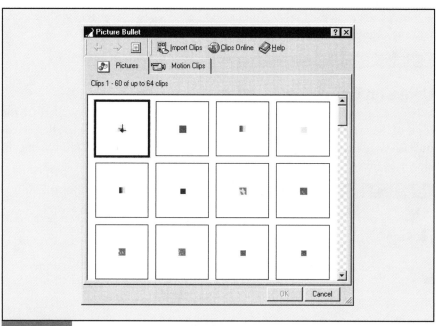

FIGURE 4-3 PowerPoint offers a selection of images that you can use as bullets

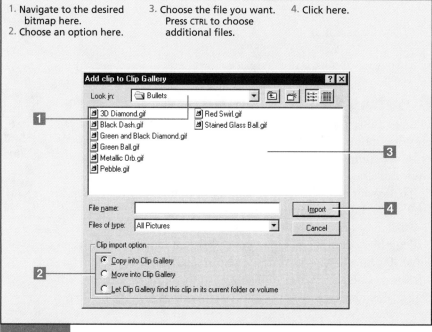

FIGURE 4-4 Use the Add Clip to Clip Gallery dialog box to find bitmap files to use as bullets

left, you see the whimsical result of choosing Red Swirl and several other bitmap files:

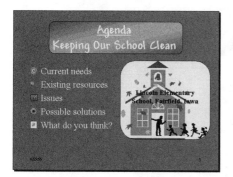

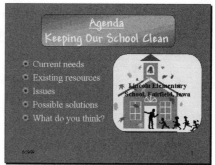

Don't use lots of different bullets on one slide.

Do find one appropriate bullet and use it consistently.

Instead, choose one appropriate bullet, as shown on the right, and use it consistently. To view this slide in color, refer to number 21 in the Slide Gallery.

If you copied or moved the file(s) into the Clip Gallery, you can find what you need again by opening the Picture Bullet window and scrolling to the bottom. Then click More Clips. Figure 4-5 shows an example of picture bullets. Refer to number 22 in the Slide Gallery to view it in color.

To create these bullets, you have to jump through a few hoops. Some of these steps involve manipulating the graphic file, which is covered in Chapter 5. Refer to that chapter for more information on these steps:

Tip: Unfortunately there is no preview feature as you try to find bitmap files to import into the Clip Gallery. Instead, choose Insert | Picture | From File and start searching. The Insert Picture dialog box that opens contains a preview box. Once you have found the bitmap file that you want, remember where it is. You can then import it into the Clip Gallery.

- The bullet originated from flower.wmf, a Windows Metafile in C:\Program Files\Microsoft Office\Clipart\Popular. (Your location may be different.) It must be rotated, which can't be done directly in PowerPoint. (If you have a program that can rotate the file, great.) To import it into PowerPoint, choose Insert | Picture | From File.

- PowerPoint can't rotate imported pictures, so the picture was turned into a PowerPoint object. To do this, select it and choose Draw | Ungroup on the Drawing toolbar. Then immediately choose Draw | Group. This process is like traveling on a transporter beam in *Star Trek*—the parts of the picture get broken down into components and then assembled again into one object.

- To rotate the picture, choose Free Rotate on the Drawing toolbar and drag on one of the green dots until you see the result you like. In this case, the idea was to have the head of the rose point more to the right, toward the text, at an angle often used for displaying roses.

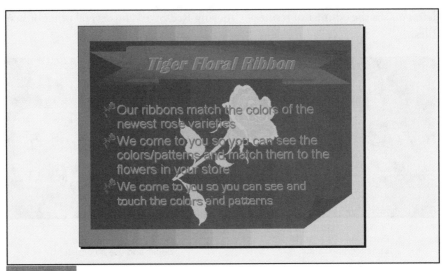

FIGURE 4-5   This slide uses an image of a rose for bullets

- The image then has to be saved in a new file. With the image selected, press CTRL-C. Then open Microsoft Paint, which comes with Windows (choose Start | Programs | Accessories | Paint). Press CTRL-V. Click Save, give the file a new name in a convenient location, and close Paint.

- The work you've done thus far would usually be enough, but this graphic now has a white background that will show up on your slide. You can change the background color in Photo Editor, which is part of Microsoft Office. Start Photo Editor and open the file. Choose Set Transparent Color on the toolbar and click the white background. Click OK. Then choose File | Save As. This file was saved in GIF format to save space.

- To use the GIF file as a bullet, select the desired text and choose Format | Bullets and Numbering. Click Picture. In the Picture Bullet dialog box, choose Import Clips. Find the GIF file, choose it, and click Import.

- Click the picture and click the top icon to insert the picture. PowerPoint creates the bullets.

- In this case, the picture was much too small. You often need to adjust picture bullets. With the text still selected, choose Format | Bullets and change the size. These bullets were changed to 175 percent of the text size. Click OK.

Cross-Reference: To change the bullets for an entire presentation, you have to change the slide master. Slide masters are covered in Chapter 7.

Creating Numbered Lists

Use a numbered list when your items have a logical sequence. To create a numbered list, select the bulleted items you want to number and click Numbering on the Formatting toolbar. PowerPoint knows to restart numbering for subheadings, as shown here. You can change the numbering back to bullets by clicking Bullets on the Formatting toolbar.

New in 2000: PowerPoint 2000 introduces the capability of using numbered lists instead of bullets.

To format the numbering, select the text and choose Format | Bullets and Numbering. Then click the Numbered tab, shown in Figure 4-6.

The AutoFormat as you type feature starts a numbered list when you type the number 1, a period, a space, and some text. Instead of the number 1, you can type **A**, **a**, **I**, or **i**. You can also use a closing parenthesis in place of the period. If you don't want automatic numbering, choose Tools | Options and click the Edit tab. Uncheck AutoFormat as You Type and click OK.

Using Bullets and Numbering in AutoShapes and Text Boxes

You can create bulleted text in AutoShapes and text boxes. For best results, the text should be left-aligned. To left-align selected text, click Align Left on the Formatting toolbar.

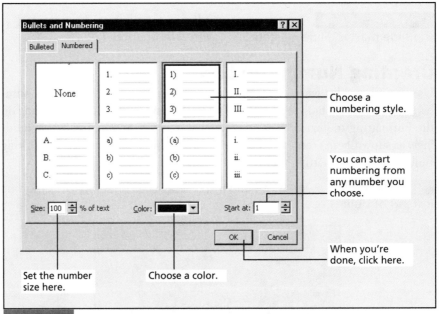

Set the number size here.

Choose a color.

Choose a numbering style.

You can start numbering from any number you choose.

When you're done, click here.

FIGURE 4-6 Use the Numbered tab of the Bullets and Numbering dialog box to format numbered text

To add bullets to selected text, click Bullets on the Formatting toolbar. To add numbering, click Numbering on the Formatting toolbar. To create bullets or numbering as you type, click Bullets or Numbering first and then start typing. Click Bullets or Numbering again when you want to return to regular text. You can use all the features of the Bullets and Numbering dialog box as described earlier, including custom bullets. Select the text and choose Format | Bullets and Numbering.

There is no automatic way to create bullets in WordArt text. You can, however, insert a bullet symbol and use this technique to create bulleted text in WordArt.

Cross-Reference: See Chapter 3 for instructions on inserting symbols into WordArt.

Working with Paragraphs

In Chapter 3, I explained how to format the characters in your text—by choosing the fonts, font size, and so on. A different aspect of formatting text involves formatting text as paragraphs. Paragraph formatting includes indentation, tabs, alignment, and line spacing. To lay out text on your slide in the most pleasing, legible manner, you need to know about paragraph formatting.

A paragraph is any single line of text or multiple lines of text followed by a return. A return character, which moves text to the next line, is created when you press ENTER on your keyboard.

Occasionally you may want text to be treated as one paragraph but look like two paragraphs. You can start a new line without using a return by pressing SHIFT-ENTER (instead of just ENTER) at the end of a line. PowerPoint interprets both lines as one paragraph. For example, to create a separate, unnumbered line within numbered text, as shown in Figure 4-7, you press SHIFT-ENTER.

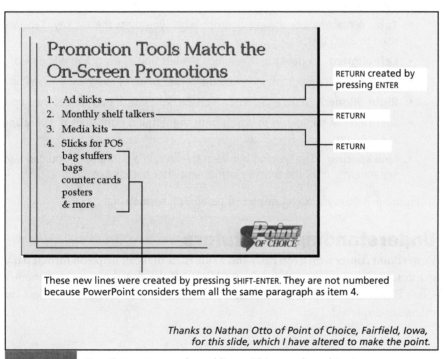

FIGURE 4-7   Creating an unnumbered line within numbered text

Understanding Paragraph Formatting

Before leaping in, you may want to understand some terms that are commonly used for paragraph formatting:

- **Margin**   The space between the edge of your working area and your text. In a text placeholder, the margin is the space between the edge of the place-holder and your text. The left margin of a paragraph is the left edge of the text.

- **Indent**   The amount that text is moved to the right of the left margin.

- **First line indent**   An indent for the first line of a paragraph. Subsequent lines are not indented.

- **Hanging indent**   A first line that is indented less than the subsequent lines of a paragraph. The first line "hangs out" from the rest of the para-graph. Bulleted text is formatted as a hanging indent. The bullet is at the left margin and hangs out from the rest of the paragraph, which is indented, as shown in Figure 4-8.

- **Tab**   A place where the cursor stops when you press the TAB key. Tabs are used to align text.

- **Left-aligned**   A paragraph in which the left side of every line is lined up.

- **Centered**   A paragraph in which the center point of every line is lined up.

- **Right-aligned**   A paragraph in which the right side of every line is lined up.

- **Justified**   A paragraph in which both the left and right sides of every line are lined up.

- **Line spacing**   The spacing between the lines in a paragraph. You can also separately control the spacing before and after paragraphs.

Figure 4-8 shows some examples of paragraph formatting.

Understanding the Rulers

PowerPoint comes with a top ruler and a side ruler that can help you format para-graph text. To view the rulers, choose View | Ruler (on the expanded menu). Click Ruler again to hide the rulers. You cannot format paragraphs unless the rulers are displayed.

This paragraph has a first line indent, created using a tab.

- Bulleted text uses a hanging indent. The bullet is at the left margin and the rest of the paragraph is indented.

This paragraph is right aligned.

Examples of paragraph formatting

The display of the rulers depends on what object you select. If you select any object other than a text placeholder, the rulers look like this:

The financial system:
Brings together individuals or businesses who have a surplus of money with those who have a productive use for this surplus.

This kind of ruler is called a *slide ruler*. It has a zero point at its middle and measures the entire slide. You can use this kind of ruler for judging layout and distances for objects. In the next chapter, I cover how to lay out and align objects on a slide.

If you select a text placeholder, the rulers look like this:

These rulers look like the rulers you see in your word processor. The zero measurement starts from the left or the top and continues from there. The white portion measures only the area of the text. The ruler's length adjusts automatically if you click on another, differently sized placeholder.

Unlike most word processors, such as Word, PowerPoint has no dialog box that you can use to format paragraphs. You must format paragraph text using the top ruler. The side ruler is mostly used to judge size and distance and contains no controls.

Let's take a closer look at the ruler, shown in Figure 4-9. To move the indent markers, drag them to the left or right. There's something of an art to dragging the markers because they are so small. It's easy to grab the Left Indent marker (the rectangle) instead of the Hanging Indent marker (the lower triangle). After a little practice, you'll get better at it. Until then, remember the Undo button on the Standard toolbar!

Indenting Text

The most common use for the ruler is to move bullets and to change the spacing between a bullet and its text. However, you can use the ruler to indent any paragraph text—in to the right or out to the left.

Cross-Reference: To change the paragraph indentation for all the slides in your presentation, you need to make the change on the slide master. Masters are covered in Chapter 7.

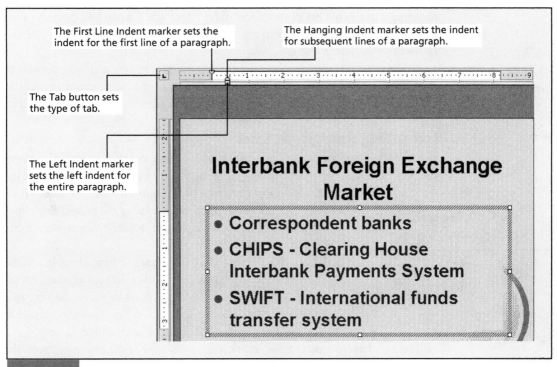

The First Line Indent marker sets the indent for the first line of a paragraph.

The Hanging Indent marker sets the indent for subsequent lines of a paragraph.

The Tab button sets the type of tab.

The Left Indent marker sets the left indent for the entire paragraph.

Interbank Foreign Exchange Market

- Correspondent banks
- CHIPS - Clearing House Interbank Payments System
- SWIFT - International funds transfer system

FIGURE 4-9   You use the top ruler to format tabs and indentations

Moving bullets

While the default distance between the bullets and text is usually acceptable, you may want to move the bullets to the right, closer to the text. If the text is too far from the bullets, it seems disassociated, and your audience may not be sure where one item ends and the next begins.

In bulleted text, the first line of a paragraph is the line with its bullet. To move a bullet, first select the text placeholder containing the bullet. Then drag the First Line Indent marker to the right. The upper indent marker moves independently of the other markers, so the indentation of the rest of the paragraph is unaffected. Therefore, moving the First Line Indent marker to the right brings the bullet closer to the text. While you are dragging the marker, PowerPoint places a dashed guideline from the marker to your text so you can gauge the effect of your dragging. All the bullets in the placeholder are affected when you drag the First Line Indent marker. If you have numbered items instead of bullets, you can move the numbers in the same way.

By default, the bullet is already at the left margin, so you can only move it to the right. Of course, once you've moved a bullet to the right, you may want to move it back to the left again. In that case, drag the upper indent marker to the left.

Indenting paragraph text

Instead of moving the bullets, you may want to move the text instead. The alignment of the text is controlled by the Hanging Indent marker, which controls the indentation of lines in a paragraph after the first line. However, since the text of the first line (after the bullet) also aligns with the subsequent lines, you actually affect the entire paragraph.

Professional Pointer

Don't move the text so far from the bullet that you lose the connection between each bullet and its text.

To move the text, drag the Hanging Indent marker to the left or the right. Be careful not to drag the rectangular Left Indent marker. Figure 4-10 shows how to move the text in a text placeholder away from its bullets. To view these slides in color, refer to numbers 23 and 24 in the Slide Gallery.

The Left Indent (rectangular) marker maintains the relationship between the first line and the subsequent lines of a paragraph. Therefore, the indentation of the entire paragraph changes as you drag the rectangular marker. As you drag, both the First Line Indent and Hanging Indent markers come along for the ride.

When your slide has more than one level of bulleted text, PowerPoint shows upper and lower indent markers for all the levels, as shown here. You can therefore adjust the indentation of any level of bulleted text you wish.

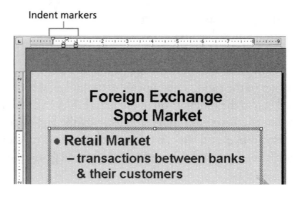

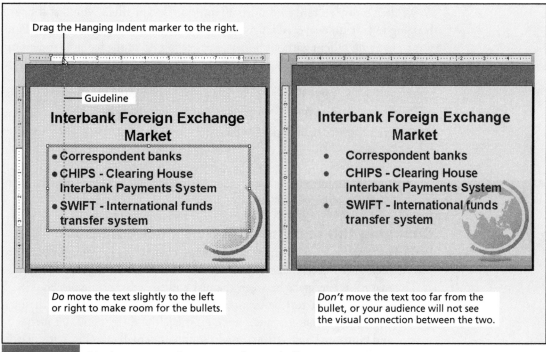

Drag the Hanging Indent marker to the right.

Guideline

Do move the text slightly to the left or right to make room for the bullets.

Don't move the text too far from the bullet, or your audience will not see the visual connection between the two.

FIGURE 4-10 Moving paragraph text away from a bullet

Creating paragraphs with no hanging indent

Sometimes you may want plain block text instead of bulleted text. For example, you might have only one statement to make on a slide, as shown here. To view this slide in color, refer to number 25 in the Slide Gallery.

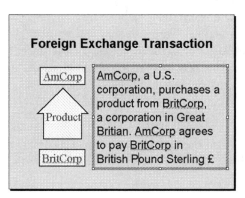

While it's easy to remove bullets if you don't want them, you'll still have a hanging indent unless you change the paragraph formatting. You usually don't want a hanging indent without bullets, but getting rid of the hanging indent can be frustrating. Here are the steps to change bulleted text to block paragraphs:

1. Select the text placeholder for which you want to create block paragraphs.

2. Click Bullets on the Formatting toolbar to remove the bullets.

3. Drag the First Line Indent marker to the right until it is aligned with the Hanging Indent marker. Now the hanging indent is gone, but the paragraphs are indented.

4. Drag the bottom rectangular indent marker to the left until the paragraphs are at the left margin again.

Changing the margins in a text placeholder

In the last chapter, I briefly mentioned how to change the margins for both text placeholders and objects that contain text. Here I explain the concept more fully.

The margin is the space between the text and the edge of the placeholder. If you want to center the text better in the placeholder, you can increase the margins. By default, the margins are .1 inch on the left and right and .05 inches on the top and bottom. These settings might sound like small margins, but since the borders of the placeholder are usually invisible on your slide, it doesn't make any difference. However, if you choose to place a visible border around your text, you may wish to increase the margins.

Cross-Reference: Creating borders is covered in Chapter 6.

Another reason to increase the margins is to move a small amount of text farther down the slide so that the text is more centered. Centered text catches the audience's eye more quickly than text stuck in one corner of a slide. Note that you can also move and resize the placeholder to move the text down the slide.

To change the margin between the text and its placeholder, right-click the placeholder and choose Format Placeholder. In the Format AutoShape dialog box that opens, click the Text Box tab, shown in Figure 4-11. Change any of the numbers in the Internal Margin section and click OK.

Tabs

You probably don't use the TAB key on your keyboard to align text anymore. That was the original purpose of the TAB key, but now that word processors offer

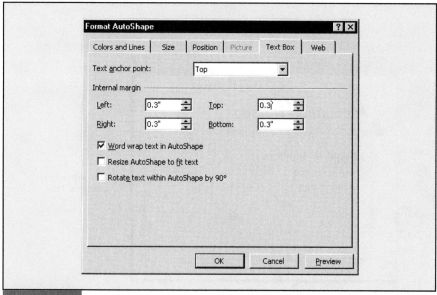

Use the Text Box tab of the Format AutoShape dialog box to increase the margins between the placeholder and the text

tables, which align text more easily, the TAB key is used mostly to move the cursor from cell to cell in a table. Nevertheless, you may sometimes wish to use a tab to align a small amount of text when a table is not needed.

There are four types of tabs. Each type has its own marker at the left of the ruler.

LEFT TAB   This marker aligns the left edge of text with the tab.

CENTER TAB   This marker centers the text at the tab.

RIGHT TAB   This marker aligns the right edge of text with the tab.

DECIMAL TAB   This marker aligns decimal points with the tab. In Figure 4-12, you see an example of text aligned with a decimal tab.

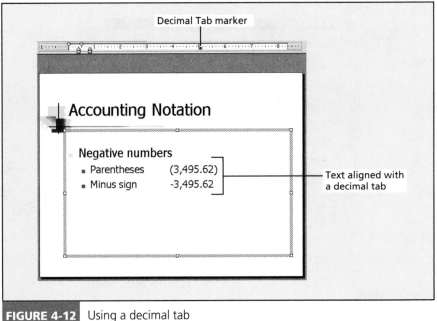

FIGURE 4-12 Using a decimal tab

To set a tab, follow these steps:

1. Select a text placeholder. Tab markers are not displayed unless a text place-holder is selected.
2. Click the tab button at the left of the top ruler until you see the type of tab you want.
3. Click the ruler where you want to place the tab.
4. Use the TAB key before the text that you want to align at the tab.

To remove a tab, select a placeholder and drag the tab marker off the ruler.

Aligning Text

Aligning text refers to how the text is lined up in reference to the margins. Bulleted text is left-aligned by default. However, you may sometimes want to use another alignment. For example, it is common to center titles. Text in text boxes or

AutoShapes also is often centered. Figure 4-13 shows some examples of various paragraph alignments. To view this slide in color, refer to number 26 in the Slide Gallery.

The procedure for aligning text is the same for placeholder text, text in text boxes, and text in AutoShapes:

 LEFT-ALIGNING   To *left-align* text, select the text and click Align Left on the Formatting toolbar (or press CTRL-L).

 CENTERING   To *center* text, select the text and click Center on the Formatting toolbar (or press CTRL-E).

 RIGHT-ALIGNING   To *right-align* text, select the text and click Align Right on the Formatting toolbar (or press CTRL-R).

JUSTIFYING   To *justify* text, select the text and choose Format | Alignment | Justify. (There is no toolbar button for justifying text.)

Cross-Reference: Refer to Chapter 2 for instructions on aligning WordArt text, which has additional alignment options not available for any other text.

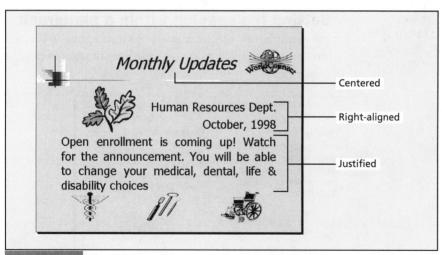

FIGURE 4-13 While most bulleted text is left-aligned, you can also center, right-align, and justify your paragraphs

In Chapter 3, I explained how to change the text anchor point of text in text boxes and AutoShapes using the Text Box tab of the Format Text Box or Format AutoShapes dialog box. The anchor point is also a form of text alignment. You can choose from the following anchors:

- Top
- Middle
- Bottom
- Top Centered
- Middle Centered
- Bottom Centered

When working with text in text boxes or AutoShapes, you may want to consider both types of alignment to get the exact result you need.

Professional Pointer

This type of setting gives you a great deal of control over how much text you can fit onto a slide.

Setting Line Spacing

The final aspect of paragraph formatting involves setting how much space you want between lines within a paragraph and between paragraphs.

Setting the spacing within a paragraph

For example, one way to fit more text into a placeholder, text box, or AutoShape is to squeeze the lines of text together, as shown here:

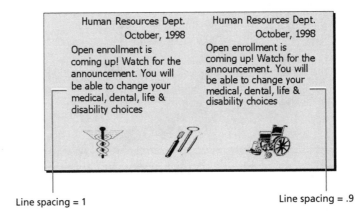

Line spacing = 1   Line spacing = .9

Of course, you don't want to put the lines too close together or your audience will have trouble reading the text.

To set line spacing within a paragraph, select the text and choose Format | Line Spacing. (This command is only on the expanded menu, so point to the down arrows at the bottom of the menu if you don't see the command at first.) PowerPoint opens the Line Spacing dialog box, shown in Figure 4-14.

Setting the spacing between paragraphs

You can also specify how much space PowerPoint places before and after paragraphs. The most common use for this feature in word processing is to set off a heading by increasing the space before the heading. In PowerPoint, you rarely use headings and several paragraphs within a text placeholder, text box, or AutoShape. However, you may still want to increase the spacing between two paragraphs to separate them in your audience's awareness.

To set the spacing between paragraphs, you use the Line Spacing dialog box, shown in Figure 4-14. The controls are the same ones you use to set line spacing. As with line spacing, you can measure by lines or points. You can separately control the spacing before and after a paragraph. You probably don't want to add

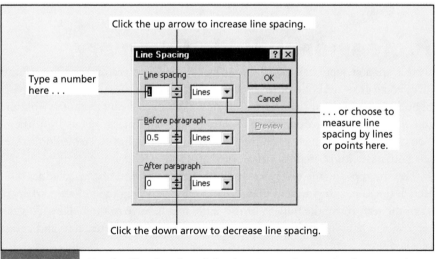

FIGURE 4-14 Use the Line Spacing dialog box to set the spacing between the lines within a paragraph

extra spacing both before and after a paragraph, because the two measurements are added together. Add spacing before *or* after your paragraphs, but not both.

Here you see an example of the effect of increasing the space following a paragraph:

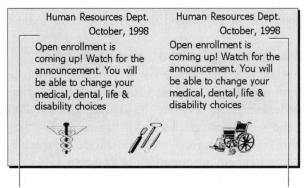

Spacing after paragraph = 1 line   Spacing after paragraph = 0 lines

By adding a 1-line space after the first paragraph, the second paragraph stands out more. You could obtain the same effect by adding a 1-line space before the second paragraph.

Professional Skills Summary

In this chapter, you learned all about bullets and paragraph text. PowerPoint gives you a great deal of control over bullets. You can choose from various types of bullets, change their size and color, or use no bullets. You can choose a picture to use as a bullet or create your own bitmap files and make bullets from them. You can also create bulleted text in text boxes and AutoShapes. PowerPoint 2000 lets you create numbered lists, too.

To format paragraph text, you use the top ruler. When a text placeholder is selected, the ruler shows indent markers and tabs. You drag the indent markers to align the text, move the bullets, or move the text relative to the bullets. You can remove the hanging indent automatically created for bulleted text and create blocked text.

Tabs are used to align text. PowerPoint lets you choose from four types of tabs: left, right, centered, and decimal. To add a tab, choose the type of tab you want on the tab button to the left of the ruler and click anywhere on the ruler.

PowerPoint offers four types of paragraph alignment. You can left- or right-align text, center it, or justify it.

You can squeeze lines in a paragraph together to fit more on a slide or spread them out to make them more readable, using the Line Spacing dialog box. You can also add space before or after a paragraph using the same dialog box.

This chapter ends Part I. Part II explains how to work with art, objects, color, 3-D effects, and slide masters—all the finishing touches you need to make your presentation truly professional.

**Congratulations on completing Part I!
Now you're ready to take what
you've learned and create a
professional-looking presentation.**

Part II

Adding Dazzle
to a Presentation

Chapter 5: **Creating an Impact with Art and Objects**

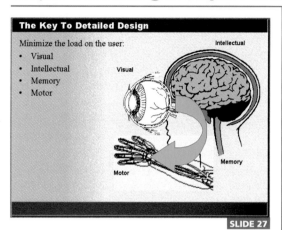

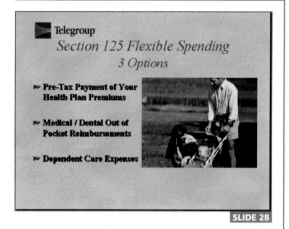

The choice of a strong graphic will have a powerful effect on its audience. How do you choose a graphic? See "Understanding the Impact of Graphics."

Thanks to Human Factors International (HFI) for this slide. You can contact HFI at 800-242-4480 or visit its Web site at www.humanfactors.com.

Here a photograph was used to evoke emotions related to caring for a family. Learn what works best. See "Understanding the Impact of Graphics."

Thanks to Telegroup for this and other slides. You can contact Telegroup at 800-393-3000 or visit its Web site at www.telegroup.com.

The dice were close together in the original graphic but were separated for maximum impact. Manipulating graphics is an important part of creating a standout presentation. See "Grouping and Ungrouping Graphics" and Figure 5-6.

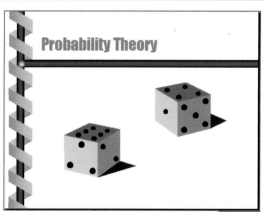

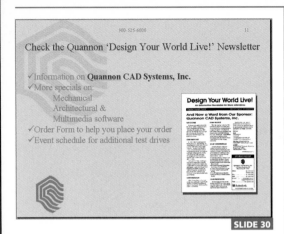

SLIDE 30

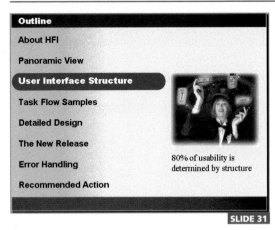

SLIDE 31

This slide uses a watermark of a company logo for its background. You can modify graphics to suit your needs. See "Image Control, Contrast, and Brightness."

Thanks to Jeff Walton at Quannon CAD Systems for this and other slides. You can contact Quannon at 800-467-3467 or visit its Web site at www.quannon.com.

Decrease the contrast of a graphic to show more subtle details and soften the look. See "Image Control, Contrast, and Brightness" and Figure 5-7.

This graphic's border was cropped off and the picture brightened to match the soft, light colors of the slide. See "Cropping a Graphic" and Figure 5-8.

Thanks to Hararit for this and other slides.

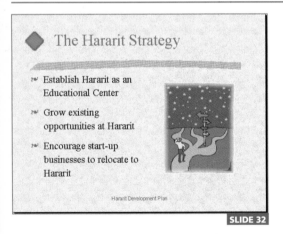

SLIDE 32

The graphic originally had autumn colors—an unfortunate impression for a slide on life insurance . . .

. . . so it was recolored to use lively summer greens and match the rest of the slide. See "Recoloring Pictures."

You can add a background to a graphic, but it usually doesn't look very good.

This graphic makes a better impression—it looks as if it was cut out and pasted directly on the slide. See "Formatting Pictures."

Photo Editor, which comes with Microsoft Office 2000, can add special effects to bitmap graphics. Here you see a photo before . . .

. . . and after being texturized to look like a Home Sweet Home needlepoint. See "Using Photo Editor."

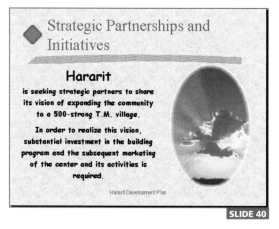

PhotoDraw, Microsoft Office's newest application, was used on this dark photo . . .

. . . to brighten it, soften it around the edges, and crop it to an oval shape. See "Getting Professional with PhotoDraw."

SLIDE 41

This black-and-white graphic . . .

SLIDE 42

. . . was easily colored in Microsoft Paint, which comes with Windows. See "Working with Color in Microsoft Paint."

This slide uses AutoShapes to create focus and interest for the client, Robert Oxley. See "Inserting AutoShapes."

Thanks to Jennifer Rotondo for this and other slides.

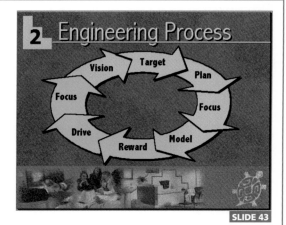

SLIDE 43

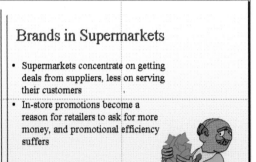

SLIDE 44

PowerPoint's visible guides help you judge the placement of objects and text. Asymmetrical Layouts often fool the eye. See "Using Guides."

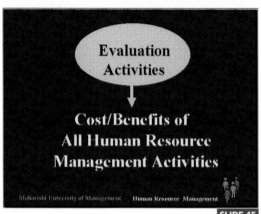

SLIDE 45

Here the oval and the arrow touch precisely. See "Snapping to the Grid and to Objects."

Thanks to the Maharishi University of Management's School of Business and Public Administration for this slide.

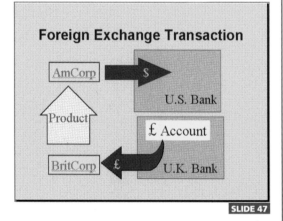

SLIDE 46

Make sure your objects are perfectly aligned and evenly distributed, as you see in the first slide.

SLIDE 47

This slide was changed to show the sloppy look that results when objects are not perfectly aligned. See "Aligning and Distributing Objects" and Figure 5-21.

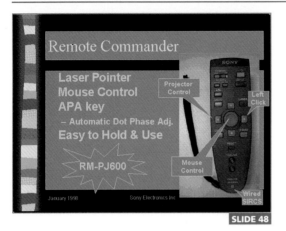

SLIDE 48

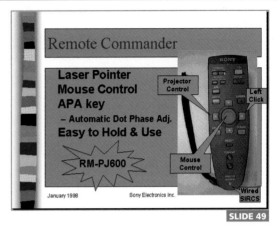

SLIDE 49

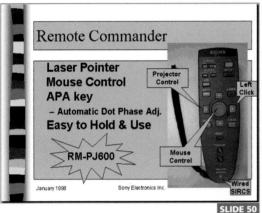

SLIDE 50

SLIDE 51

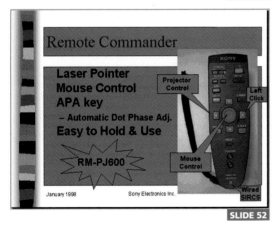

SLIDE 52

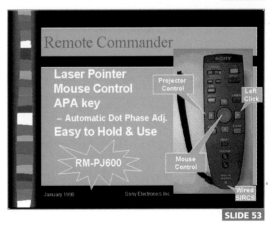

SLIDE 53

Each design template comes with several color schemes that you can use to instantly change the look of the presentation. You can also create a custom color scheme for a unique look. See "Choosing a Color Scheme."

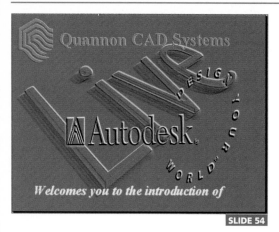

SLIDE 54

SLIDE 55

Here a picture is used to create a subtle but impressive background.

This background was created using a picture that contains only texture and shade variations. See "Changing Backgrounds."

The Hararit Advantage

- Strong development team committed to making the Hararit dream a reality
- Sole T.M. village in Israel; stable, self-sustaining, well-situated
- Ample land available for immediate development

Hararit Development Plan

SLIDE 56

Microsoft Photo Editor's tools were used on a picture of a sky to create a custom background. See "Creating Picture Backgrounds" and Figure 6-10.

SLIDE 57

A semi-transparent fill is used here for the text box in order to increase the legibility of the text while allowing the beautiful background to show through. See "Formatting Fills in the Dialog Box."

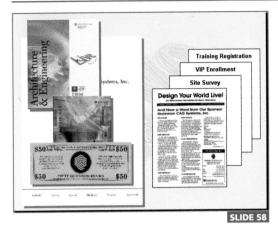

SLIDE 58

Shadows can be used to create a layered, three-dimensional effect. See "Creating Shadows."

3-D AutoShapes and text boxes create a sense of substance. See "Creating 3-D Shapes."

SLIDE 59

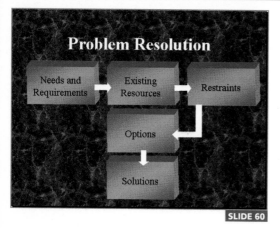

SLIDE 60

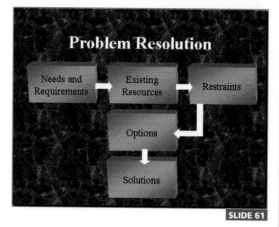

SLIDE 61

Control the properties of 3-D objects such as tilt, direction, and lighting. Here you see 3-D AutoShapes in parallel view . . .

. . . and in perspective view. See "Changing the Direction."

SLIDE 62

Format the slide master to control the look of your entire presentation. You can change the background, text formatting, and graphics. See "Entering Slide Master View" and Figure 7-1.

SLIDE 63

If you want to make sure your audience never forgets your corporate logo, place it on the slide master so that it appears on every slide. See "Adding Repeating Objects" and Figure 7-2.

SLIDE 64

When you have a great graphic, flaunt it by removing the slide master's background graphics (such as a corporate logo) on that slide . . .

SLIDE 65

. . . instead of obscuring your graphic and text message. See "Hiding the Background Graphic on a Slide" and Figure 7-4.

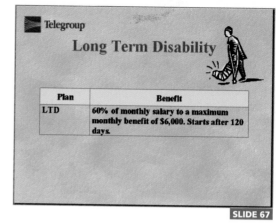

By combining one of PowerPoint's design templates and adding your own graphics and formatting, you can create a simple but effective custom design template. This master slide was used as a basis for a presentation on a new employee benefits program. See "Creating Your Own Design Templates" and Figure 7-10.

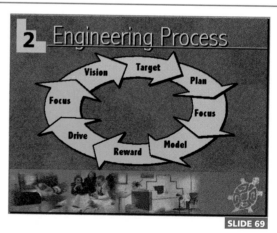

A custom background and custom-designed graphics can be combined for a completely new look. This presentation was created for Robert Oxley, a trainer and consultant for kitchen designers. See "Creating Your Own Design Templates" and Figure 7-10.

Important Statistics
(in thousands)

	1993	1994	1995	1996	1997
Total revenues	29,790	68,714	129,119	213,208	337,432
Retail customers	7,021	16,733	17,464	34,294	54,266

SLIDE 70

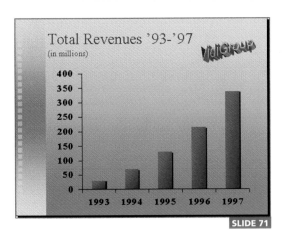

SLIDE 71

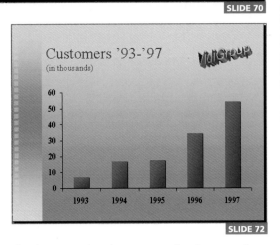

SLIDE 72

You might be accustomed to using tables of numbers in printed reports, but for presentations the message needs to be expressed more simply. Here you see the data from a table split up onto two slides and converted to charts. See "Presenting Data Simply."

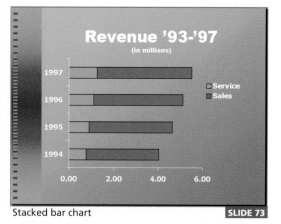

Stacked bar chart — **SLIDE 73**

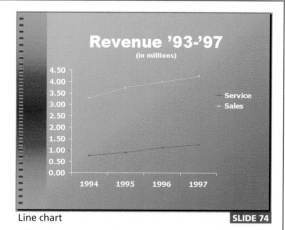

Line chart — **SLIDE 74**

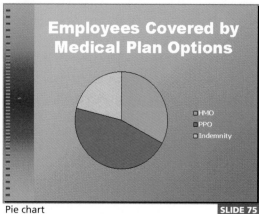

Pie chart — **SLIDE 75**

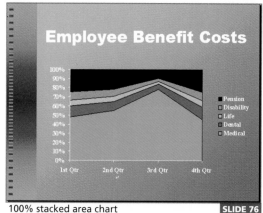

100% stacked area chart — **SLIDE 76**

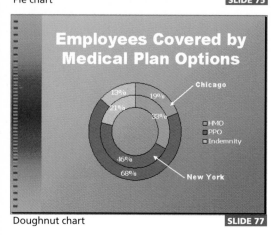

Doughnut chart — **SLIDE 77**

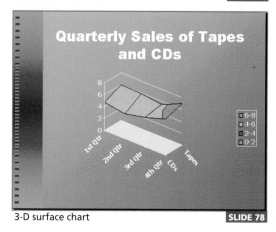

3-D surface chart — **SLIDE 78**

How do you choose which type of chart to use? You have to know your data and the strengths and weaknesses of each chart type. See "Choosing the Right Chart Type." Here you see just a small sampling of your choices.

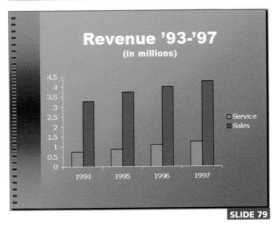

The experts say, "Keep your charts simple and uncluttered."

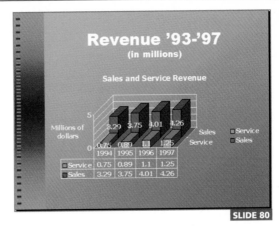

Don't put in too much detail, or your audience won't get the message. See "Chart Options Dialog Box" and Figure 8-7.

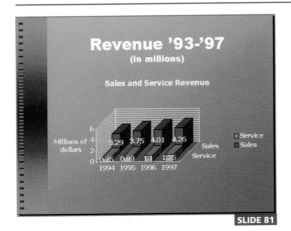

Three-dimensional charts are flashy, but two-dimensional charts are often easier to understand.

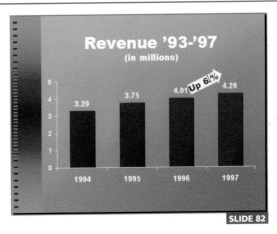

If the point still isn't clear, add AutoShapes, text, or graphics to make it clear. See "Formatting Chart Elements" and Figure 8-9.

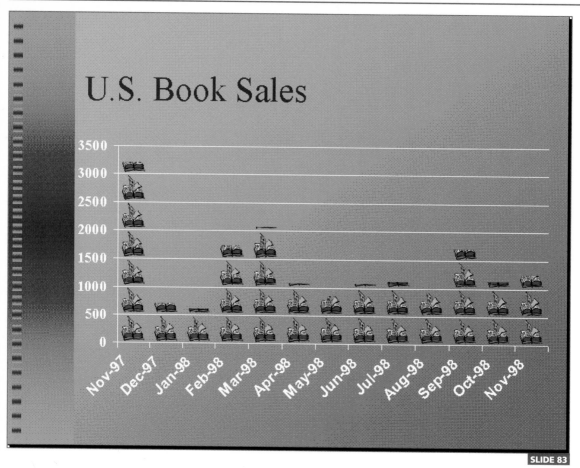

U.S. Book Sales

There are some flashy effects that don't obscure the point. One example is using a graphic to make a column chart. Here a picture of a book is used to indicate book sales. See "Formatting Chart Elements."

1996 Financial Results
($ Millions)

	1995	1996
Gross sales	438.1	413.1
Net income (loss)	(30.1)	26.6
Earnings Per Share	(1.03)	1.12

SLIDE 84

This table, a summary of a company's income statement, doesn't make its point clear. And red is a no-no for financial statements. See "Advice from a Pro: Charting a Clear Course for Better Graphics."

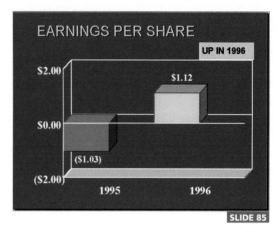

SLIDE 85

Here you see the first draft of a chart that replaces the table; but the colors are wrong, there is unnecessary clutter, and the 3-D effect is confusing. Where is the top of the bar? See "Advice from a Pro: Charting a Clear Course for Better Graphics."

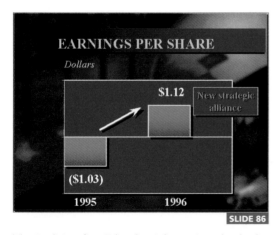

SLIDE 86

The simplicity of a 2-D bar chart is better. A text box has been added, the bars filled with a gradient, and a soft background added. See "Advice from a Pro: Charting a Clear Course for Better Graphics."

SLIDE 87

This final chart is still better. By removing the box around the chart with its background, the slide is clear and simple. See "Advice from a Pro: Charting a Clear Course for Better Graphics."

SLIDE 88

A table is used to tell employees about their new medical plan options. Find out when a table is the best option in "Presenting Data in a Table."

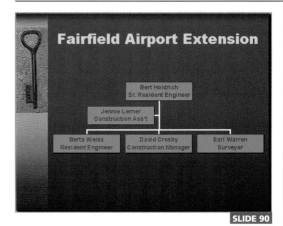

SLIDE 90

Here you want the audience to focus on two numbers, rather than the trend, which is obvious. A table requires expert formatting to transform it from PowerPoint's default style to a bold and simple statement. See "Making the Point Plain."

Organization charts help you manage people. You can create simple organization charts that get the job done using Microsoft's Organization Chart applet. See "Working with Organization Charts."

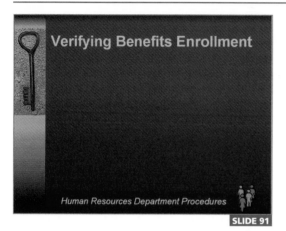

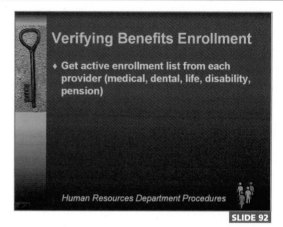

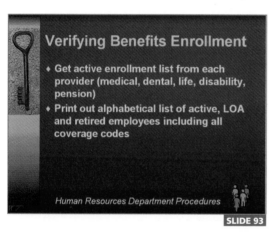

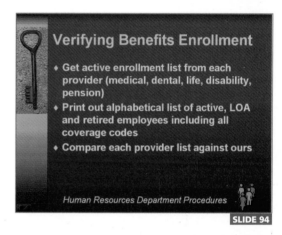

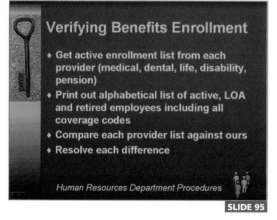

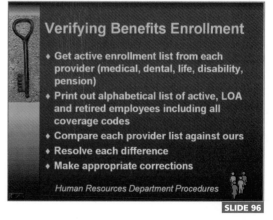

To focus your audience's attention on the item you are talking about *now*, you can animate a slide so that objects appear when you want them to. On the other hand, too much animation has the opposite effect, distracting your audience instead. This slide uses the simple Appear preset animation effect. See "Using Preset Animation Effects for Quick Results" and Figure 9-1.

Read Real World Case, p. 8
Identify these issues in the case

• Link IT Investment to Business
Strategies

Management Information Systems

SLIDE 97

Read Real World Case, p. 8
Identify these issues in the case

• Link IT Investment to Business
Strategies

• Reengineer Administrative Processes

Management Information Systems

SLIDE 98

Read Real World Case, p. 8
Identify these issues in the case

• Link IT Investment to Business
Strategies

• Reengineer Administrative Processes

• Improve Management Information
Throughout the Organization

Management Information Systems

SLIDE 99

Read Real World Case, p. 8
Identify these issues in the case

• Link IT Investment to Business
Strategies

• Reengineer Administrative Processes

• Improve Management Information
Throughout the Organization

• Retrain IS Staff and All Personnel in
New Technologies

Management Information Systems

SLIDE 100

You can dim an animated object to a different color after it is animated, or hide it completely to make sure your audience isn't thinking about your last point. In this management information systems course, previously animated bulleted items dim to white. See "Dimming After Animation" and Figure 9-3.

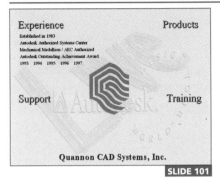

SLIDE 101

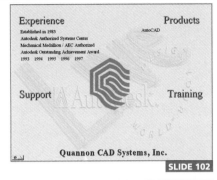

SLIDE 102

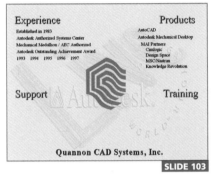

SLIDE 103

SLIDE 104

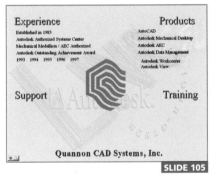

SLIDE 105

SLIDE 106

SLIDE 107

SLIDE 108

An advanced dimming technique is to hide previously animated text completely and place new text in the same location, letting you cover a topic in more detail without cluttering up the slide. This technique is used here to discuss a company's products. See "Dimming After Animation" and Figure 9-4.

Thanks to Jeff Walton at Quannon CAD Systems for this presentation. You can contact Quannon at 800-467-3467 or visit its Web site at www.quannon.com.

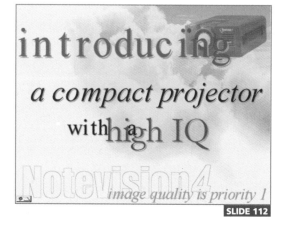

Animation can be used to create a multimedia effect. Each text object flies in from a different corner in continuous animation. See "Setting the Order and Timing of Animation" and Figure 9-6.

Thanks to Sharp Electronics for this presentation, which was used to advertise Sharp's new projector. You can contact Sharp about its projectors at 888-LCD-SHARP or visit its Web site at www.sharp-usa.com.

SLIDE 113

SLIDE 114

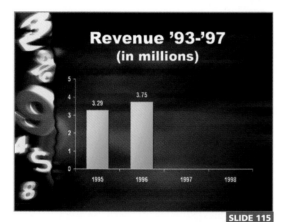

SLIDE 115

SLIDE 116

SLIDE 117

SLIDE 118

You can animate a chart in the same way you animate other slide objects. PowerPoint offers several options for animating the parts of the chart so that your audience can follow you as you discuss it. This chart animates each year in turn, ending up with an AutoShape arrow that highlights the last year's results. See "Animating Charts" and Figure 9-8.

SLIDE 119

SLIDE 120

You can create a special mood by inserting a sound from the Clip Gallery or from a file. PowerPoint inserts a sound icon on the slide. You then specify how the sound will play during the presentation. See "Inserting a Sound or Music File."

You can set a sound icon to hide while the sound is playing. You can also camouflage the icon. Here the sound icon is hidden behind the top right side of the AutoShape banner. See "Using Action Settings."

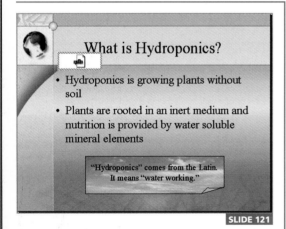

SLIDE 121

SLIDE 122

You can insert a Media Clip on your slide. Here you see a MIDI Sequencer icon on the slide. You can specify how this MIDI file will play in your presentation. See "Adding Sounds and Music with Media Clips" and Figure 10-2.

You can play an electronic video clip on a slide. Here you see an animated AVI video clip, but you can also create a customized video—for example, of your CEO explaining the company's P&L, a production technique, or a testimonial about your product. See "Showing Movies with Video Clips."

Creating an Impact with Art and Objects

In this chapter, you:

- Find the right clip art from the Clip Gallery

- Add clip art to the Clip Gallery

- Find clip art on the Internet

- Add your own art for a customized look

- Use scanned art

- Edit pictures like the pros

- Attract attention with AutoShapes

- Edit drawing objects for a great impression

- Draw your own made-to-order shapes

- Use precision tools for perfect results

Until now, you have mostly worked with text, but a presentation is much more than words. Without adding appropriate art and objects to your slides, you cannot create the impact needed for an effective presentation. The visual effect of art helps your audience remember and understand your message more quickly and easily. In fact, one of the main differences between amateur and professional presentations is the quantity and quality of the graphics. This chapter is all about graphics, including clip art, photos, and shapes.

Understanding the Impact of Graphics

When your viewers first see a slide, they scan the slide quickly before focusing on specific elements. The mind first focuses on large, simple shapes. Shapes can include the obvious AutoShapes but can also include lines, rows of bullets, and borders. Then viewers move to shapes and patterns that are more complex, and finally they focus on the text. You can use this tendency to increase your audience's understanding of your material. If you ignore this pattern, your audience is likely to be confused or slow to comprehend your point.

In addition, graphic elements wake up your audience by grabbing their attention. Perhaps from our continual immersion in television and movies, we're used to constantly changing input. A presentation consisting only of text soon becomes boring, and viewers tune out. Offering a changing menu of shapes and pictures keeps your audience engaged. A good guide is that at least half of your slides should include graphics. Note that graphics that are displayed on each slide, such as a company logo, don't count here. The audience learns to ignore repeating graphics—they soon become as boring as the text. It's the contrast and newness that works wonders. On the other hand, overloading a presentation with graphics soon negates the alertness effect. Vary your presentation so that there is some alternation between quiet and active slides—and your audience will take note. In Figure 5-1, you see a slide on the topic of Web page design that uses a strong graphic of an eye, a brain, and a hand. To view this slide in color, refer to number 27 in the Slide Gallery.

Art has a more subtle effect than simple graphic shapes. The right art can evoke a mood the supports your message. Think of how your audience might react to:

- A flag
- A dollar sign
- A happy family
- A pastoral farm scene
- The floor of the New York Stock Exchange

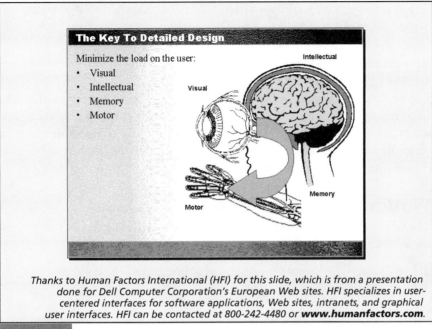

*Thanks to Human Factors International (HFI) for this slide, which is from a presentation done for Dell Computer Corporation's European Web sites. HFI specializes in user-centered interfaces for software applications, Web sites, intranets, and graphical user interfaces. HFI can be contacted at 800-242-4480 or **www.humanfactors.com**.*

FIGURE 5-1   Choose your graphics carefully for maximum effect

Each picture has a different effect. Even the manner in which the art is rendered has an effect—a photo makes a different impression than a rough sketch. An example of a photo used to explain an employee benefit feature covering dependent care costs is shown here. To view this slide in color, refer to number 28 in the Slide Gallery.

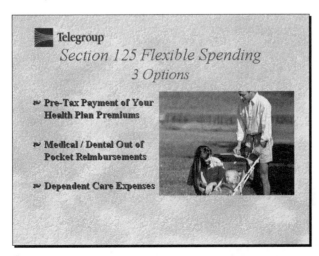

The colors you use are important too. The next chapter is all about using colors and other effects.

Using Clip Art

Clip art is ready-made art that you can simply choose and insert onto a slide. The Clip Gallery is shared by Microsoft Office applications, Microsoft Publisher, and several other Microsoft applications. You probably have other art available on your computer or network. You can also find clip art on the Internet or buy your own clip art collection, usually on a CD-ROM.

Working with the Gallery

The Clip Gallery organizes your graphics by category and keyword. You can also use the Clip Gallery for sounds/music and video clips.

Cross-Reference: See Chapter 10 for lots more about sound, music, and video.

There are two ways to add clip art to a slide, as follows:

- Choose a slide layout that includes a clip art placeholder. Then double-click the clip art placeholder to open the Microsoft Clip Gallery, shown in Figure 5 -2.
- Click Insert Clip Art from the Drawing toolbar (or choose Insert | Picture | Clip Art) to open the Insert ClipArt dialog box, which is the same as the Microsoft Clip Gallery dialog box that you see in Figure 5-2.

Once you have chosen a category, PowerPoint displays the available clip art in that category. When you click a piece of art, you see this shortcut menu:

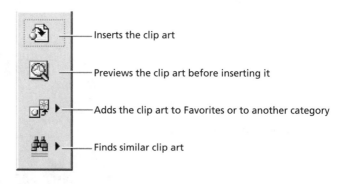

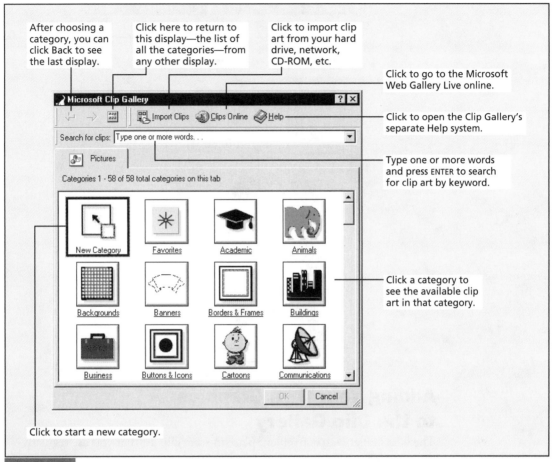

After choosing a category, you can click Back to see the last display.

Click here to return to this display—the list of all the categories—from any other display.

Click to import clip art from your hard drive, network, CD-ROM, etc.

Click to go to the Microsoft Web Gallery Live online.

Click to open the Clip Gallery's separate Help system.

Type one or more words and press ENTER to search for clip art by keyword.

Click a category to see the available clip art in that category.

Click to start a new category.

FIGURE 5-2 Use the Clip Gallery to insert clip art onto a slide

When searching for clip art by keyword, don't expect to find anything exotic. If you try searching for "trash," you will come up empty. On the other hand, if you're looking for clip art about money, you will get a good selection of possibilities, as shown next.

Tip: When you are in the Insert ClipArt dialog box, you can also drag a picture from the Clip Gallery to your slide. This method doesn't work when you double-click a clip art placeholder.

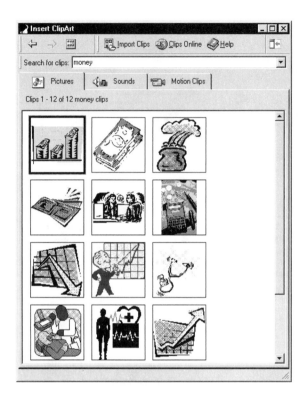

Adding Your Own Graphics
to the Clip Gallery

The Clip Gallery is a convenient place to store clip art that you use regularly—a company logo or a purchased clip art collection are good candidates. You can add this clip art to the gallery, place it in a category, and give it searchable keywords. You can then use this clip art in any of the Microsoft applications that share the gallery.

When you click Import Clips, PowerPoint opens the Add Clip to Clip Gallery dialog box, shown in Figure 5-3. You can choose to either copy or move the file to the Clip Gallery, or to have the Clip Gallery find the file in its current location.

You can add your own pictures in the following formats to the Clip Gallery:

- Windows Metafile (.wmf), a vector format that looks good even when scaled
- Bitmap (.bmp)
- Computer Graphics Metafile (.cgm)
- Graphics Interchange Format (.gif), the most common graphics format on the Web
- Joint Photographic Experts Group (.jpg)
- Portable Network Graphics (.png)

FIGURE 5-3   In the Add Clip to Clip Gallery dialog box, find a file and click Import

By default, PowerPoint uses a file type called "All Pictures" that searches for several types of graphic files. You can also choose All Sound Clips, All Motion Clips, All Clip Gallery Catalogs, or All Files. When you have selected the file you want to import, double-click it, or click Import. PowerPoint opens the Clip Properties dialog box. The Description tab is shown here:

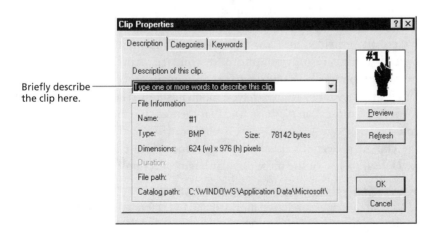

When you have completed the description, follow these steps to organize the clip art:

1. Click the Categories tab. Choose as many categories as you think apply to the clip art.

2. Click the Keywords tab. PowerPoint automatically provides the type of graphic file as the first keyword, because you may want to search by file type.

3. To add a keyword, click New Keyword. Then, in the New Keyword dialog box, type the keyword and click OK. Do this for each keyword.

4. When you have finished setting up the clip art, click OK. Your clip art has been added to each of the categories you chose, and you can search for it by the keywords you entered.

You can change any of the properties you specify when you add clip art to the Clip Gallery. Find the display of the art and right-click it. Choose Clip Properties from the shortcut menu, and you are back in the Clip Properties dialog box. You can change the description, categories, and/or keywords.

Finding More Clip Art

There are many sources for clip art. One of the simplest is to buy a clip art collection. You can also find free graphics on the Internet. Finally, Microsoft offers a Web site where you can download free images.

Purchasing a clip art collection

Clip art collections offer both bitmap and vector images. Bitmap (or raster) images are based on dots (bits) and don't scale up very well, because you start to see the dots and the image looks grainy. However, you can more easily add special effects to bitmap images. Vector images are based on lines and scale well, an important factor when you need to fit an image onto a slide. Most clip art collections separate bitmap and vector images so you can choose the image type you need. Photos are often divided into low-resolution and high-resolution sections. You may need a high-resolution photo if you are printing handouts, but low-resolution photos look fine on-screen. The main problem with clip art collections is that they rarely seem to have enough business-related images—just the kind users need most. You may also find that there are too many cartoon graphics for your taste.

The clip art collections usually include some sound clips and may include video. Here are a few of the most popular large collections:

- *Brøderbund ClickArt 200,000* comes on 14 CD-ROMS and offers a variety of clip art in many categories. Included are 1,800 fonts and 2,000 sound clips. There's also a 125,000 version, with fewer images. Brøderbund provides two paper image catalogs and an image browser to help you find the image you need. Call 415-382-4400 or go to **www.broder.com**.

- *Corel Gallery Magic 200,000* has one of the best collections of business-related images. It includes a paper catalog and photo browser. However, the catalog lacks an index, making it sometimes hard to find the image you want. Call 807-772-6735 or go to **www.corel.com**.
- *Nova Art Explosion 250,000* comes on 21 CDs. There is a paper black-and-white catalog and a browser for the photographs. There are no sound files. Call 818-591-9600 or go to **www.novadevcorp.com**.
- *IMSI MasterClips 202,000* comes with a paper black-and-white catalog and online search engine for photos. IMSI has an Instant 3D feature that creates 3-D images. The images are more realistic than those of most large collections. Call 415-247-3000 or go to **www.imsisoft.com**.

Using Microsoft's Clip Gallery Live Web site

If you have an Internet connection, click Clips Online in the Microsoft Clip Gallery or Insert ClipArt dialog box. If you usually connect by dialing from a modem, you will be prompted to make the connection, or you can connect in advance. PowerPoint seamlessly transports you to Clip Gallery Live, a Microsoft Web site (shown in Figure 5-4) where you can find and download picture, music, sound, video, or animation clips.

You can search the gallery by keyword or choose a category. The Web site then displays the applicable clips. Once you download them, PowerPoint automatically places them in the PowerPoint Clip Gallery.

Finding other clip art sites

You can find many clip art sites on the Internet—some free and some not. You can do a search on "clip art" to find them. Be sure to check the terms of use—some are available for private use only, others can be used for advertising brochures and the like but not in an item you are going to sell, and there are other variations. Many of the Web sites naturally emphasize Web art—but often that just means the graphics are in GIF format, which PowerPoint accepts. Here are a few sites that you might find helpful. Happy hunting!

- *Zedcor's ArtToday* at **www.arttoday.com** has over 750,000 clip art images, including photos and lots of fonts. You pay $29.95 annually. The collection is continually being updated so that you can always find something new.
- *Brøderbund's PrintShop Connection* at **www.printshop.com/graphcon.html** has free clip art each month as well as plenty of collections for sale.
- *Barry's Clip Art Server* at **www.barrysclipart.com/mdex.html** offers a good selection of free clip art on certain specialized topics, as well as animations. You can drag clip art directly onto your slide.

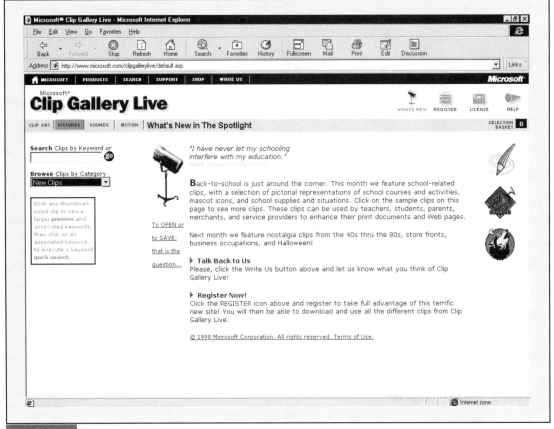

FIGURE 5-4 You can find additional graphics at Microsoft's Clip Gallery Live

- Go to **www.successinformation.com/common/freegifs.htm** for free clip art that you can drag onto a slide.
- *FX Media* at **www.fxmm.co.uk** is a multifaceted Web site that includes clip art and banners. You can drag items directly onto your slide.

To drag clip art onto a slide, you can use one of two methods:

- Adjust the size of your browser window so you can see the slide at the same time and drag.
- Drag the clip art down to the Windows taskbar onto your presentation's button, wait until the presentation appears, and drag directly onto the slide.

Using shareware clip art collections

Shareware is a method of marketing computer software, including clip art. You "try it before you buy it." If you like it, you must register it, usually for a fee. Here are a few shareware clip art collections:

Name	Number of Images	Cost	Format	Contact
Artpals for Children	100 when you pay	$25	PCX and BMP, b&w	800-524-2307
CMU English Server Clip Art	589	Free	GIF, b&w	Geoffrey Sauer: postmaster@english-server.hss.cmu.edu
Color Bits	425+	$24.95	PCX, color	800-4WEBTEC or WEBTEC@delphi.com
M&M Software Zodiac Clip Art	21	Free	BMP, b&w	800-642-6163 or **www.mm-soft.com**
SpriteLib	Over 700	Free	BMP, color	**www.walrus.com/~ari/register.htm** Note: These are characters and objects meant for creating computer games.

Using Scanned Art

If you have a scanner or digital camera connected to your computer, you can import a picture directly from your scanner or camera. Follow these steps:

1. Place the cursor where you want to insert the scanned art.

2. Choose Insert | Picture | From Scanner or Camera (on the extended menu).

3. Use the scanner to scan the picture or follow the camera instructions to transfer the picture to your computer.

4. Microsoft Photo Editor opens with your image displayed. You can use Photo Editor to edit the picture, as discussed later in this chapter.

5. In Photo Editor, choose File | Exit and Return To. Your picture appears on your slide.

Inserting Picture Files

You don't need to use the Clip Gallery to insert a picture. You may never want to use a particular graphic again so there's no point adding it to the Clip Gallery. To insert a picture, choose Insert | Picture | From File to open the Insert Picture dialog box, shown in Figure 5-5. You can also click Insert Picture from File on the Picture toolbar.

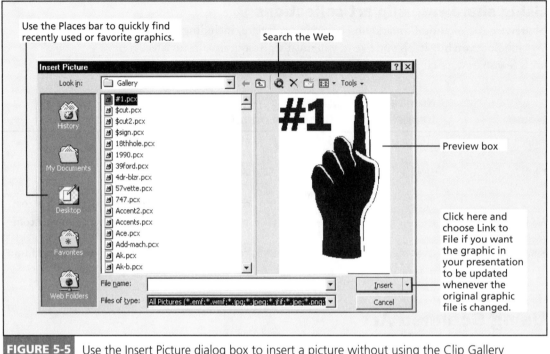

Use the Insert Picture dialog box to insert a picture without using the Clip Gallery

By default the Files of Type is set to All Pictures. Navigate to the file you want to insert and double-click it. When you insert a picture onto a slide with no clip art placeholder, you need to make room for it. You may need to resize or move an existing text placeholder.

Editing Pictures

The truth is that you may need to edit graphics to get the look you want. Most professionally created presentations include images that have been edited using separate software. The premier example of this type of software is Adobe Photoshop, a high-end graphic file-editing program that can create just about any effect you want for a bitmap graphic.

For those of you who don't happen to have the high-end Photoshop, other cheaper, simpler alternatives are available, such as Photoshop Deluxe, which allows you to do almost everything you want. In this section I explore all the ways to edit graphics.

Using PowerPoint's Basic Tools

You may be able to edit the graphic from within PowerPoint. PowerPoint can't save a graphic as a separate file but does allow you to modify most graphics that you insert. Sometimes the type of editing available depends on the type of graphic—bitmap or vector.

Resizing and duplicating graphics

When a graphic—clip art or other graphic file—appears on your slide, it may be much too big or small. You can quickly resize it using the handles. To maintain the proportion of the picture, drag one of the corner handles in the desired direction.

You can duplicate any selected graphic by choosing Edit | Duplicate or pressing CTRL-D. PowerPoint creates a copy of the graphic slightly overlapping the original. Drag it to a new position. You can also copy it to the Clipboard and paste it—either on the same slide or another one.

Grouping and ungrouping graphics

Some vector-based art can be ungrouped into individual drawing objects. (Drawing objects are discussed fully later in this chapter.) Right-click the graphic and choose Grouping | Ungroup. (Or choose Draw | Ungroup on the Drawing toolbar.) Sometimes you can even ungroup the art twice, once into a few larger objects and again into many smaller ones. When you choose Ungroup for an imported picture, PowerPoint converts it to a Microsoft Office drawing.

You can manipulate the art in unusual ways using this technique. For example, in Figure 5-6 you see a picture of two dice on the left. On the right, the two dice have been moved farther apart—something that you could do only by ungrouping the picture. You can also rotate or resize one or both dice. You can then regroup the picture for easier handling. To view this slide in color, refer to number 29 in the Slide Gallery.

This picture had to be ungrouped three times before all the elements were separated. Then the elements in the left die were selected together and grouped. The same was done with the right die. Once they were two separate objects, they could be moved farther apart. The color was lost, which was okay since dice are white and black anyway.

On the other hand, you may discover that you now have a few hundred drawing objects, which are awkward to work with. If you lose the colors, you may be able to recolor the object from scratch, but that process may be difficult and not entirely satisfactory.

Professional Pointer

Save your presentation before you start making major changes to a picture, then have a little fun. If you don't like the results, you can undo all your changes or close the presentation without saving them.

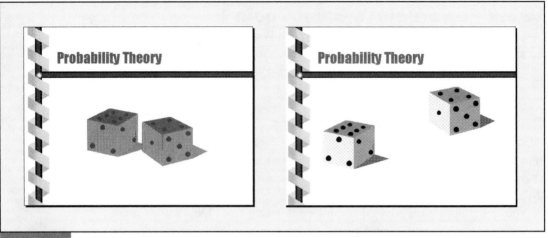

FIGURE 5-6   You can manipulate vector art by ungrouping it and converting it to drawing objects

Using the Picture Toolbar

For more precise tools, you can use the Picture toolbar, shown here in vertical shape for easy labeling. The Picture toolbar is your key to editing graphics. Many users are not aware of the depth of these editing tools and miss opportunities to manipulate their graphics effectively.

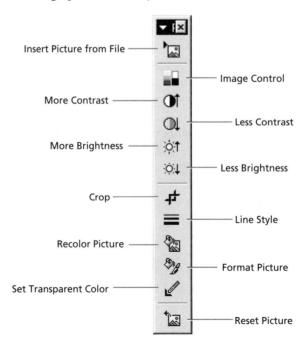

The first tool, Insert Picture from File, opens the Insert Picture dialog box, which has already been discussed. See Figure 5-5.

Image control, contrast, and brightness

You can convert images to grayscale, black and white, or a watermark. Watermarks—light-toned graphics—are often used as backgrounds behind text. When you choose Image Control, PowerPoint opens the short menu shown here:

- Automatic is the default and uses the image type that came with the graphic.
- Grayscale changes the graphic to shades of gray. Colors are assigned a shade of gray in relation to their intensity.
- Black & White converts your graphic to black and white, with no shading.
- Watermark creates a light-toned graphic. An example is shown here. A watermark is not transparent, and you often need to move it behind text as explained later in this chapter.

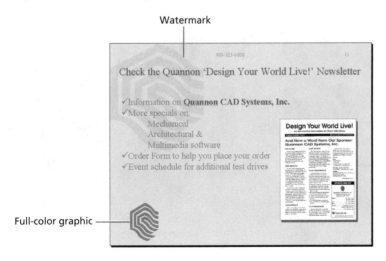

To view this slide in color, refer to number 30 in the Slide Gallery. To create a watermark like this, you may need to first ungroup the graphic. If it is in color, first change it to grayscale and then to a watermark. You may want to adjust the brightness slightly as well. You can then group the graphic again and resize it. If you want it to appear as a background on every slide, place it on the slide master.

Cross-Reference: Chapter 7 discusses slide masters.

 The next two buttons on the Picture toolbar, More Contrast and Less Contrast, increase and decrease contrast. Increasing contrast makes dark colors darker and light colors lighter. Increase contrast when a graphic is not clear enough. Decreasing contrast makes dark colors lighter and light colors darker. If you continue to decrease a graphic's contrast, you end up with all grays. Decrease contrast when you want a softer effect.

Figure 5-7 shows a graphic before and after adjustment for contrast. The contrast was originally very high, so the presenter reduced the contrast to get a softer look and clearer details. Note that this graphic was created and modified using a photographic editing program; as a result, there are several other special effects that cannot be created in PowerPoint. To view a slide that contains this image, refer to number 31 in the Slide Gallery.

 The fifth and sixth buttons increase and decrease brightness. Increasing brightness lightens all the colors in the graphic. You can increase brightness to correct a dark graphic. Decreasing brightness darkens all the colors. You may find that a graphic that looks good on paper, but your screen is too bright when you shine it on a wall screen with an LCD projector—in that case, decrease its brightness.

Before adjustment, the contrast is very high and you see few details.

After reducing the contrast, the photo looks softer and the subtle details are clearer.

FIGURE 5-7 You can get a softer look by reducing contrast

Cropping a graphic

You often want to use only a portion of a graphic to emphasize the main focus. For example, you may want only the flower without its surroundings. Another good use for the crop tool is to get rid of an unwanted black border. Choose Crop on the Picture toolbar. The cursor changes to look like the Crop button. Move the cursor to one of the handles on the graphic and drag inward. Release the mouse button when you have cropped enough. The Crop button stays depressed so you can crop from more than one side. When you are done, click Crop again to stop cropping. Figure 5-8 shows an example of a graphic before and after cropping. To see in color the slide showing the graphic after cropping, refer to number 32 in the Slide Gallery.

To create this graphic, first the black border was cropped on all four sides. Then the brightness was increased until the picture was light enough to blend in with the rest of the slide. Note that to create the soft edges, you can open the graphic first in PhotoDraw 2000. Choose Outline on the Visual Menu toolbar and then Soft Edges, and drag the Soft Edges marker to the right until you get the desired result. While this softens the black border, it does not eliminate it. PhotoDraw is briefly described later in this chapter.

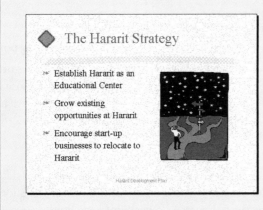
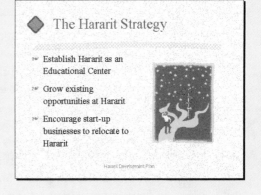

This graphic came with a black border.

To match the light, soft colors of the slide, the black border was cropped and the graphic was lightened.

FIGURE 5-8 If you need only part of a graphic, you can crop it

Changing line style

You can place a border around a graphic. PowerPoint calls this border a "line," and you can choose the color, weight (thickness), and type of the line. In practice, most professional presenters' graphics do not use a border because it looks formal and artificial.

To place a border around a graphic, choose Line Style on the Picture toolbar. PowerPoint opens the list shown here, which lets you quickly choose from a number of line weights and styles:

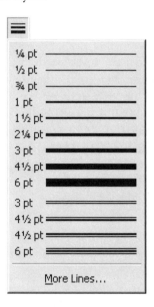

To gain more control, choose More Lines. PowerPoint opens the Format Picture dialog box, with the Colors and Lines tab on top, as shown later on in Figure 5-10. Here you can control the border's color, create a dashed border, choose a double- or triple-lined border, and change the line's weight, as measured in points.

Recoloring pictures

What if you find a graphic that is perfect in its subject but the wrong color? The colors of a graphic should blend nicely with the colors of the rest of the slide. (There's more about color in the next chapter.) PowerPoint can change the colors of a vector graphic, color by color, giving you incredible control. To change the colors in your picture, choose Recolor Picture. PowerPoint opens the Recolor Picture dialog box, shown in Figure 5-9.

PowerPoint defines a picture as having lines, fills, and backgrounds. Lines create edges—when you draw a picture with a pencil you are creating lines, even if

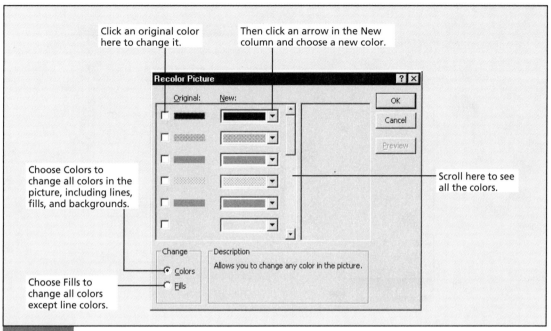

Click an original color here to change it.

Then click an arrow in the New column and choose a new color.

Choose Colors to change all colors in the picture, including lines, fills, and backgrounds.

Scroll here to see all the colors.

Choose Fills to change all colors except line colors.

FIGURE 5-9 Use the Recolor Picture dialog box for total control over colors in your graphics

they are curves. Fills fill in enclosed spaces created by lines. Backgrounds fill the space around the picture. The Recolor Picture dialog box lets you work with all these colors (choose Colors in the Change section) or only fills and backgrounds (choose Fills). The purpose of working with fill and background colors only is so that you can exclude lines of the same color. For example, if your picture has black lines and black fill—a common situation—by choosing the Fill radio button, you can change the black fill to another color, yet leave the black lines alone.

Tip: You cannot recolor bitmaps in PowerPoint. You need to use a separate image-editing program, as discussed later in this chapter. If you try to recolor a bitmap, PowerPoint displays a message telling you to use an image-editing program.

Cross-Reference: For more on colors, borders, and fills, see Chapter 6.

Once you have made any changes, as described in Figure 5-9, the Preview button appears, and you can preview your picture. Click OK when you have finished recoloring your picture. To see an example of a graphic before and after recoloring, refer to slides 33 and 34 in the Slide Gallery.

Formatting pictures

For general graphic editing, choose Format Picture on the Picture toolbar to open the Format Picture dialog box, shown in Figure 5-10 with the Colors and

Format Picture ? X

| Colors and Lines | Size | Position | Picture | Text Box | Web |

Fill

Color: [▼]   ☑ Semitransparent

Line

Color: [No Line ▼]   Style: [▼]

Dashed: [▼]   Weight: [0.75 pt ▼]

Connector: [▼]

Arrows

Begin style: [▼]   End style: [▼]

Begin size: [▼]   End size: [▼]

☐ Default for new objects

[OK]   [Cancel]   [Preview]

FIGURE 5-10   The Format Picture dialog box lets you format many properties of a picture

Lines tab on top. You can also right-click any picture and choose Format Picture on the shortcut menu. The Picture tab is displayed initially.

This dialog box may look familiar because it is very similar to the Format AutoShape and Format Text Box dialog boxes discussed previously in Chapters 3 and 4 in relation to editing text. Use the Colors and Lines tab to format fill color. In this instance, *fill color* refers to the background. Generally, you can add a fill color only to vector graphics. When you click the Color drop-down box, you see the menu shown here:

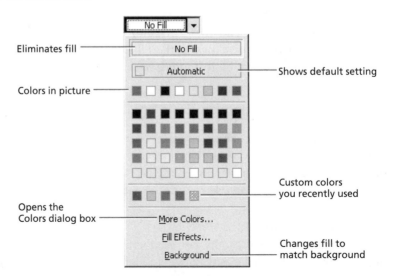

Eliminates fill ——— No Fill

Shows default setting ——— Automatic

Colors in picture ———

Custom colors you recently used ———

Opens the Colors dialog box ——— More Colors...

Fill Effects...

Background ——— Changes fill to match background

Cross-Reference: The Colors dialog box and fill effects are covered in the next chapter.

Usually, adding a fill makes the graphic look awkward and stilted, as shown at left in the following illustration. To view these slides in color, refer to numbers 35 and 36 in the Slide Gallery.

Don't add a fill to the background of a graphic—it usually looks awkward.

Do use a graphic without a fill. The graphic looks more professional when it appears to be cut out and pasted directly on the slide.

The Size tab of the Format Picture dialog box is shown in Figure 5-11. You can type a height and width in inches to get precisely the measurement you need. In the Scale section, choose a scale for the height and width. Check Lock Aspect Ratio to keep the height and width in proportion. Check Relative to Original Picture Size to calculate the scale based on the original picture size. Choose Best Scale for Slide Show to set the screen resolution you will use for the slide show and size the picture appropriately for that resolution. Click the Reset button to return the picture to its original size.

The Position tab lets you precisely set the position of the picture vertically and horizontally. You can measure from the top-left corner or the center of the slide.

The Picture tab lets you use precise measurements for cropping. You can also choose the image type here, duplicating the controls available on the Image Type button of the Picture toolbar. Finally, you can control contrast and brightness by percent.

When you have completed editing your picture, click OK to return to your slide.

You cannot crop, group, or change the fill, border, shadow, or transparency of an animated GIF image with the Picture toolbar in PowerPoint. Use an animated GIF editing program, and then insert the file on the slide again.

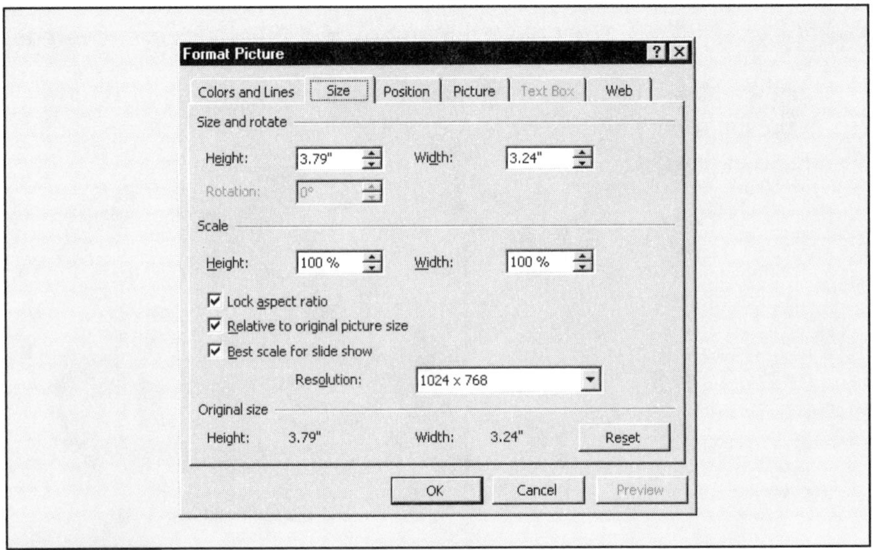

FIGURE 5-11 The Size tab lets you set the size and scale of your picture

Editing Graphic Files

Unfortunately, you may not be able to get the results you want within PowerPoint. When you want to edit graphic files, you need to find a graphic-editing program that can do the job and save the results in a file format PowerPoint can accept. Fortunately, there are many such programs.

Tip: From within PowerPoint, you can choose Insert | Object (on the expanded menu), and choose Microsoft Photo Editor Photo. Once in Photo Editor, open the graphic and edit it. Then choose File | Exit and Return To at the bottom of the menu (your presentation name will be inserted on the menu) to return to PowerPoint.

Using Photo Editor

If you have Office 2000, you probably already have a program you can use to edit graphics—Microsoft Photo Editor. (If you don't have it, use Office Setup to install it.) Despite its name, Photo Editor can edit any bitmap image. It contains a number of tools that are not found in PowerPoint for manipulating bitmap images. Photo Editor specializes in the types of effects often used on photographs, but you cannot change colors or modify individual pixels in the image. Start Photo Editor by choosing Start | Programs | Microsoft Photo Editor. You can then open any bitmap image, edit it, and save it. Return to PowerPoint and choose Insert | Picture | From File to open the graphic.

In this section, I give a brief overview of the features of this application. For more information, consult Photo Editor's help system.

- To change image type, choose File | Save As. In the Save as Type drop-down list, you can choose a new file type. For example, you can change a TGA image to a GIF image in this way.

- To convert an image's color type (true color, 256 color, grayscale, or monochrome), choose File | Properties and select from the items in the Type drop-down box. Click OK.

- Use the Image menu to crop, resize, rotate, transpose, invert, or mirror an image.

- You can create transparent areas in an image, using the Set Transparent Color tool on the toolbar. (PowerPoint's Picture toolbar also contains this tool, but PowerPoint doesn't let you save the image as a separate file.) If you don't want the background of your graphic to show up on your slide, make the background transparent.

- Choose Image | Balance to adjust brightness, contrast, and gamma. While you can adjust brightness and contrast in PowerPoint, gamma, which controls contrast in dark areas, is a Photo Editor feature that gives you increased control over your images.

- What do you do if you want to cut out an internal area of your picture? Use the Select tool to select a rectangular area anywhere within your picture. Then choose Edit | Cut.

The most exciting features of Photo Editor are its way-cool artistic and special effects, which you find on the Effects menu. The first set of commands—the *artistic* effects—are sharpen, soften, negative, despeckle, posterize, and edge. The second set are the *special* effects—chalk and charcoal, emboss, graphic pen, notepaper, watercolor, stained glass, stamp (like an ink stamp), and texturizer. The best way to get familiar with these effects is to take a couple of pictures and try them all! You can get some very artsy results. Here you see an original photo and a version that has been texturized in Photo Editor to give the effect of being embroidered or painted on burlap. You can see both versions in color—refer to numbers 37 and 38 in the Slide Gallery.

To create the graphic on this slide, choose Insert | Object and choose Microsoft Photo Editor Photo. In Photo Editor, open the graphic you want to use. Choose Effects | Texturizer. To save the graphic in its new permutation, choose File | Save As and give it a new name (and location, if you want). Then choose File | Exit and Return To. Photo Editor closes and returns you to your presentation with the graphic on the displayed slide. Resize and place the graphic as you wish. To create the frame, choose AutoShapes | Basics Shapes on the Drawing toolbar and choose the shape in the fourth row, third column. Drag from one corner to the opposite corner so that the inside rectangle frames the graphic. Now choose Draw | Order | Send to Back to move the AutoShape behind the graphic. Right-click the graphic and choose Format Picture.

Cross-Reference: Fill effects are covered in detail in the next chapter.

In the Fill section on the Colors and Lines tab, click the drop-down box and choose Fill Effects. On the Texture tab, choose the last option, Medium Wood. Click OK twice. To create the text, choose Text Box on the Drawing toolbar and drag the box along the bottom edge of the frame. Type **Home Sweet Home**. Select the text and change it to Lucida Casual (or another script-type font), at 22 points (which you need to type in) or an appropriate size for your frame. Finally, hold down Shift and select the text box, the AutoShape frame, and the photo. From the Drawing toolbar, choose Draw | Group. Voilà!

Getting Professional with PhotoDraw

If Photo Editor doesn't quite do the trick, you can get even more professional and use PhotoDraw, the newest member of the Microsoft Office family. However, PhotoDraw comes only with the Premium edition of Microsoft Office. PhotoDraw can create many special effects and supports a wide variety of graphic file types. Here are some of its capabilities:

- You can add text and create fancy text effects similar to WordArt.
- You can crop and create cut outs in various shapes.
- You can draw lines and shapes and create painting effects.
- You can fill in areas with solid colors, gradients, pictures, and textures.
- You can modify the outer edges of the graphic with soft edges or brush effects.
- You can recolor pictures, which includes changing brightness, changing to grayscale, and several types of colorization.
- You can correct defects, such as red eye and dust spots.
- You can create 3-D, shadow, and distortion effects.

PhotoDraw comes with its own tutorial—choose Help | Tutorial. Here you see the result of two simple effects, colorization and soft edges, before and after. Refer to numbers 39 and 40 in the Slide Gallery, since the black-and-white images don't do it justice.

The original photo is too dark, and the sharp edges don't blend with the rest of the slide.

Here, the photo has been modified in PhotoDraw. The colors are lighter and softer, and the edges have been softened to look more visionary, to match the text.

To create this effect, open a photograph in PhotoDraw. With the photo selected, choose Color | Brightness and Contrast from the Picture menu and adjust the settings until the photo is lighter but not too washed out. Then choose Outline | Soft Edges and increase the setting slightly. Finally, choose Cut Crop | Crop and choose the circle. Then click Stretch to Fit to stretch the circle out to the edges of the photo. Save the photo with a new name and suitable location. You can use the default file type, .mix, if you only need to import the drawing into PowerPoint. In PowerPoint, choose Insert Picture from File on the Picture toolbar and open the graphic. Resize and move it until you have the results you want.

Professional Pointer

If the details of the graphic are not significant, you can brighten and reduce contrast until you have a watermark. Then, enlarge the graphic and place it behind the text, using Draw | Order on the Drawing toolbar.

Working with color in Microsoft Paint

One more tool for editing bitmaps is Microsoft Paint, which is included with Windows. Paint is a simple program, but it is especially useful for coloring in black-and-white clip art. As long as an area is enclosed, Paint can fill it with color. You can also easily touch up a drawing by adding your own freely drawn lines. To open Paint, choose Start | Programs | Accessories | Paint.

To fill in an area with color, choose a color from the color palette at the bottom of the screen. Then choose the Fill with Color tool. Then

Tip: Paint is an old program and freezes if you try to open up newer file types such as GIF files. To use a GIF file, open it in PhotoEditor, choose File | Save As, and save it in BMP format. You can then open it in Paint.

Tip: To add a
custom color, choose
Options | Edit Colors and
click Define Custom
Colors in the dialog box.

click in any enclosed area of the picture. To enclose an area, choose a
color, and use the Line tool.

Here you see a drawing in its original black-and-white form (on the
left) and after being colored using Paint (on the right). To view these
slides in color, refer to numbers 41 and 42 in the Slide Gallery.

To create the graphic in this slide, fill in each area in Paint, using the procedure previously explained. Save the graphic and import it into PowerPoint. Then
use the Set Transparent Color tool on the Picture toolbar and point to the white
background. (Many graphics come in with a white background.) Finally, resize,
crop, and place the graphic as desired.

Vector files can usually be edited with success within PowerPoint, but drawing
programs such as CorelDraw can edit vector files as well and may have better tools.

Creating Drawing Objects

Microsoft Office 2000 has its own drawing tools that you can use to create graphics on your own. While you won't be able to create sophisticated drawings or art-
work, you can create some useful shapes to add focus and impact to your slides.
In addition, you can manipulate these shapes to create some great effects, such as
shadows and 3-D.

Using the Drawing Toolbar

The Drawing toolbar, shown in Figure 5-12, is your gateway to creating drawing
objects. By default, it is at the bottom of the screen. In this chapter, I explain
most of the tools on the Drawing toolbar. Note that a few of the features of the
Drawing toolbar relating to text were discussed in Chapters 2 and 3.

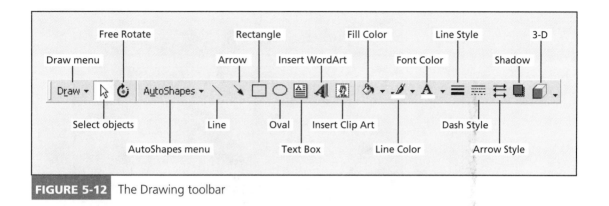

FIGURE 5-12   The Drawing toolbar

Cross-Reference: I cover the tools relating to colors, borders, fills, and 3-D effects in the next chapter.

The next section covers inserting AutoShapes from the Draw menu. The following section tells you how to draw your own shapes using the tools on the Draw menu. The section "Editing Drawing Objects" covers the Draw menu tools that deal with manipulating existing drawing objects.

Inserting AutoShapes

The simplest function of the Drawing toolbar is to let you insert AutoShapes. AutoShapes are surprisingly flexible, and there are loads of them. In Figure 5-13, you see a slide that makes creative use of AutoShapes: one is a curved arrow that is repeated and rotated to create a circular shape, and the other is a series of squares that have been combined to create a step shape. To view this slide in color, refer to number 43 in the Slide Gallery.

To create this circle, use the last block arrow AutoShape, a curved arrow. Reshape it by dragging on the diamonds (explained later in this chapter); then resize and place it as desired. Choose Edit | Duplicate to create a second arrow and click Rotate on the Drawing toolbar to rotate it. Choose Draw | Order | Send Backward to move the second arrow behind the first, and move it so it appears to come out of the first arrow. Then select both arrows and choose Draw | Group to group the two arrows. Duplicate them, and repeat the process of sending it backward, rotating it, and moving it. Continue until you are finished. Then ungroup (Draw | Ungroup) all the arrows.

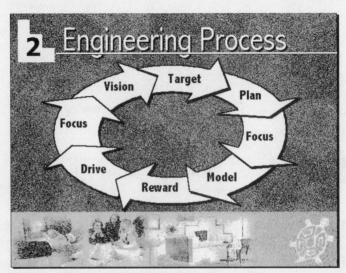

FIGURE 5-13   You can use AutoShapes to add shapes that enhance your meaning

The last arrow needs to be retouched so that its point appears to be above the end of the first arrow. To block out the end of the first arrow, insert a diamond-shaped AutoShape with no line that is the same color as the arrows. Resize, rotate, and place it so it covers the end of the first arrow. Then use the Line tool to draw over the arrow point of the last arrow so it appears to be on top. Can you see where this was done to the point of the arrow labeled Vision? The top side of the arrow point doesn't perfectly match the rest of the arrow, but you would never notice it unless it was pointed out to you. Finally, fill the arrows with a slight gradient to represent the process being described. Add the text last.

Tip: If you group the entire circle, you can then resize and move it easily on the slide.

The step shape at the top of the slide is simply six squares, with no line. Place them so they touch and look like one shape.

Click AutoShapes on the Drawing toolbar to open the AutoShapes menu, shown here in its expanded form. Each item opens to a submenu with thumbnail pictures of the AutoShapes. Here are some pointers:

- *Lines* includes simple lines, arrows, curves, free-form shapes, and scribbles.

- *Connectors* and *flowchart* symbols are used in flowcharts.

- *Callouts* are balloons that point to an object. You place text in the balloon that labels the object.

- *Action buttons* are familiar from Web sites. Some examples are back, forward, and home. You can place action buttons in a presentation and assign actions to them. For example, you can place an action button on the third slide that skips you to the last slide.

Cross-Reference: Action buttons are covered in Chapter 11.

- Choose More AutoShapes to open the window shown here with more shapes, including a number of office objects. This window works like the Clip Gallery.

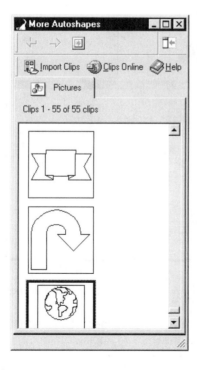

Drawing lines, arrows, and curves

Use lines and curves to create your own shapes or touch up existing ones. On the Drawing toolbar, choose AutoShapes | Lines to find the lines and curves. Each tool works slightly differently—sometimes leading to a frustrating experience. Here are precise instructions to make it easy.

- To draw a single line, choose the Line tool, move the cursor to your slide, then click and drag. The endpoint of the line is where you release the mouse button.

- To draw an arrow, choose one of the arrow tools. Click and drag to create the arrow. The endpoint of the arrow is where you release the mouse button.

- To draw a curved shape, choose the Curve tool. You can create a multicurved shape. First click at the desired start point. Then move the cursor to either the desired endpoint or to where you want to create a curve that changes the direction of the line, and click. You can continue to click at curve points. Double-click to end the curve. Here you see a curve with two vertices.

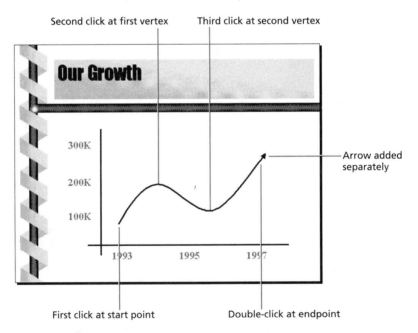

- A free-form shape is a multisegmented shape that can contain both curves and lines. Choose the Freeform tool. Then click at the desired start point. To create a line segment, move the mouse to the desired endpoint and click. You can continue drawing line segments in this way. To draw freehand shapes, which are usually curved, drag the mouse. The shape follows the cursor, as if you're drawing with a pencil. To end the free-form object, double-click.

- A scribble follows the cursor as you drag with the mouse. Choose the Scribble tool. Click at the desired start point and drag, drawing as you go. Just release the mouse button to end the scribble.

Tip: To close a free-form shape, click near its start point. PowerPoint automatically connects the endpoint to the start point.

The Line tool is also directly on the Drawing toolbar. There is one special advantage to using this tool. To draw several individual lines, double-click the Line tool on the Drawing toolbar. It stays depressed, and you can draw any number of lines without reclicking it. Single-click the Line tool again to stop drawing lines. The same applies to the Arrow tool on the toolbar.

Creating flowcharts and process diagrams

The AutoShapes menu lets you insert a variety of flowchart shapes and *connectors*. Connectors are used in flowcharts and process diagrams to connect shapes. Figure 5-14 shows a simple flowchart.

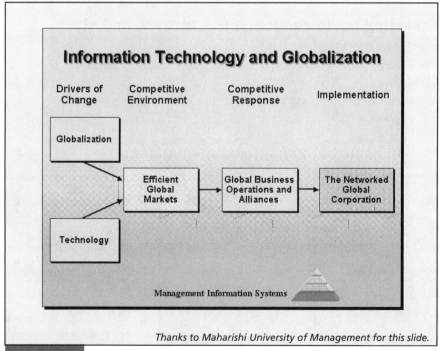

FIGURE 5-14 A flowchart diagram

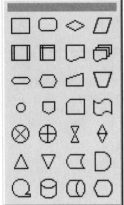

To insert a flowchart shape, choose the shape from the menu shown at the left. Then click and drag on the slide to obtain the desired size.

Once you have your shapes in place, you can use the connectors to show how the shapes relate to each other. Choose one of the connectors shown at the right.

When you place the cursor near one of the flowchart shapes, PowerPoint displays tiny blue boxes at appropriate points on the shape. Click, and the connector snaps exactly to one of the boxes. Now drag to the second shape, and the blue boxes appear on that shape. Click to snap the end of the connector to one of the boxes.

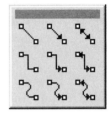

You can easily edit flowcharts and process diagrams because connectors know what they are connected to and try to remain stuck to their shapes. If you move one of the flowchart shapes, the connector readjusts its length and direction accordingly.

Tip: You can also insert a shape by simply clicking on the slide. PowerPoint inserts the shape using a predefined size.

Inserting basic shapes, block arrows, and stars and banners

PowerPoint has a generous selection of shapes that you can insert onto your slides. From the Drawing toolbar, choose AutoShapes | Basic Shapes, Block Arrows, or Stars and Banners to see the menus shown here:

Basic Shapes

Block Arrows

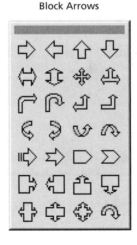

Stars and Banners

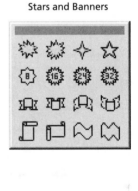

As you can see, the choice ranges from utilitarian to whimsical. To insert one of the shapes, choose it. Then click and drag on the slide until the shape is the size you need. To insert a shape with its default size, simply click the slide without dragging.

To draw a circle or oval, use the Oval tool on the Drawing toolbar. You can double-click this tool to draw several ovals at once. To draw a circle, either press SHIFT as you drag or click the slide without dragging.

To draw a square or rectangle, use the Rectangle tool on the Drawing toolbar. You can double-click this tool as well. To draw a square, press SHIFT as you drag or click the slide without dragging.

Some of the shapes display a small yellow diamond when selected. Dragging this marvelous diamond gives you extra control, enabling you to create an infinite variety of shapes. Initially, the effect of dragging the diamond in a specific direction may not be obvious, so experiment! Figure 5-15 shows some examples of these variations on a theme.

Inserting callouts

A *callout* is a combination of a text box and a line, which points to an object. Here you see an example:

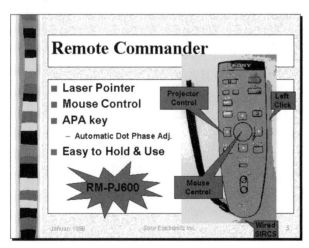

The callouts are on the expanded AutoShapes menu and are shown here. You probably don't know the right size for the callout until you have typed its text. Therefore, the easiest way to insert a callout is to follow these steps:

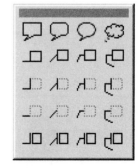

1. Choose the callout you want.
2. Click on your slide. PowerPoint inserts the callout using its default size and configuration.
3. Type the text for the callout.

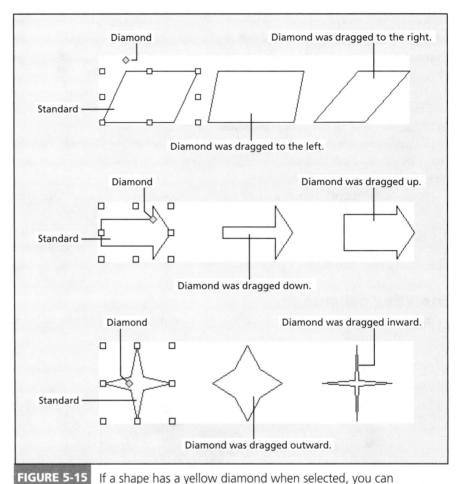

FIGURE 5-15 If a shape has a yellow diamond when selected, you can manipulate the shape's features

4. Drag on the handles to adjust the size of the callout to fit the text.

5. Move the callout to its desired location.

6. Drag the diamond(s) until the line points to the appropriate spot.

Formatting Drawing Objects

Once you have inserted an AutoShape, you usually want to format it in some way. You can change the size and shape of arrows, change the line style, or create a dashed line directly from the Drawing toolbar. You can also use the Format AutoShape dialog box to specify the properties of your AutoShape.

Cross-Reference: In the next chapter, I cover formatting AutoShapes and drawing objects with color, fills, shadows, and 3-D effects.

Formatting arrows

Choose Arrow Style on the Drawing toolbar to open the choices shown here. To change an arrow type, select the arrow and pick one of the styles on the menu. If you don't find the arrow you want, or if you want more control over arrow size and shape, choose More Arrows at the bottom of the menu to open the Format AutoShape dialog box shown in Figure 5-16.

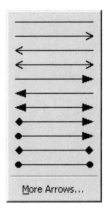

Once you've selected an arrow, this dialog box opens with the current parameters showing in the Arrows section. For example, in Figure 5-16, you see that there is no begin size, because the arrow that was selected started with a plain line, not an arrow.

Since an arrow is a combination of a line and an arrowhead, the settings in the Line section of the dialog box affect the arrow as well. The Line section controls the part of the arrow that applies to all lines:

- Choose a color from the Color drop-down list.

- From the Dashed drop-down list, you can choose from a variety of dashed and dotted lines.

- The Style drop-down list lets you choose from various line widths (weights) as well as a few double and triple lines.

- The Weight drop-down list also controls line weight (width), but you can specify an exact width in points.

Tip: Increasing the line weight affects both the arrow and the line.

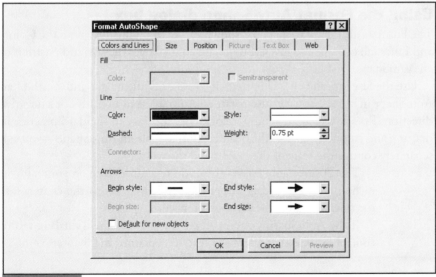

FIGURE 5-16 Use the Colors and Lines tab of the Format AutoShape dialog box to control arrows

Use the Arrows section to control the part of the arrow that is specific to arrows:

- Use the Begin Style drop-down box to create an arrow with an arrowhead at its beginning.

- If the arrow has an arrowhead at its beginning, use Begin Style to choose the type and size of the arrow.

- Use the End Style drop-down list to choose the type of arrow at the end. The choices are the same for both the beginning and the end of the arrow and are shown here.

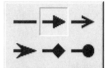

- Use the End Size drop-down list to choose a size for the arrowhead at the end of the arrow. You can choose from arrows that vary in both width and length, as shown here. Unfortunately, you cannot specify an arrowhead size in points.

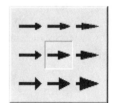

> **Tip:** If you wish, you can create your own arrowhead using the triangular basic shape and a solid fill.

Formatting lines

You format lines in the same way that you format arrows. Choose Line Style on the Drawing toolbar to choose from various line weights and a few double and triple lines. From this menu, choose More Lines to open the dialog box shown shown previously in Figure 5-16. Choose Dash Style on the Drawing toolbar to choose from various dashed and dotted lines.

Using the Format AutoShape dialog box

The Format AutoShape dialog box, shown earlier in Figure 5-16 with the Colors and Lines tab on top, also gives you precise control over the size and position of an AutoShape.

Use the Size tab, shown in Figure 5-17, to specify the height and width of an AutoShape in inches. You can also rotate an AutoShape in a positive or a negative direction. Rotation increases counterclockwise, contrary to standard practice in drafting and engineering. Use the Scale section to scale an AutoShape—you can separately control the scale of the height and the width.

> **Tip:** You can position by millimeters by typing **mm** after a measurement and by points by typing **pt**.

The Position tab lets you position the AutoShape on your slide in inches, measuring from either the top-left corner or the center. Use the rulers to judge the setting you need.

If the AutoShape contains text, you can use the Text Box tab to control settings that affect the text, as explained in Chapter 3.

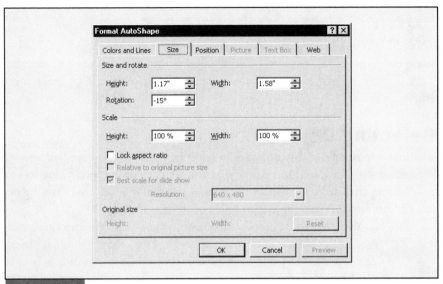

FIGURE 5-17 The Size tab of the Format AutoShape dialog box

Adding drawing objects to the Clip Gallery

When you create drawing objects using the tools on the Drawing toolbar, you can add them to the Clip Gallery. If you spent quite a bit of time creating them and might use them again, by all means place them in the Clip Gallery. Here's how:

1. First create the drawing object or objects.
2. Select the objects.
3. Press CTRL-C or click Copy on the Standard toolbar.
4. Click Insert Clip Art on the Drawing toolbar. PowerPoint opens the Insert ClipArt dialog box.
5. Choose a category.
6. Press CTRL-V.
7. When PowerPoint prompts you, type a name for the object and click OK. You can now insert the object or objects on any slide, or even in another application that supports the Clip Gallery.

Editing Drawing Objects

You will, of course, have to make changes to your drawing objects, sooner or later. No project ever seems to be completed without its fair share of changes. Take the time to learn these techniques well, and your work will go much more efficiently.

Selecting Objects

The first step in editing any object is to select it. By now, you have had enough experience with PowerPoint to know that you select an object by clicking it. You may have to click an AutoShape on its border to select it. A selected drawing object has handles that you can use to resize or reshape the object.

Tip: Press SHIFT and click a selected object to deselect an object that you selected in error.

You can choose more than one object at a time. You can then reformat all the objects with one command. First, choose the first object. Then, press SHIFT and click a second object. Keep on going as long as you like.

Another way to choose multiple objects is to use a selection box. There's no button for a selection box; to create one, you first click at one corner of the rectangular area you want to enclose. Be careful not to click an object—click only empty space on the slide. Then drag to the opposite corner of the rectangle. PowerPoint displays a dashed rectangle as you drag. Release the mouse button when the rectangle encloses all the objects you want to select. In this situation, too, you can press SHIFT and click any of the selected objects to deselect it. This is a great technique when you want to select all the objects in an area except one or two.

Tip: To select all the objects on a slide, press CTRL-A or choose Edit | Select All.

Objects are often layered on top of each other. You may find it difficult to select the object you want if it is behind another object. If the slide does not have too many objects, you may find it easier to cycle through all the objects until the object you want is selected. To accomplish this, first select any object. Then press TAB repeatedly until the object you want is selected.

Grouping and Ungrouping Objects

If you want to work with certain objects together more than once, you should group them. Grouped objects act like single objects. Common uses for grouping are text in a text box placed in a flowchart, WordArt text in an AutoShape, or a caption for a graphic image. In these instances, you want a set of objects to remain together permanently. Grouping is especially important when moving objects.

To group a set of objects, select them all. On the Drawing toolbar, choose Draw | Group. All the handles displayed by the individual objects are replaced by one set of handles for the whole group.

You can always ungroup a group. Select the group and choose Draw | Ungroup on the Drawing toolbar.

Reordering Objects

As mentioned earlier, it is common to have objects that cover one another. You often place objects on a slide in a certain order, only to find that the wrong object is on top. Reordering objects lets you specify which object appears on top. To reorder an object, select it and choose Draw | Order from the Drawing toolbar. (It's on the expanded menu.) Choose one of these options on the submenu:

- Bring to Front brings the selected object to the front of any other objects it overlaps.
- Send to Back sends the selected object behind any other objects it overlaps.
- Bring Forward brings the selected object one layer toward the front.
- Send Backward sends the selected object one layer toward the back.

In Figure 5-18, you see a slide containing several layers of pictures. On the right side of the first slide, the pictures are obviously in the wrong order.

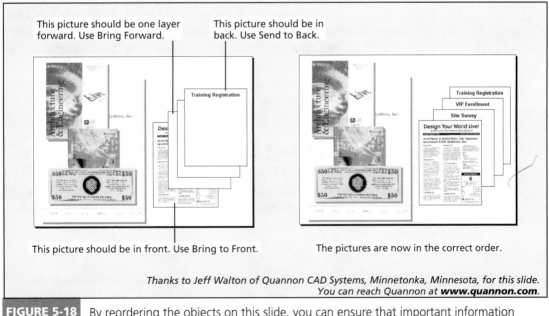

FIGURE 5-18 By reordering the objects on this slide, you can ensure that important information is not obscured

Moving Objects

You have already moved many objects in PowerPoint. Generally you select the object, move the cursor over the object until you get the crossed-arrows cursor, and then drag the object. I have already mentioned that you can precisely position an object using the Position tab of the Format AutoShape dialog box. (Right-click any object and choose Format AutoShape.) In the section, "Drawing with Precision," later in this chapter, I explain other techniques for positioning objects precisely.

Duplicating Objects

When you want two objects to be the same size and shape, you should draw the first object and then duplicate it, rather than try to draw it exactly the same the second time. There are two ways to duplicate objects:

- Select the object, copy it to the clipboard (CTRL-C), and then paste it back onto your slide (CTRL-V).
- Select the object, and duplicate it (CTRL-D or Edit | Duplicate).

You have no control over the location of the duplicate, but it appears selected so you can immediately drag it to a new location.

Deleting Objects

To delete an object, select it and press DEL. I discussed in Chapter 3 how text placeholders are in edit text mode when you select them. Pressing DEL just deletes one of the characters of the text. Callouts follow the same rule. To delete them, press ESC, and then press DEL. Pressing BACKSPACE also deletes any selected object or objects.

When you press CTRL-X (or choose Edit | Cut), the selected object is deleted and moved to the clipboard. You can then paste it on another slide or even in another application.

Resizing/Scaling Objects

When you select an object, it has eight sizing handles—four on the sides and four on the corners—creating a selection rectangle. For an irregular object such as a star-shaped AutoShape, the handles are placed on an imaginary rectangular border that bounds the object, as shown here.

When you drag on a handle, the shape resizes in the direction you drag. For example, if you drag outward on either the left or right handles, the shape becomes wider. The side of the object *opposite* the handle you drag remains fixed. The center and all other sides of the object are moved.

You can also resize an object so that the center remains fixed. To do this, press CTRL while dragging a handle.

You may want to scale an object. When you scale an object, you have the option to maintain the shape without any vertical or horizontal distortion. PowerPoint calls this *resizing proportionally* because the vertical and horizontal remain proportional to each other.

- To resize proportionally from one side or a corner, press SHIFT and drag the opposite handle.
- To resize proportionally from the center, press CTRL and SHIFT and drag any handle.

As explained earlier, you have exact control over the size of the object using the Size tab of the Format AutoShape dialog box. You can also scale the object by percentage.

Lines, arrows, and connectors have only two handles when selected. When you drag one handle, the other end remains fixed. You can change the endpoint's position freely, so that both the length and angle of the line are changed.

You can resize a line from its center by pressing CTRL as you drag. When you press SHIFT and drag, the line's angle is held constant and you can only change the line's length.

Rotating and Flipping Objects

There are several ways to rotate an object. To rotate by dragging, select the object and choose Free Rotate on the Drawing toolbar. You see four round, green handles, and the cursor takes on a spiral shape as shown here. Place the cursor over one of the handles and drag, using the dashed image as a guide. Release the mouse button when you like what you see.

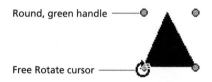

Round, green handle

Free Rotate cursor

Click Free Rotate to return your cursor to normal.

For quick rotation by 90 degrees, choose Draw | Rotate or Flip from the Drawing toolbar, and then choose Rotate Left or Rotate Right. For precise rotation, return to the now familiar Format AutoShape dialog box and click the Size tab. Here you can set the rotation to any degree, as mentioned earlier in this chapter.

Tip: You may want to create a mirror image of an object. You can then group the two objects and create a perfectly symmetrical shape.

To mirror an object (called *flipping*), select the object and choose Draw | Rotate or Flip from the Drawing toolbar. Then choose Flip Horizontal to mirror around a vertical line, or Flip Vertical to mirror around a horizontal line.

You can create a mirror image of vector-based clip art by converting it to a PowerPoint object. Select the clip art, and then choose Draw | Ungroup on the Drawing toolbar. Immediately select Draw | Group and flip the object.

Editing Points

Curve, free-form, and scribble objects are created with vertices that are located where you clicked as you created the object. You can edit these vertices to reshape these objects. Select the object, and then choose Draw | Edit Points on the Drawing toolbar (or right-click and choose Edit Points). PowerPoint now displays all the vertices, as shown in the following illustration. You can drag any vertex in any direction. This method is great for making minor corrections in these objects.

Editing Connectors

Connectors have several unique properties that make them different from lines. First, there are three types of connectors—straight, elbow (angled), and curved. You can change any connector's type by right-clicking it and choosing a different type of connector from the shortcut menu.

To disconnect one end of a connector from its object, drag the handle at that end. You can then drag the handle to another object. To move the entire connector, drag its middle, and both ends become "undone."

PowerPoint can automatically reroute connectors so they travel the shortest distance. Right-click a connector and choose Reroute Connectors from the shortcut menu. This command is also available on the expanded Draw menu on the Drawing toolbar.

Changing One AutoShape to Another

Would you like to switch AutoShapes? Maybe you think another shape would look more attractive or fit around the text better. It's easy:

1. Select the AutoShape you want to change.
2. Choose Draw | Change AutoShape on the Drawing toolbar.
3. Choose a type of AutoShape, and choose the shape you want.

Drawing with Precision

For you control freaks that like to lay out a slide precisely, a number of tools are designed especially for you. I have already discussed some of the techniques, such as using the Format AutoShapes dialog box to exactly position an AutoShape on a slide. Here are a few more pointers.

Using the Rulers

The rulers are very helpful when laying out a slide. As you move the cursor, the top and side rulers each show their position with a line. By observing the lines as you point to an object, you can know its position. You can use this information to position other objects.

Cross-Reference: The rulers are covered as they apply to text in Chapter 4.

To show the rulers, choose View | Ruler on the expanded menu.

Using Guides

Perhaps the best tools for placing objects are the guides. Guides are fine horizontal and vertical lines that cross the entire slide. To view the guides, choose View |

Guides. The default guides appear through the zero mark of each ruler, as shown here:

You can use the guides to measure distances. To do this, drag a guide. The measurement from the guide's start point appears as shown here:

To properly use guides, you often need more than one in each direction. To add a guide, press CTRL and drag any guide. PowerPoint creates a new guide.

Use the measurement to place the new guide precisely. One reason that guides are so useful is that objects snap to them as you move them. To try this, place a guide and drag any object near the guide. You will see that the object's edge snaps to the guide.

To delete a guide that you have added, drag it to its corresponding ruler. Drag horizontal guides to the top ruler and vertical guides to the side ruler.

Constraining Shape and Direction

As mentioned earlier in this chapter, you can constrain lines to be horizontal or vertical by pressing SHIFT as you draw. You can also press SHIFT to create a circle using the Oval tool and a square using the Rectangle tool. Refer back to the section "Resizing/Scaling Objects," which explains how to resize objects proportionally to prevent horizontal and/or vertical distortion.

 Tip: You can create a visible grid of guides. For example, you can create a grid whose boxes are all one-inch square.

Professional Pointer

Many slides use an asymmetric layout, and the center of the slide is not obvious. Use guides often to make sure that objects are properly centered, as shown in Figure 5-19. You can also see this slide in color—refer to number 44 in the Slide Gallery.

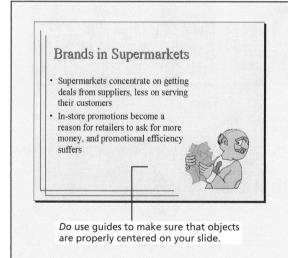

Do use guides to make sure that objects are properly centered on your slide.

Don't let asymmetric layouts fool you. The title and left placement of the bulleted text offset the graphic sufficiently; however, the bulleted text should still be centered vertically. Here, it is too high.

Thanks to Nathan Otto of Point of Choice, Fairfield, Iowa (nathan@pointofchoice.com), for this slide.

FIGURE 5-19   You can use guides to center text and objects on a slide

To constrain movement of objects horizontally or vertically, press SHIFT as you drag the object.

Snapping to the Grid and to Objects

PowerPoint has a secret—an invisible grid of evenly spaced lines that covers the entire slide. By default, whenever you draw, resize, or move an object, it *snaps* to this grid. As a result, objects tend to line up easily, without much fuss.

On the other hand, sometimes you want more control. To temporarily disable the grid snapping, press ALT as you drag or draw an object.

You can also snap one object to another. To set this up, choose Draw | Snap | To Shape on the Drawing toolbar. (If it looks like a depressed button, this feature is already active.) Note that Snap appears only on the expanded Draw menu. When Snap to Shape is on, shapes that you draw or drag automatically snap to nearby shapes. To turn off snapping to the grid or to shapes, choose the same menu items you use to turn them on.

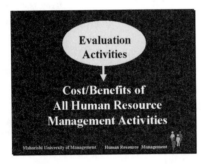

If you want objects to touch precisely, *do* use the Snap to Shape command.

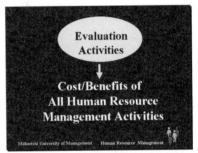

Don't let your objects almost touch— it can look sloppy and unprofessional.

To view the slide on the left in color, refer to number 45 in the Slide Gallery.

Tip: For those of you who want super control, press CTRL as you use the appropriate arrow key. PowerPoint moves your object in increments of .02 inches.

Nudging Objects

Do you find it difficult to move objects a very short distance with the mouse? You're not alone. PowerPoint lets you *nudge* objects, which means to move them a short distance. To nudge an object, select it and choose Draw | Nudge on the Drawing toolbar. Then choose Up, Down, Left, or Right from the submenu. PowerPoint moves the object one grid unit in the direction you chose.

For quicker access, you can also use the arrow keys on the keyboard to nudge objects.

Aligning and Distributing Objects

PowerPoint has two tools that help you automatically align objects and distribute them evenly across an area or the entire slide.

To align two or more objects, first decide how you want to align them. If the objects are lined up approximately vertically, you can line them up along their left sides, right sides, or through their center. If the objects are lined up approximately horizontally, you can line them up along their top sides, bottom sides, or through their middle.

To align objects, first select two or more objects. Then choose Draw | Align or Distribute. Choose one of the options on the submenu.

Figure 5-20 shows a slide that needs aligning, both horizontal and vertically. Both the shapes and the arrows should be aligned. Figure 5-20 also shows the results of the various alignment options.

Figure 5-21 shows how unaligned objects can make a slide slipshod. To view these slides in color, refer to numbers 46 and 47 in the Slide Gallery.

Another slick trick is to distribute three or more objects equidistant from each other, either horizontally or vertically. This saves you lots of calculations and is often a must for a neat-looking slide. In Figure 5-22, you see the same slide shown in Figure 5-21. The objects on the left are aligned but not evenly distributed. To distribute objects, first choose three or more objects. Then choose Draw | Align or Distribute on the Drawing toolbar. From the submenu choose either Distribute Horizontally or Distribute Vertically.

To arrange objects equal distances from each in relation to the entire slide, first click Relative to Slide on the expanded submenu of the Align or Distribute menu. Then start again, choosing Draw | Align or Distribute and choosing Distribute Horizontally or Distribute Vertically.

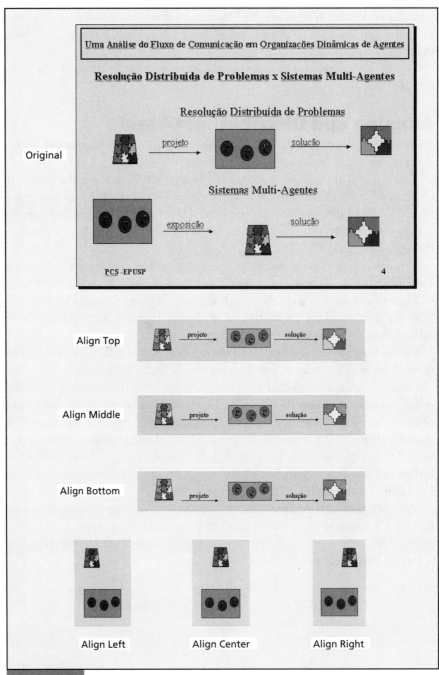

FIGURE 5-20 You can align two or more objects on a slide

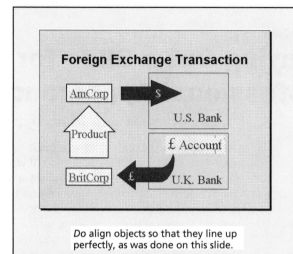
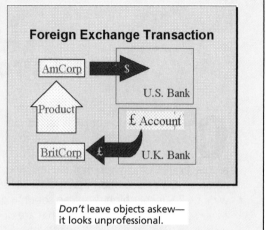

Do align objects so that they line up perfectly, as was done on this slide.

Don't leave objects askew— it looks unprofessional.

FIGURE 5-21   Use the Align and Distribute command to align two or more objects for a professional look

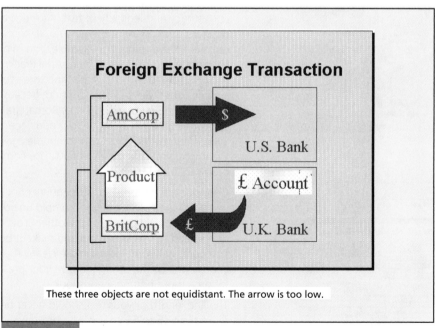

These three objects are not equidistant. The arrow is too low.

FIGURE 5-22   Whenever you have three or more objects, you can distribute them evenly from each other or across the entire slide

Laying Out a Slide for a Professional Appearance

from an interview with Stuart Friedman

One of the most important techniques you can use to lay out a slide is to set up a grid of evenly spaced guides. For example, by default, PowerPoint creates slides for an on-screen presentation that are 10 inches wide by 7.5 inches high. You can set up a grid of vertical and horizontal guides that are one inch apart. (Unfortunately, PowerPoint limits the number of guides to eight in each direction.) It's also helpful to create a margin around edges. Here you see a slide in its draft form with guides and then in its final form.

Once you have the grid, use it as a guide to place text, charts, graphics, and so on. If you choose, you can violate the grid, but always use it as your starting point. Think of your text in terms of how many columns of the grid it requires. To adjust vertical spacing, set the line spacing or add spacing between paragraphs. Once you get used to working with a grid, you'll be amazed at how easy it is to lay out a slide. The more columns in your grid, the more flexible it will be. You can use smaller gridded areas for subtext, footnotes, or small graphics.

In addition, pay a great deal of attention to consistency and legibility of text. As much as possible, stick to the same type family throughout the presentation. For example, you might consider using Arial, Arial bold, Arial Black, and Arial Narrow. Don't use more than three fonts. Include font styles in your counting, because Times Roman regular and Times Roman italic appear as different fonts to your audience. Even different font sizes can sometimes give the impression of a different font. Use common sense and keep it simple.

Consider the old belt and suspenders principle: you don't want to wear both to hold up your trousers—it's either one or the other. You don't need to use large type *and* make it bold. The point will come across more clearly if you choose one or the other and give your presentation a more homogeneous look.

The line length of your text should never be more than 45 to 55 characters, including spaces. More than that is difficult for audiences to read. In most cases, the type will be large enough so that this is not a problem. The general principle is to use shorter lines rather than longer lines of text.

When mixing two different fonts, consider the x-height of the font. The *x-height* is the height of the lowercase *x* as well as of many lower-case letters, such as *a*, *c*, and *e*. Two fonts may be the same point size but have different x-heights. For example, Garamond (shown in the following slide on the right) has a much smaller x-height than Arial (shown on the left):

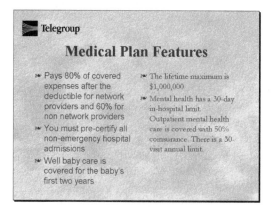

As a result, the entire font looks smaller and is harder to read. To compensate, you could increase the font size of the Garamond text.

Organize the elements of your slide in advance. Decide which elements are most important and which least important, and design them accordingly. Numbering and footnotes should be least important. If your headings are 44 points and bold and body copy is 28 points, create footnotes that are 18 points. Don't forget to stand back and take a look at your slides. If some minor element jumps out at you, adjust it as necessary—remove the bold, make it smaller, or change the color.

Create a visual theme. A visual theme allows the graphic representation to express the content. For example, if you're giving a lecture on herb gardening, you might want to use

natural-looking colors that emphasize the illustrations and photographs, leaf borders, leaf bullets, or pictures of finished recipes that express the theme visually.

If your slides are busy, with lots of text and graphics, make the background simple. The more contrast you create between your text and your background, the easier your slides will be to read. If you use a 3-D or shadow effect, use it as emphasis. It's the belt and suspenders principle again—don't overdo special effects, or they lose their impact. The same principle works for highly saturated colors—use them in small areas for emphasis.

Audiences naturally read from left to right and from top to bottom. Audiences also notice dark or bright areas before light ones. So place and emphasize items with those two principles in mind. If you have a dark background, lighter areas stand out more because of the brightness and contrast.

Use cooler, muted colors for backgrounds, light or dark. Brighter warmer colors are "sweet,"—they're hard to look at for a long time. Light text on a dark background looks a little larger than vice versa. But don't be afraid to use lighter backgrounds with dark text—they create a softer look that is appropriate for many messages.

Think about the rhythm of the entire presentation. Like a piece of music, your presentation should have a regular beat without getting boring. For example, your slides could go like this: text, text, image, text. You can also create a rhythm such as large image, text, text, smaller images, text, text. To give the eye a rest and keep your audience attentive, you need to create variety.

Do a usability test. You can even learn from a six-year-old's comments on your work. Then do the same with your colleagues at work. These people can point out issues that you missed, such as "This slide is about gardening. Why are the slides red?" or "This part is too small for me to read." You'll get a lot of useful feedback and bring in an important element of objectivity. Don't be shy—people love to tell you what they think!

TIP: Another way to create a grid is to draw it on the slide master using the Drawing toolbar. First create your guides. Then draw a line along the first guide. (Grids are traditionally light blue.) By default, the line snaps to the guide. Choose CTRL-D to duplicate the line and drag it to the second guide. Now continue to duplicate the last line you've created, and PowerPoint gets the message, placing them automatically on your guides. When you've done this in both directions on the slide master, use the Rectangle tool to create a margin all around the slide. Select all the lines and the rectangle, and group them. Return to your presentation, and you will see the grid on all your slides. You can create a template containing only a slide master with this grid and use it for all your presentations. (Or once you've created this grid, you can copy it from one presentation to another.) When you have finished the presentation, go to the slide master and delete the grid.

Stuart Friedman has over 20 years of professional graphic design experience and has completed numerous print and electronic media projects for commercial clients such as Dell Computer, Federal Express, Bell Canada, MCI, and Apache Medical Systems. Areas of expertise include typography, information design, and graphic user interface design. Since 1985 he has focused on educational and scientific software design. In 1992 he received his MFA degree from Yale University School of Art, specializing in graphical user interface and information design. He currently is Senior Visual Designer with Human Factors International. He can be reached at 515-472-4480 or stuart@humanfactors.com.

Professional Skills Summary

In this chapter you learned all about graphics. The first part of the chapter covered how to insert clip art on your slides. I discussed using the Clip Gallery, finding clip art, inserting graphic files, and editing pictures. You can edit many pictures using the Picture toolbar. Other tools often available are Microsoft Photo Editor, PhotoDraw, and Paint.

The second part of the chapter was about AutoShapes, including inserting, formatting, and editing them. This section also described the functions of the Drawing toolbar in detail. Finally, I reviewed some special techniques for laying out a slide with precision.

The next chapter is all about colors, borders, fills, and 3-D effects.

chapter 6

Working with Colors, Borders, Fills, and 3-D Effects

Color is an essential element of a presentation. Different colors send different messages to your audience. By the use of colors in borders, fills, backgrounds, and the slides as a whole, you can transform a ho-hum presentation into a force-ful one. Add fills, shadows, and 3-D effects to realize the full power of your message.

Working with Color Schemes

Every design template includes a default *color scheme*. A color scheme is a set of eight colors that are automatically applied to the following features:

- Title text
- Text and lines
- Shadows
- Background
- Fills
- Accent
- Accent and hyperlink (The color scheme is only applied to hyperlinked text, not to objects.)
- Accent and followed hyperlink (The color scheme is only applied when a hyperlink is clicked to show that the hyperlink has been followed.)

Cross-Reference: Hyperlinks are covered in Chapter 11.

In addition, design templates include a set of alternate color schemes that you can choose. The purpose of a color scheme is to ensure that your presentation has a coordinated look—not only should all titles look the same, but the colors should work well with each other.

You don't have to do anything to work with the default color scheme for your design template. PowerPoint automatically assigns the appropriate colors to the elements in your presentation based on the color scheme.

Choosing a Color Scheme

Professionals choose a color scheme to match the message. You can imagine that you would not want to use the same color scheme for selling vacation packages to Hawaii as for selling long-term care insurance. Even the same presentation might use different color schemes for different situations. For example, if a presentation to employees on their employee benefits program is good news, you might use brighter colors compared to the softer colors you would use if the new program represented a cutback.

To choose a different color scheme, choose Format | Slide Color Scheme to open the Color Scheme dialog box shown in Figure 6-1. Note that some templates offer more color scheme options than others.

To see a slide rendered with all six standard color schemes available with the presentation's template, refer to numbers 48 to 53 in the Slide Gallery. As you look at the color schemes, you'll see that the colors in each scheme are related. One scheme might feature blues, greens, and grays—soft colors—while another uses warmer greens, oranges, and browns. One color scheme is always in shades of gray. Each color scheme is designed to create an overall impression that applies to your entire presentation.

Note the tip at the bottom right of the Color Scheme dialog box (shown in Figure 6-1), which advises using a light background for overheads and a dark background for on-screen presentations. Changing backgrounds is covered later in this chapter.

Professional Pointer

Backgrounds that are neither very light nor very dark can work well for both situations. A very dark background is usually used with white or yellow text for contrast, but the result can be harsh. When you want to create a softer effect, use a mid-range green or blue. However, be sure the text contrasts sufficiently with the background for good legibility.

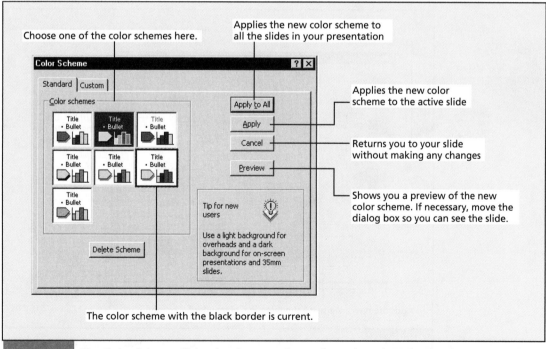

FIGURE 6-1 The Color Scheme dialog box lets you choose from the color schemes that come with each design template

Creating Your Own Color Scheme

If you looked at the six color schemes in color (numbers 48 to 53 in the Slide Gallery), you probably thought that some (or most) of them were pretty ugly. Luckily, you have the flexibility to create any color scheme you can think up, using the Custom tab of the Color Scheme dialog box, shown in Figure 6-2.

Tip: To apply the change to several, but not all, slides, select the slides in Slide Sorter view before opening the dialog box.

While you can use the Custom tab to change the background of the color scheme, PowerPoint also has a separate Background command on the Format menu that offers more capabilities.

When you click Change Color in the Color Scheme dialog box, PowerPoint opens the dialog box shown in Figure 6-3. You can choose any of the color mosaics for your color scheme. When you click OK, you return to the Color Scheme dialog box. You can make changes to other items of the color scheme or click OK again to return to your presentation.

Like the Color Scheme dialog box, the Color dialog box has both a Standard and a Custom tab. When it comes to color, the Custom tab, shown in Figure 6-4, is where the fun is.

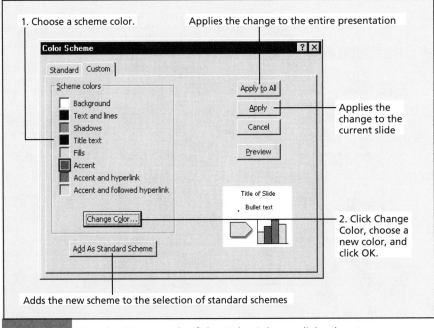

FIGURE 6-2   Use the Custom tab of the Color Scheme dialog box to create your own color scheme

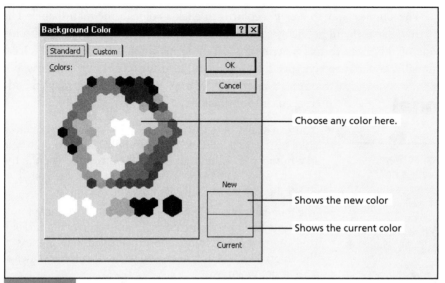

FIGURE 6-3 You can choose any color for any item in the color scheme from this dialog box

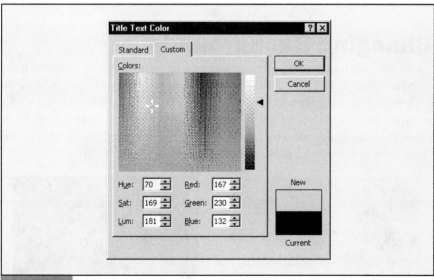

FIGURE 6-4 The Custom tab lets you create any color

The simplest way to create a color is to click a color in the main panel. The narrow bar at the right changes the *luminosity*—the brightness. You can also use one of the more formal systems for determining color: RGB or HSL. Occasionally, you may receive specifications for colors using one of these systems. For example, a company logo or a country's flag may include precise color specifications.

Professional Pointer

Use the standard color schemes as a guide when creating new color schemes. Remember that the colors should fit well together and yet provide enough contrast so that text is easy to see against the fill and background colors.

- You can use the red-green-blue (RGB) system to define a color by the amount of each primary light color. You can type in a number for each color or use the arrows to change the color by small increments. The numbers must be from 1 to 255; when all three colors are 255, you get white.

- The hue-saturation-luminosity (HSL) system of defining a color lets you choose a color by hue (the color), saturation (the intensity of the color), and luminosity (the brightness of the color). In the HSL system, you also set all three values at 255 to get white.

Click OK to return to the Color Scheme dialog box.

The RGB and HSL systems are used by PowerPoint (and all Microsoft Office applications) whenever you need to choose a color. For example, if you click the Fill Color arrow on the Drawing toolbar and then choose More Colors, you get the same dialog box.

Changing Backgrounds

Each slide has a background. The background is the bottommost layer and is not an object that you can manipulate. You can never place anything behind the background, and it always covers the entire slide. A background can be a solid color, or you can use one of the fill effects discussed later in this chapter. Backgrounds certainly don't have to be dull! Here you see some examples. To view these slides in color, refer to numbers 54 and 55 in the Slide Gallery.

As mentioned earlier, you can change the background color in the Color Scheme dialog box, but you have many more options if you choose Format | Background (or right-click the background of any slide and choose Background) to open the Background dialog box shown here:

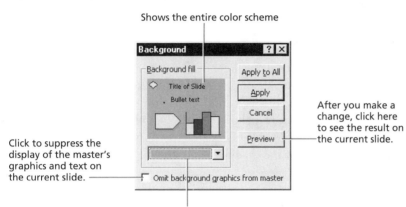

Shows the entire color scheme

Click to suppress the display of the master's graphics and text on the current slide.

After you make a change, click here to see the result on the current slide.

Shows the current background color.
Click the down arrow to change the background.

The Background Fill box display looks just like the one in the Color Scheme dialog box, as you saw in Figures 6-1 and 6-2. You see the entire color scheme so that you can see if your new background will match and contrast appropriately with the other elements on your slide. You can also click Preview, but if the current slide does not contain all the elements, you could miss a potential problem.

Click Apply to change only the selected slide or slides. Click Apply to All to change all the slides.

The background is one aspect of the slide master, which controls the look of all the slides in your presentation. Masters can include graphics and text. The Background dialog box lets you suppress the master's graphics and text by checking the box at the bottom of the dialog box.

Cross-Reference: Slide masters are covered in the next chapter.

When you click the down arrow in the Background dialog box, you see the menu shown here:

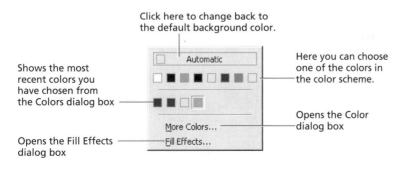

Click here to change back to the default background color.

Shows the most recent colors you have chosen from the Colors dialog box

Here you can choose one of the colors in the color scheme.

Opens the Color dialog box

Opens the Fill Effects dialog box

This small menu hides a world of opportunities! To choose a color not available on this menu, click More Colors to open the Colors dialog box, where the tabs look like the ones you saw in Figures 6-3 and 6-4. To create a more elaborate background, choose Fill Effects to open the Fill Effects dialog box, shown with the gradient tab on top in Figure 6-5.

Creating Gradient Backgrounds

In a *gradient,* the colors vary across the slide. In a one-color gradient, the intensity of the color varies. In a two-color gradient, the background changes from one color to the second. Choose Preset to give yourself the choice of a number of preset gradients, with names like Early Sunset, Nightfall, and Desert.

The one- and two-color gradients also offer a number of shading styles that determine the direction of the shading. Each shading style then has two to four variants.

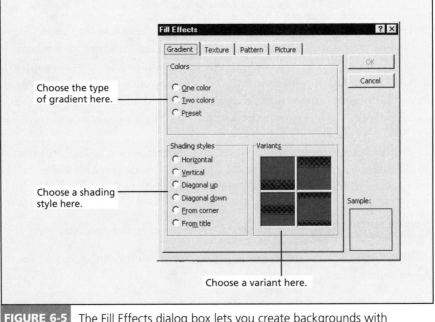

FIGURE 6-5 The Fill Effects dialog box lets you create backgrounds with gradients, textures, patterns, and pictures

Once you choose a type of gradient, new opportunities appear in the Colors section of the dialog box. If you choose One Color, you see the section shown here:

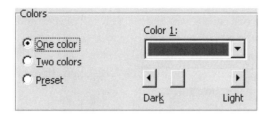

Click the Color 1 down arrow to choose from color scheme colors, recently used colors, or any color in the Colors dialog box. Then choose how the gradient varies the basic color by using the dark/light slider bar. If you slide the box all the way toward dark, the basic color grades to black. If you slide the box to the light end, the basic color grades to white. A setting in the middle eliminates the gradient because the color grades with itself.

If you choose Two Colors, the Colors section of the dialog box looks like this:

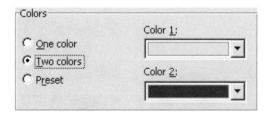

Choose the two colors from the drop-down boxes. You can choose two similar colors to create a subtle impression or contrasting colors for a bolder effect.

If you choose Preset, the Colors section of the dialog box displays a drop-down box letting you choose from any of 24 gradient backgrounds. Here's what you see:

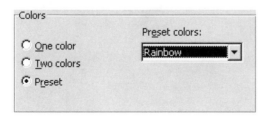

I recommend trying out the preset gradients. Gradients can create a professional look and range from soft to exciting. Some of the preset gradients are quite beautiful.

Whichever type of gradient you choose, you still have to choose a shading style and one of the variants. With so much choice, it's a good thing there's a sample at the bottom-right of the dialog box.

When you have chosen a gradient, click OK. Then choose Apply or Apply All in the Fill Effects dialog box.

Tip: On the Internet, use any search engine to search for the words *backgrounds* and *download*. Other words to look for are *textures* and *free*. Some of the clip art Web sites mentioned in the previous chapter also have backgrounds designed for use on Web sites.

Creating Texture Backgrounds

Texture backgrounds look as if you have placed your slide on a physical object with a texture, such as wood, marble, or water droplets. Textures are pictures, and you can find your own, if you like. To use a texture background, click the Texture tab of the Fill Effects dialog box, shown in Figure 6-6.

Textures generally provide an understated, dignified impression. You can choose from the textures provided or click Other Texture to open the Select Texture dialog box shown in Figure 6-7.

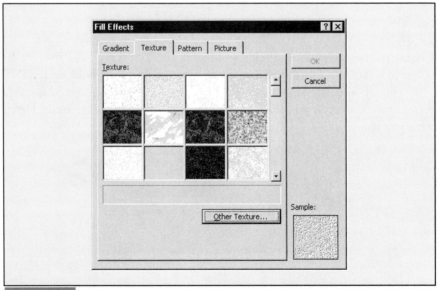

FIGURE 6-6 Use the Texture tab of the Fill Effects dialog box to create a textured background for your slides

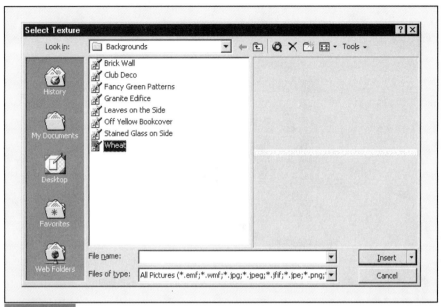

FIGURE 6-7 You can choose from many picture files to create your own texture

Not all graphic files will work as textures. If you try a large file, PowerPoint will display a message that the file is too large to use as a texture. I've tried .bmp, .jpg, and .gif files with success. Although a background may only show as a strip in the preview box of the dialog box, PowerPoint uses it to create a background covering the entire slide.

When you have chosen a texture, click OK. Then choose Apply or Apply All in the Fill Effects dialog box.

Professional Pointer

For a one-of-a-kind look, make your own textures using Photo Editor (try taking a picture or solid fill and texturizing it) or PhotoDraw (fill any picture with one of the supplied textures). Save the texture as a .gif or .bmp file.

Creating Pattern Backgrounds

Pattern backgrounds are created from repeating patterns of lines or dots on a background. You choose from the patterns shown in Figure 6-8. You can choose the background and foreground colors. The foreground color generally creates the lines or dots, although some of the patterns are in reverse—see the second column of patterns in Figure 6-8.

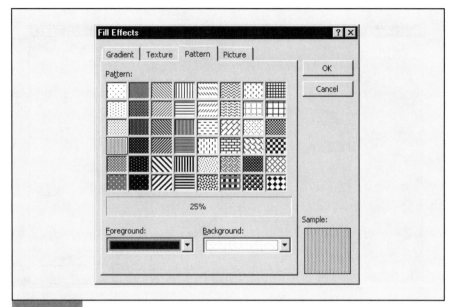

FIGURE 6-8   Choose a patterned background from the Pattern tab

Using contrasting foreground and background colors gives you a different effect than using similar colors. Be careful to check that your text is fully legible on a patterned background. The finer patterns work better than the more obvious patterns.

When you have chosen a pattern, click OK. Then choose Apply or Apply All in the Fill Effects dialog box.

Professional Pointer

Most pictures are too distracting to use as a background. Legibility suffers. To use pictures effectively, you often need to turn them into watermarks.

Creating Picture Backgrounds

The last tab of the Fill Effects dialog box, shown in Figure 6-9, lets you use a picture as a background. As you can see, the only thing you can do on this tab is to click Select Picture, which opens the Select Picture dialog box. Navigate to the picture you want and click Insert. Your picture will now be shown on the Picture tab. Click OK, and then click Apply or Apply All in the Fill Effects dialog box.

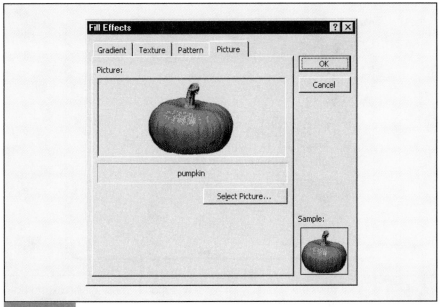

FIGURE 6-9   The Picture tab of the Fill Effects dialog box lets you choose any graphic file as a background

To create a watermark in Photo Editor, open the graphic and choose Image Balance on the toolbar. Increase the brightness and reduce the contrast until you get the results you want. If necessary, click Set Transparent Color and click the background of the picture. Click OK. Save the file under a new name.

PowerPoint automatically covers the entire slide with your picture, so you don't need to worry about its size.

As you can see, you need to experiment to get the effect you want. Have fun! A picture can create a sophisticated effect on a slide, so it's worth the effort. Figure 6-10 shows an example of a sky and clouds picture used as a background. To view this slide in color, refer to number 56 in the Slide Gallery.

Professional Pointer

Some pictures get distorted or show lots of white space when turned into a background and are therefore not suitable. You'll get the best results if the shape of the picture is close to the shape of a slide. You may be able to crop a picture to the proper shape. Pictures with little detail also work well.

Professional Pointer

A watermarked company logo can be effective as the background on each slide.

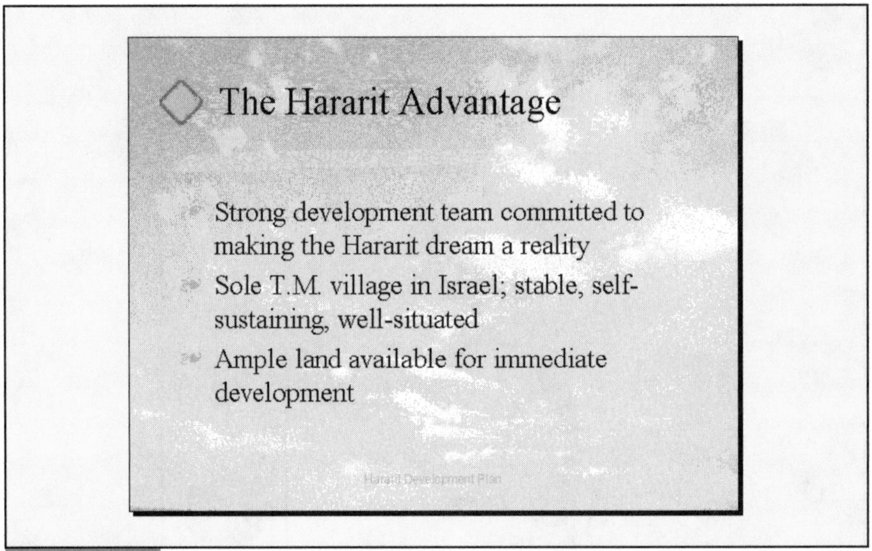

The Hararit Advantage

Strong development team committed to making the Hararit dream a reality

Sole T.M. village in Israel; stable, self-sustaining, well-situated

Ample land available for immediate development

Hararit Development Plan

FIGURE 6-10 In this slide, a picture of a sky was modified using Microsoft Photo Editor to create a watermark effect; the text shows nicely against the sky

Formatting Lines and Borders

Every color scheme includes a color for text and lines. You can change the text color in the Font dialog box by selecting text and choosing Format | Font. A simpler way is to use the Font Color button on the Drawing toolbar. Either click the button to change the text to the most recently chosen color, or the down arrow to choose any color you wish.

Lines include the edging around an AutoShape and the border around a text box, text placeholder, or picture. The line color also applies to lines that you draw using the tools on the Drawing toolbar. You can change the line color or choose not to use a line at all.

The easiest way to format a line or a border is to right-click the object and choose Format AutoShape (or Format Text Box or Format Picture, depending on the type of object). PowerPoint opens the appropriate dialog box; in Figure 6-11 you see the Format AutoShape dialog box with the Colors and Lines tab on top.

Most of the features of this dialog box related to formatting lines are covered in the section "Formatting Arrows," in Chapter 5. Following are a few additional

[Format AutoShape dialog box]

or text box

FIGURE 6-11 Use the Line section of the Format AutoShape dialog box to format the color and style of the edging around the AutoShape; the same section formats the border around text boxes and pictures

suggestions from the point of view of color. When you click the Color drop-down box, you see the now-familiar choices shown here. The top choice is No Line, which is often the right choice. You rarely want a border around a picture, for example, unless you want to create a picture-frame effect. Text placeholders usually don't have borders, but text boxes can go either way: use a border when you want the text to stand out from the rest of the slide's text. Omitting the line in an AutoShape creates a subtle effect; on the other hand, a line can make the AutoShape more powerful.

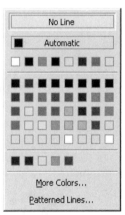

As previously explained in the discussions of color schemes and backgrounds, you can choose from the automatic color scheme color, another color in the color scheme, recently selected colors, or any color in the Colors dialog box.

Patterned Lines is the last of the Color choices. Click to open the Patterned Lines dialog box, which looks exactly the same as the Pattern tab of the Fill Effects dialog box, shown earlier in Figure 6-8. Choose foreground and background colors, choose any pattern, and click OK. However, note that line patterns don't show up very well unless the line is quite thick. Use the Weight drop-down box to create a thick line.

You can use the Line Color button on the Drawing toolbar to make quick, simple changes to line color. To change any line or border to the current color, select its object and click the main part of the button. For more options, click the down arrow at the right to see the options shown here:

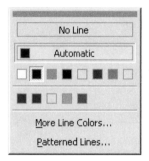

As you can see, the options on the Drawing toolbar are more limited than those in the Format AutoShape dialog box. You can choose any color or a patterned line, but you can't change line weight or style.

To change line weight and style, use the Line Style button on the Drawing toolbar. Choose from the list of line weights and styles. The last option includes a More Lines item that brings you to—guess what?—the Format AutoShape dialog box. (Moral: Simple line changes are easier from the Drawing toolbar, but if you want to make two or more adjustments with full control, open the Format AutoShape dialog box.) Figure 6-12 shows some AutoShapes using various line options.

Working with Fills

A *fill* fills an enclosed space, such as the inside of an AutoShape or a text box. Every color scheme includes a fill color, but you can change any fill. You can also create the same fill effects for fills as you can for backgrounds.

Changing Fill Color

To change the fill color quickly, use the Fill Color button on the Drawing toolbar. This button can be used in two ways. Beneath the image of the paint can is a line filled with the current fill color. To change any fill to the current color,

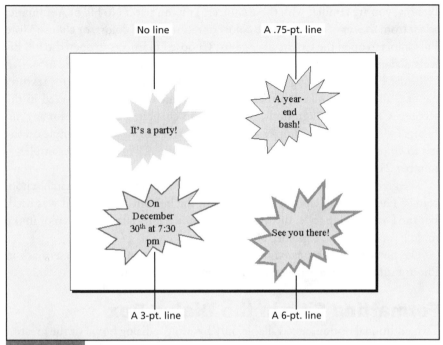

FIGURE 6-12   Each of the AutoShapes uses a different line format

select its object and click the main part of the button. For more options, click the down arrow at the right to see the options shown here:

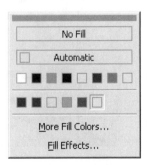

By now, you are familiar with these choices. You can select No Fill or Automatic, select from the set of color scheme colors or recently used colors, or choose More Fill Colors to open the Colors dialog box. Choose Fill Effects to open the Fill Effects dialog box, which I introduced earlier in this chapter (see Figure 6-5).

In the Fill Effects dialog box, as you know, you can create gradient, texture, pattern, and picture fills. In other words, the same effects that I covered in the section "Changing Backgrounds," earlier in this chapter, are available for any fill. Figure 6-13 shows two examples of fill effects. You can view the example on the left in color by referring back to one of the Chapter 4 Slide Gallery examples— number 21.

The gradient was created with a one-color gradient in a color to match school colors. The Diagonal Up shading style with the bottom-right variant was used. For the Diagonal Up style, this variant places the lighter shade of the color in the middle for maximum legibility of the text.

The picture fill was created by modifying a graphic to create a watermark in Photo Editor. The watermark was then chosen as a picture fill.

Formatting Fills in the Dialog Box

Two additional options are available only by using a dialog box. For the greatest control, right-click any object and choose Format AutoShape (or Format Text

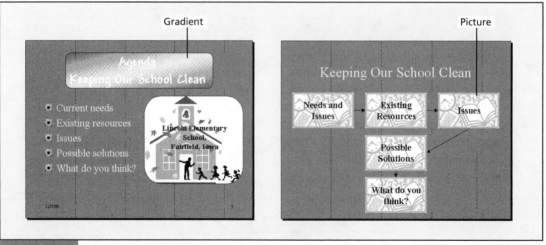

FIGURE 6-13   Fills are often used in AutoShapes and text boxes

Box, etc.). You've already seen the Format AutoShape dialog box in Figure 6-11. Here you see the options when you click the Color drop-down box in the Fill section. The color choices are similar to those available on the Drawing toolbar. However, one new choice, Background, is now available. Choose Background to set the fill to the same color (or effect) as the slide background. Be careful, though! If your object has no line, it promptly disappears because you can't distinguish it from the background! If you don't like the result, click Undo on the Standard toolbar.

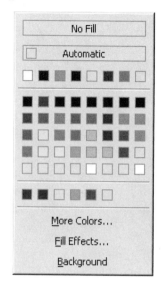

In the Fill section of the Format AutoShape dialog box is another option we have not yet discussed—the Semitransparent check box. Check this box if you want objects behind the selected object to show through slightly. Your slide background will show through as well. Here you see a text box with a semitransparent fill:

The fill makes the text more readable but still lets the beautiful picture background show through. To view this slide in color, refer to number 57 in the Slide Gallery.

It's always a good idea to use the Preview button before clicking OK, although you can undo any change you make. If you don't like the result, you can quickly try something else. Move the dialog box to see the slide, if necessary.

The Psychology of Color

Adapted from an article in Presentations *magazine by Jon Hanke, Senior Editor*

The most important factor is legibility, which should never be sacrificed merely for the sake of a pleasing color combination. Colors for graphics and text need to contrast sufficiently with the background to be easily read. It's generally a good idea to use darker colors for backgrounds, because light backgrounds can cause an uncomfortable glare and make audiences restless. For similar reasons, consultants also caution against using highly saturated primary colors as backgrounds. For presentation slides, yellow text on a black background provides the ultimate contrast; use this as a benchmark.

Due to the way our eyes work, and because color-perception deficiencies are common, certain color combinations, including red/green, brown/green, blue/black, and blue/purple, should be avoided.

Red should be handled with care. Red is one of the most influential colors in your software palette—it can elicit such emotions as desire, passion, and competitiveness. However, it also carries negative cultural attachments; in the business world, it connotes financial loss—so use it carefully.

Don't forget your basic black. Often overlooked, black is a background color with useful psychological undertones; it connotes finality and also works well as a transitional color.

Green is another background color with positive associations. It is believed to stimulate interaction, which makes deep greens and teals good colors for trainers, educators, and others whose presentations are intended to generate discussion.

Calming and conservative are some of the adjectives most commonly associated with blue.

Studies have also shown that blue has the power to slow our breathing and pulse rates. However, due to blue's popularity for business presentations, some business audiences now equate blue backgrounds with staleness and unoriginal thinking. When corporations specify blue backgrounds, professional presentation designers typically try to infuse them with some originality. Purple can imply immaturity and unimportance, while brown connotes uneasiness and passivity.

While background colors help set the emotional tone for your presentation, the colors you use for text, tables, charts, and other graphic elements have a bearing on how well the audience understands and remembers your message. Research has shown that the effective use of selective contrast, known as the *von Restorff* (or *isolation*) *effect,* makes audiences *remember* the outstanding item better as well. A 1982 Daemon College study concludes that highlighting or emphasizing meaningful text results in better retention—not just for the highlighted item, but for the *entire message.*

Arrange colors from dark to light, placing light colors on top of darker ones. We perceive dark colors as being "heavier" than light ones, so graphic elements that are arranged from darkest to lightest are the easiest for the eyes to scan.

Most consultants agree that your palette should include one or two bright colors for emphasis—but to preserve the power of these colors, use them with restraint.

You can contact Jon Hanke at jhanke@presentations.com. Contact Presentations at 800-328-4329, or visit the Web site at **www.presentations.com**.

Creating 3-D Effects

PowerPoint can create 3-D graphics for you on the fly. A simple type of 3-D is shadows, which give the impression that the AutoShape or other object is raised off the slide's surface. True 3-D effects are more complex and actually draw in a third dimension. Both shadows and 3-D effects come with loads of options and settings and can quickly improve the quality of your presentation's graphics.

Creating Shadows

Shadows create a subtle, yet effective 3-D impression. You may have noticed that PowerPoint displays slides on your screen with a slight shadow. Here you see a slide with several graphics. The ones on the left use shadows and look much more three-dimensional than the newsletters on the right.

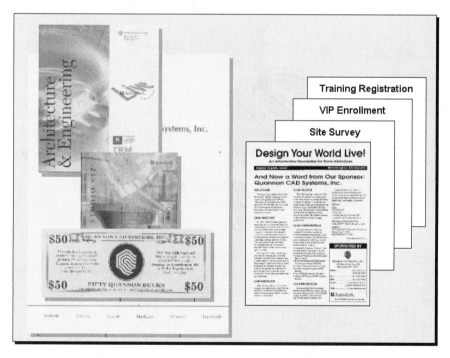

The graphics here were created by scanning the actual documents, inserting them as pictures, and then adding shadow effects, as discussed next. To view this slide in color, refer to number 58 in the Slide Gallery.

To create a shadow, select any object (except text), and use the Shadow button on the Drawing toolbar. (To shadow text, use the Text Shadow button on the Formatting toolbar.) PowerPoint displays the choices shown in the following illustration. Choose No Shadow to eliminate a shadow you have created previously.

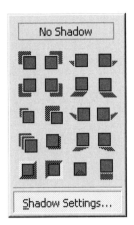

Otherwise, choose any of the options. Notice that the options come in groups, which are generally based on four different lighting angles—top left, top right, bottom left, and bottom right. Even within these angles, there are variants. Generally, you will need to try a few shadows out before you find what you like.

Some colors and shapes show up a shadow better than others. A shadow that looks great on an orange, rectangular AutoShape may be scarcely noticeable on a green, star-shaped AutoShape. Semitransparent fills let the shadow show through, which can be confusing.

The color of the shadow is important. Often the shadow's color is too similar to either the object's fill or the slide background. Every color scheme has a shadow color, but you can change the color.

Professional Pointer

If you want to add a shadow to more than one object, you usually want to add the same type of shadow to all. When you create 3-D effects, they should mimic the real world to some extent; otherwise, the effect is confusing to your audience.

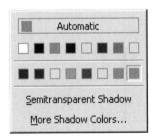

Using the Shadow Settings

If a shadow doesn't turn out to your satisfaction, you still have a lot more options. On the menu that pops up when you click Shadows on the Drawing toolbar, choose Shadow Settings to display the Shadow Settings toolbar shown in Figure 6-14.

Nudging a shadow makes it bigger or smaller. If the shadow appears to the right of the object, nudging its shadow to the right makes the shadow bigger. Nudge the same shadow to the left to make it smaller.

When you click the down arrow to the right of the Shadow Color button, you see the typical color selections shown here. Typically, shadows are gray, as you have probably noticed in real life. However, other colors can create a fun effect. Remember that the shadow needs to contrast with both the object's fill color and the slide's background to be noticed. On the other hand, you don't want the shadow effect to distract your audience from the shape. Remember that the main purpose of a shadow is to make the shape itself appear to stand out from the surface of the slide.

Choose More Shadow Colors to open the Colors dialog box. Nothing is new here except that for the first time you might notice quite a nice selection of grays at the bottom of the dialog box. (Figure 6-3, earlier in

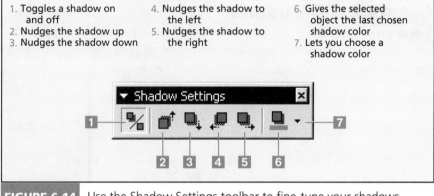

1. Toggles a shadow on and off
2. Nudges the shadow up
3. Nudges the shadow down
4. Nudges the shadow to the left
5. Nudges the shadow to the right
6. Gives the selected object the last chosen shadow color
7. Lets you choose a shadow color

FIGURE 6-14   Use the Shadow Settings toolbar to fine-tune your shadows

this chapter, shows the Background Colors dialog box, which looks the same.) These grays are great for shadows. You may want to choose a lighter gray for a dark background or a darker gray for a light background. Figure 6-15 shows four of the available shadow effects against a white background.

FIGURE 6-15   You can create both subtle and dramatic shadow effects

Creating 3-D Shapes

You can take a further step and create realistic 3-D shapes. A 3-D shape displays sides and shading like a real three-dimensional object. Here you see a slide with a 3-D AutoShape:

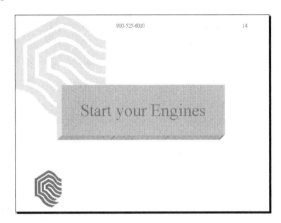

This is the final slide of the presentation and invites the audience to "test drive" the new software that the company is selling. To view this slide in color, refer to number 59 in the Slide Gallery. This 3-D AutoShape was easily created by inserting a rectangle, choosing a solid fill color and no line, and then adding a 3-D effect, as discussed next.

You always start with a 2-D shape. Select a shape and choose the 3-D button on the Drawing toolbar. PowerPoint displays the pop-up menu shown here:

As with the shadows, the 3-D options come in groups based on the direction of the *extrusion*—the side of the object that appears pushed out into the third dimension. The extrusion creates the depth of the object. The choices have rather unhelpful names such as 3-D Style 1, 3-D Style 2, and so on. Choose one of the options and let PowerPoint create the 3-D effect for your object.

Each 3-D option assumes that the viewer is standing in a different position vis-à-vis the object. As with shadows, you don't want to use differing 3-D effects on several objects on a slide—it could give your audience vertigo! You can create classy effects using 3-D, but use it with constraint.

Choose No 3-D to remove the 3-D effect on the selected object or objects. The top-right effect, 3-D Style 4, creates a wire-frame effect as if the shape is made of wire and has no solidity. You will probably try out a few effects before settling on one you like.

Controlling the 3-D Settings

To have more control over a 3-D effect, choose 3-D Settings to display the 3-D Settings toolbar shown in Figure 6-16. You'll find quite a bit to sink your teeth into on this little toolbar, but the settings are actually fairly simple. After all, PowerPoint is not like a professional rendering program where you can specify the lighting location of dozens of lights by x,y,z coordinates accurate to six decimal places. So here goes!

> **Tip:** You can use the 3-D and shadow settings to format WordArt text.

Tilting a 3-D object

The four tilt buttons on the 3-D settings toolbar change the rotation of the object. Imagine holding a cube in your hand and tilting the side facing you up, down, left, or right—now you have the idea. The only thing that changes about the object is its position relative to your eyes. Try selecting an object and clicking these buttons, and their functions will soon be clear. Here you see the result of tilting in the four directions.

Original object using 3-D Style 1

Tilt Down clicked three times

Tilt Up clicked three times

Tilt Left clicked three times

Tilt Right clicked three times

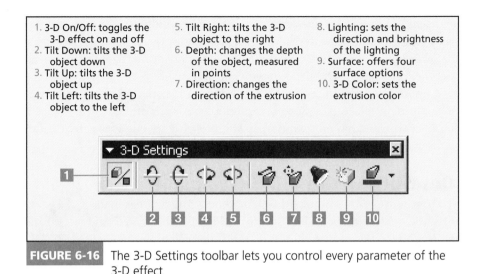

1. 3-D On/Off: toggles the 3-D effect on and off
2. Tilt Down: tilts the 3-D object down
3. Tilt Up: tilts the 3-D object up
4. Tilt Left: tilts the 3-D object to the left
5. Tilt Right: tilts the 3-D object to the right
6. Depth: changes the depth of the object, measured in points
7. Direction: changes the direction of the extrusion
8. Lighting: sets the direction and brightness of the lighting
9. Surface: offers four surface options
10. 3-D Color: sets the extrusion color

FIGURE 6-16 The 3-D Settings toolbar lets you control every parameter of the 3-D effect

The effect of tilting depends on the original style you chose. For some styles, a certain tilt looks good; for others, it doesn't.

Changing a 3-D object's depth

When you click Depth on the 3-D Settings toolbar, you see the options shown here. When you change an object's depth, you are actually changing its characteristics. The tilt stays the same, but the depth of the object that extrudes into the third dimension becomes greater or smaller. You specify the depth in points—remember that 72 points equals one inch. You can type any point value you want in the Custom box. Again, try out a few settings, and see what you like. Once you find what you want, you can use the same setting for other objects. Here you see some examples using different depth settings:

- 0 pt.
- 36 pt.
- 72 pt.
- 144 pt.
- 288 pt.
- Infinity
- Custom: 36.00 pt

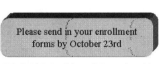

Original 3-D object (36-pt. depth)

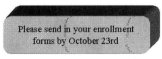

72-pt. depth

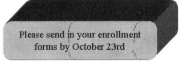

144-pt. depth

Changing the direction

When you click the Direction button on the 3-D Settings toolbar, the options shown here pop up. The effect of these options is to change the viewer's position relative to the object. It's like holding a cube steady and moving your head in one of eight directions. That might be hard to do in real life, but in PowerPoint, it's as easy as clicking one of the options.

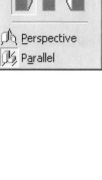

At the bottom of the pop-up menu, you have two different view choices—Perspective or Parallel. In a perspective view, parallel lines—in this case the lines that create the depth of the object—converge as they go off into the distance. The typical example is railroad tracks appearing to touch in the distance. In a parallel view, parallel lines always remain parallel.

Try out both types of views—you'll be surprised at the difference. Here you see some AutoShapes that use the bottom-center 3-D direction, to create the impression that you are looking at the shapes from the front top. The slide on the left uses a parallel view, while the slide on the right uses a perspective view. While here the perspective view looks more realistic, from other directions, the parallel view gives a more "normal" impression. To view these slides in color, refer to numbers 60 and 61 in the Slide Gallery.

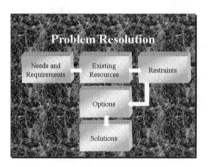

Parallel view

Perspective view

Setting the lighting direction and brightness

When you choose Lighting on the 3-D Settings toolbar, PowerPoint opens the pop-up menu shown here. At the center is a cube that represents your 3-D object. The current lighting is depressed, and the cube shows the result. Without clicking, move your mouse cursor from light to light and watch the difference on the cube. Click when you like what you see. At the bottom, you have three brightness options: Bright, Normal, and Dim.

If you include shadows on the same slide with a 3-D object, you might want to coordinate the two. If the light on your 3-D object is coming from the right, sides facing left will be darker. Shadows will be thrown to the left as well.

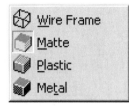

Choosing a surface type

The Surface button offers the four options: Wire Frame, Matte, Plastic, and Metal. A wire frame has no solidity—it looks like you fashioned the shape out of wire, as you can see here:

> ## Start your Engines

A matte surface, the default, is bright but has no reflection. A plastic surface shows a slight reflection along one edge. The metal surface is the darkest, for some reason.

Setting the 3-D color

You can change the color of the extrusion portion of the 3-D object, the part that shows the object's depth. The 3-D Color tool works the same as other color tools you have worked with in this chapter. Click the tool to apply the most recently chosen color or click the down arrow for a greater choice of colors.

The 3-D color does not affect the color of the front face of the object, which is controlled by the fill color. However, the wire frame display shows only the wire frame without any fill—there is no color.

Professional Skills Summary

This chapter started off by exploring color schemes and how you can use them to create a uniform look in your presentation. Then I explained how to create any background you want—from plain colors to gradients to textures, from patterns to pictures.

I discussed formatting lines and borders for AutoShapes, text boxes, and pictures. Then I covered how to work with fills. You can create a fill of any color and use the same fill effects that are available for backgrounds.

The simplest 3-D effects are shadows, which give the impression that an object is raised off the surface of the slide and therefore casts a shadow. The chapter ended with a complete discussion of 3-D objects, including the various 3-D styles and all the settings on the 3-D Settings toolbar.

The next chapter explains how to coordinate elements throughout an entire presentation with slide masters.

chapter 7

Coordinating Presentations with Slide Masters

The past few chapters have covered a lot about creating a presentation, but PowerPoint has a secret hidden beneath the text and objects you add to each slide. A slide master is a layer that's underneath all the slides in your presentation. In this chapter you learn how to use masters to coordinate and polish the look of an entire presentation.

Understanding the Slide Master

A slide is made up of three major layers—the background, the slide master, and objects. The background was discussed in the last chapter; it is a rectangle at the bottommost layer of each slide. Objects are the top layer; you can easily move, resize, or format them. Objects include AutoShapes, text boxes, graphics, and WordArt. The object layer is the default mode of functioning in PowerPoint. When you work on your slide, you most often work on this object layer.

The slide master is between the background and the objects. You need to go into a special slide master view to access the master.

The slide master includes any text or graphics that you want to appear on every slide. Slide masters are used to create uniform features throughout a presentation. For example, you may want the company's logo on each slide. Although the logo is an object, because you insert it on the slide master, it appears on each slide and you cannot select or manipulate it in any way except from the slide master view.

In addition, the slide master acts like a template to control most text properties, such as font, font size, color, bullet style, and shadowing effects. These properties are attached to the text placeholders, which are also on the slide master. However, you can move, resize, and delete the text placeholders as if they were objects on your slide. Of course, because text is on the object layer, you can change these properties directly on each slide. However, to make global changes to the entire presentation, you need to use the slide master.

The settings on the slide master are saved with each design template. You can make changes to a slide master and save the resulting presentation as a design template. Then, each time you start a new presentation based on that template, your text is formatted the way you want. Any other changes you made to the slide master, such as inserting a logo, slide numbers, or your name, also appear in the new presentation. At the end of the chapter, I explain how to use the master to create your own design template.

You don't need to use the slide master to create a presentation. Often, the design template is all you need. You can also make changes to the color scheme and background and quickly apply them to the entire presentation, as explained in the last chapter. Because you need to know all about slide formatting to work with slide masters, I have waited to explain them until you had a good grasp of all the essential features of PowerPoint.

However, when you decide to use the slide master, you should use it early in the creation process. Set up the global features you want first and make as few exceptions to individual slides as possible. This procedure saves you from making changes to many individual slides. It also ensures a uniform look for the entire presentation.

Entering Slide Master View

To enter slide master view, press SHIFT and click the Slide View button, which appears with other view buttons at the bottom-left corner of your screen. You can also choose View | Master | Slide Master. PowerPoint opens the slide master view, shown in Figure 7-1 with the High Voltage design template applied to it. You can control formatting for your entire presentation from this view. To see this slide master in color, refer to number 62 in the Slide Gallery.

Changing the Background

Although the background can be considered its own layer, you can format it from the slide master to affect the entire presentation. The relationships between the background, the color scheme, the design template, and the slide master can be confusing.

The design template contains the settings for the master, including the background and the color scheme. When you assign a design template, PowerPoint always remembers that template and displays the design template name on the status bar. PowerPoint continues to remember the design template even if you end up changing everything about it—the background, the text properties, and so on.

If you change the background from the master slide view (by choosing Format | Background), your changes affect every slide, even if you click Apply, not Apply to All. Your presentation may no longer look anything like the original design template, but that's okay. If you change the background from normal view or any other view, the background affects only the active slide, unless you choose Apply to All.

However, the color scheme controls the master, not vice versa. If you change the color scheme for text, background, and titles, for example, from any slide and click Apply to All, the entire presentation is

Tip: Graphics that appear on the design template are actual objects on the slide master that you can delete or change if you wish.

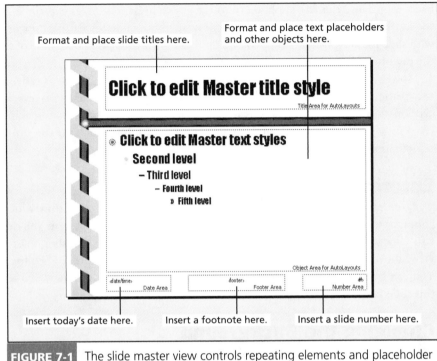

Format and place slide titles here.

Format and place text placeholders and other objects here.

Click to edit Master title style

Title Area for AutoLayouts

⊛ **Click to edit Master text styles**
- **Second level**
  – **Third level**
    – **Fourth level**
      » **Fifth level**

Object Area for AutoLayouts

‹date/time› Date Area   ‹footer› Footer Area   # Number Area

Insert today's date here. Insert a footnote here. Insert a slide number here.

FIGURE 7-1 The slide master view controls repeating elements and placeholder text formatting for the entire presentation

affected. If you view the slide master, you will see that the slide master has been changed to reflect your changes. If you try it the other way around—view the master and change the background, title color, and bulleted text color, the changes affect all your slides but the color scheme has not been changed. The color scheme is more tightly connected than the slide master to the design template. If you have a presentation whose slides don't reflect the color scheme, remember—someone could have made changes to either the master or to individual slides that overrode the color scheme.

Formatting Headings and Bulleted Text

At the top of the master, in the area labeled "Title Area for AutoLayouts," you format slide titles. The text, "Click to edit Master title style," not only gives you an instruction, but also shows you the current text properties. Text color, font, size, alignment, and case are some of the properties you can change. You make the changes as you would on the object level. The techniques for editing text properties were discussed in Chapter 3. The only difference is that any change you make affects every slide in the presentation.

In the middle of the master is an area called, "Object Area for AutoLayouts." Here you find the formatting for five levels of bulleted text. You can format the text and the bullets, as well as the paragraph alignment and indentation. See Chapter 4 for information on formatting bullets and paragraphs. If you like fancy bullets and want to use them throughout your presentation, here's the place to create them.

Adding Placeholders

You may have wondered why there is no way to add a text place-holder. Suppose you delete one from the slide master. How do you get it back? PowerPoint knows that every master can have a title area, an object area, a date area, a footer area, and a number area. If you delete one or more placeholders, choose Format | Master Layout to open the dialog box shown here. Only the placeholders that you have deleted are available. Check any placeholders that you want to reinstate, and click OK.

Adding Repeating Objects

You can add any other objects to the slide. A company logo is probably the most common example, as shown in Figure 7-2. (To view this slide in color, refer to number 63 in the Slide Gallery.) To create this effect, open the slide master and choose Insert | Picture | From File. Locate and choose the graphic file and click Insert. Then move and resize the graphic as necessary.

Remember that you can't see the actual text on each slide on the slide master. Since the logo will appear on every slide, be careful to place the object where it won't interfere with your text. Remember to double-check this placement after you have completed the presentation. The easiest way to check is to go to slide sorter view, where you can get a bird's eye view of the entire presentation. If the object collides with text on one or more slides, return to the master and move it to a better location.

Tip: Insert the logo on the slide with the most text. If it fits, press CTRL-X to cut it to the clipboard, open the slide master, and press CTRL-V to paste it onto the master.

Since objects that you insert on the slide master are not on the object layer, you cannot select them unless you are in slide master view. If you are unable to select an object, try going to slide master view. The Office Assistant will probably advise you of this if you try to click a slide master object from one of the other views.

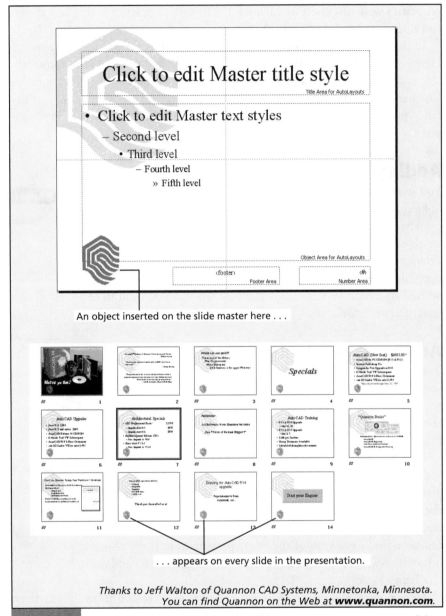

Adding a Footer

The slide master comes with placeholders for the date, a text footer, and the slide number. Many users add the date for documentation purposes. A text footer can specify your name or department without being obtrusive. Slide numbers are especially helpful if you might need to go back and forth in your presentation while you present. Slide numbers are also invaluable in the creation process, while you are still deciding on the order of your slides. You can change the location and formatting of these footers directly on the slide master.

Tip: There are no separate headers and footers, but you can move the placeholders on the slide master to the top of the slide and turn them into headers.

Adding footers to the entire presentation

To add or change one of the footers, display the slide master and click in one of the placeholders. Choose View | Header and Footer.

PowerPoint opens the Header and Footer dialog box shown in Figure 7-3 with the Slide tab on top.

Adding the date or slide number to one slide

To add the date or slide number on one slide only, follow a different procedure. (Of course, you don't want to add the date or slide number to a slide if you've done so on the slide master, because you'll end up with the date or slide number twice on a slide.) Click Text Box on the Drawing toolbar to create a text box. To insert a slide number, choose Insert Slide Number. PowerPoint inserts the slide number in the text box. To insert the date, choose Insert | Date and Time to open the dialog box shown here:

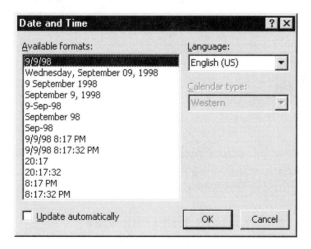

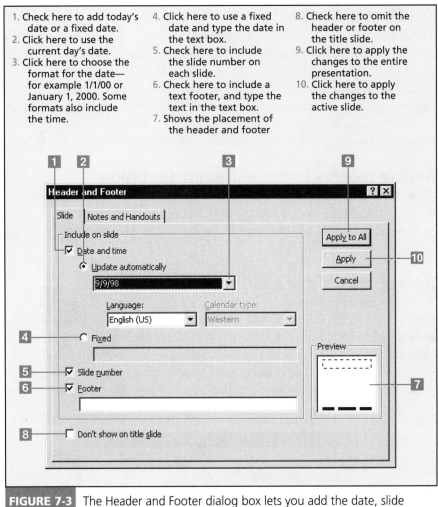

1. Check here to add today's date or a fixed date.
2. Click here to use the current day's date.
3. Click here to choose the format for the date— for example 1/1/00 or January 1, 2000. Some formats also include the time.
4. Click here to use a fixed date and type the date in the text box.
5. Check here to include the slide number on each slide.
6. Check here to include a text footer, and type the text in the text box.
7. Shows the placement of the header and footer
8. Check here to omit the header or footer on the title slide.
9. Click here to apply the changes to the entire presentation.
10. Click here to apply the changes to the active slide.

FIGURE 7-3 The Header and Footer dialog box lets you add the date, slide number, and a text footer to all your slides

Choose the format you want. Check Update automatically to always show today's date. In the English version of PowerPoint, you can choose from U.S., U.K., and Australian English to format the date properly. Click OK when you're done.

Changing the starting slide number

Occasionally, you may want your slide numbers to start with a number other than one. Perhaps your presentation is the second half of a larger presentation.

To change the starting slide number, choose File | Page Setup to display the Page Setup dialog box shown here:

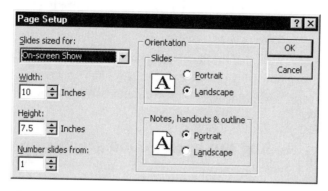

Under Number Slides From, type a new starting number or use the arrows to change the starting number. Click OK.

Making Exceptions

You aren't locked in to the slide master. You may want to make exceptions to the formatting you have created in the slide master. In fact, most of the formatting already covered in this book has had the effect of making exceptions to the master. Any time you reformat bulleted text on a slide, change font color, or change the background for a slide, you are creating an exception to the master.

Any change you make on a slide overrides the master. Even if you change the master, your changes remain. That's because although the slide master is the master of the presentation, you, dear user, are the master of the slide master. What you say, goes. Therefore, if you make changes to a slide, PowerPoint always respects those changes.

The advantage of the slide master is that you can make changes that affect the entire presentation. It is certainly much easier to change text color once than to change it individually on each slide. Moreover, if you need to change the text color again, as long as you made the change on the master, you need only change the master. If you made the change on each slide, guess what? Now you have to go back to each slide and change it individually.

Reapplying the design template to a presentation

There is one technique to get around this problem. You can reapply the design template to your presentation. All the settings, including the master, the background, and the color scheme are reapplied to the presentation. You lose any formatting changes you have made. However, objects that you added to the design template, such as a logo or text box, are retained. To reapply the design template, choose Format | Apply Design Template. In the Apply Design Template dialog box, choose the original template you used (its name is on the status bar if you forget), and click Apply.

Once you have reapplied the design template, you can start from scratch making changes, this time using the slide master. Any changes you made on individual slides have been eliminated, so they won't interfere with your global changes on the master.

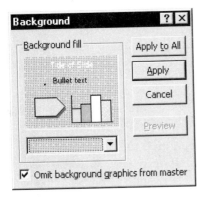

Hiding the background graphic on a slide

Suppose you want to create a slide without any background graphics. You might want to do this for a great graphic that will look best taking up the entire slide. You can easily do this. Figure 7-4 shows such a slide without and with a background graphic. To view these slides in color, refer to numbers 64 and 65 in the Slide Gallery.

First display the slide, then choose Format | Background and check Omit Background Graphics from Master in the Background dialog box, as shown here. Click Apply so that the background graphics are omitted from the active slide only.

Do remove background graphics, such as a corporate logo, from a slide to make room for a striking graphic and to emphasize your message.

Don't put background graphics on every slide when doing so detracts from your main graphic and textual message.

FIGURE 7-4   Although the other slides in this presentation have a corporate logo at the bottom left corner, the logo would detract from this graphic, so it has been omitted

This technique deletes all the background graphics from the slide, including the graphics that make up the design template and any graphics you may have added to the master. This all-or-nothing approach may not work in your situation. Let's say you want to see the design template's graphics but not a graphic you added, such as your company's logo. (Perhaps it doesn't fit on one slide.) Here's how to accomplish the task:

1. Display the slide you want to work on.

2. Choose Format | Background, check Omit Background Graphics from Master, and then click Apply.

3. Press SHIFT and click the Slide View button to open the slide master.

4. Select the graphics that make up the background design for the design template. Remember that on the slide master, they are objects just like objects you create on a slide. You might have to select several objects.

5. Press CTRL-C to copy them to the clipboard.

6. Click Normal View to return to normal view and display the slide you were working on.

7. Press CTRL-V to paste the graphics onto the slide. You now have your background graphics but not any additional objects you added to the master, in this case your company's logo.

Understanding the Title Master

The title master is just like the slide master, but it applies only to slides that you created using the Title Slide AutoLayout. Just as the title page of a book often has a different format from the rest of the book, title slides often use different formatting from the rest of your presentation. Most presentations only have one title slide at the beginning, but you can have as many as you want. Changes made on the title master affect only title slides.

Entering Title Master View

If, and only if, you are displaying a slide using the Title Slide AutoLayout, you can press SHIFT and click the Slide View button to enter title master view. If you are viewing any other slide, choose View | Master. On the expanded submenu, choose Title Master.

If you open a blank presentation, there is no title master. To create one, press SHIFT and click the slide view icon to enter the slide master. Then choose Insert | New Title Master.

Tip: If you are already in the slide master, scroll down to see the title master. From the title master, you can scroll up to get to the slide master.

Figure 7-5 shows a title master. As you can see, it looks much like a slide master, except that there is no placeholder for bulleted text. Instead, the title is centered vertically on the title master, and there is a subtitle. This formatting reflects the typical structure of title slides.

Formatting Title Slides

You format title slide masters in the same way you format slide masters. However, bear in mind that the slide master controls the title master to some extent. For example, if you change the color of the title text on the slide master, you will find that the title text will also change on the title master. The opposite does not hold true—changes to the title master have no effect on the slide master.

While this can be confusing, the general rule is to change the slide master first. Then make changes to the title master. If you make changes to the title master first, you may find them overridden by changes you subsequently make to the slide master.

FIGURE 7-5   Use the title master to format slides using the Title Slide AutoLayout

Understanding Handout Masters

You can create printed handouts of your presentation to give to your audience to take home or to show your boss during the approval process. Handouts show your slides in groupings of two to nine per page. Handouts are covered in Chapter 16. However, since we are on the topic of masters, you may want to know about the handout master.

The handout master controls the formatting of handouts. You can add art, text, the date, and page numbers to your handout master, and they will display on the handouts, in addition to your slides, which are automatically included. Settings on the handout master have no effect on your slide master or slides.

Entering Handout Master View

To enter handout master view, press SHIFT and click the Outline icon at the bottom right of your screen. You can also choose View | Master | Handout Master. Figure 7-6 shows a typical handout master, formatted to print six slides per page. By default, the handout master contains a header area for text, a date area, a page number area, and a footer area for text.

Formatting the Handout Master

When you open the handout master, PowerPoint automatically displays the Handout Master toolbar shown here. The toolbar lets you easily change the number of slides that the handouts include on a page. The three-per-page choice prints lines to the right of each slide so the reader can jot down notes. You can also print the outline. Click the format you want, and the handout master will change automatically.

As mentioned previously, you don't have to limit yourself to the standard format. You can add graphics, text boxes—anything that you could add to a slide. For example, you can create captions for each slide or callouts pointing out features of a slide. You can add your phone number or e-mail address—the possibilities are limitless.

To add a header, footer, the date, or page numbers, choose View | Header and Footer while in handout master view. PowerPoint opens the Header and Footer dialog box, with the Notes and Handouts tab

Tip: You can use many of the techniques you use when you create a slide. For example, you can display the guides to help you place a graphic more precisely.

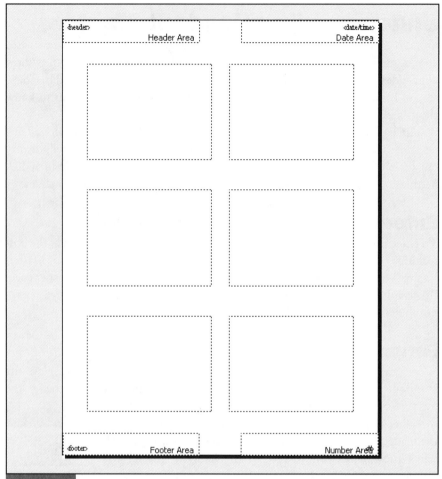

Header Area
Date Area
Footer Area
Number Area

FIGURE 7-6 The handout master controls the formatting of printed handouts

on top, as shown in Figure 7-7. This tab is almost the same as the Slide tab. The only differences are the following:

- You can specify both a header and a footer.
- You must choose Apply to All. You cannot separately format the various pages of the handouts.

Refer back to Figure 7-3 for more information on using this dialog box. When you have finished formatting your handouts, click the Close button of the Master toolbar. Then return to any view by clicking its icon.

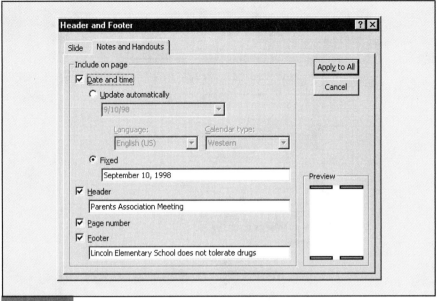

Use the Notes and Handouts tab of the Header and Footer dialog box to create headers and footers for your handouts

Understanding the Notes Master

As explained in Chapter 1, you can create notes to accompany your presentation. Traditionally, notes are used by the speaker during the actual presentation. For example, notes are a good place to put your jokes, so that you won't forget the punch lines. Printed notes contain one slide per page and a large area for text—your notes. However, you can use notes for other purposes, such as to write down ideas for the presentation as you are creating it, or to create and print comments for your supervisor who is reviewing the presentation.

You create the notes by typing in the notes pane. Chapter 16 contains more information about creating and using notes.

The notes master formats these notes. Notes are generally text, and PowerPoint provides an outline format that is similar to the slide master.

Entering Notes Master View

To enter notes master view, choose View | Master | Notes Master. PowerPoint opens the notes master view, as shown in Figure 7-8.

Because the actual notes page includes a picture of a slide on the top and your notes at the bottom, the top of the notes master shows the slide master. You can only move and resize the slide master.

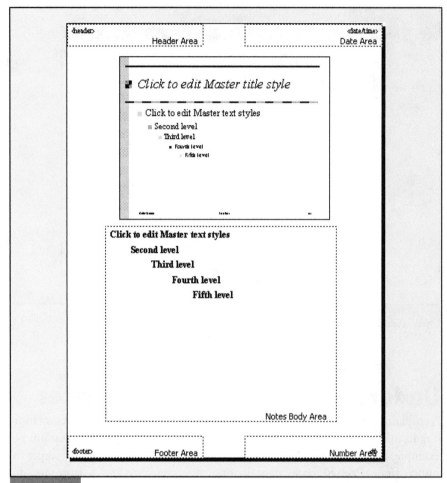

FIGURE 7-8 Notes master view lets you format the look of your notes when printed

Formatting the Notes Master

Although notes are usually just text, you can add graphics. For example, if you are preparing a presentation for a client, you might send the client your preliminary presentation for review in the form of notes pages. You might want to add your company logo in the notes area. Graphics, headers, and footers don't appear in the notes pane when you are in normal (or a similar) view. You see them on the notes master, in notes pages view, and when you print notes. Printing notes is covered in Chapter 16.

To add a header, footer, the date, or a page number, use the same procedure explained previously for the handout master.

Setting Page Size

Another way of formatting an entire presentation is to set the page size. Choose File | Page Setup to display the Page Setup dialog box shown in Figure 7-9. By default, PowerPoint sizes your slides for an on-screen slide show. Slides are 10 inches wide by 7.5 inches high. When you click the Slides Sized For drop-down arrow, you see the choices shown here. Once you choose the type of presentation, you can customize the size using the Width and Height text boxes.

On the right side of the dialog box, you can set the orientation of the slides separately from the notes, handouts, and outline. By default, slides are in landscape orientation (the width is longer than the height), and everything else is in portrait orientation.

Tip: If you want to change the default slide size and orientation, do so before you start working on your presentation. Otherwise, text and graphics may not fit as you would like after you make the change.

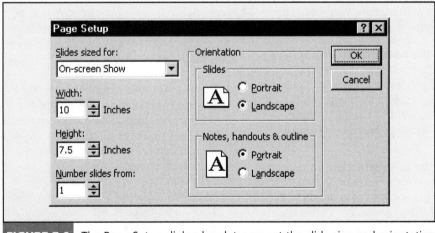

FIGURE 7-9   The Page Setup dialog box lets you set the slide size and orientation

Using the Slide Master to Control Your Presentation

by Jennifer Rotondo

The master of a PowerPoint presentation is a powerful tool if used to its maximum potential. Consider it the skeleton of a presentation. Just as our skeleton supports our bodies, so should the master support the presentation.

There are two masters that affect what you see in the presentation: the slide master and the title master. The title master defines only the style for the title slides, which are usually used to open or close the presentation and for transitioning to another section. The slide master defines every other layout option. On both of the masters, you can define the style for the entire presentation, which makes it easy for you to change something in one location—that is, on the master—and have it affect the whole presentation. You should do the following on the master:

- **Format the background.** This is where you insert your background. Whether you select a PowerPoint design or create a custom template, this is where you want to place it. It copies to every slide and keeps the file small in size.

- **Define the color scheme.** Format your slide color scheme on the master. Here, in one location, you decide all the colors of the presentation. Define the colors of the text, shadows, fills for charts, and even hyperlink colors.

- **Select fonts and bullets.** Apply your fonts to the masters. These will take effect for any slide in the presentation. Try to stay clear of serif fonts and

use no more than two fonts per presentation. You should also select what bullets you want in the body text.

- **Add consistent animation.** (Animation is covered in Chapter 9.) Use the master to set the animation for the presentation.

- **Add logos or elements you want to appear on each slide.** Anything you need on every slide should be placed on the master. A company logo, slide numbers, copyrights, and so on—all of these should be placed once on the master, so they will be displayed on every slide.

The masters usually aren't used to their full potential. They are powerful tools making you more efficient in creating your presentations. Anything consistent you need in your presentation should be incorporated into the masters!

Jennifer Rotondo, founder and president of Creative Minds, is a "new media" consultant specializing in electronic presentations. She creates custom-designed PowerPoint presentations, as well as projects in multimedia design, Web site design, and graphic concepts. Jennifer is a "Microsoft Certified Expert PowerPoint User" and teaches her own "Advanced PowerPoint Design" seminar. She also critiques presentations in Presentations *magazine. You can contact her at 770-421-2776 or rotos@mindspring.com, or visit the Creative Minds Web site at* **www.creativemindsinc.com***.*

Creating Your Own Design Templates

Now that you understand about masters, you have the tools to create your own design templates from scratch.

Most design templates are simply a slide master, including a background. The background can include graphics that make up a design like the ones in PowerPoint's design templates. If you create your own slide master, you can save it as a design template. You can then use that template for other presentations. You can include fonts, bullets, a color scheme, and other formatting in your template. You can even include text and shapes—in other words, you can develop some actual content for your template that you may want to reuse in the future.

Creating your own design template is really a must if you create a lot of presentations and want the highest-quality results. Having your own template means that everything is already set to your specifications, and you can start to work right away. Here are the steps you need to take:

1. Open a blank presentation. From within PowerPoint, choose File | New. Click the General tab and double-click Blank Presentation. When the New Slide dialog box appears, you can click Cancel (or choose an AutoLayout and click OK). You can also open an existing presentation that has many of the features you want and modify it.

2. Open the slide master.

3. Choose Format | Slide Color Scheme. Choose the color scheme closest to the one you want. Then click the Custom tab and change the colors as you wish. Click Apply to All. You immediately see the changes on the master.

4. If you want to add a fill effect to the background, choose Format | Background. In the Background dialog box, click the down arrow and choose Fill Effects. Create the effects you want. Click OK and then Apply to All.

5. Now add any graphics that you want to appear on every slide. These can be a creative design, a company logo, or both. Format the graphics with color, fill effects, shadows, and/or 3-D effects.

6. Change the font if you like. Choose Format | Replace Fonts to globally change the font.

7. Change the font color and size if you want.

8. Format the bullets and the indents.

Tip: To find additional PowerPoint design templates, choose Help | Office on the Web while connected to the Internet.

Tip: If you want to create a background with a design, open some of the design templates and go to slide master view. Select the graphics on the slide master. You may need to ungroup them several times to break them down to individual objects. By looking at the shapes and fills, you will see that many of them have been created using simple AutoShapes and fills. These designs should give you some ideas for creating your own backgrounds. Some useful design templates to look at are Azure, Checkers, and High Voltage.

9. You can resize and format the text placeholders.

10. If you want footers, choose View | Headers and Footers and choose the options you want. You can also delete any of the footers from the master.

11. To create a title master, choose Insert | New Title Master.

12. Use the same procedures described in the previous steps to format the title master.

13. If you wish, add content to your template. A template with suggested text is called a *content template*.

14. Choose File | Save As. In the Save as Type drop-down box, choose Design Template (*.pot). In the Save In box at the top of the dialog box, navigate to the desired folder. By default, design templates are in C:\Program Files\MSOffice\Templates\Presentation Designs.

15. Type a name for the template in the File Name text box and click Save.

To use your template, start PowerPoint. In the Startup PowerPoint dialog box, choose Design Template and choose the template from the list. From within PowerPoint, choose File I New. Choose the Design Templates tab and choose your template. If your template is not on the list, you probably saved it in a different location. Open a blank presentation and choose Common Tasks I Apply Design Template from the Formatting toolbar. If necessary, browse until you find your template.

Figure 7-10 shows some examples of slides created using custom-made design templates and their slide masters. To see these slides in color, refer to numbers 66 to 69 in the Slide Gallery.

If you want the extra professional touch that a graphic artist can provide, you can find a professional who specializes in creating PowerPoint presentations. You can also purchase design templates. An example is PresentationPro from Interactive (**www.interactivevision.com**).

You can add a template of your own to the AutoContent Wizard. Here's how:

1. Choose File | New.

2. Click the General tab.

3. Double-click AutoContent Wizard, shown in Figure 7-11.

4. Click Next.

5. Choose a category except for All or Carnegie Coach.

6. Click Add, as shown in Figure 7-12.

7. Find your template, choose it, and click Open.

8. Click Cancel if you don't want to continue with the AutoContent Wizard. Or choose the new template and click Next to start a new presentation using the template.

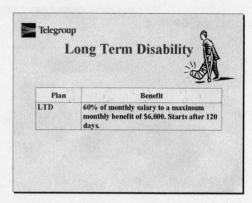

You don't always have to reinvent the wheel. This slide master starts with one of PowerPoint's design templates and adds a corporate logo and a special bullet.

The company wanted a soothing effect for this presentation, which was good news to most employees but bad news to employees at one corporate location.

Thanks to Telegroup of Fairfield, Iowa, for these slides.

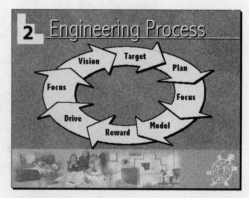

This slide master includes a customized background, as well as graphics designed for a specific client.

The graphics on this slide master still leave plenty of room for the slide's main message. They don't detract from the slide because of their soft color and treatment.

Thanks to Jennifer Rotondo for these slides. Jennifer is a consultant specializing in custom-designed and multimedia presentations, Web sites, and graphics. Thanks also to Robert Oxley of Training & Consulting, Inc.

FIGURE 7-10   Custom-made slide masters and sample slides

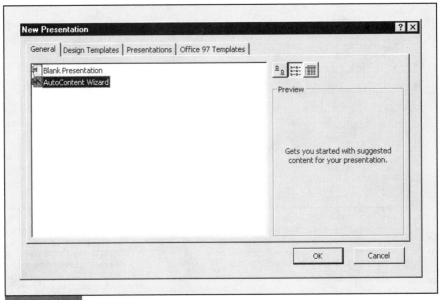

FIGURE 7-11 To add your own template to the AutoContent Wizard, start the wizard

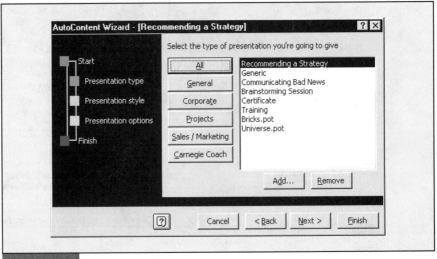

FIGURE 7-12 In the AutoContent Wizard, choose a category and click Add

Professional Skills Summary

In this chapter you put together all the knowledge you have learned about creating presentations and put it to use to create masters. Masters control the overall look of a presentation.

The slide master controls all slides except for those using the Title AutoLayout. In the slide master you can change the background, format titles and bulleted text, insert objects and graphics that will appear on every slide, and add footers.

The title master is like the slide master, but it only controls slides using the Title AutoLayout. This chapter also explained how to use handout masters to format handouts and notes master to format notes.

The Page Setup dialog box lets you format the size and orientation of your slides.

Once you can create masters, you have the tools you need to create your own design templates. The chapter wound up with a description of how to create design and content templates.

In the next chapter, you learn how to incorporate graphs, tables, and organization charts into your presentations.

chapter 8

Incorporating Graphs, Tables, and Organization Charts

In this chapter, you:

- Create a graph from within PowerPoint
- Import a Microsoft Excel graph
- Add a table to a slide
- Import a Word table
- Add an organization chart to a slide

Effective presentations sometimes require more than pictures, and PowerPoint lets you add graphs, tables, and organization charts to your slides. In this chapter you learn how to present complex data as simply and clearly as possible.

Presenting Data Simply

The more complex the data you need to present, the more you should plan ways to present that data so that your audience can comprehend it at a glance. While long tables of data are okay for printed reports, they are not effective on slides. A slide is not big enough, and the audience doesn't have enough time to read through lots of numbers. You may need to present less data, but you may also be able to find a way to format the data more simply. For example, the table shown next doesn't make the trends immediately obvious. (To view this slide in color, refer to number 70 in the Slide Gallery.)

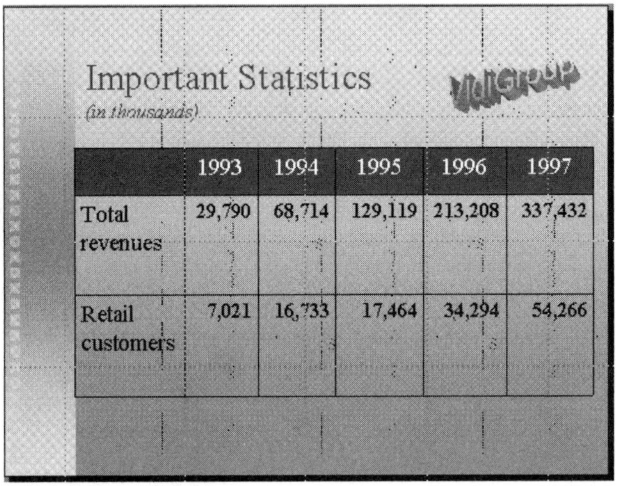

Important Statistics
(in thousands)

	1993	1994	1995	1996	1997
Total revenues	29,790	68,714	129,119	213,208	337,432
Retail customers	7,021	16,733	17,464	34,294	54,266

If your point is the growth of the company, you could split the data onto two slides and use these two charts instead. To view these slides in color, refer to numbers 71 and 72 in the Slide Gallery.

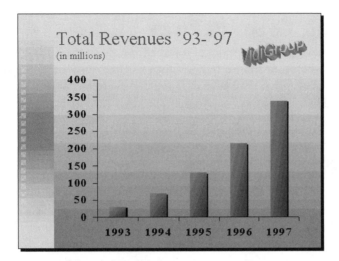

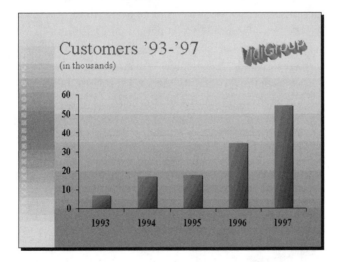

Your audience doesn't see the exact numbers, but the overall message is much clearer—the company is growing!

Adding Graphs to a Slide

A graph visually portrays a series of numbers. Graphs are usually more effective than tables when they show a trend. Your audience can see the direction of the trend at a glance rather than have to figure out the trend by analyzing the numbers in a table.

New in 2000: PowerPoint 2000 now generates its own graphs.

The most direct way to add a graph to a slide is to use a graph placeholder and PowerPoint's own graph module. Later in this chapter I explain how to import a graph from a spreadsheet application such as Microsoft Excel.

To create a graph using a graph placeholder, create a new slide with the Chart & Text (the chart is on the left), the Text & Chart (the chart is on the right), or the Chart (chart only) AutoLayout. PowerPoint uses the term *chart,* which is another word for *graph.* PowerPoint displays the new slide, shown in Figure 8-1.

The instructions are clear—double-click to add a chart. The text placeholder works just like the text placeholders you have used earlier.

 Another way to insert a chart is to click Insert Chart on the Standard toolbar. For example, to create a slide that includes clip art and a chart, use one of the clip art AutoLayouts, delete the text placeholder and click Insert Chart. You'll have to resize both objects so they fit together on the slide.

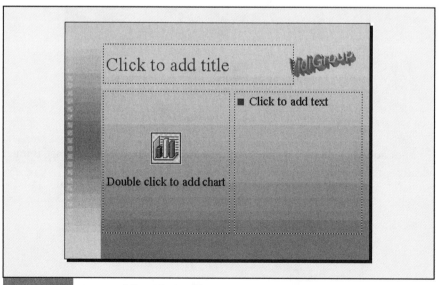

FIGURE 8-1 A new slide with the Chart & Text AutoLayout

Once you have the proper layout, you can create a chart. Although the order of the steps you use to create a chart is flexible, in general you should proceed as follows:

1. Resize the chart placeholder to the desired size on your slide. Resizing a placeholder after you have created the graph often does not provide satisfactory results.

2. Enter the data you want to use.

3. Choose a chart type.

4. Format the graph.

Entering Data on the Datasheet

Once you have sized the placeholder appropriately, it's time to enter your data. When you double-click the chart placeholder, your screen looks like Figure 8-2. Where did those numbers come from?!

The datasheet looks just like a worksheet in any spreadsheet application. Columns are labeled A, B, C, and so on, and rows are numbered 1, 2, 3, and so on. A cell is called by its column and row, so that the active cell in Figure 8-2—the one

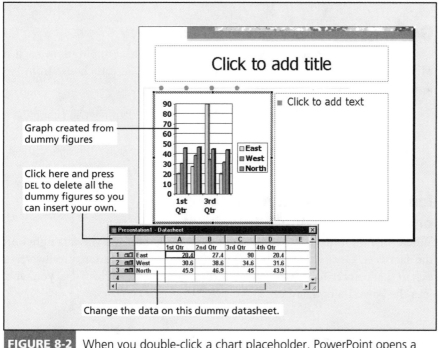

FIGURE 8-2 When you double-click a chart placeholder, PowerPoint opens a dummy chart and datasheet

with the black border—is cell A1. Unlike most spreadsheets, however, PowerPoint's datasheet has an unlabeled first column and top row that you use for labeling the columns and rows. You can delete all the dummy data first, as explained in Figure 8-2, or just replace the data. Move from left to right across a row by pressing TAB, or click the cursor in any cell to type there. If you need to enlarge the datasheet to see more of your data, place the cursor over an edge or corner until you get the two-headed arrow cursor, and drag outward.

As you type, PowerPoint modifies the graph so that you instantly see the results of your data. However, the graph usually needs to be formatted to customize your presentation.

In most cases, the columns of the datasheet are *categories* of data (such as 1st Qtr and 2nd Qtr) and the rows are *data series,* which contain the actual data (such as 43,279 and 45,292). When you start formatting the chart, you will find it helpful to keep these terms in mind.

While you are working in a datasheet, you might notice that PowerPoint's toolbars have changed and two new menu items, Data and Chart, have been added. The new menu and toolbar items are especially for working with graphs. These items will be covered throughout the rest of the section on graphs.

Getting Your Data the Easy Way

Of course, if you already have the data in a spreadsheet application, such as Microsoft Excel, you don't need to retype the data. You can choose from two ways to import existing spreadsheet data:

- Import the spreadsheet data onto the PowerPoint datasheet and continue to work in PowerPoint.
- Insert a spreadsheet as an object and modify it using the spreadsheet's menus and toolbars.

Importing spreadsheet data onto the PowerPoint datasheet

When you import data onto the datasheet, PowerPoint places the data right onto the datasheet. Once you've imported the data, PowerPoint automatically creates a chart that you can format just as you format a chart created from data you typed into the PowerPoint datasheet.

You can import data from programs with the following extensions:

Extension	Description
.txt, .csv	Delimited text (text separated by tab characters, commas, or spaces)
.wks, .wk1	Lotus 1-2-3
.xls	Microsoft Excel worksheet or workbook
.xlw	Microsoft Excel version 4.0 workbook
.xlc	Microsoft Excel version 4.0 or earlier chart

Here's how to import your data:

1. In PowerPoint, double-click the chart to open it. If the datasheet is not visible, click View Datasheet on the Formatting toolbar.

2. Choose Edit | Import File.

3. In the Import File dialog box, check the file format in the Files of Type drop-down list and, if necessary, change it. Navigate to the file you want to import and double-click it.

4. If you selected a Microsoft Excel workbook created with version 5.0 or later, the Import Data Options dialog box appears, as shown in Figure 8-3.

Tip: If you are importing a Microsoft Excel worksheet, you can click the cell where you want the imported data to begin.

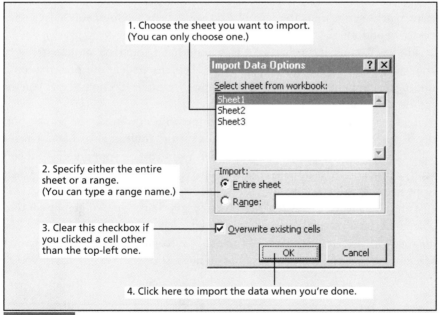

1. Choose the sheet you want to import. (You can only choose one.)

2. Specify either the entire sheet or a range. (You can type a range name.)

3. Clear this checkbox if you clicked a cell other than the top-left one.

4. Click here to import the data when you're done.

FIGURE 8-3 Use the Import Data Options dialog box to specify exactly which data you want to import and how

Inserting a spreadsheet as an object

When you insert, or *embed,* a spreadsheet as an object, you edit the object by double-clicking it. The menus and toolbars change to those of the original spreadsheet application, which you use to make changes. Here's how to embed a spreadsheet:

1. Display the slide you want to add the spreadsheet to.

2. Choose Insert | Object.

3. To create a new chart, click Create New, and then choose your spreadsheet from the list. For example, choose Microsoft Excel Chart if you have Excel. To insert a chart you've already created, click Create from File, and then click Browse. Locate and double-click the file. (If you created a new Excel chart, you see dummy data and a chart, similar to the datasheet.)

You can now use your spreadsheet's tools to edit the data and the corresponding chart. When you're done, click anywhere outside the chart to close it.

Choosing the Right Chart Type

While you have the datasheet open, the entire graph object is open and available for formatting. One of the first tasks is to choose the chart type. By default, PowerPoint creates the column chart you saw in Figure 8-2. However, not every chart type is suitable for the type of data you have; therefore, you have a wide choice of options.

The key to choosing a chart type is to understand your data and the strengths and weaknesses of each chart type. The ideal chart type for your presentation is the one that presents the data most clearly. In the next few sections, I give you the information you need to understand each chart type.

To change the chart type, right-click in the white area inside the graph's border. Choose Chart Type from the shortcut menu. You can also choose Chart | Chart Type to open the dialog box shown in Figure 8-4. If your graph is not currently open, you must double-click it to open it before you can access the Chart Type menu item.

You can't always use any chart type you want. Some types of graphs are suitable for data with several rows; others shouldn't have more than one row. Several are used only for scientific data. If you aren't sure what kind of chart to use, try several to see which seems to make the point most clearly.

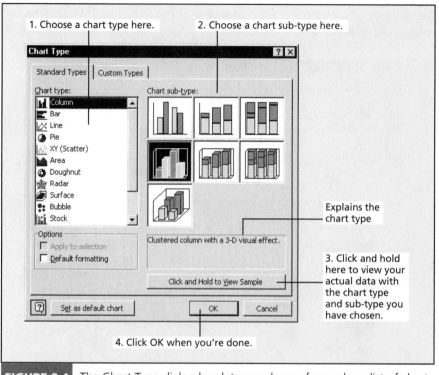

1. Choose a chart type here.

2. Choose a chart sub-type here.

Explains the chart type

3. Click and hold here to view your actual data with the chart type and sub-type you have chosen.

4. Click OK when you're done.

FIGURE 8-4   The Chart Type dialog box lets you choose from a long list of chart types and sub-types

New in 2000:   PowerPoint 2000 has added new options for bubble, radar, and doughnut charts.

Column

Column charts are among the most common. You often see them showing financial data over time, where quarters or years are the categories in the datasheet. On the graph, these time categories are shown across the bottom (on the X axis) and the data for each time category is along the left side (on the Y axis). If you are showing data for more than one item (such as several products or locations), you will see as many vertical bars as you have items. Here you see an example of a datasheet and its corresponding column chart showing income for both sales and service over four years:

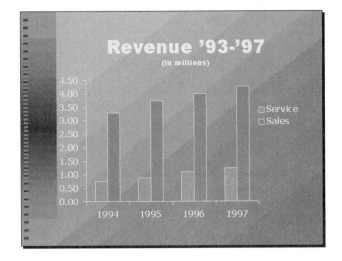

Professional Pointer

To leave more room for the graph, you can omit the chart title and use the slide title to describe the graph instead.

If you want to show the relationship of your data to totals, try one of the stacked column charts. And if you have more than one series and want to show relationships both across categories and across series, try the last 3-D Column type.

Bar

Bar graphs also compare data across categories, but the categories are shown along the left (Y) axis and the data is shown along the bottom (X) axis, as shown next with the Stacked Bar sub-type. This graph used the same datasheet as the column graph. To view it in color, refer to number 73 in the Slide Gallery.

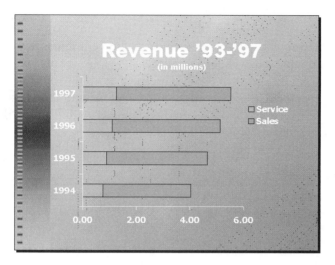

Column and bar graphs are visually impressive and easy to understand. You can use fill effects on the bars for a sophisticated look.

Line

A line graph is similar to a bar graph, but instead of creating bars, a line is drawn from value to value. Line graphs are especially good at showing trends—your audience immediately grasps if the line is going up, down, or remaining flat. However, they are not as visually impressive as column or bar graphs.

You can add markers at each data point to make the actual values on the line graph stand out. The 3-D sub-type creates ribbons instead of lines. Here you see a line graph using the same datasheet used for the bar and column graphs. To view this slide in color, refer to number 74 in the Slide Gallery.

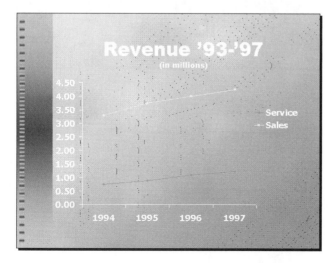

Pie

A pie chart shows what percentage each data value contributes to the whole pie. For this reason, pie charts are suitable for datasheets with only one row, that is, one data series. They are often used for breaking down revenues or expenses. Pie charts look great on slides, but keep the number of items to six or less, if possible. Here you see a datasheet and its corresponding pie chart. To view this slide in color, refer to number 75 in the Slide Gallery.

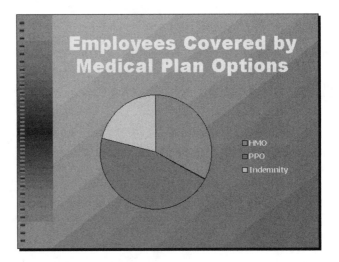

PowerPoint offers some great-looking 3-D pie charts. You can also create exploded pies (messy!) and pie charts that break down one of the chart's components into subcomponents.

Scatter

A scatter chart (also called an XY chart) is used when both the categories (columns) and the series (rows) are numbers, to draw conclusions about the relationships in the data. It is an effective way to present many data values at once. Here you see a datasheet showing average annual salaries based on age and years of college education completed.

		A	B	C	D	E	F	G	H	I	
	X Values	0	1	2	3	4	5	6	7	8	
1 ◆	25	18.1	19.1	20.2	21	25.5	25.7	27.9	28	30	
2 ■	30	19.2	19.3	20.4	21.1	25.7	25.9	28	28.5	30.5	
3 ▲	35	20.1	20.3	20.5	22	26	26.1	28.7	29.1	31	
4 ■	40	22.5	22.7	23.1	23.2	27.1	27.3	28.9	30.1	32.1	

Duffy HR2 - Datasheet

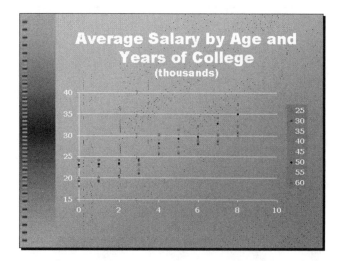

The scatter chart shows years of college education along the X axis and annual salary along the Y axis. Each marker type in the legend indicates a different age. You can clearly see how salary goes up with age and education, including a jump for those with four years of college. (This chart uses dummy data.)

Area

An area chart is plotted like a line chart, but the area under the lines is filled in. Because of the fill, an area chart shows up better on a slide. Another advantage of an area chart is that you can use one of the stacked sub-types, which show the relationship of the data series to their total. Here you see a 100% Stacked Area chart, which shows the trend in the percentage that each value contributes across the categories.

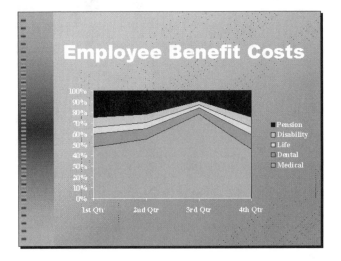

In this case, you clearly see how much each of the five employee benefits categories contributes to the total employee benefits cost over the four quarters of the year. Your audience would immediately understand that medical expenses are the largest part of the total cost, with pension expenses coming second. To view this slide in color, refer to number 76 in the Slide Gallery.

Doughnut

A doughnut chart is like a pie chart, but it can be used for data with more than one series (row). You can also use the exploded doughnut option. Here you see an unexploded doughnut, showing medical plan choices made by employees in two offices.

			A	B	C	D	E
			HMO	PPO	Indemnity		
1	🕐	New York	325	456	210		
2	🕐	Chicago	25	92	18		
3							
4							

The point is to show the proportions between the choices, not the total numbers. Since the Chicago office has fewer employees than the New York office, a chart type emphasizing totals, such as a bar chart, would not make the point clearly. To view this slide in color, refer to number 77 in the Slide Gallery.

Radar

A radar chart compares the values of several data series. Each category (column) has its own value axis radiating out from the center. Lines connect all the values in a series. A radar chart is usually used for scientific data and may be confusing for a presentation. Here you see a radar chart showing average annual temperature and rainfall for three U.S. cities.

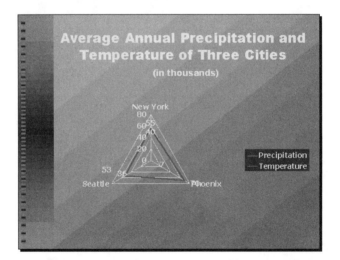

Surface

You can use a surface chart when you have two series (rows). The surface chart plots both series as it would with a line graph and connects lines to create a ribbon-like surface. The topology of the surface shows the combined value of both series. Here you see a surface chart showing quarterly sales of tapes and CDs.

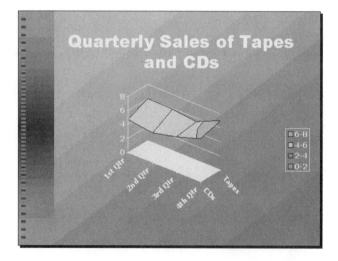

You can see that in the fourth quarter, the combined sales were the highest for the year. To view this slide in color, refer to number 78 in the Slide Gallery.

Bubble

A bubble chart lets you plot three series (rows) of data. The first row becomes the horizontal (X) axis, the second row becomes the vertical (Y) axis, and the third row is indicated by the size of the bubbles. In the next example, you see data for four U.S. cities—the X axis is precipitation, the Y axis is temperature, and the size of the bubbles indicate population (as of 1990) in thousands. In which city would you rather live? (Try to guess which city is which. The answer is at the end of the chapter.)

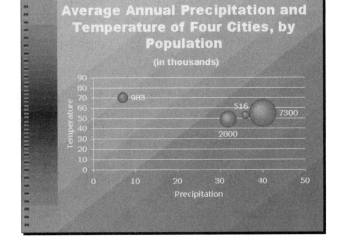

Tip: You could add text boxes to the graph to label the cities.

Stock

A stock chart is specifically designed to plot stock prices. The simplest version plots high, low, and closing prices, which must be located in rows in the datasheet in that order. The first row can be the names of stocks, sectors, dates, and so forth. Here you see a datasheet with dummy data for three sectors and the corresponding stock chart.

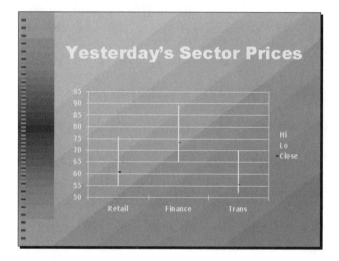

Cylinder, Cone, and Pyramid

These charts are just like bar or column charts, but PowerPoint uses cylinders, cones, or pyramids rather than bars to create the graph. These charts use 3-D effects that look good if the exact numbers are not important. In the next example you see a cone chart displaying data about employee benefits costs. You get the main idea—medical/dental costs are the highest of the three costs listed and are most variable.

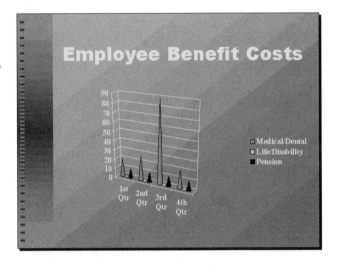

Creating a Clear Chart

Rarely is the default version of the chart acceptable for a slide. The charts you have seen in this chapter were formatted after their initial creation. Sometimes the labels aren't readable. Perhaps the scale of the axes is not appropriate. PowerPoint gives you a great deal of control over the format of a chart.

Charts have a number of elements that can be formatted individually. Not all charts have every element. For example, only 3-D charts have a floor. Other elements are optional, such as axis titles. The type of formatting available depends on the type of element. Obviously, you can only change the font, font size, and font color for elements that contain text. The following table lists chart elements and their descriptions.

Element	Description
Category axis	Usually (but not always) the horizontal (X) axis
Value axis	Usually (but not always) the vertical (Y) axis
Series axis	A third axis (on some 3-D charts), labeled with the names of the data series being plotted
Chart title	A title for the chart
Axis titles, if any	Titles for the axes
Data labels, if any	Labels containing the actual values
Plot area	The area within the axes
Each series of data	Each row of data (there may be several) that is plotted on the graph
Chart area	The entire chart, including the plot area, the legend, and a chart title, if any
Corners	The corners of the floor and walls in 3-D charts
Floor	In a 3-D chart, the floor that creates the chart's depth
Walls	In a 3-D chart, the two walls that create two of the three dimensions
Legend	The labels that indicate the names of the series
Tick marks	Marks that divide the axes into regular units
Gridlines	Lines running perpendicular to the axes from the tick marks, which help the viewer visualize the values plotted on the graph

Figure 8-5 shows a simple datasheet, its 3-D chart, and its elements.

Chart Options dialog box

Perhaps the simplest way to change a chart's elements is to use the Chart Options dialog box, which gives you access to the entire chart and its many elements at once. To open this dialog box, shown in Figure 8-6, open a chart and choose Chart | Chart Options.

Each tab in this dialog box lets you format one of the features of the chart. As you make changes, the simplified image of the chart previews the effect of the change. Here's how to use the tabs:

- **Titles**   Add an overall chart title or add titles to the series, category, and/or value axes.
- **Axes**   Check if you want each of the available axes. If you uncheck an axis, PowerPoint removes its labels, for example, the years on a category (X) axis.
- **Gridlines**   Check if you want major and minor gridlines for each axis. Major gridlines mark off larger intervals. Minor gridlines mark off smaller intervals between the major gridlines.

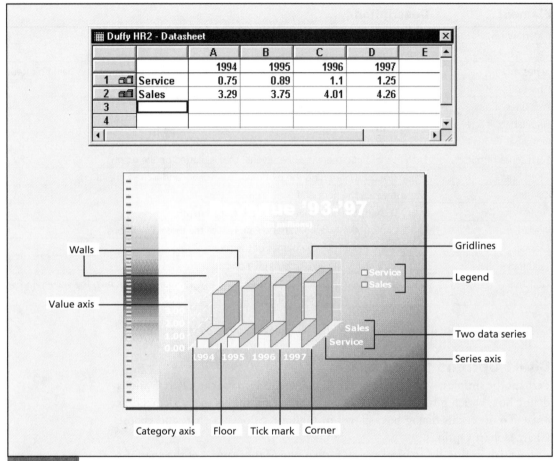

FIGURE 8-5   A chart is made up of several elements, each of which can be formatted

- **Legend**   Check if you want a legend and choose where you want it to be placed. (You can always drag it elsewhere.)
- **Data Labels**   Data labels usually show actual values. For example, you can place the actual number represented by a column at the top of the column. You can choose from several formats.
- **Data Table**   You can include with the chart a table of the data in your datasheet.

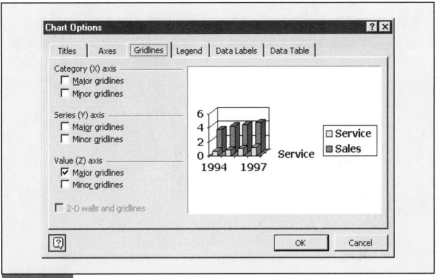

FIGURE 8-6 The Chart Options dialog box with the Gridlines tab on top

As a general guideline, include as few features as possible without sacrificing clarity. For example, titles, gridlines, and a data table often clutter up a chart without providing any additional necessary information. Save the fine details for a printed report. Figure 8-7 shows two versions of a chart. One is easy to understand, but the other has too much information for an audience to quickly grasp. To view these charts in color, refer to numbers 79 and 80 in the Slide Gallery.

Formatting chart elements

Once you have determined which features to include in your chart, you also want to individually format those features. Each element of a chart has its own customized Format dialog box that fine-tunes that element. To format an element, first make sure that the chart is open and active.

Then, double-click an element to open its Format dialog box. For example, if you double-click one of the axes, you see the Format Axis dialog box, shown in Figure 8-8.

Tip: As you move the mouse cursor around the chart, ToolTips pop up telling you what object you are passing over. To get an idea of the available elements in your charts, click the Chart Objects drop-down list on the Formatting toolbar that appears when you double-click a chart. You can choose any element from this list to select it.

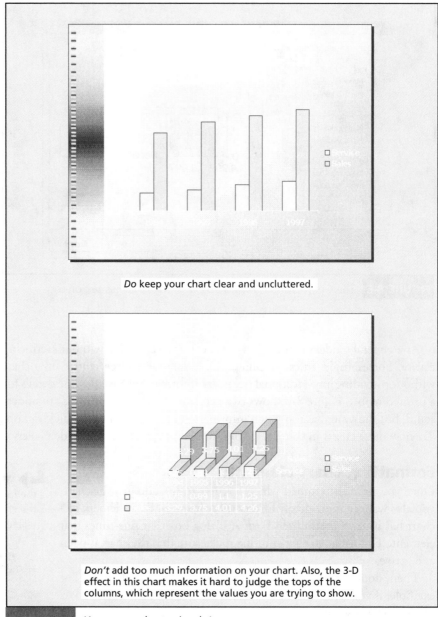

Do keep your chart clear and uncluttered.

Don't add too much information on your chart. Also, the 3-D effect in this chart makes it hard to judge the tops of the columns, which represent the values you are trying to show.

FIGURE 8-7 Keep your charts simple!

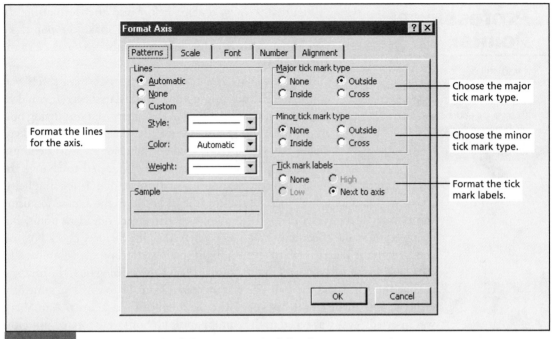

Format the lines for the axis.

Choose the major tick mark type.

Choose the minor tick mark type.

Format the tick mark labels.

FIGURE 8-8 The Patterns tab of the Format Axis dialog box

All the Format dialog boxes have a Patterns tab that lets you change colors, apply a texture or pattern (by using the Fill Effects pull-down menu), or change the line width or border style. Here are some of the other items you can format:

- **Axes** You can format the scale of the axes, setting the minimum and maximum numbers as well as the intervals for major and minor units. Use the Font tab for formatting the font of the axis labels. The Number tab lets you format exactly how numbers will appear. The Alignment tab aligns the text—great for fitting axis labels into tight spaces.

- **Data series** The data series is the part of the chart that plots the values, such as the columns, bars, or lines. For certain charts you can set which axis PowerPoint uses to plot the data series and format Y error bars, which indicate standard deviation or some other type of error value. You can format the data labels and set options for the spacing between the data series (for example, the columns). You will often want to change the color and width of bars or columns.

- **Chart area** Besides the Patterns tab, there's a Font tab where you can format the font for text in the chart area, as well as background and foreground colors.

- **Legend** You can format the patterns, font, and placement of the legend.

- **Gridlines** You can format the patterns and the scale of the gridlines.

Professional
Pointer

If you still don't think your chart conveys the message adequately, feel free to add AutoShapes, arrows, or text boxes. You can animate elements of a chart—see Chapter 9.

Figure 8-9 shows a chart before and after formatting. In addition, an arrow has been added to make the point. To view these charts in color, refer to numbers 81 and 82 in the Slide Gallery.

To create this chart, first the Service data series was eliminated by deleting its row in the datasheet. (It could be placed on a separate slide.) In the Chart Options dialog box, all the titles and gridlines were eliminated. The Chart Type dialog box was used to change the chart to a 2-D column format. The value (Y) axis was reformatted to change the major unit to 1 (from .5) and the maximum to 5 (instead of 4.5) for simplicity. The font was changed to Arial. A gradient fill was added to the data series, using the Format Data Series dialog box. (You can also select one data point, but changes you make affect only that data point.) Also, the Shadow check box was checked on the Patterns tab to create a slight shadow effect on the columns. The data labels were selected, and in the Format Data Labels dialog box, the font was changed to Arial, and the font size was increased from 18 to 22. The same font changes were made to the category (X) axis. Finally, a block arrow AutoShape was inserted. Text was typed in the AutoShape, and both were rotated using the Free Rotate button on the Drawing toolbar. This AutoShape emphasizes the increase in revenue from 1996 to 1997.

On the other hand, sometimes you want to be dramatic. For example, PowerPoint's chart feature lets you fill columns or bars with a picture that can be either stretched to fill the column or bar or stacked as many times as necessary. Here you see an example of using a graphic of a book to indicate book sales. To view this slide in color, refer to number 83 in the Slide Gallery.

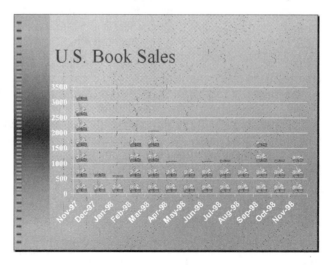

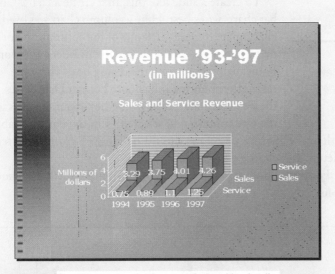

Don't let your point be overwhelmed by details.

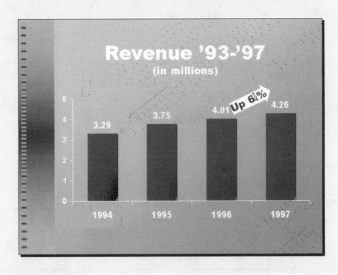

Do eliminate any unnecessary details and add
AutoShapes or other graphics to emphasize the main

FIGURE 8-9   Format your chart's elements to make it simple and clear

Professional Pointer

Use a very simple picture—a complex image doesn't show up very well inside the narrow columns.

To create a slide like this, first create a chart. Column and bar charts work best. Here a column chart was used. With the chart open, double-click one of the columns to open the Format Data Series dialog box. (If this opens the Format Data Point dialog box, close the dialog box. This time, right-click one of the columns and choose Format Data Series. If you use the Format Data Point dialog box, your changes affect only the one column you selected.) On the Patterns tab, click Fill Effects, then the Picture tab. This should be familiar from Chapter 6. Click Select Picture and choose a picture.

In the Format section of the Picture tab, shown in Figure 8-10, choose one of the options.

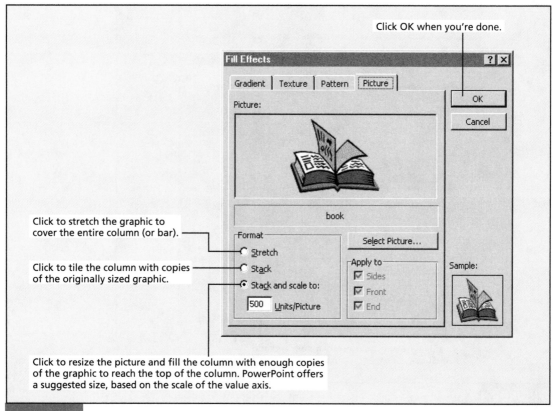

Click OK when you're done.

Click to stretch the graphic to cover the entire column (or bar).

Click to tile the column with copies of the originally sized graphic.

Click to resize the picture and fill the column with enough copies of the graphic to reach the top of the column. PowerPoint offers a suggested size, based on the scale of the value axis.

FIGURE 8-10   Use these options to format your graphic

Click the Options tab of the Format Data Series dialog box and reduce the gap width—this chart used a gap width of 20. This widens each column, making the graphic larger. In the Format Plot Area dialog box, the border was removed to make the chart as simple as possible. In the Category Axis dialog box, on the Alignment tab, the text was rotated to 45 degrees.

Saving chart properties
You can save all your hard work formatting a chart if you think you might use the same formatting in the future. Follow these steps:

1. Open the chart.
2. Right-click the chart and choose Chart Type.
3. In the Chart Type dialog box, choose the Custom Types tab.
4. Choose User-Defined at the bottom of the dialog box.
5. Click Add.
6. Name the chart type and add a more detailed description, if you wish.
7. Click OK twice to return to your presentation.

To use this chart type, follow steps 1 to 4 in the preceding list. Then choose the chart type you created. Click OK.

Inserting a Chart from Microsoft Excel
If you have already created and formatted a chart in Excel, for example, you can insert it onto a slide. This works best when you created the chart on a separate sheet in Excel. Follow these steps:

1. Choose Insert | Object.
2. Click Create from File in the Insert Object dialog box.
3. Click Browse, locate the file, and double-click it.
4. Click OK.

When you use this method, you double-click the chart to open it and use Excel's menus and toolbars to edit the graph for your presentation.

Charting a Clear Course for Better Graphics

by David Fine

Creating charts is an essential part of most presentation design. But all too often, rather than highlighting key points clearly, charts are unclear and end up needing a lengthy explanation to be understood.

A chart is created for a reason. The most common mistake is to simply put a chart showing sales or earnings into a presentation without identifying the reason for its existence. For example, let's say you're making a presentation about your company's financial results. You could include a summary of the company's balance sheet on the slide. However, if what your financial analysts really want to see is the company's debt-to-equity ratio, which is buried somewhere in the balance sheet, a simple pie chart of the debt-to-equity ratio would do the trick.

A table containing a summarized income statement doesn't make the point clear. Are you trying to show improved efficiency (higher earnings on lower sales) or simply a turn-around in the bottom-line earnings? (Of course, using red is a no-no in financial presentations.) See the example shown here, which you can also see in color—refer to number 84 in the Slide Gallery.

1996 Financial Results ($ Millions)	1995	1996
Gross sales	438.1	413.1
Net income (loss)	(30.1)	26.6
Earnings Per Share	(1.03)	1.12

Having decided that the key point is to show the improvement in earnings per share, let's say, create your chart, perhaps a column chart. But here, too, you can break the rules. Choose your colors so that your audience's eye is drawn to improvement, rather than past losses. Also, if you place data values on the top of each column, the data on the Y axis is redundant and therefore unnecessary clutter. The lines around the chart that PowerPoint creates by default are also unnecessary. Also, 3-D bar charts are notoriously confusing—it's difficult to see exactly where the top is, as you can see in the example here. (Look for this in color—it is number 85 in the Slide Gallery.)

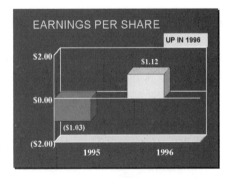

EARNINGS PER SHARE

UP IN 1996

$2.00

$1.12

$0.00

($1.03)

($2.00)

1995   1996

The simplicity of a 2-D bar chart would work better. If you wish, add an arrow to guide the eye to the latest earnings, highlighting the improvement. If there is a reason for the turn-around, add a text box or AutoShape to explain it in a few words. A few basic design effects such as shadows and shaded fills on the columns enhance the visual appeal. By all means, add a custom background, perhaps a softly colored photo representing the product or service of your company. Animation (discussed in Chapter 9) will further upgrade the visual appearance and focus the attention of the audience on what the speaker is saying. These improvements are shown here and in color as number 86 in the Slide Gallery.

Here are some handy rules of thumb for charts:

1. Guide the eye to the main point: The key point should jump out at the audience. Use arrows, animation, or a different color to guide the eye to the main point.
2. The fewer lines the better: A chart should be clear and simple. One powerful data series (line or row of bars) per chart is preferable. Using too many lines, or using different axes for multiple lines, is confusing.

3. Use an axis scale or data points—but not both: If you are putting data points on the actual line or bar, there is no need to clutter the axis with a scale. It is redundant.
4. Remove details: Grid lines, footnotes, and other details detract from the key point. Remove them whenever possible.

Here you see the final chart. To see this slide in color, refer to number 87 in the Slide Gallery.

David Fine is founder of Fine Communications, an investor relations firm specializing in high-quality laptop presentations for annual meetings, road shows, and investor conferences. He is also the coauthor of Point, Click and Wow! A Quick Guide to Brilliant Laptop Presentations. *Contact him at 416-489-6110 or finecome@interlog.com.*

Presenting Data in a Table

Using a table is an easy way to present lots of text or to summarize complex information that you want your viewers to remember. Use a table to make your point quickly and succinctly when you are not trying to show relationships or trends. Another good use of a table is to supplement a chart to show your audience the details. Show them the chart first so they get the main point, and then let them focus in on all the nitty gritty. To view this slide in color, refer to number 88 in the Slide Gallery.

Telegroup

Medical Plans

Plan	Deductible	Out-of-Pocket Maximum
High	$300 single; $600 family	$1,300 single; $2,600 family
Medium	$600 single; $1,200 family	$1,600 single; $3,200 family
Low	$1,000 single; $2,000 family	$3,000 single; $6,000 family
Basic	$5,000 single	None

Creating a Table

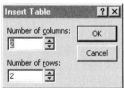

The simplest way to create a table is to create a new slide using the Table AutoLayout. Double-click the table placeholder, and PowerPoint opens the Insert Table dialog box, shown here, where you specify the number of columns and rows you want. When you click OK, PowerPoint creates the table on your slide.

You can create a table on a slide without a table placeholder by choosing Insert Table on the Standard toolbar. (Depending on the way your toolbars are configured, you may have to click the arrow at the end of the toolbar to display this button.) A grid appears. Drag down and to the right to fill in the number of columns and rows you want. You can always change the table later.

You also use the Tables and Borders toolbar, shown in Figure 8-11, to create a more complex table, varying the size and shape of the columns and rows. Here's how to use the Tables and Borders toolbar to create a table on a slide:

1. Click Tables and Borders on the Standard toolbar. The cursor changes to a pencil. (If it doesn't, click Draw Table.)

2. Create the outer boundaries of the table by dragging from the top-left corner to the bottom-right corner. (Yes, you can do it from right to left if you want.)

3. Drag across to create rows. You can stop in the middle to create a partial row.

4. Drag vertically to create columns. You can similarly create a partial column.

5. To erase a line, click Eraser and drag across the line.

Here you see an empty table created using this method. This table would be difficult to create starting with the Insert Table button.

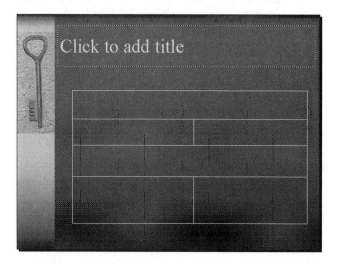

1. Draw Table
2. Eraser
3. Border Style
4. Border Width
5. Border Color

6. Outside Borders
7. Fill Color
8. Table drop-down menu
9. Merge Cells
10. Split Cell

11. Align Top
12. Center Vertically
13. Align Bottom

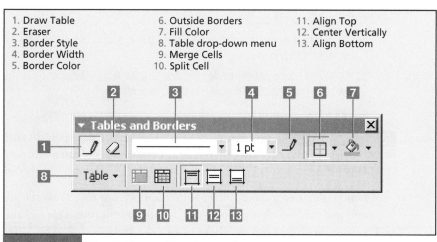

FIGURE 8-11   The Tables and Borders toolbar

Once you have created a table, click in the first cell and start typing data. Press TAB to move from cell to cell. You can click in any cell to type in that cell. If you press TAB from the bottom-right cell, PowerPoint creates a new row so you can add more data.

If necessary, use the Tables and Borders toolbar to add, delete, split, or merge cells, rows, and/or columns.

Taking Advantage of Your Previous Work

As with charts, you don't have to reinvent the wheel. If you have already created the table, for example, in Word, Excel, or Access, you can import it onto your slide. If you wish, you can start in PowerPoint, embed an object from one of those programs (or another program of your choice), and use the toolbars and menus of that program to create the table in PowerPoint. Remember these points when deciding what program to use:

- Word allows for more graphics formatting within its tables, including bulleted lists, numbering, and individual cell formatting.
- Use Excel when you want to include calculations, statistical analysis, or sorting and search features.
- If you need the power of a relational database, use Access.

PowerPoint has a special procedure for importing a new Microsoft Word table. Choose Insert | Picture | Microsoft Word Table. (It's on the expanded menu.) In the Insert Table dialog box, enter the number of rows and columns you want and click OK. Here's the general procedure for importing a table:

Tip: To import a table contained as part of a file, such as a word processing document, open the file, select the table, and copy it to the clipboard. Display the slide that you want to import the table to and choose Paste from the Standard toolbar.

1. Choose Insert | Object.
2. To create a new table, choose Create New and choose the type of object from the list.
3. To import an existing table, choose Create from File and type the filename or choose Browse to locate the file.
4. Click OK.

Cross-Reference: For more information about sharing information between PowerPoint and other applications, see Chapter 11.

When you embed a table from another application into PowerPoint, you need to double-click it to open it. The other application's menus and toolbars appear so you can use them to edit the table.

Making the Point Plain

Assuming you have created a table within PowerPoint, you now need to format it. The default table that PowerPoint creates, shown here, doesn't stand out at all!

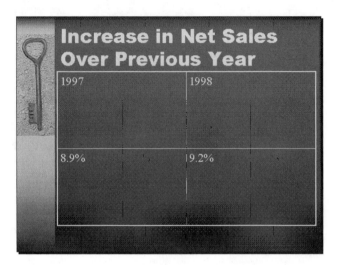

One way to format a table is to use the Format Table dialog box, shown in Figure 8-11. Choose Format | Tables. On the Borders tab, you can change the style, color, and width of the borders. You can also use the diagram on the right to create and delete borders. The Fill tab just lets you set the fill color, if any. The Text Box tab is like the Text Box tab of the Format Text Box dialog box discussed in Chapter 3. Here you set the text alignment and internal margins.

On the other hand, you can also format a table using the Tables and Borders toolbar, which I recommend because it contains all the tools you need in one place.

Tip: You can open the Format Table dialog box from the Tables and Borders toolbar. Choose Table | Borders and Fill.

The following are probably the minimum things you need to do to get a professional-looking table:

- Resize and place the table.
- Select the entire table and format the font, font size, and font color. Use the Formatting toolbar to center the text if you want. Use the Tables and Borders toolbar to center the text vertically, if desired.
- Change the borders: On the Tables and Borders toolbar, set the border style, width, and color. Then click the Pencil tool and redraw over the borders. You may want to make the outer borders thicker. If your table has a heading, it is common to place a heavier line under the first row. To delete borders, click the Border Style drop-down list and choose No Borders. You can also create

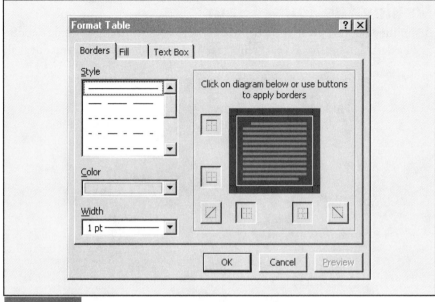

FIGURE 8-12 The Format Table dialog box

Tip: To easily select an entire row or column, or the entire table, choose the appropriate item from the Table drop-down menu on the Tables and Borders toolbar.

individual borders using the drop-down arrow next to the Outside Border button, which opens to give you a choice of border arrangements.

- If you wish, use the Fill Color button to choose a fill. You can use any of the fill effects discussed in Chapter 6.

Here you see the simply formatted chart. The point is clear—we're going up, where do we go from here? To view this table in color, refer to number 89 in the Slide Gallery.

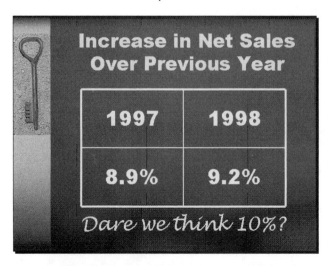

Working with Organization Charts

An organization chart shows the structure of an organization and where members of the organization fit in. Many professional presentations include an organization chart. It pulls employees and viewers into the presentation and shows how management is committed to a project or program. Organization charts are often used for project management and employee orientations.

To create organization charts, PowerPoint (and other Microsoft Office applications) uses a small application (*applet*) called Microsoft Organization Chart (what else?). When you use Organization Chart for the first time, you may be prompted to install it. This applet is very easy to use because its only function is to create organization charts.

The easiest way to start an organization chart is to use the Organization Chart AutoLayout. Double-click the layout to start Organization Chart, shown in Figure 8-13. You can also choose Insert | Picture | Organization Chart. (You'll find it on the expanded menu.)

Once you have designed your organization chart, as explained in Figure 8-12, and typed in all the data, you can format it as follows:

- To delete a box, click it and press DEL.
- Choose Styles to choose a chart structure type.
- Choose Text to format the font, size, color, and alignment of the text.
- Choose Boxes to format the boxes' color and shadow, as well as their border style, border color, and border line style.
- Choose Lines to format the thickness, style, and color of the lines. First select a line. You can select lines by clicking them and add to the selection by holding down SHIFT as you click. Or drag across the entire chart with the arrow cursor to select all the lines.
- Choose Chart to specify the background color of the entire chart.

To return to PowerPoint, choose File | click Exit and Return to presentation. You will be prompted to update the organization chart. Once you see how your chart looks on

Professional Pointer

Organization Chart offers only simple formatting options. If you want a more sophisticated look, you can buy another application that creates organization charts.

Tip: By default, the arrow button is depressed, meaning that you can drag across the chart to select objects. Use this technique when you want to format several or all the boxes at once.

Professional Pointer

When formatting the background color, choose the bottom-right option for no color. Your chart will then look like it has been drawn directly on your slide.

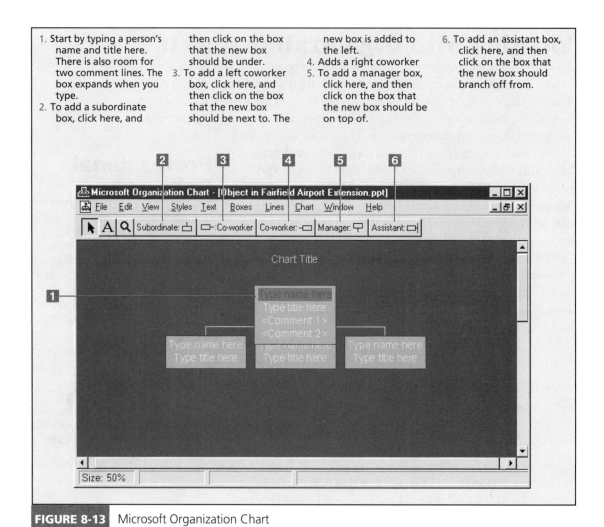

1. Start by typing a person's name and title here. There is also room for two comment lines. The box expands when you type.
2. To add a subordinate box, click here, and then click on the box that the new box should be under.
3. To add a left coworker box, click here, and then click on the box that the new box should be next to. The new box is added to the left.
4. Adds a right coworker
5. To add a manager box, click here, and then click on the box that the new box should be on top of.
6. To add an assistant box, click here, and then click on the box that the new box should branch off from.

FIGURE 8-13 Microsoft Organization Chart

your slide's background, you will probably go back and make some more changes. The following illustration shows an organization chart for an airport extension project. The organization chart title was deleted, and the slide title was used instead to label the chart. To view this slide in color, refer to number 90 in the Slide Gallery.

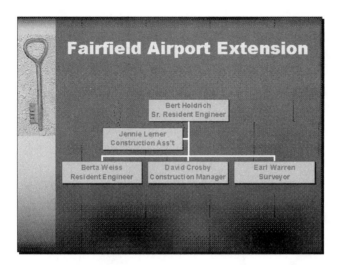

Professional Skills Summary

In this chapter, you learned how to present complex information clearly using graphs, tables, and organization charts.

PowerPoint lets you create or insert a graph (or chart) to suit your presentation needs. To determine the type of chart, you need to understand the structure of your data and the specific qualities of the types of charts PowerPoint offers. Once you have chosen a chart type, you should format it for maximum simplicity and impact.

Tables add clarity to complex information, and PowerPoint lets you draw a simple or complex table to present information. You can also embed tables from other applications. Tables also need to be well formatted to deliver the message loud and clear.

Organization charts show the structure of an organization. PowerPoint lets you insert and edit organization charts easily and quickly.

In the next chapter, you learn how to animate slides and create electronic transition effects between slides.

Answer to the question under "Bubble," the section on bubble charts: The cities are New York, Phoenix, Seattle, and Chicago.

chapter 9

Adding Animation to a Presentation

In this chapter, you:

- Animate individual objects
- Use preset and custom animation
- Animate text
- Animate charts
- Add transitions from slide to slide
- Add a sound to a presentation

To add the finishing touches to a presentation, you can include two types of animation—within a slide and from slide to slide. Animation on a slide, often called *builds*, determines how and when objects on the slide appear. Animation from slide to slide, called *transitions*, specifies how a new slide appears after the previous slide disappears.

Creating Professional Animation

To animate a presentation in a professional manner, it has to have a purpose beyond the Wow! effect. Animation can certainly enliven a presentation, but too much animation will distract your audience from your main message. All professionals say the same thing about animation—pick one or two effects and stick to them. This principle applies both to animation on a slide and transitions.

Animating Objects the Right Way

Animating objects has an additional purpose—to focus your audience's attention on what you're saying. In order to animate a slide, you need to know what you are going to say while that slide is displayed—and in what order. You then use that order to determine the order that the objects appear on the slide. Object animation is sometimes called a *build* because the objects build up on the screen, one after another. You can control the following aspects of the animation:

- How the object appears—for example, from which direction
- In what grouping the object appears—for example, text most often appears paragraph by paragraph but can appear by the word or even by the letter
- Whether the animation occurs when you click the mouse or automatically after a preset number of seconds
- Whether a sound plays during the animation
- What happens, if anything, after the animation—for example, you can change the color of a previously displayed object when the next object appears or hide it completely

Using preset animation effects for quick results

For a quick solution, PowerPoint offers *preset* animation. These animation options offer a complete group of settings that you can quickly assign to an object. While you can select several objects for animation, you cannot control the order of their animation. PowerPoint automatically animates them in the order in which they were created.

You can use preset animation either in slide sorter or in normal view. For some reason, PowerPoint offers more preset animation types in slide sorter view—and you can also animate more than one slide at once.

When you animate placeholder text, all the text in the placeholder is considered one object. However, it is automatically animated paragraph by paragraph—that is, bullet by bullet, which is usually what you want.

Don't forget that you can also animate objects such as AutoShapes and text boxes. Since these objects often serve to draw attention anyway, adding animation to them only increases the effect.

To add preset animation in slide sorter view, follow these steps:

1. Select the slide (or slides) for which you want animation.

2. Choose the type of animation you want from the Preset Animation drop-down list on the Slide Sorter toolbar.

To add preset animation in normal view, follow these steps:

1. Display the slide for which you want animation.

2. Select the object or objects you want to animate.

3. Choose Slide Show | Preset Animation.

4. Choose the type of animation you want from the submenu.

A number of the preset animations include a sound effect. For example, the Camera effect sounds like the shutter of a camera. Using sound is discussed later in this chapter, but here you should be aware that the effect of sound is usually humorous. If that is not what you want, don't use sound in your animation effects.

To see the result of an animation effect, you have three options:

- In normal view, choose Slide Show | Preview Animation. PowerPoint opens a small window that runs through the entire animation effect. This window stays open until you close it. As you experiment with different types of animation, you can keep the window open and just click anywhere in the window to run the animation.

- If you would like to see the effect of animation on more than one slide, switch to slide sorter view. Then click the animation icon at the bottom left of the slide, shown here, or click Animation Preview on the slide sorter toolbar.

- Switch to slide show view. Click the mouse to see each successive step of the animation.

Tip: Don't forget to use the expanded menu for more options. You can also open the Animation Effects toolbar by right-clicking any toolbar and choosing it; however, the toolbar only contains some of the available preset effects.

Professional Pointer

Most of the preset animations are not suitable for professional business use, especially those with sound effects. They are too distracting. Use them on one or two slides at most. The most appropriate ones are Wipe Right, Dissolve, and Appear. In slide sorter view, Fly from Left and Peek from Left are also suitable.

Tip: To see an overview of the animation effects for the whole show, in slide sorter view select all the slides (Edit | Select All), and then click Animation Preview. This gives a quick view of the whole presentation.

Figure 9-1 shows the effect of the Appear preset animation on a slide of bulleted text. Each bulleted item appears in order at the click of the mouse. At the end of the process, the entire slide's contents are visible. To view these frames in color, refer to numbers 91–96 in the Slide Gallery.

Using custom animation for maximum control

For more control over animation, you need to create your own settings. It's not hard once you've done it once or twice; you'll soon be

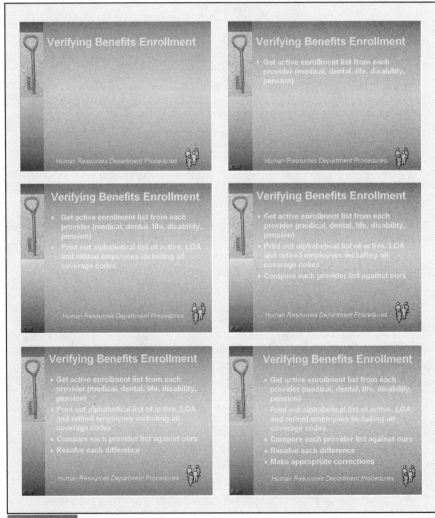

FIGURE 9-1   The simplest preset animation, Appear, displays each paragraph in order

able to get exactly the effects you want. To specify a custom animation, you must be in normal or slide view. Choose Slide Show | Custom Animation to open the Custom Animation dialog box, shown with the Effects tab on top in Figure 9-2. The Effects tab is a good place to start.

Tip: Before adding custom animation to a slide, remove any preset animation you may have added. Choose Slide Show | Preset Animation | Off.

Dimming after animation

Dimming text after animation is especially effective in focusing your audience's attention on the current point. You can dim to a lighter color by choosing the color on the After Aimation drop-down list. You can also hide the object

1. Check the objects you want to animate. Don't worry about the order.
2. As you check an object, PowerPoint selects it here (and on the slide) for confirmation.
3. Click here to see the results of your choices.
4. Choose how you want text introduced—all at once, by word, or by letter.
5. If you want to group the animation by level, specify it here.
6. Check to reverse the order of text animation (from bottom to top).
7. Choose what you want to happen after animation

here. Choose Don't Dim for no change after animation.
8. Choose a sound here.
9. Choose a variant of the animation effect here.
10. Choose the animation effect from this drop-down list.

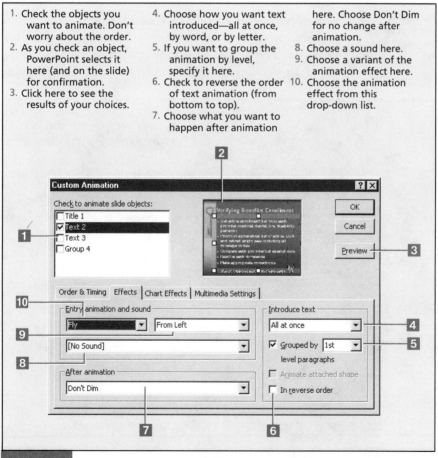

FIGURE 9-2 Use the Custom Animation dialog box for complete control over animation

Professional Pointer

completely immediately after the animation (which doesn't leave it on the screen for very long) or on the next mouse click. Just as your audience can wander ahead of you when all the text is visible at once, your audience may start thinking about the points you just finished if they are still clearly visible on the slide. You can dim to a softer, lighter color to emphasize your current point. The advantage is that the previous items are still visible enough to discuss if someone in the audience asks a question about a previous point. You can hide previous text completely, if you wish.

Figure 9-3 shows a slide that is animated with a dim to a lighter color. All the bulleted items are still visible, but the current item is much more obvious. To view these frames in color, refer to numbers 97–100 in the Slide Gallery.

An interesting use of the Hide on Next Mouse Click feature, one of the After Animation options, is to enable you to cover a great deal of information on one slide. This advanced

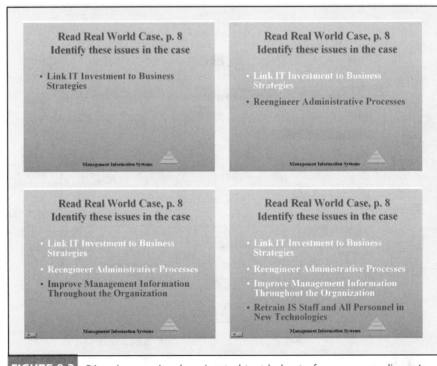

FIGURE 9-3 Dimming previously animated text helps to focus your audience's attention on the current point

technique lets you hide text and then display new text in the same location as the previous text, which is now invisible. You get to use the same "real estate" twice—or more. Figure 9-4 shows a slide that uses this technique. This slide contains 28 text objects, all animated. Figure 9-4 focuses only on the text in the top-right corner of the slide. The presenter wanted to discuss the products that his company offers, but more details than a basic list were necessary to attract the audience's interest. This slide includes some complex animation, in which major topics are animated on the presenter's mouse click and the subtopics are displayed automatically afterwards. See if you can follow the frames in Figure 9-4 to get a sense of the flow of the slide. To view these frames in color, refer to numbers 101–108 in the Slide Gallery.

If you are animating only one text placeholder (a common situation) and you want each item to appear when you click the mouse (giving you control over when each line of text appears), you're done. Click OK to close the dialog box.

Setting the order and timing of animation

When you are animating more than one object, you often need to change the order of animation. You can also decide whether to animate according to preset timing or only when you click the mouse button. These settings are on the Order & Timing tab and are explained in Figure 9-5.

> **Tip:** When using automatic timing, set the number of seconds to 00:00 for continuous animation.

When you are done, choose OK to close the dialog box.

To use the On Mouse Click setting on the Order & Timing tab or the Hide on Next Mouse Click setting on the Effects tab (in the After Animation section), you must also have the On Mouse Click check box checked in the Slide Transition dialog box. If On Mouse Click is not checked, your mouse click will have no effect when you run the presentation. The Slide Transition dialog box is covered later in this chapter.

Animation can be a major influence in a presentation that is not meant to tell a simple story but instead used to create a visual impression. For example, some presentations are used as an impetus for a subsequent workshop or brainstorming session. In these cases, you want to excite or inspire your audience, rather than systematically move from text item to item.

Professional Pointer

If you have created automatic timing and decide that you need more time while you are presenting, you can pause the presentation. See Chapter 16 for details.

Figure 9-6 shows a presentation on one of Sharp Electronics' projectors. While it provides information, there is no bulleted text in the entire presentation. The purpose of the presentation is to excite potential customers about a new product. In other words, this is advertising. The last slide invites the audience to visit Sharp's Web site (at **www.sharp-usa.com**). Although you can't see the actual animation in

FIGURE 9-4 This slide uses the Hide on Next Mouse Click feature to display subtopics that could not otherwise fit on the slide

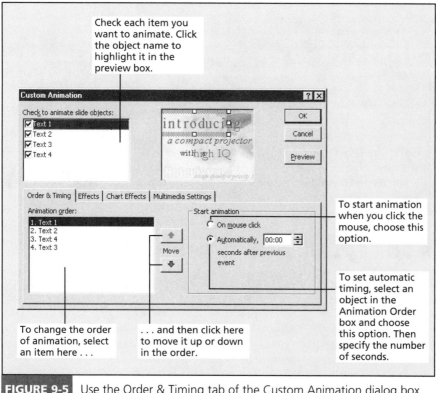

Check each item you want to animate. Click the object name to highlight it in the preview box.

To start animation when you click the mouse, choose this option.

To set automatic timing, select an object in the Animation Order box and choose this option. Then specify the number of seconds.

To change the order of animation, select an item here . . .

. . . and then click here to move it up or down in the order.

FIGURE 9-5 Use the Order & Timing tab of the Custom Animation dialog box to determine in which order the objects are animated and choose automatic timing

the figure, you can get an idea of how the first slide presents the material. This presentation is meant to run automatically, with preset timing. To view these frames in color, refer to numbers 109–112 in the Slide Gallery.

You can animate organization charts like any graphic objects, such as an Auto-Shape. The organization chart is considered one object.

Animating Charts

You can animate a chart created within PowerPoint or with Microsoft Excel. As with other objects, animating a chart can help to focus your audience's attention on a specific portion of the chart. Because charts often represent growth over time, building the chart over several steps is appropriate. You can animate a chart in the following ways (refer to the chart shown here as you read):

- **All at once** The entire chart appears at once with the animation effect.

"introducing" flies in from the top left.

"a compact projector" flies in from the top right.

"with a" flies in from the bottom left.

"high IQ" flies in from the bottom right.

Thanks to Gerry Ganguzza of Sharp Electronics Corporation for this presentation.

FIGURE 9-6 The first slide of the Notevision presentation

- **By series** For a chart with more than one series (in the sample chart on the preceding page, the two series are Total revenue and Retail customers), first one series appears, then the next, and so on, with the animation effect. All of the elements of the series (the breakdown by years) appear together as a group. Use this when you want to discuss each series separately.

- **By category** Each category (in the sample chart, each year is a category) appears together. Use this option when you want to discuss the chart year by year.

- **By element in series** This option breaks down the animation by each element in each series. In the sample chart, first you see 1993 total revenue, then 1994 total revenue, and so on until 1997 total revenue. The animation continues with 1993 retail customers, 1994 retail customers, and so on until 1997 total customers.

- **By element in category**   The elements of each category appear in order. In the example, first you see 1993 total revenue, then 1993 retail customers, then 1994 total revenue, then 1994 retail customers, and so on through 1997 total revenue and 1997 retail customers.

Tip: If you forget to select the chart before opening the dialog box, click the chart's name (usually something like Chart 2) in the Check to Animate Slide Objects box.

These options will not all be available if your chart doesn't contain all these features. For example, a simple pie chart will only have the All at Once and the By Category options.

If these options aren't enough for you and you must animate a chart in more detail, you can ungroup the chart. You can then animate each individual object as you wish. But beware, ungrouping a chart turns it into an Office drawing object, and it loses its connection with the underlying data. Also, any link to another file is severed. Another disadvantage is that you will probably end up with more objects than you want to deal with. But you *can* do it!

To animate a chart, select the chart and choose Slide Show | Custom Animation. Then click the Chart Effects tab, shown in Figure 9-7.

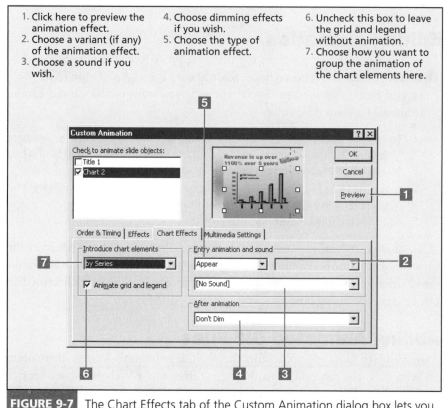

1. Click here to preview the animation effect.
2. Choose a variant (if any) of the animation effect.
3. Choose a sound if you wish.
4. Choose dimming effects if you wish.
5. Choose the type of animation effect.
6. Uncheck this box to leave the grid and legend without animation.
7. Choose how you want to group the animation of the chart elements here.

FIGURE 9-7   The Chart Effects tab of the Custom Animation dialog box lets you specify how you want to animate your chart

Professional Pointer

While dimming to a lighter color may work for text, hiding previously discussed chart objects makes it difficult for your audience to comprehend the chart, which usually needs to be seen as a whole by the end of your discussion of the slide.

If you have more than one object to animate, use the Order & Timing tab as described earlier. For example, if you have an AutoShape that points out an aspect of the chart, you might want to animate that as well. You can also choose whether to animate automatically or when you click the mouse. Click OK when you're done.

When you add animation to charts, you can use the Multimedia Settings tab of the Custom Animation dialog box to allow you to edit a chart during a presentation. You might do this for an in-house presentation, where you want to get input from others and make the changes on the spot. In the Object action drop-down list, choose Edit. You can use this setting for organization charts as well.

Figure 9-8 shows the steps to animating a simple column chart. Each column uses the Wipe Up animation type, appropriate for a column chart. The AutoShape appears last with the Zoom In animation type. To view these frames in color, refer to numbers 113–118 in the Slide Gallery.

Editing Animation

To edit animation, you generally use the same procedure as is used to create it. To remove preset animation, choose Slide Show | Preset Animation | Off.

To edit custom animation, display the slide you want to change and choose Slide Show | Custom Animation.

- To remove animation from an object, uncheck it in the Check to Animate Slide Objects box. Choosing No Effect for the Entry Animation and Sound box on the Effects tab for a selected object has the same effect.
- To remove a sound, click the object's name in the Check to Animate Slide Objects list to select the object (or select the object before opening the dialog box). Then choose No Sound from the list of sounds on the Effects tab.

To change any other setting for an object, select the object's name in the Check to Animate Slide Objects list. Then choose the appropriate tab and make the changes you want. You can click Preview to preview the new effects. Click OK to close the dialog box.

Adding Animated GIF Files

Animated GIF files are graphics files that include animation. You see them often on Web sites. You can easily download them from many Web sites that offer free Web graphics. Try a search in your favorite search engine on "free animated gif."

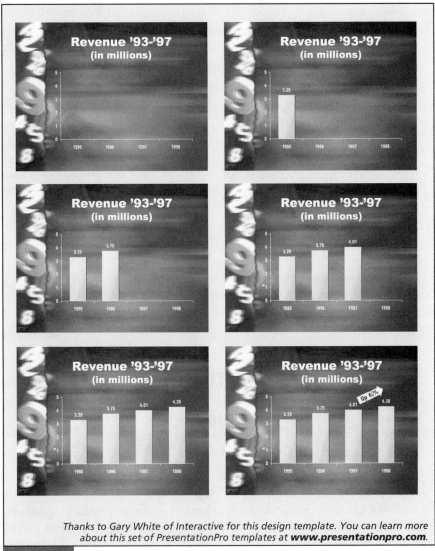

Thanks to *Gary White* of *Interactive for this design template. You can learn more about this set of PresentationPro templates at* **www.presentationpro.com.**

FIGURE 9-8 In an animated chart, each bar appears individually, in order, followed by the arrow

Among the more useful animated GIFs are animated bullets. However, be aware that, like sound, the effect will usually be humorous. If you want to use animated GIFs in a business presentation, keep it low key. You may be able to take an animated logo from your company's Web site. Perhaps you could draw attention to one especially noteworthy or exciting item with an animated arrow. Too many animated GIFs make a presentation look like a cartoon.

You insert an animated GIF like any image. Follow these steps:

1. Display the slide you want to add the animated GIF to.

2. To insert an animated GIF from a file, choose Insert | Picture | From File. Then navigate to the file, select it and choose Insert.

3. To insert an animated GIF from the Clip Gallery, choose Insert | Picture | Clip Art or click Insert Clip Art on the Drawing toolbar. Click the Motion Clips tab. You can select from a category if you have added animated GIFs to the Clip Gallery. If not, type **animated gif** in the Search for Clips text box to find what is available. Choose the animated GIF and choose Insert Clip from the submenu that appears.

Cross-Reference: For information on adding graphic files to the Clip Gallery, see Chapter 5.

Animated GIFs move only in slide show view. In normal or slide sorter view, they are frozen. You cannot edit an animated GIF image with the Picture toolbar in PowerPoint. To edit an animated GIF, you need an animated GIF editing program.

Transitioning from Slide to Slide

Another type of animation controls how each new slide appears. Because these effects control the transition from one slide to another, they are called *transitions*. While some of these effects have the same names as animations, they look quite different when applied to an entire slide.

Using Transitions Wisely

Transitions, like slide animation, need to be used with reserve. Many options are available, but that doesn't mean you should use them all in one presentation. One of the best solutions is to choose a simple transition and apply it to every slide in the presentation. If your presentation is divided into sections, you could use a second transition to introduce each new section.

Choosing the Ideal Transition Style

The ideal transition style heightens your audience's attention without your audience noticing why. If the transition style is too active, your audience will get a headache looking at it. PowerPoint offers a transition style for every possible purpose.

Transitions are usually set in slide sorter view where you can get a sense of the flow of the entire presentation. PowerPoint places a transition icon beneath each slide with a transition so you can easily see which slides have transitions and which don't. However, you can add transitions in normal view.

When you add a transition to a slide, the transition determines how that slide appears after the previous slide is removed from view.

To add a transition, follow these steps:

1. Select the slide or slides you want to add a transition to.

2. To quickly add a transition setting without any options, choose it from the slide sorter toolbar's Slide Transition Effects drop-down box (if you're in slide sorter view). Otherwise, choose Slide Show | Slide Transition to open the Slide Transition dialog box, shown in Figure 9-9.

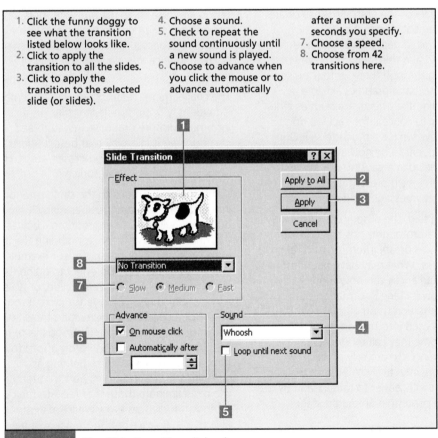

1. Click the funny doggy to see what the transition listed below looks like.
2. Click to apply the transition to all the slides.
3. Click to apply the transition to the selected slide (or slides).
4. Choose a sound.
5. Check to repeat the sound continuously until a new sound is played.
6. Choose to advance when you click the mouse or to advance automatically after a number of seconds you specify.
7. Choose a speed.
8. Choose from 42 transitions here.

FIGURE 9-9   The Slide Transition dialog box

Animations and Transitions

by Jim Endicott

When our presentation software programs introduced movement into their feature sets, it became the best of times and the worst of times. Not that the ability to make text and graphics move was inherently a bad thing, it's just that those who create presentations forgot to ask one key question . . . why? It's not enough that we animate objects because we can; our audiences simply grow weary of the gratuitous use of any presentation element. The first time we animate some clip art, it gets a few oohs and aahs; the second and third time some yawns. And after sitting through three or four presentations that fly text and graphics like in a George Lucas film, the effects are seen as a diversionary tactic to conceal the fact we don't necessarily believe we have much to say. Our flying objects appear to be nothing more than a multimedia shell game causing our audiences to wonder under which presentation component does the real message reside?

With that being said, the proper use of movement can have a profoundly positive affect on how our audiences grasp, interpret, and retain our key messages. What may have been lost in a sea of data, audiences can now more easily assimilate when we stage information during the actual presentation using animations. The use of sensory-based information in a presentation (which some may call *multimedia*) causes our audiences to actually process the information more effectively. A busy chart can be made significantly easier to understand by introducing the content in animated stages.

Mirroring how the presenter addresses the information (quarter by quarter or category by category) is essential in making the point. Text-based information creates its own inherent challenges. This left-brain appeal often goes through a filtering process by the audience when they have a chance to read ahead, and a presenter may find that quick judgments are made. By at least staging the bullets to enter on a mouse click, the presenter gets an opportunity to articulate the points before judgment is passed, providing the best chance of the audience staying with the flow of information.

The challenge in creating a quality presentation is to identify opportunities for making text-type information more graphical in nature and introducomg it in a way that best supports the presenter. This could be processes, steps, chronologies, or other similar topics.

Transition effects fall into the same category. Presentation software provides many more options than will ever be appropriate. Look at transition effects as a tool for guiding the audience's eye or creating interest. For example, you could use a Wipe Up effect to guide the eye back to the top after each slide, or possibly a Wipe Left to reset the eye for more information. Pick a specific nondistracting transition and stick with it. After all, if our goal is to really communicate, we can hardly afford to distract our audiences with something as insignificant as a transition. Sort through the choices, eliminate those that fall into the cute category (audiences grow weary of "cute" very quickly) and throw in a change-up once in a while. Introducing a new topic in the presentation may be a time to "box out" a transition and then get back into your standard transition effect.

Let's face it: Animations and transitions are just electronic effects. A wise presenter will realize that the stage lights don't make good presenters, compelling stories do.

Jim Endicott is owner/manager of Distinction, a business communications company that provides creative and consulting support services. He assists business professionals in enhancing the content, tools, and techniques of effective presenting. Jim regularly writes articles for Presentations *magazine. He can be reached at 503-554-1203 or jim.endicott@distinction-services.com.*

Professional Pointer

Once you have both animation and transitions, preview your presentation in slide show view to see how they work together. When the animation and transitions blend together without an obvious distinction, you will create a truly professionally animated impact.

The Advance section of the Slide Transition dialog box affects animations as well when you are in slide show view. If On Mouse Click is not checked, your mouse will not work while you present! (You can still use the keyboard.) As a result, you should keep this box checked even if you also check the Automatically After check box. At the bottom of the Sound drop-down box, choose Other Sounds to locate other WAV files on your hard drive or network in the Add Sound dialog box. You can choose Tools | Find in this dialog box to search for WAV files.

Cross-Reference: Chapter 15 covers setting automatic timing for a presentation.

After you close the Slide Transition dialog box, you can preview transitions in two ways:

- In slide sorter view, click the transition icon, shown here.
- Select a slide or slides and choose Slide Show | Animation Preview. You see both animation and transition effects.

To remove a transition, select the slide or slides you want to work with. Either from the Slide Sorter toolbar or the Slide Transition dialog box, choose No Transition. To remove a sound, open the Slide Transition dialog box and choose No Sound in the Sound drop-down list.

Knowing When to Add Sound

As you have seen earlier in this chapter, you can attach sound to both animation and transition effects. Sound adds a totally new dimension to a presentation. Sound is especially useful for presentations that run automatically, without a presenter, such as presentations used at kiosks and trade shows.

Cross-Reference: The next chapter explains how to add music, CD soundtracks, and narration to a presentation.

PowerPoint comes with a few sound effects, such as applause, a drum roll, or a cash register. These sounds tend to have a humorous effect, which is fine if that's what you want. For a presentation given by a real person, sound effects tend to distract from the presenter. They can also be annoying. You certainly don't want to attach a sound to a transition on every slide in your presentation unless you want your audience to walk out! The same is true for adding a sound to an animation effect on a slide. Imagine the same sound repeating as each bulleted item of text appears. Only in rare circumstances would that be appropriate.

Professional Pointer

Use sound effects only rarely.

The first and last slides are two places where sound can be useful. For example, you might want music to be playing as the audience trickles in before the presentation or as they leave after the last slide (if you won't be taking questions). A drumroll on the first slide can get your audience's attention in a humorous way—but leave it at that.

PowerPoint can play any WAV sound file attached to a transition or animation effect. Use the Windows Find feature (Start | Find | Files or Folders) to search for WAV files on your hard drive or network. Don't forget to look on your Microsoft CD-ROM. Finally, Microsoft offers a modest number of sound files in its Clip Gallery Live at **www.Microsoft.com/clipgallerylive**. You'll probably be surprised at what you find. Unfortunately, WAV files are much more limited than some other formats of sound files such as MIDI or MPEG files. (See the next chapter for more information about playing other types of files.)

To repeat a sound continuously throughout several slides or an entire presentation, you can attach the sound to a slide transition, as explained earlier in this chapter. Follow these steps:

1. Select the first slide to play the sound.
2. Choose Tools | Slide Transition.
3. In the Sound section, choose the sound you want to play. To play a WAV file not on the list, choose Other Sound. Locate the WAV file and choose Open.
4. Choose Loop Until Next Sound.
5. Choose Apply.

Don't try this with most of the sounds that come with PowerPoint. They're much too annoying! The only usable sound is the bird chirping, which you could use in a self-playing presentation on gardening, for example.

Professional Skills Summary

In this chapter you learned how to animate text and objects on a slide, both to help focus your audience's attention on what you're saying and to add interest and excitement to a presentation. Animation options including building text and objects with various effects, dimming or hiding objects after animation, and adding WAV sound effects.

You can also add animated GIF files to a slide.

Add transitions from slide to slide for a professional effect. PowerPoint offers many transition effects to choose from. For both animation and transitions, the main principle is to keep it simple.

In the next chapter I explain how to add other types of sound as well as music to your presentation. In addition I cover using a CD soundtrack, video clips, and narration.

Joining the Multimedia Revolution

More and more, multimedia effects are showing up in PowerPoint. While PowerPoint does not yet offer the flexibility of creating a full-fledged video or movie, you can add some of the same features. You can include sounds, music, or CD soundtracks to your presentations. Short sounds can be used with any presentation, but continuous music or soundtracks work best for unattended presentations, where the music doesn't compete with the presenter. For a self-running presentation, music can add a professional effect.

Video clips can be inserted onto a slide and shown at any time during a presentation. They don't turn your presentation into a video but add the element of video where the static quality of a slide is not enough. These video clips are usually quite short—less than a minute—but they pack quite an impact.

For self-running presentations, you can record narration. Narration replaces what you would say if you were making the presentation and is appropriate whenever viewers will view a presentation on their own. As with music, the impact of the narration adds a professional quality to your presentation.

Creating a Mood with Sounds and Music

When you stand in front of an audience, you generally want the audience to pay attention to *you*. You talk, which is probably the best sound effect your presentation can have. But when you create a self-running presentation for a kiosk or the floor of a trade show, you often need to replace your words with some type of sound, music, or narration. Music, especially, creates a mood that can add a lot to the overall impression of your presentation. You've probably heard of research done by retailers showing how the music often played in stores increases sales. Music can have a powerful effect on your presentation because music has an emotional effect on people. Of course, you need to choose appropriate music for your message. In this section, I explain how to add sound and music to a presentation. Later in this chapter, I explain how to add narration to a presentation.

Cross-Reference: Chapter 15 covers how to create a self-running presentation.

Inserting a Sound or Music File

In Chapter 9, I explained how you can add WAV sound files to animation and transitions. For more options, you can insert a music or sound file into your presentation. You have many more file type options when you use this method. For example, you can play MIDI files (which usually have a filename extension of .mid or .mri). MIDI (Musical Instrument Digital Interface) files are more compressed than WAV files and are used for the full sound of longer instrumental musical pieces. When you insert a MIDI file, PowerPoint places an icon on the slide. The music or sound can be set to play automatically or only when you click its icon. Here's how to insert music or sound on a slide:

1. Display the slide you want to add the sound or music to.

2. Choose Insert | Movies and Sounds.

3. On the submenu, choose either Sound from Gallery or Sound from File.

4. If you choose Sound from Gallery, you see the Insert Sound window, which looks just like the Clip Gallery. You can choose from a category or type in a keyword to locate a sound. Choose the sound you want and choose Insert Clip from the submenu.

5. If you choose Sound from File, locate the file, choose it, and click Insert.

6. PowerPoint puts a sound icon, shown here, on the slide.

7. PowerPoint asks you if you want the sound to play automatically. Click Yes to play the sound automatically when the slide is displayed. Click No to play the sound only when you click the sound icon while you are presenting. If you click Yes, PowerPoint creates an animation setting for the icon. You can change it by choosing Slide Show | Custom Animation and removing the checkmark next to the sound icon object.

Cross-Reference: See Chapter 5 for instruction on adding clips to the Clip Gallery. You add sounds in the same way.

Most music files come in MIDI format. Search your hard drive and network for .mid files. The Windows Media folder has additional sounds and music that you can use. Don't forget to look on the Office CD and on the Web. Microsoft's Clip Gallery Live at **www.Microsoft.com/clipgallerylive** has a few sounds that you can download. Be especially careful when searching the Web for music—much of it is copyrighted.

Note that if you already have a sound icon on a slide, PowerPoint usually places a new sound icon on top of the previous one, making it hard to find. Just select it and drag it to a new location, and you immediately see that you have two sound icons on the slide.

You can play the sound or music at any time by double-clicking the sound icon. The next illustration shows a slide with a sound icon on it. (Thanks to Gary White, of Interactive, for this design template, part of Interactive's PresentationPro collection. Visit Interactive's Web site at **www.presentationpro.com**.) To view this slide in color, refer to 119 in the Slide Gallery.

Specifying How Sound or Music Plays

Once you have inserted a sound or music file, you need to specify how it will play. These settings give you a great deal of control over the sound in your presentation. Here are your options:

- You can play the music or sound before or after other animation on the slide.
- You can choose whether to play the music or sound automatically or when you click the mouse button.
- You can continue the presentation while the sound or music is playing, or pause it.
- You can stop the sound or music after the current slide or after any number of slides that you specify. If you specify the last slide in the presentation, the sound or music plays to the end of the presentation.
- You can choose to start the sound or music file from the beginning again when it reaches the end, called *looping*.
- You can hide the sound icon before and after it plays.

Using custom animation settings

To set the options for playing sound or music, select the sound icon. Then choose Slide Show | Custom Animation and click the Multimedia Settings tab, shown in Figure 10-1. Most of the settings on this tab are available only when you have selected a sound or a video.

Your decisions will depend on whether you are playing a short sound effect or a long piece of music. Is the sound or music appropriate for just this slide or do you want to continue it throughout part or all of the presentation?

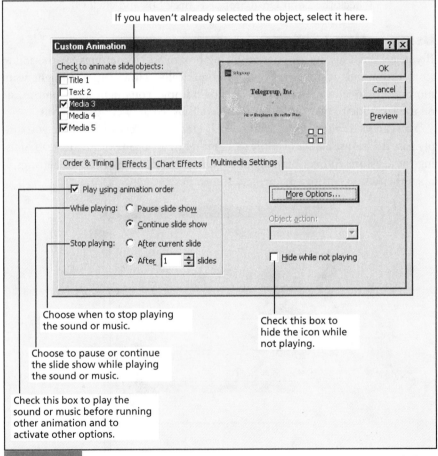

FIGURE 10-1   Use the Multimedia Settings tab of the Custom Animation dialog box to specify how sound plays

How do you find out how long the sound or music will last? One way is to choose More Options on the Multimedia Settings tab to open the Sound Options dialog box, shown here. Notice that the playing time, in this case 1 minute and 35 seconds, is displayed. You now have the information you need to decide if you want to repeat the sound or music over and over. For example, if you want the music to play throughout the entire presentation and since the presentation will obviously take more than 1.5 minutes, you need to loop it. Check the Loop Until Stopped check box and click OK.

Using action settings

If you use the Custom Animation dialog box to specify settings for the sound icon, the sound or music will play automatically. However, you might want more control over when a sound plays. For example, you might want some music on the last slide to play only after you have finished answering questions.

You can set a sound or music file to play either when clicked or when you simply pass the mouse cursor over the icon, rather than automatically. Instead of using the Custom Animation dialog box, choose Slide Show | Action Settings to open the Action Settings dialog box, shown here:

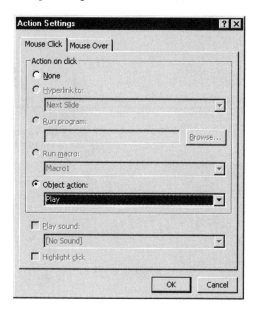

Cross-Reference: This dialog box is covered in detail in Chapter 11.

On the Mouse Click tab, you specify what action you want to occur when you click an object. In the case of a sound icon, check Object Action and choose Play from the drop-down list. The Mouse Over tab determines what action, if any, occurs when you pass the mouse over an object. For a sound icon, check Object Action and choose Play. You can set the icon to play for both a mouse click and a mouse over.

Instead of hiding the object while not playing it, you can format it with the same background color and hide most of it behind the object. Your audience is unlikely to notice the icon and if you set it to play on a mouse over, your audience will think you made magic! Here a sound icon is slightly peeking out from the AutoShape. To view this slide in color, refer to number 120 in the color Slide Gallery.

Professional Pointer

When you use a mouse over setting, your audience is less likely to see the mechanics behind the playing of the sound or music. However, for a self-playing presentation where you want someone at a kiosk to control the presentation, a mouse over setting is too subtle.

A sound icon is almost completely hidden behind the AutoShape banner, but it can still be played when you pass the mouse over it.

Adding Sounds and Music with Media Clips

When you insert sound files onto a slide, they become PowerPoint objects. Sometimes you might have a file that PowerPoint can't play. In this situation, you can try using Media Player, a Windows program that plays many types of sound and video files. Media Player can play CD and videodisk music, and it offers you more control over playback of the sound file.

To insert a media clip, choose Insert | Object and choose Media Clip from the Insert Object dialog box. Leave Create New selected. Choose OK. Your screen now looks like the illustration shown here, which shows a large media clip icon and a new menu:

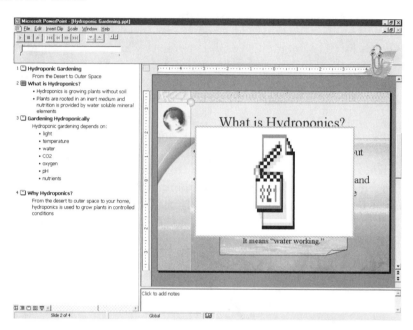

Choose Insert Clip on the menu. Then choose either MIDI Sequencer (MID or RMI files) or Sound (WAV files). In the Open dialog box, locate the file you want to insert and choose Open. PowerPoint reduces the size of the icon, and your screen now looks like Figure 10-2. (Figure 10-2 shows the MIDI Sequencer icon. The sound icon is different.) You can now try out the sound or music. To view this slide in color, refer to number 121 in the Slide Gallery.

Media Player works like a tape recorder. You can play, pause, stop, rewind, and fast forward. To play a portion of a multimedia file, called a *selection,* click at the starting point, click at the desired end of the selection, and then click Play. The Window/Media folder contains some MIDI files that you can play with Media Player.

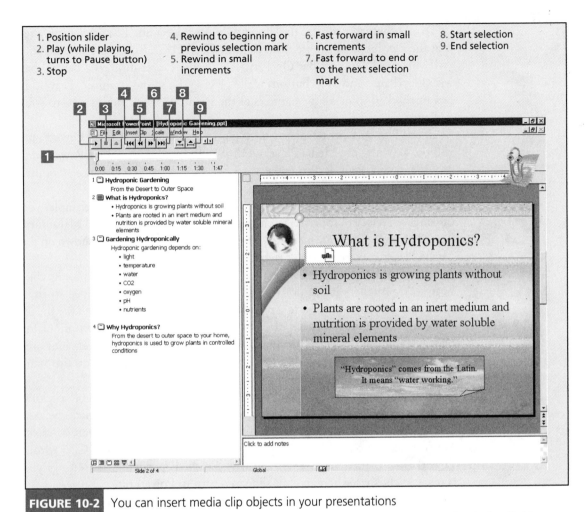

1. Position slider
2. Play (while playing, turns to Pause button)
3. Stop
4. Rewind to beginning or previous selection mark
5. Rewind in small increments
6. Fast forward in small increments
7. Fast forward to end or to the next selection mark
8. Start selection
9. End selection

FIGURE 10-2 You can insert media clip objects in your presentations

The Media Clip window also tells you how long the clip is. Use this information to decide if you want to repeat the clip over and over. To set options for playing media clips, double-click the media clip object to open it and choose Edit | Options on the Media Clip menu to open the Options dialog box, shown here to the right.

To automatically rewind the file, choose Auto Rewind. To automatically repeat the file (loop it), choose Auto Repeat. Click OK.

If you check Control Bar On Playback, Media Player displays a control bar with Play/Pause and Stop buttons while playing the sound or music. Leave this box unchecked to make the controls of the sound or music transparent to your audience.

Check Play in Client Document to play the file directly within PowerPoint without showing the Media Player controls. Playing the file within PowerPoint avoids showing your audience the source of the file and results in a smoother presentation.

Explore the other Media Player menus for more options. For example, you can choose Device | Properties to change the properties of WAV and MIDI files. You can also use the Scale menu to change the time and frame scale shown on the Media Player controls during playback.

You can also insert a media clip file into a document by copying it to the clipboard. You might want to do this when you have Media Player open to copy more than one file at once into a presentation. In Media Player, open the file by choosing File | Open, locating the file, and clicking Open. Set the options for playing the file as described previously. Choose Edit | Copy Object. In your presentation, display the slide where you want the file and click Paste on the Standard toolbar.

Once you have closed Media Player, you can play the file by double-clicking its icon or frame. If you want to change some of the settings, right-click the icon and choose Media Clip Object | Open to open Media Clip as a separate window. You can also choose Media Clip Object | Edit to open Media Clip within PowerPoint. In that case, when you have finished specifying the settings you want, just click elsewhere in your slide to return to PowerPoint.

During a presentation, in slide show view, click the media clip icon to play the file. It changes color when you play it. If you choose Hide While Not Playing in the Custom Animation dialog box (see Figure 10-1) and place the icon in a location whose color is similar to the media clip's color during playback, the icon will be barely visible. This type of technique hides the mechanics behind the playing of the media clip for a smoother-looking presentation.

Playing a CD Soundtrack

As you may know, you can play an audio CD in your CD drive. (Try it, you might enjoy working that way! However, it can also slow down your computer.) Just put the CD in your CD drive, and it will start playing automatically. You'll find a CD Player button on the Windows taskbar. Click it to reveal the CD Player controls, which are like those of any tape recorder.

You can insert a CD audio track on a slide. The sound that you'll get will be much superior to either WAV or MIDI files, for a more professional result. As with other electronic files, be careful about copyright issues when using an audio CD track. Inserting a CD audio track is like inserting any sound. Follow these steps:

1. Display the slide on which you want to place the CD audio track.

2. Choose Insert | Movies and Sounds | Play CD Audio Track. (The Play CD Audio Track is on the extended menu.)

3. In the Movie and Sound Options dialog box, shown here, set the options you want for playing the CD audio track:

You can choose to loop the CD until it is stopped. You can also specify the exact tracks with minutes and seconds that you want to play. You can generally find this information on the CD itself. Be sure to change the End Track setting.

If you leave it at 1, PowerPoint stops and ends the play in the same place—that is, it doesn't play anything. To play the first track, start at track 1 and end at track 2.

4. PowerPoint asks if you want the CD to play automatically when you display the slide. Click Yes to play the CD automatically. Click no if you want the CD to play only when you click the mouse.

PowerPoint places a CD icon, shown here, on the slide. To listen to the CD audio track in normal view, double-click the CD icon. Don't forget that you need to put the CD in your CD-ROM drive. If you are traveling, remember to take the CD with you!

Tip: To make the CD icon as inconspicuous as possible, you can animate it with the Appear effect and then set After Animation to Hide After Animation. The CD icon appears automatically for a second, starts to play the audio track, and then disappears.

You can change the play settings that you created. Choose Slide Show | Custom Animation and choose the Multimedia Settings tab. You will see settings just like those in the Movie and Sound Options dialog box. Here you can change the tracks you want to play, for example. You can also check the Play Using Animation Order check box to make available the options to continue playing the audio track as you change slides.

To play an audio track automatically when a slide starts and continue playing it to the next slide, use these settings:

1. On the Order & Timing tab, in the Start Animation section, check Automatically and set the seconds to 00:00.

2. On the Effects tab, set the Entry Animation & Sound to No Effect. (You can, if you wish, animate the icon.)

3. On the Multimedia Settings tab, check Play Using Animation Order. Also choose Continue Slide Show to continue the slide show while playing the audio track. Set the Stop Playing setting to After 2 Slides.

Test your settings in slide show view to make sure you like the results.

Showing Movies with Video Clips

You can also play video clips in your presentations. Video clips are AVI, MOV, or MPG (.mpeg, .mpe, or .mpg) files—electronic movies. They are usually videos of live scenes but can also be animated. Examples of videos you might use in a presentation are a short message from your CEO, a demonstration of a product, an example of how a product is produced, or a testimonial of a customer. Most videos should be custom-made to suit your needs. There are three ways to create a video clip:

- Internet video-camera kits let you record a video while sitting in front of your PC. They're intended mostly for sending videos of yourself while calling someone over the Internet. They include a small camera with a built-in microphone that you place on top of your monitor, facing you, and software to record the video into a digital file format. Prices range from under $100 to about $200. One example is QuickCam Home from Logitech (**www.Logitech.com**), but it works only with Windows 98.

- You can use a video capture device that captures analog videos created with a video camera or camcorder and converts them into digital format. Examples are Logitech QuickClip, Iomega Buz (**www.iomega.com**), or Alaris Quick-Video Transport (**www.alaris.com**). This software also compresses the video files, which is generally important since they quickly grow to an unmanageable size.

- You can create a video with a digital camcorder, which is like a digital camera except that it creates videos instead of photographs. Canon, Sony, Hitachi, and Sharp, among others, make these camcorders, which are quite expensive.

Most likely, you'll do none of the above and instead look for a professional service bureau that specializes in creating business or educational videos. To look on the Web, use a search engine to search for *digital video* and *service bureau*. If you already have a video that you want to use, you can convert it yourself using one of the video capture devices or ask a service bureau to convert it for you.

Video clips are typically compressed because without compression they are too large to store. There are many types of compression called *codecs* (which stands for compression/decompression). To see how many are on your system, choose Start | Settings | Control Panel. Double-click Multimedia. In the Multimedia dialog box, choose the Advanced tab and click the plus sign next to Video Compression Codecs to see a list. The beauty of codecs is that they decompress your video on the fly and then display it.

Once you have the video, you can add it to the Clip Gallery. See Chapter 5 for instructions.

To insert a video on a slide, follow these directions:

1. Display the slide.

2. Choose Insert | Movies and Sounds.

3. Choose Movie from Gallery if the video clip is in the Clip Gallery. Then locate the file you want, click it, and choose Insert Clip. Otherwise, choose Movie from File, locate the file, choose it, and click Open.

4. PowerPoint asks you if you want the movie to play automatically. Click Yes if you do. Click No if you want the movie to play only when you click its image.

You see the first frame of the video on your slide, as shown here. (Thanks to Kelly Planer of MBC Teleproductions [**www.mbctv.com**] for this animated video clip.) To view this slide in color, refer to number 122 in the Slide Gallery.

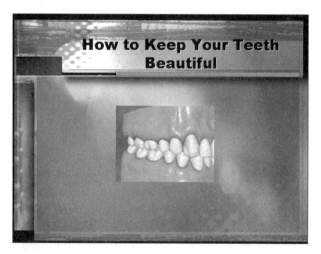

Once you have inserted the movie, you can watch it by double-clicking it.

Note that if the codec used by your video clip is not recognized by PowerPoint, you may still be able to insert it by choosing Insert | Object and choosing a different video player application. You can also use an AutoLayout that includes a video clip to insert a video.

The video clip will never cover your entire slide. In general, you won't get good results by enlarging it—you lose too much resolution, and the video starts to look grainy. However, you can adjust the video clip for the resolution of your screen. This is especially important if you are creating your presentation on a desktop with 1024×768 resolution but presenting it on a laptop with 800×600 resolution, for example. Follow these steps:

1. Choose Format | Picture to open the Format Picture dialog box.
2. Choose the Size tab.
3. Check the Best Scale for Slide Show box. This box scales any picture to the best scale for your screen's resolution. Then choose the proper resolution from the resolution drop-down box.
4. Click OK.

As with media clips, sounds, and so on, you can specify play settings. Choose Slide Show | Custom Animation and click the Multimedia Settings tab. You can choose to rewind the video, which is useful if you might play the video more than once during a presentation. You can also check Hide While Not Playing to hide the entire image until you click.

Professional Pointer

You need to test how this looks in slide show view. If hiding the image simply leaves a blank screen, you might want to keep the image on the screen.

Adding a Professional Touch with Narration

For a presentation that will run unattended at a kiosk or trade show, you may want to add narration to replace what you would say if you were there. PowerPoint lets you record narration that plays when you run the presentation.

Narration can add a professional touch. The problem is that poor narration is usually worse than no narration. Unless you can sound like those announcers on the radio, you should seriously think about hiring a professional to record the narration for your presentation. Remember that an unattended presentation will play over and over again. Not only will a professional have a better sounding voice, but he or she will likely have the use of a sound studio, professional recording equipment, and the best sound-editing software. You can contact a sound studio yourself to make the arrangements although your narrator probably has good contacts.

If you are looking for a professional narrator, you can try doing a search on the Web—use the keywords *professional, narrator,* and *announcer.* A number of individual narrators have their own Web sites. You may also want to consider a professional scriptwriter. An experienced outsider can often more easily envision the point of view of your intended audience and avoid technical language that you use everyday, but your audience may not understand.

You should ask for the recording in digital format, rather than on a cassette tape. (Otherwise, you need to digitize the tape yourself.) When you make arrangements for the narration, remember that you will eventually need a separate file for each slide. If necessary, you can divide the file yourself using sound-editing software, such as Creative WaveStudio. Most sound cards come with some sound-editing software.

While the exact steps depend on the software you are using, you can generally divide a file as follows:

1. Select part of the file and click Play. Do this, adjusting the amount you select, until you have the snippet you want.
2. Copy it to the clipboard.
3. Open a new file.
4. Paste the clipboard contents into the new file.
5. Save that file as slide 1, for example.

Once you have sound files for each file, you can attach them to the transition of each slide by choosing Slide Show | Slide Transition. In the Sound section of the Slide Transition dialog box, choose Other Sound at the bottom of the drop-down list. In the Add Sound dialog box, locate and choose your sound file and click OK. PowerPoint plays the slide file. Click Apply to return to your presentation.

If you do decide to record your own narration, here's the procedure:

1. Attach a microphone to the proper connector at the back of your computer. You may have to check with your computer manufacturer.
2. Choose Slide Show | Record Narration to open the Record Narration dialog box, shown in Figure 10-3. This dialog box displays the amount of free disk space and the number of minutes you can record before using up that space.

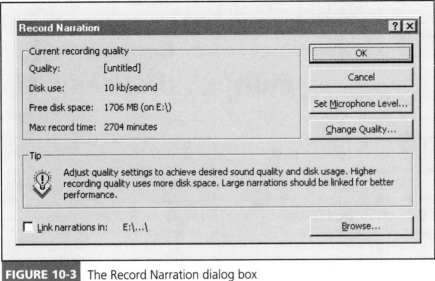

FIGURE 10-3 The Record Narration dialog box

3. Click Change Quality to open the Sound Selection dialog box, shown here:

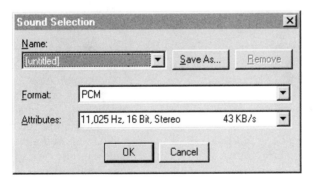

You can choose a sound quality from the Attributes drop-down box. Then click OK. Of course, the higher the quality, the fewer minutes you can record. Sound files take up a great deal of space.

4. For the first time you record, choose Set Microphone Level and follow the directions to set the proper microphone level for recording. Click OK.

Case Study in Multimedia Presenting

by Jim Endicott

It was February 1999—the event, the first year of the Presentation 99 Conference in Chicago. I had been asked to deliver three high-powered seminars to the conference attendees entitled "Presentation Survival Skills Seminars." Each dealt with different facets of presentation design, development, and media integration. There are several inherent challenges in this kind of assignment. First of all, some presenters don't have any idea that they're even in a jungle, and if they did, many don't care to be rescued. They're very comfortable with what they're doing. In the first few minutes, I clearly needed to reframe the role of the business presentation in corporate America today.

The second challenge of this type of seminar is that it's not like doing a presentation on rebuilding an automobile engine. Delivering presentations on the topic of dynamic presenting becomes somewhat of a self-fulfilling prophecy. If you can't deliver it, you sure as heck can't teach it. I think I'd rather that the hypothetical engine I just rebuilt broke down on a quiet country road—not in downtown Chicago!

Any good presentation is targeted at the specific expectations of your audiences. I needed to exceed their expectations from their initial entry into the room through my final closing comments. Here is what I did:

- **The template design**   I designed a unique presentation template background in Adobe PhotoShop. No off-the-shelf stock templates would fly with this audience. The template would quickly form their first impressions of my topic credibility and of me, before I could even say my first words. I played off the jungle metaphor while subtly integrating presentation-related elements and some key themes that we would cover. Doing this required not only having an understanding of the room environment issues but also an understanding of the electronic projector that would be used to support the event. Creating a template background that was too dark would ensure that all the creative, subtle detail would all but disappear in a lighter room or a dim projector image.

- **Ambiance created with music**   From the moment the attendees entered the room before the seminar, they were engaged not only with a uniquely designed template but also presentation-embedded jungle sounds. They looped continuously in the first frame until I made a mouse click to continue on. Engaging the senses is always key to creating interest with an audience, and it did the trick. Whenever possible I try to stack the deck in my favor to create positive impressions as a preemptive presentation tactic. Too often we wait well into the presentation to integrate elements that get our audience excited about things to come.

- **Strong use of graphical information** As a consultant, you don't stay in this industry very long unless you can challenge individuals and companies to move beyond the typical bullet slide into a stronger graphical reinforcement of their topics. You need to approach the slide content with bullets as a last resort. You need to challenge yourself to think about the word pictures the bullets are painting and how you can better portray the information as images that might be built on screen. My presentation focused on graphical portrayals of my content and design concepts at every opportunity. Lest anyone think you need only back up the clip art dump truck, believe me, this impresses no one. When's the last time you saw cheesy clip art in your company-printed collateral?

- **Video integration** As much as I'm comfortable in front of an audience, it's important to throw "change-ups" to an audience just like a baseball pitcher. If the audience knows where you're going with your presentation and how, it leaves very little for them to anticipate. For this reason, I scripted four sequences for a very funny friend, named Todd, to videotape. I gave him a jungle pith helmet, and he put on some jungle fatigues. Then, in a jungle-type outdoor setting, he delivered hilarious dialogs (with appropriate gaps left for my live responses). I later edited in my jungle sounds using Adobe Premier and created four final .AVI movie files that I embedded at strategic places during the presentation. I created a mock video-conference frame triggered automatically after entering the slide for the digital videos and practiced until my crisp responses created doubt in my audiences mind as to whether it was "live or Memorex." Todd introduced topics, and I delivered the content to

my audience. It was a very entertaining team effort.

- **The close** It's very true that the final impression you make during a presentation tends to last a long time in the hearts and minds of your audience. For that reason, I spent the last 60 minutes before my final seminar practicing a five-minute close. I'm sure the hotel workers wondered who this guy was pacing their back hallways talking to himself, but it was time well spent. Your close becomes equivalent in importance to the dismount for an Olympic gymnast: the audience may be impressed with your presentation, but you can ill afford not to "stick the landing." If you either fall flat on your face on the close—or worse yet, walk away from your "routine" with no close at all—it becomes a weak finale that will be judged harshly.

The feedback from the conference indicated I'd hit a home run and exceeded audience expectations, but preparing for the presentation took a great deal of time. Whether we like it or not, being a good presenter simply takes work. I've had some hits, and I've fallen short of my own expectations at times. But one thing is for sure—there's no such thing as *just* a presentation anymore. Careers and reputations hang in the balance more frequently than we'd like to admit.

Jim Endicott is the owner/manager of Distinction, a business communications company that provides creative and consulting support services. He assists business professionals in enhancing the content, tools, and techniques of effective presenting. Jim regularly writes articles for Presentations *magazine. He can be reached at 503-554-1203 or jim.endicott@ distinction-services.com.*

5. If you want to link narration as a separate file, check Link Narrations In and click Browse to choose the desired folder. If you use separate files, you have greater control, especially if you want to make changes in the file. Otherwise, narration is inserted on your slides as OLE (embedded) objects. Click OK.

6. PowerPoint puts you into slide show view automatically. Start narrating. Move through the slide show, narrating on each slide as desired. Note that other sounds do not play while you're recording. If you have other sounds in your presentation, run through the presentation afterward to make sure there are no conflicts.

7. When you reach the end of the presentation, PowerPoint asks you if you want to save the slide timings as well as the narration. If you save the timing, you can play the presentation automatically using the exact same timings for each slide. Click Yes to save the timings. Click No to save only the narration.

Professional Pointer

Even if you are going to present your slide show yourself, you can record narration for practice purposes. When you run through the presentation and listen to the narration you created, you will get an excellent idea of how it all will sound. Awkward moments will become apparent, and you will notice which slides (and their accompanying narration) are boring or unclear. You can then go back and make adjustments.

Cross-Reference: Setting timing for a presentation is covered in Chapter 15.

Run the presentation in slide show view again to listen to the narration. It's a lot of fun!

Cross-Reference: In Chapter 15, I recommend recording narration as a practice technique when preparing for actual presentation.

It's easy to make a mistake while narrating, and you might want to make changes, just as you make changes to any other part of your presentation. However, you wouldn't want to have to record the entire narration over from the beginning. Because the narration for each slide is separate, you can edit existing narration. You display the first slide that you want to edit and use the regular narration procedure for the slides you want to edit. Then advance to the next slide and press ESC.

Let's say you want to redo the narration for slides 2 and 3. Display slide 2. Start narrating using the steps just previously listed. Narrate for slides 2 and 3. When you get to slide 4, press ESC.

You have the option to run the presentation without the narration if you want. For example, you might want to record narration only as a backup (for when you go on vacation) for a presentation that you usually present yourself. You might also have a presentation that is sometimes run automatically and sometimes given by a presenter. Or, as explained earlier, you might record narration as practice to see how long the presentation will take and how it will sound. To run the slide show without the narration, choose Slide Show I Set Up Show. Check Show Without Narration and click OK.

Professional Skills Summary

In this chapter you learned how to add sounds, music, video, and narration to include multimedia effects in a presentation. You can use PowerPoint's sound effects, sounds or music from files, or sounds or music from the Clip Gallery. The most common type of sound and music files are WAV and MIDI files. You can insert a media clip object that the Media Player program can play on a slide. PowerPoint can play a CD soundtrack as well for a full-length, full-bodied sound.

You can show a small video clip on a slide. The video clip is attached to an individual slide and played when you display that slide. Video clips can add an extra dimension to a presentation, which is, in essence, mostly static.

You can record narration for all the slides in a presentation. Narration is usually used for self-running presentations. Your presentation will then play with that narration.

In the next chapter, I explain how to create hyperlinks, use action buttons to control your presentation, and move data in and out of PowerPoint.

Part III
Effectively Managing and Conveying Your Presentation

Chapter 11: Interacting with the Rest of the World

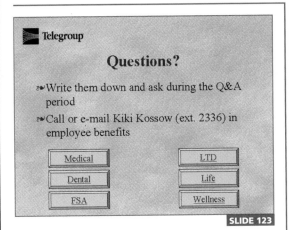

SLIDE 123

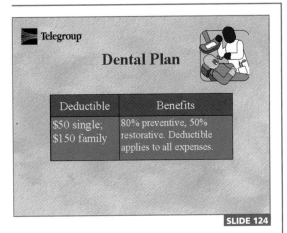

SLIDE 124

You can create hyperlinks to anywhere else in your presentation, to another presentation, to another file, or to the Web and attach them to text or objects. This slide uses text on AutoShapes to provide an easy way for the presenter to go back to earlier sections of a presentation during the question and answer period. See "Creating a Hyperlink to Another Slide in Your Presentation."

When you create a hyperlink to another slide in a presentation, you need a return trip ticket. Here, the presenter wanted the hyperlink to be unobtrusive so the audience wouldn't be distracted during the presentation. The hyperlink is attached to the graphic of the dentist. See "Creating a Hyperlink to Another Slide in Your Presentation."

In an audience-controlled presentation, such as one at an employee information center, you can include an e-mail link that instantly opens a new message to the specified individual. Here, employees can e-mail a representative in the Human Resources department if they have questions on the new employee benefit plan. See "Creating an E-mail from a Slide" and Figure 11-3.

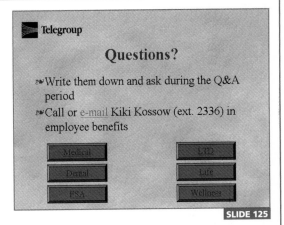

SLIDE 125

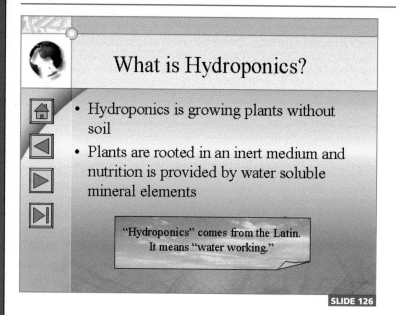

You can create action buttons with familiar navigation symbols. They are especially valuable for self-running presentations where you want to give some control to your viewers. Here you see actions buttons that will take you home (to the first slide), to the previous and next slides, and to the last slide. See "Using Action Buttons to Move Around in a Presentation."

Chapter 12: **Collaborating with Other People**

PowerPoint offers several features to help you collaborate on a presentation. You can insert comments for others to read. Comments are usually simple text boxes, but you can reformat them as whimsical callouts, as shown here. See "Adding Comments to a Presentation."

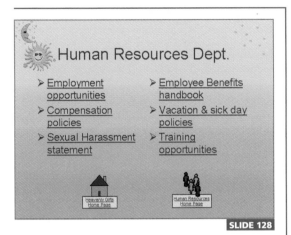

SLIDE 128

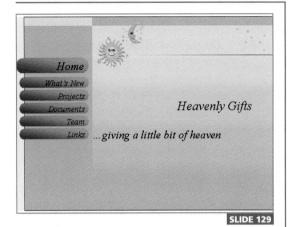

SLIDE 129

When you use PowerPoint to create a Web site, you need to include links on each page so viewers can navigate to other pages. Most pages should also have a hyperlink back to the home page. See "Using PowerPoint to Create Web Pages" and Figure 13-1.

You can use PowerPoint's Corporate Web Site presentation as a starting point for creating your own presentation. See "Using PowerPoint to Create Web Pages" and Figure 13-2.

SLIDE 130

SLIDE 131

Even before you publish a presentation in HTML format, you can preview it as a Web page. PowerPoint creates navigational aids for your viewer. See "Using PowerPoint to Create Web Pages" and Figure 13-3.

When you want to place a presentation on a Web site, browsers can view your presentation using the navigational tools. See "Creating a Viewer-Controlled Presentation" and Figure 13-7.

Chapter 14: **Customizing PowerPoint**

SLIDE 132

You can customize PowerPoint's menus to serve you better. You can add an entirely new menu or just add a menu item to an existing menu. Here you see a shortcut menu that has been customized by adding the Slide Master item. This menu appears when you right-click a slide's background.

Thanks to Human Factors International (HFI) for this slide. You can contact HFI at 800-242-4480 or visit the Web site at www.humanfactors.com.

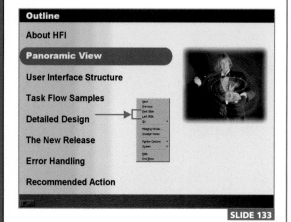

SLIDE 133

Here is another example of a shortcut menu. This shortcut menu appears when you right-click during a slide show. Two menu items, First Slide and Last Slide, have been added to help you more easily navigate through your presentation. Such customization can help you create a more professional impression by offering you quick, smooth alternatives during a presentation.

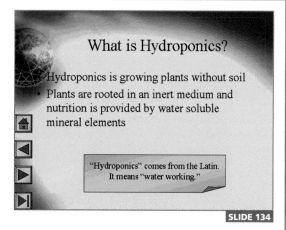

SLIDE 134

You can record macros to automate the repetitive tasks of creating and editing presentations. Here you see the results of a macro that formats the fill of selected objects with a two-color gradient. For more information on recording and using macros, see "Working with Macros."

Chapter 15: **Preparing for the Perfect Presentation**

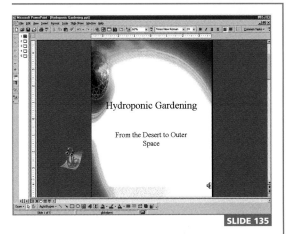

SLIDE 135

If you want to present using overhead transparencies, you should use a lighter background than you would when presenting from a computer. Here you see a design template that has been designed specifically for printing overheads and handouts. See "Using Overhead Transparencies."

Thanks to Gary White of Interactive, Inc. (404-262-8784 or www.interactivevision.com) for this template, part of Volume I of their PresentationPro Library Series.

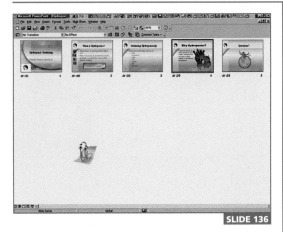

SLIDE 136

Rehearsing the timing of slide display is an important part of preparing for the actual presenting process. Here you see a short slide show with timing icons under each slide. See "Rehearsing Timings."

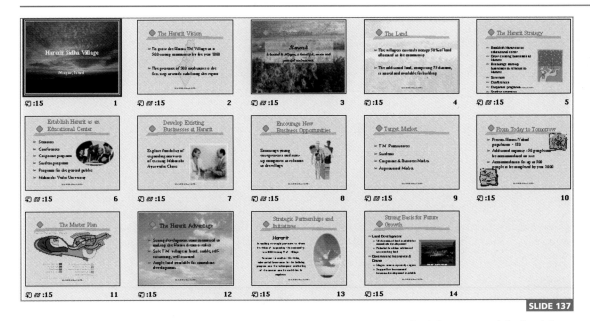

SLIDE 137

You can quickly specify the timing of slides in your show using the Apply to All button on the Slide Transition dialog box. Then make modifications as needed. Here, timings were set for 15 seconds with one click of a button. See "Assigning Timing to Slides" and Figure 15-3.

Thanks to Lee Cohen of Trendlines and Shorashim and David Doron of Hararit for this presentation.

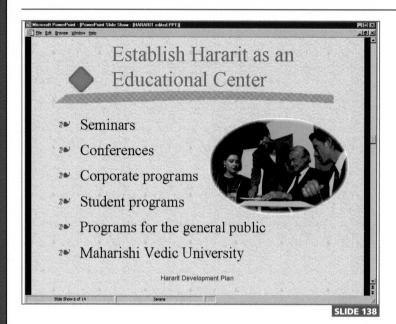

SLIDE 138

If your presentation will be viewed at a kiosk or a computer station, you can display the presentation in a window with a scrollbar, as shown here. The scrollbar lets individuals navigate through the slide show by themselves. See "Setting Slide Show Parameters" and Figure 15-5.

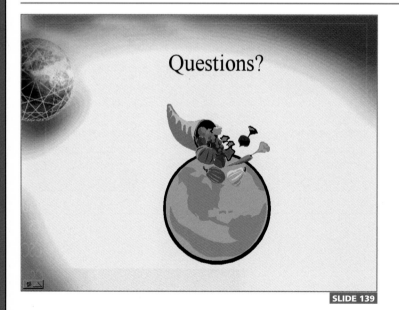

SLIDE 139

You can customize your presentation with a *custom show*, a presentation containing one or more slides that you show only when you choose to. Here you see a slide that can be used when you have time to take corrections. See "Creating a Custom Show" and Figure 15-8.

To emphasize certain points, you can annotate your slides as you present. These annotations are temporary. See "Marking Slides as You Present" and Figure 16-4.

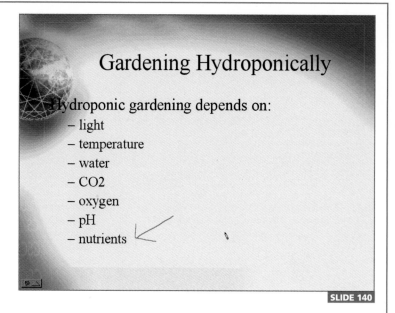

SLIDE 140

Because you don't have much control when you draw with a mouse, be careful not to scribble!

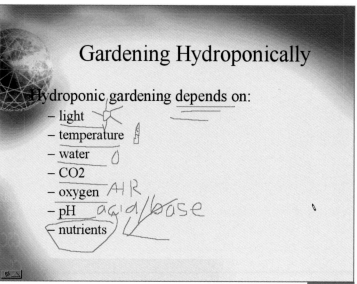

SLIDE 141

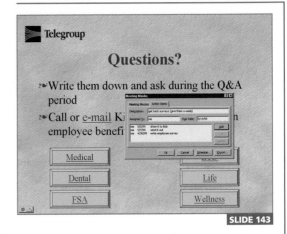

SLIDE 142

During your presentation, you can open the Meeting Minder to take minutes. Learn when this is appropriate and useful—see "Taking Minutes" and Figure 16-5.

SLIDE 143

If your presentation is part of a brainstorming session or department meeting, you might want to jot down action steps that arise during the discussion. You can specify a task and a due date, and then assign the task. See "Creating an Action List" and Figure 16-6.

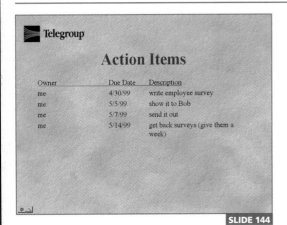

SLIDE 144

When you create action items, PowerPoint automatically places them on a new slide at the end of the presentation. Action item slides come without fancy formatting, but your attendees can view them and discuss their contents easily. See "Creating an Action List" and Figure 16-7.

chapter 11

Interacting with the Rest of the World

In this chapter, you:

- Hyperlink to anywhere
- Use action buttons to control your presentation
- Move data from application to application

These days, the whole world is interconnected. A presentation cannot stand isolated any longer. A question from the audience can bring up the need to access data from another presentation, another application (such as a spreadsheet), or from your company's Web site. If you're making a presentation to a customer, your customer might express an interest in any number of other products you sell, and you need to be ready to provide pertinent information at a moment's notice. However, you don't want to create a huge presentation with all the possibilities and make your customer sit through everything. In this chapter you learn how to use hyperlinks and action buttons to create the ultimately flexible presentation. You also learn how to manage data from other presentations and applications.

Hyperlinking to Anywhere on Command

A hyperlink is a command to go to another location. That other location can be another slide in the same presentation, a slide in another presentation, a file in another application, or a location on a Web site or intranet. You can even go to an e-mail address. In other words, you can go anywhere.

You attach a hyperlink to an existing object—text, AutoShapes, a table, a chart, or a picture. Click the hyperlink to go to the specified location. When you attach a hyperlink to text, PowerPoint underlines the text and displays it in the accent and hyperlink color of the presentation's color scheme. When you click a text hyperlink, PowerPoint changes the color of the text to the accent and followed hyperlink color of the color scheme. Be sure to check out how this these two colors look in your presentation. They may lack the necessary contrast to show up clearly.

Cross-Reference: Chapter 6 explains how to customize the colors in a color scheme.

You can use hyperlinks only in slide show view. They are not active in normal, slide sorter, or the other views.

Adding Flexibility with Hyperlinks

Think of hyperlinks as a way of providing supporting information for a presentation. In the days of paper presentations, you carried along with you reams of additional data—perhaps sample swatches, price sheets, delivery schedules, and so on. Now you can include hyperlinks to the electronic versions (although nothing beats the feel of a real piece of carpet). Moreover, you can include hyperlinks to various pages on your Web site to add a truly unlimited potential for information.

Creating a hyperlink to another slide in your presentation

A common use for hyperlinks is to let you quickly jump around in a complex presentation. You may be able to anticipate that your audience will have additional questions on a topic when you're done. On the last slide, for example, you can provide hyperlinks back to each major section of the presentation. You can also create a custom presentation that lets you show some slides to one audience and other slides to another audience.

Cross-Reference: Custom presentations are covered in Chapter 15.

To attach a hyperlink to an object that connects to a location in the current presentation, select the object to which you want to attach the hyperlink. Then choose Insert | Hyperlink (or press CTRL-K) to open the Insert Hyperlink dialog box. In the Link To bar on the left of the dialog box, click Place in This Document to display the options shown in Figure 11-1.

Professional Pointer

When you add a hyperlink to a presentation, you must be careful that the target of the hyperlink is available. If you are giving the presentation offsite using a laptop, all the targets need to be on the laptop as well, unless your laptop is actively connected to the Internet. An alternative is to copy the Web site documents you think you will need to your laptop and hyperlink to those documents. The advantage is that you don't have to depend on getting a good connection to the Internet.

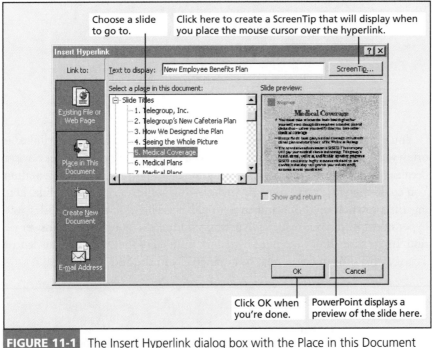

Choose a slide to go to.

Click here to create a ScreenTip that will display when you place the mouse cursor over the hyperlink.

Click OK when you're done.

PowerPoint displays a preview of the slide here.

FIGURE 11-1 The Insert Hyperlink dialog box with the Place in this Document button active

You should now switch to slide show view and test the hyperlink. If you selected text, make sure it is still readable in its new color, both before and after you click it, as mentioned earlier.

When you test the hyperlink, you will end up in the new location. You might wonder how you get back again. Usually you want to create a complementary hyperlink to bring you back to the original location.

There's an art to designing hyperlinks. You may want some hyperlinks to be obvious. You may wish others to be undetectable until you use them. (You may not want your potential client asking where each and every hyperlink goes to.) For example, you can place several obvious hyperlinks on a slide near the end of the presentation that simply says "Questions?" Here you pause and answer questions. You might have a series of text boxes, naming the topics you covered, hyperlinked back to those topics, as shown in the example here. To view this slide in color, refer to number 123 in the Slide Gallery.

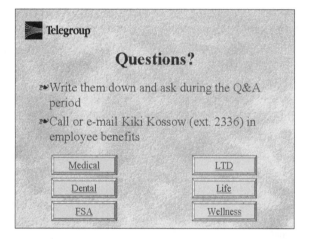

You should have hyperlinks on each of the slides to which you hyperlinked to bring you back to the Questions slide, but you wouldn't want them to be obvious because they might be distracting during the main portion of the presentation. You could therefore attach those hyperlinks to graphic objects on the slide. During the presentation, your audience would have no clue that the slides were hyperlinked until you used the hyperlinks during the question and answer period. In the slide shown next, the hyperlink is added to the graphic of the dentist. To view this slide in color, refer to number 124 in the Slide Gallery.

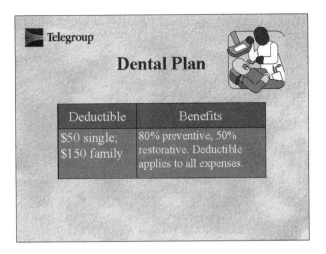

Creating a hyperlink to a slide in another presentation

You can create supporting presentations that contain information that you think you may need. You can then hyperlink to those presentations as long as they are available from the computer you are using.

To create a hyperlink to a slide in another presentation, select the text or object you want to attach the hyperlink to. Choose Insert Hyperlink to open the Insert Hyperlink dialog box. In the Link To bar, choose Existing File or Web Page, as shown in Figure 11-2.

When you click Bookmark in the Insert Hyperlink dialog box, PowerPoint opens the Select Place in Document dialog box, shown here:

Professional Pointer

Remember that hyperlinks attached to text clearly appear as hyperlinks. Hyperlinks attached to graphic objects are not obvious until you use them.

Select Place in Document

Select an existing place in the document:

- Slide Titles
  - 1. Hararit Sidha Village
  - 2. The Hararit Vision
  - 3. The Environment
  - 4. The Environment
  - 5. The Hararit Strategy
  - 6. Establish Hararit as an Educational Center
  - 7. Grow Existing Opportunities at Hararit
  - 8. Encourage start-up businesses to relocate to Hararit
  - 9. Target Market
  - 10. From Today to Tomorrow
  - 11. From Today to Tomorrow
  - 12. The Hararit Advantage
  - 13. Strategic Partnerships and Initiatives
  - 14. Strategic Partnerships and Initiatives
  - 15. The Leadership

OK   Cancel

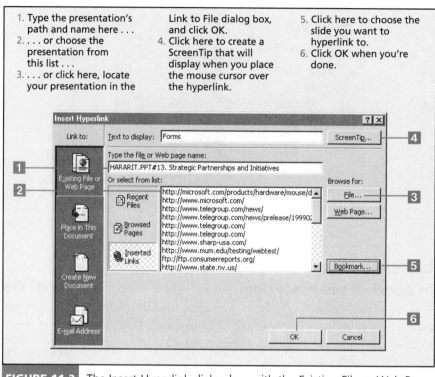

1. Type the presentation's path and name here . . .
2. . . . or choose the presentation from this list . . .
3. . . . or click here, locate your presentation in the

Link to File dialog box, and click OK.
4. Click here to create a ScreenTip that will display when you place the mouse cursor over the hyperlink.

5. Click here to choose the slide you want to hyperlink to.
6. Click OK when you're done.

FIGURE 11-2 The Insert Hyperlink dialog box with the Existing File or Web Page button active

Tip: When you hyperlink to another presentation, you can feel free to go to any slide in that presentation and even page through the entire presentation. Pressing ESC brings you back to your original point in the first presentation.

Choose the slide you want to hyperlink to and click OK. PowerPoint identifies the slides by their number and title. If your slides don't have titles, you'll need to know the slide number.

Switch to slide show view to test out the hyperlink. When you click the hyperlink, PowerPoint sends you to the specified slide in the other presentation. Press ESC to automatically return to your original point.

Creating a hyperlink to another file or a Web page

You can hyperlink to any other file, even in another application. For example, you can hyperlink to a word processing document, a spreadsheet, or a CAD drawing that might contain additional details your audience may be interested in. You can also hyperlink to a Web page, which is, after all, just another file.

Hyperlinking to another file or Web page is similar to hyperlinking to another slide in a presentation. Follow these steps:

1. Select the object you want to attach the hyperlink to.

2. Choose Insert | Hyperlink. (You can refer back to Figure 11-2 for the Insert Hyperlink dialog box.)

3. In the Link To bar, choose Existing File or Web Page.

4. Type the filename and path in the text box, choose it from the list, or click either File or Web Page to browse to the file or Web page. If you click Web Page, you should already be connected to the Internet. PowerPoint opens your browser. In your browser, locate the Web page you want, by typing the URL, using the Favorites feature, or using the list of recently visited Web sites. Then switch back to PowerPoint by choosing your presentation's button on the Windows taskbar or by closing your browser. The URL is now displayed in the text box.

5. Click ScreenTip to enter a label that will be displayed when you place the mouse cursor over the hyperlink. Without a ScreenTip, PowerPoint uses the path or URL of the file or Web page.

6. Click OK when you're done.

As with all hyperlinks, you should go into slide show view and test the hyperlink. PowerPoint opens your browser and links you to the URL. You can close your browser to return to your presentation or use the Windows taskbar button.

> **Tip:** You can type a URL on a slide. PowerPoint recognizes URLs and automatically creates a hyperlink.

Creating a hyperlink to a new file

You can also use a hyperlink to open a new file. You might want to open a new file if your presentation is part of an in-house working session and you want to have a place to enter ideas as they come up. Here's how it works:

1. Select an object for the hyperlink.

2. Choose Insert Hyperlink.

3. In the Link To bar, choose Create New Document. The Insert Hyperlink dialog box looks like this:

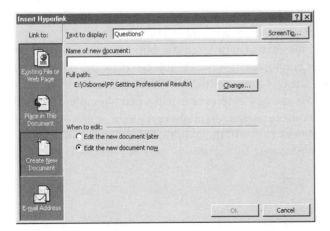

4. In the Name of New Document text box, type the name of the file you want to create. You determine the type of document by the filename extension. For example, if you name the file **New Ideas.doc**, then you will create a Microsoft Word document. To change the location from the path listed, click Change. You can then find a new location and type a name for the file in a dialog box.

5. Choose when to edit the file. If you choose to edit the file now, PowerPoint opens the file. You can create a framework for inserting those new ideas, for example, such as headings of your major topics. Save the file and close it. When you show the presentation, your hyperlink will open the file again as you saved it. If you choose to edit the document later, PowerPoint will open it the first time you try out the hyperlink in slide show view (which should be before you actually give the final presentation). (If you are opening a new PowerPoint presentation, choose to edit the slide now. If you try to edit it later in slide show view, PowerPoint creates a new presentation with no slides and immediately returns you to your original presentation.)

6. Click OK when you're done.

Once you create the new document, the hyperlink is connected to it. You can open the file any time you use the hyperlink. To return to your presentation, use the Windows taskbar. Be sure to choose the taskbar button that says PowerPoint Slide Show, not the button that says Microsoft PowerPoint.

Creating an e-mail from a slide

You have probably seen Web sites that let you instantly e-mail the sponsoring company. You click an image on the Web page, and your e-mail software opens with the correct e-mail address already in the message dialog box. You can do the same on a PowerPoint page. You would use this technique for self-running presentations when you want potential customers or other viewers to e-mail you with questions or for further information. Be sure to check that this works properly. Obviously, you need an e-mail program and an active Internet connection for this to work. Once you get it working, it's a great tool for creating an interactive presentation.

You'll find it easy to set up this kind of system over a company intranet. For example, you may have a networked computer set up with presentations on various topics for employees to view. Or you can place the presentations on an employees-only area of your company's Web site or intranet. One could be a presentation on the new employee benefits plan—employees could e-mail their questions. Another presentation might present the employee suggestion program and ask employees to e-mail their suggestions. The possibilities are endless.

Here are the steps:

1. Select any object on a slide.
2. Choose Insert | Hyperlink.
3. In the Insert Hyperlink dialog box, choose E-mail Address from the Link To bar. You see the dialog box shown here:

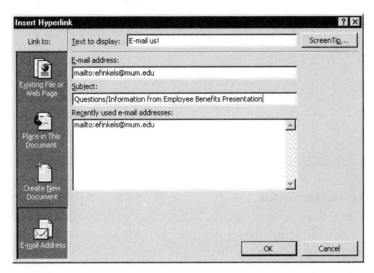

4. In the E-mail Address text box, type the e-mail address you want the e-mail to go to.
5. In the Subject text box, type a subject. You can insert a general subject that will let you know which presentation the e-mail came from so that you can distinguish it from other e-mail you receive.
6. If you wish, choose ScreenTip and type a ScreenTip to appear when you place the mouse cursor over the hyperlink. Otherwise, PowerPoint uses the e-mail address and subject.
7. Click OK.

Figure 11-3 shows an example of a slide with an e-mail link. Employees viewing the presentation on their own can click to e-mail the appropriate person in the Human Resources department. To view this slide in color, refer to number 125 in the Slide Gallery.

The following illustration shows a new message created using an e-mail hyperlink.

Editing hyperlinks

You will sometimes need to edit a hyperlink. Any of the settings that you create in the Insert Hyperlink dialog box can be changed. To edit a hyperlink, right-click it and choose Hyperlink | Edit Hyperlink. PowerPoint opens the Edit Hyperlink dialog box, which is the same as the Insert Hyperlink dialog box. Make any desired changes and click OK.

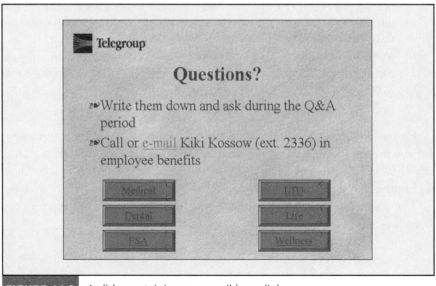

FIGURE 11-3 A slide containing an e-mail hyperlink

To remove a hyperlink, right-click it and choose Hyperlink | Remove Hyperlink. You can play a sound or highlight a hyperlink to draw attention to its action. The next section explains how to attach actions to a hyperlink.

Using Action Buttons for Ultimate Control

Action buttons are graphics on a slide that control actions you specify. You can use them to create hyperlinks, to play movies or sounds, or to open applications. Action buttons have the following advantages:

- They include graphic symbols that are familiar to users from Web sites for going back, forward, to the first slide (home), and so on. Action buttons are therefore ideal for self-running presentations at a kiosk or on a Web site because their controls are familiar.

- They often look more professional than graphics you would create yourself. When they are used during a presentation, they appear to be depressed, similar to buttons that have been clicked on Web sites.

- You can play a sound while executing an action.

- You can use action buttons to run movies or play music.

- You can use action buttons to run macros or programs.

- You can choose whether clicking the button or passing the mouse cursor over it executes the action.

Using Action Buttons to Move Around in a Presentation

Action buttons don't need to be limited to self-running presentations. You can also use them for presentations that you show. The buttons are cute but professional looking. Whenever you want navigation in a presentation to be obvious, you can use an action button. Here's how to add an action button:

1. Display the slide where you want to place the action button.

2. Choose Slide Show | Action Buttons. (It's on the extended menu.) On the submenu shown next, choose one of the buttons. Each button has a ScreenTip so you can tell its intended purpose.

Tip: Don't forget to align and distribute your action buttons. You can format them just like any other AutoShape. Chapter 5 explains how.

3. To insert the button in the default size, click the slide. Otherwise, drag the shape to the desired size. You can adjust the size and shape later.

4. PowerPoint opens the Mouse Click tab of the Action Settings dialog box, shown in Figure 11-4, with a suggested hyperlink based on the action button you inserted. If necessary, click the Hyperlink To drop-down list and choose another option. Click OK.

When you use the Hyperlink To drop-down list, not only can you choose another slide option, but you have all the options you would have if you attached a hyperlink to an existing object, as described earlier in this chapter:

- **Slide**   Choose any slide in the presentation by its number and title.

- **URL**   Type a URL.

- **Other PowerPoint Presentation**   You can locate any other presentation and can then choose any slide from that presentation.

- **Other File**   You can choose any file you have access to.

As with regular hyperlinks, you should always go to slide show view and test how the hyperlink works and how to get back to your presentation. Here you see

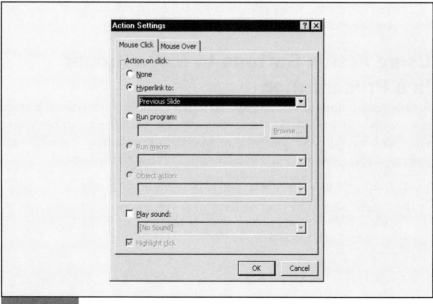

FIGURE 11-4   The Action Settings dialog box with the Mouse Click tab on top

a slide with a set of action buttons along the left side. It looks somewhat like a Web page. To view this slide in color, refer to number 126 in the Slide Gallery.

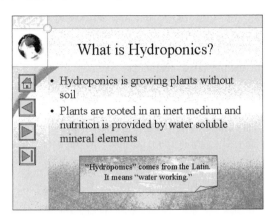

By default, the Action Settings dialog box opens with the Mouse Click tab on top. You activate the hyperlink you create by clicking it with the mouse. The Action Settings dialog box also has a Mouse Over tab, which is identical to the Mouse Click tab except that it creates actions that you activate by passing the mouse cursor over the action button.

Most of the time, you'll use the Mouse Click tab. You certainly don't want to accidentally move elsewhere in a presentation because you (or someone else if you have a self-running presentation) happen to move the mouse over the action button.

> **Tip:** You can put an action button on the slide master so it will appear on every slide.

A good use for the Move Over tab might be to play a sound file that says, "We need your comment" or something similar. (You probably have this file, ycomment.wav, on your hard drive. Look in C:\Multimedia Files\Music.) The next section explains how to attach a sound to an action button.

Playing a sound for an action button

At the same time that the action button executes a hyperlink, it can play a sound. While you can attach only one action to an object, playing a sound is an exception. To make an action button play a sound, check Play Sound on either the Mouse Click or the Mouse Over tab. Then choose a sound from the drop-down list. Choose Other Sound at the bottom of the list to locate any sound file on your system.

Using action settings for hyperlinks

You can use the Action Settings dialog box for hyperlinks that you create with the Insert | Hyperlink command. Select the hyperlink and choose Slide Show | Action Settings. You can then add a sound, for example.

If the hyperlink is an object (that is, not text), you can highlight it when it is clicked or when the mouse cursor is passed over it. This technique is a traditional way to emphasize a hyperlink. Here's how highlighting is generally used:

- If you choose to highlight the object when the mouse cursor is passed over it, the object blinks once in a contrasting color any time the mouse cursor passes over the object. The highlighting confirms to the user that this object is active and suggests that clicking it will perform some action.

- If you choose to highlight the object when it is clicked, the object blinks once when clicked and then immediately performs the action. This confirms to the user that the click "took," that is, was successful.

Using action settings to run a macro

You can run a run a macro by clicking or passing the mouse cursor over an object. Using an object or an action button to run a macro lets you execute complex actions with a click of a button. To do this procedure, you first need to create the macro.

Cross-Reference: For more about macros, see Chapter 14.

Here's how to use action settings to run a macro:

1. Select the text or object you want to use.
2. Choose Slide Show | Action Settings.
3. Choose Run Macro on either the Mouse Click or Mouse Over tab.
4. From the drop-down list, choose the macro you want to use.
5. You can also play a sound if you wish.
6. Click OK.

Test the macro in slide show view. Note that some macros do not work in slide show view. For example, macros that edit a slide will not work in slide show view because you cannot edit in that view.

Using action settings to run a program

You can also use action settings to run a program. This technique simply opens another application—you can't open a specific file. Select an object, choose Slide Show | Action Settings, and choose Run a Program. Then click Browse. In the dialog box, locate the executable file (for example, winword.exe) in the Select a Program to Run dialog box, choose it, and click OK.

When you click the object in slide show view, PowerPoint opens the application. You can then use that application in any way you want. For example, you could record data in a spreadsheet file. Save the file and close the program to return to where you left off in your PowerPoint presentation.

Moving Data from Here to There

When you create a presentation, you often use data from other applications. You can copy data from other documents and paste it into PowerPoint, or you can drag-and-drop it. You can also import and export entire files. Another way to use data from other applications is to embed an object, such as a spreadsheet, into a presentation. Finally, you may want to investigate linking data from another document, so that it is always updated as the other document changes. Linking is especially valuable for price lists that change regularly.

Using the Clipboard and Drag-and-Drop

The Windows and Office clipboard lets you copy data from place to place, whether within a presentation, from one presentation to another, or from one application to another.

Cross-Reference: See Chapter 3 for more about the Windows and Office clipboards.

While I have already covered using the clipboard within PowerPoint, I have not talked much about using it to insert data from other applications. Deciding how to best bring data into your presentation will be based on an understanding of how PowerPoint formats it.

When you paste data from another application via the clipboard, it becomes part of your presentation. PowerPoint creates PowerPoint objects. For example, if you paste data from an Excel spreadsheet, PowerPoint creates text boxes and groups them. You can ungroup them if you wish. You can then format them as you would any other text boxes. However, if you want to enlarge the text, a common requirement, you then lose all the nicely lined up rows and columns. For this reason, you'll get best results when importing only a small amount of data from a spreadsheet. When pasting in text from a word processing document, keep in mind that you can't fit very much text on a single slide. Remember that spreadsheet and word processing documents almost always contain text that is too small for a slide—you'll need to enlarge the text once you paste it into your presentation.

You'll have different considerations when pasting in graphics. You often can't determine the size the graphic will be until it's pasted into PowerPoint. Enlarging a small bitmap graphic may make it grainy. Sometimes there will be a background that you don't want. You may need to make the background transparent. An outside graphic editing program may help you get the results you want.

Drag-and-drop works just like the clipboard. You can select data, text, or a graphic from one application, drag it down to the Windows taskbar onto your presentation's taskbar button, and your presentation will open. Continue to drag the data onto the slide and release the mouse button.

You can drag-and-drop an entire file onto a PowerPoint slide from Windows Explorer. Locate the file in Windows Explorer and size the window so that you can see both your slide and the icon for the file. Then drag the file onto your slide. This technique works well for graphic files.

Importing and Exporting Files

A different way of sharing information is to import and export files. For example, you might need to import a presentation created in another presentation program. You might also need to export a PowerPoint presentation into another format.

Importing files

You can create a PowerPoint presentation by simply opening a file from another application. This doesn't provide satisfactory results in many cases, but occasionally it will be just what you need to start you off on a presentation. For example, you can open a Microsoft Word document in PowerPoint, and PowerPoint converts it to a presentation. Don't forget to change the Files of Type drop-down list to All Files in the Open dialog box.

PowerPoint uses file converters to accomplish this conversion, and the converters are not all installed automatically. You may see the message shown next. Put your Microsoft Office CD in your CD-ROM drive and click Yes. PowerPoint will install the converter and convert the file.

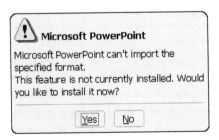

PowerPoint can also import presentations created in Harvard Graphics and Lotus Freelance. Usually PowerPoint can convert both the text and the graphics satisfactorily. If you have a presentation created in another program, you may have to convert the text and the graphics separately. You can probably save the presentation as a text (.txt) or Rich Text Format (.rtf) file. You can also use a graphics converter, but this converts an entire slide into a graphic file. You may not be able to edit or manipulate the slide in a meaningful way.

PowerPoint can open presentations saved as .wmf or .pct files. If the program can't save in those formats, try one of the other formats that PowerPoint can import.

PowerPoint can import the following graphic types without a filter:

- Enhanced Metafile (.emf)
- Graphics Interchange Format (.gif)
- Joint Photographic Experts Group (.jpg)
- Portable Network Graphics (.png)
- Windows Bitmap (.bmp, .rle, .dib)
- Windows Metafile (.wmf)

PowerPoint can also open graphic files in the following formats, but these require a special graphics filter. These are generally not installed automatically. When you try to open them, PowerPoint generally displays a message offering to install the filter. If not, you can start Setup from the Office CD-ROM and install the filter yourself.

- Computer Graphics Metafile (.cgm)
- CorelDRAW (.cdr)
- Encapsulated PostScript (.eps)
- FlashPix (.fpx)
- Hanako (.jsh, jah, and .jbh)
- Kodak Photo CD (.pcd)
- Macintosh PICT (.pct)
- PC Paintbrush (.pcx)
- Tagged Image File Format (.tif)
- WordPerfect Graphics (.wpg)

> **Tip:** The Microsoft Office Update Web site has additional graphics filters. Start at **www.microsoft.com**.

Exporting files

PowerPoint can also export to different file types. Typically, PowerPoint is not as generous in export capabilities as it is in its importing capabilities. For example, PowerPoint can't save a presentation as Harvard Graphics or Lotus Freelance presentations. However, you do have a number of options when exporting to different file types, as explained next.

- Web page (HTML)—for more information, see Chapter 13.

- Several older versions of PowerPoint so you can give your presentations to users who don't have the latest version. (Remember that PowerPoint 2000 is compatible with PowerPoint 97. You only need to save in an older version for someone using a version prior to PowerPoint 97.)

- Several graphic formats: GIF, JPEG, PNG, BMP, TIFF, TGA, and WMF. PowerPoint asks if you want to save the entire presentation or only the current slide. Whichever you choose, PowerPoint creates a graphic file from an entire slide. If you save the entire presentation, PowerPoint automatically creates a subfolder with the same name as your presentation and places the graphic files in the subfolder.

- Rich Text Format (RTF). Saves only the text, but preserves some of the text formatting.

Cross-Reference: These options are discussed in more detail in Chapter 1.

Inserting OLE Objects

When you insert an object into PowerPoint, you are embedding the object. The object, while part of your presentation, retains an "awareness" of its original application. When you double-click the object, the original application opens within PowerPoint and you use the menus and toolbars of that application to edit the object. To return to PowerPoint menus, click anywhere outside the objects. Embed an object when you have no need to update the data from the original source document. There are three main ways of embedding an object:

Tip: If you insert a Microsoft Excel worksheet, PowerPoint inserts the entire workbook but can display only one worksheet at a time. To display a different worksheet, double-click the object and click a different worksheet tab to activate it. Click outside the object to return to PowerPoint. You will now see the new worksheet displayed.

- Choose Insert | Object. In the Insert Object dialog box, either choose Create New to create a new object and choose the type of object you want to create, or choose Create from File to embed an existing file and choose an existing file (using the Browse button). Click OK.

- Double-click a placeholder on a slide—chart, organization chart, media clip, or object.

- Go to the source document, select the data you want to embed, and copy it to the clipboard. Return to PowerPoint and choose Edit | Paste Special. In the Paste Special dialog box, choose Paste. In the As box, choose the type of object you want to create. Click OK. Use this method to create an object from part of a file.

Inserting objects has been discussed in several chapters in this book. For example, Chapter 8 discussed inserting organization chart and chart objects, and Chapter 10 covered inserting Media Clip objects.

Linking Objects

If you need to update the data from its original source, you should link an object. Linked data is not actually part of your presentation. Instead, PowerPoint stores the location of the data and only displays it. Linked objects can help reduce the size of a file, but the main reason to link is to keep your data current. Each time you open the presentation, PowerPoint reloads the file from the source, giving you the most current data. Also, if the source changes while the presentation is open, PowerPoint updates the data on the spot. There are two ways to insert a linked object:

- Choose Insert | Object. In the Insert Object dialog box, either choose Create New to create a new object and choose the type of object you want to create, or choose Create from File to embed an existing file and choose an existing file (using the Browse button). Check Link and click OK.

- Go to the source document, select the data you want to embed, and copy it to the clipboard. Return to PowerPoint and choose Edit | Paste Special. In the Paste Special dialog box, choose Paste Link. In the As box, choose the type of object you want to create. Click OK. Use this method to create an object from part of a file.

Links need to be well taken care of. Because PowerPoint stores the location of the source file, if that source file is moved, PowerPoint cannot maintain the link. If your slide doesn't properly display a linked object, or you get a message that PowerPoint cannot find the object, you have a broken link. Choose Edit | Links. Use the Links dialog box as shown in Figure 11-5 to reconnect the linked object. You can choose whether to update the link automatically or manually.

Managing Files

When you create presentations, you often collect numerous supporting files as well, especially graphic files. Managing your files is an important part of creating a presentation. Chapter 1 contains some tips for saving files so you can easily find them again. Here I discuss techniques for finding files.

Finding files

You can use the Open dialog box to search for files either on your hard drive or on a network. In the Open dialog box, choose Tools | Find to open the Find dialog box, shown in Figure 11-6.

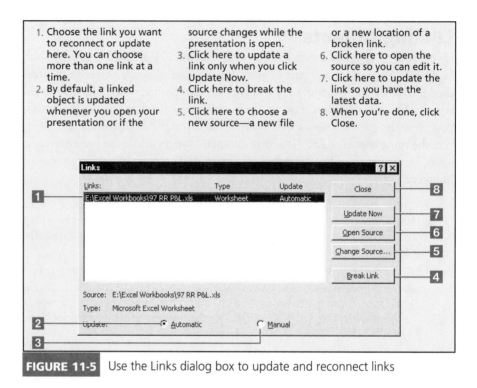

1. Choose the link you want to reconnect or update here. You can choose more than one link at a time.
2. By default, a linked object is updated whenever you open your presentation or if the

source changes while the presentation is open.
3. Click here to update a link only when you click Update Now.
4. Click here to break the link.
5. Click here to choose a new source—a new file

or a new location of a broken link.
6. Click here to open the source so you can edit it.
7. Click here to update the link so you have the latest data.
8. When you're done, click Close.

FIGURE 11-5 Use the Links dialog box to update and reconnect links

Once you have specified the criteria in the Find dialog box and clicked Find Now, PowerPoint reopens the Open dialog box with a list of presentations, or other files, that meet your criteria so you can open the file you want.

Many of the properties in the Properties drop-down list come from the Properties dialog box, discussed in the next section.

Setting file properties

You can set properties for any Microsoft Office file to help you find the file again later, using the Find dialog box. There are two ways to open the Properties dialog box shown here:

- From within the file, choose File | Properties. (It's on the expanded menu.)

1. PowerPoint provides a default criterion here.
2. Choose an operator here. "And" means the search must fulfill all criteria. "Or" means the
   search must fulfill any of the criteria.
3. Choose a property from the drop-down list.
4. Specify the condition here.
5. Enter a value here.
6. Click here to add the critera to the list at the top.
7. Specify where to look here.
8. Check this box to search subfolders.
9. Click here to save the search criteria.
10. Click here to edit saved search criteria.
11. Click here to start searching.

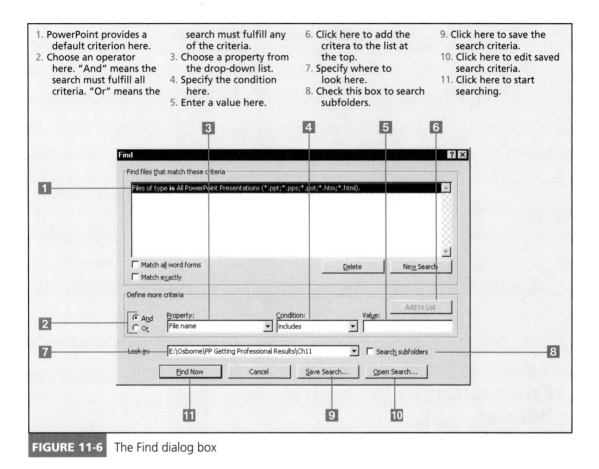

FIGURE 11-6   The Find dialog box

- From another file, click Open on the Standard toolbar and navigate to the file. In the Open dialog box, choose Tools | Properties.

Most often, you will use the Summary tab. Here you can add the properties listed, such as subject, manager, company, and category. You can also add keywords. You can then search for the presentation by any of these properties. For more control, choose the Custom tab, shown next with two custom properties added.

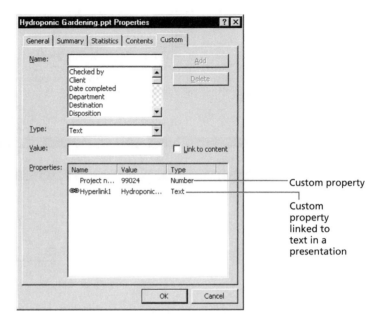

Custom property

Custom property linked to text in a presentation

PowerPoint offers a long list of suggested properties, such as Checked By, Client, Department, Document Number, and Project. You can create your own properties as well. For example, you could use custom properties to assign project numbers.

An interesting feature of the Properties dialog box is the ability to link properties to text in your presentation. (Unfortunately, you cannot link properties to anything except text.) Once you create this link, you cannot only use the property to find the presentation, but you can quickly go to the linked text. Choose Edit | Go to Property. In the Properties dialog box, choose the property you want and click OK.

To add a custom property, choose File | Properties and click the Custom tab. If you want to link a property, select the desired text first. Then follow these steps:

1. In the Name text box, choose a property from the list or type in your own property name.

2. In the Type drop-down list, choose Text, Date, Number, or Yes or No.

3. In the Value text box, type the value for the property. For example, if your property is a project number, type the project number for the presentation.

4. Click Add.

5. To link the property, check Link to Content. (This checkbox is available only if you previously selected some text in the presentation.)

6. Click OK.

Cross-Reference: Chapter 15 explains how to use Pack and Go to collect all the files you need when you go on the road with a presentation.

Using the Find and Properties features of PowerPoint will go a long way to helping you keep track all your presentations.

Professional Skills Summary

In this chapter, you learned how to create hyperlinks to other slides, other presentations, other files, or the Web. You can even create a hyperlink that opens a new e-mail message. Action buttons provide a professional way to display hyperlinks as well as other actions, such as opening a program, playing a macro, or playing a sound.

Part of managing the relationship between your presentation and the rest of the world is knowing how to move data in and out of files. You can use the clipboard or drag-and-drop to paste in data. You can embed objects with or without a link to the source document.

This chapter ended with a discussion of techniques for managing files, including finding files and setting file properties.

The next chapter covers the process of collaborating with others in the creation of a final presentation.

chapter 12

Collaborating with Other People

In this chapter, you:

- Share a presentation on a network
- Send and route a presentation via e-mail
- Send a list of action items to Outlook
- Track revisions with Outlook
- Let non-PowerPoint users view your presentation

Whether you are creating a presentation for your company or for a client, you usually need to collaborate with others and share your ideas before the presentation is finalized. The old-fashioned way of collaborating involved printing out the presentation, mailing it to everyone, getting their feedback via return mail or phone, and making the necessary changes. Nowadays, you can collaborate online via a network or the Internet. These options make it easier to control the flow of comments. Collaborating online also allows you to keep up with the fast pace of today's electronically enabled businesses.

Many of the techniques described in this chapter require that you be connected to a network or an intranet. You will probably need to work with your system administrator to put some of the techniques into place. However, some of the techniques are applicable to everyone, so browse through them and see what will work for you.

Working with Others

How you collaborate with others will depend largely on the systems you have where you work. In this chapter, I review some of the options you have to enable you to work with colleagues, managers, and clients on a presentation.

Sharing Your Presentation

Windows contains a built-in feature that lets you give others on a network access to files on your hard drive. It's called *file sharing*, and it creates a special shared folder. If you are on a network, you should ask your system administrator about using this method. Follow these steps:

1. Close all applications.
2. If you wish, create a folder that you want to use for shared presentations. You can do this in Windows Explorer. Select the drive you want to use and Choose File | New | Folder. Type a name for the new folder and press ENTER. Otherwise, you can use an existing folder that you want to designate as shared.
3. Choose Start from the Windows taskbar, and then choose Settings | Control Panel.
4. Double-click Network in the Control Panel.
5. On the Configuration tab, choose File and Print Sharing.
6. Check the check box labeled I Want to Be Able to Give Others Access to My Files.
7. Click OK twice to close the dialog box and the Control Panel.
8. Click Yes in response to the message asking you to restart your computer.
9. On the desktop, double-click My Computer, and then double-click the drive containing the presentation.
10. Move or copy the presentation to the folder you want to use or the folder you created in step 2.

11. Still in My Computer, right-click the folder and choose Sharing.

12. On the Sharing tab, click Shared As.

13. In the Share Name box, give the folder a name—Usually the actual name of the folder. You can also add a comment.

14. If your network uses user-level access control, click Add and select the names of those with whom you want to share the presentation. If your network uses share-level access control, choose an access type from the list.

15. Click OK.

Sending and Routing Presentations via E-mail

You will often want to send a presentation via e-mail. You may already have an e-mail system set up that you can use. You can also send a presentation via e-mail directly from within PowerPoint.

In order to use this method, you need Microsoft Outlook, Microsoft Exchange, or a MAPI-compliant e-mail program. This method also works with Lotus cc:Mail or VIM-compliant e-mail programs. If you have one of these, you will have an e-mail button on the Standard toolbar, as shown here.

E-mailing a presentation as an attachment

To mail an entire presentation as an e-mail attachment, follow these steps:

1. Open the presentation and choose File | Send To | Mail Recipient (as Attachment).

2. PowerPoint opens a new message window, as shown here. Complete the names in the To and Cc boxes.

3. If you wish, select the name of your presentation in the Subject box and type a new subject.

4. Click Send to send the e-mail.

E-mailing one slide as an e-mail message

You can also send a slide in the body of the e-mail message. If your recipient does not have Office 2000, check if your recipient's e-mail system can accept e-mail in nontext format. (The best way to find out is to try it and see what happens.)

New in 2000: PowerPoint 2000 lets you send a single slide in the body of the e-mail. Previously, you needed to send it as an attachment to retain the formatting.

Here's how to send a slide as an e-mail message:

1. Display the slide you want to send.

2. Click the e-mail button from the Standard toolbar. PowerPoint displays the message shown here:

3. Choose Send the Current Slide as the Message Body. PowerPoint turns the entire screen into one big e-mail message.

4. Complete the names in the To and Cc boxes.

5. If you wish, change the subject by typing over the one PowerPoint has suggested.

6. Choose Send This Slide.

Routing a presentation

Microsoft Office 2000 lets you add a routing slip to an e-mail message so that your presentation can be sent to more than one person, in a specified order. Each person receives the e-mail message and when finished with it, continues the routing process to the next person. If you are sending the e-mail, you start the process by creating a routing slip, the electronic version of the little yellow "Route to" piece of paper that used to accompany interoffice mail (especially magazines). Here's how to start the process of routing a presentation:

1. Open the presentation.

2. Choose File | Send To | Routing Recipient.

3. PowerPoint opens the Add Routing Slip dialog box, shown here:

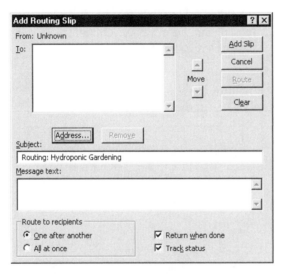

4. Click Address to choose recipients from the address book on your system.

5. In the Type Name or Select from List text box, type a name or choose one from the list. Click To. Continue to do this for each recipient. You can change the routing order by choosing a recipient and clicking either the up or down Move arrows. Click OK.

6. Add message text if you wish. You can also change the subject.

7. Choose to route to recipients one after another or all at once. Choose if you want the e-mail to come back to you at the end. If you check Track Status, you will get an e-mail message each time the e-mail gets routed to the next recipient (so you can see who is holding things up).

8. Click Route.

When you receive a routed presentation, you should make any changes or comments, and then choose File | Send To | Next Routing Recipient. Then click Route Document to (Name).

Adding Comments to a Presentation

What do you do with a presentation when it is routed to you? Well, it depends who you are. If you're the boss, you can probably just make changes. On the

Tip: Comments are AutoShapes. You can format them. To change the shape, select a comment and choose Draw | Change AutoShape from the Draw menu. Choose a new shape from the submenu.

other hand, you might want to delegate that job to the creator of the presentation. If you're a colleague, you probably just get to make comments. Anyone can add comments to a presentation. Each comment contains the name of the commentor so you'll always know who made the comment. If you have created a presentation and receive it back full of comments, you can then incorporate the suggestions (or perhaps ignore them). To insert a comment, follow these steps:

1. Choose Insert | Comment. (It's on the extended menu.)

2. PowerPoint opens a new comment with your name on it. Just start typing your comment.

Here you see a whimsical thought bubble comment. To view this slide in color, refer to number 127 in the Slide Gallery.

When you insert a comment, PowerPoint automatically opens the Reviewing toolbar, shown here. The Reviewing toolbar lets you easily add comments, show/hide comments, delete comments, and move from comment to comment throughout a presentation.

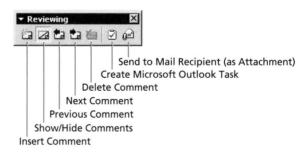

The two processes of routing a presentation and commenting on it go together. You prepare a draft presentation, route it to others who add comments, and then get it back again with all the comments. You then use the Reviewing toolbar to show the comments (if they're hidden) or move from comment to comment, making any necessary changes as you go. You can then delete the comments as you incorporate their suggestions.

Collaborating with Online Meetings

Microsoft Office includes NetMeeting, a program for online meetings. While it is beyond the scope of this book to go into detail about how to use NetMeeting, you should know about its capabilities for collaboration. Other online collaboration programs are also available, which you may have available to you at your company. NetMeeting includes the following features:

- Audio capability so participants can talk to each other during the meeting
- Application sharing so participants can share access to the presentation
- Whiteboard that lets you paste data into the whiteboard and mark up the image for all to see
- Text chat where you can type comments that all can see and reply to
- File transfer so that participants can send presentations and other documents to each other

You can start NetMeeting from within PowerPoint by choosing Tools | Online Collaboration. Then choose either Meet Now or Schedule Meeting. To use the Meet Now option, all the participants need to have NetMeeting running and be on your network. When you choose Schedule Meeting, you use Microsoft Outlook to schedule the time of the meeting. Of course, you can also e-mail or phone people to set up the meeting. The first time you use NetMeeting, you need to complete the Microsoft NetMeeting dialog box where you fill out information that NetMeeting needs to connect everyone. You will probably need to contact your system administrator to complete the information.

Once you are ready to start the meeting, you choose the Meet Now option to open the Place a Call dialog box where you select people you want to invite. Then click Call. The people you invite receive a message inviting them to participate. When they accept, they are in on the meeting and can see the shared presentation on their screens. During the meeting, the host starts out with control over the presentation, although everyone sees it. When the collaboration feature is on, participants can take turns controlling the presentation, which means that they can edit it. Only one person can edit the presentation at a time. During an online meeting, you can send text messages to each other in the Chat window and work on the Whiteboard, where you can type, draw, copy and paste objects, and mark up text and graphics. The host of the meeting has controls for ending the meeting when everyone is done.

Creating Discussions on a Presentation

Microsoft Office includes a discussions feature; however, it requires Microsoft Office Server Extensions, which can only be set up by your system administrator on a network. If you've ever participated in a newsgroup discussion group, you are familiar with discussions.

Discussions let collaborators add comments to a presentation. Discussions are different from comments. They can be much longer, and they are *threaded,* which means that people can reply to the comments. Related comments and replies are kept together, so you can follow the thread of the discussion. If you have Office Server Extensions installed, you have a Discussions toolbar that facilitates sending and replying to messages in the discussion.

You can also use a browser to start a discussion about a presentation that you have posted on a Web page.

For more information about using discussions, speak to your system administrator.

Sending Action Items to Outlook

Microsoft Outlook is a program included with Microsoft Office that you can use to keep track of to-do items. You can automatically send action items from PowerPoint to Outlook. Of course, you would use this technique only if you and your colleagues regularly use Outlook to keep track of tasks. PowerPoint includes a feature called the Meeting Minder that lets you write down notes and to-do items. It is usually used during a slide show, when follow-up tasks come up during the conversation. However, you can use it at any time as a collaboration technique to send others tasks in Outlook.

Cross-Reference: The Meeting Minder is covered in Chapter 16.

Let's say you are creating a presentation and you want to tell a colleague to send you a TIF file of the company's logo. Choose Tools | Meeting Minder and choose the Action Items tab, shown here:

Here's how you use send an action item to Outlook:

1. Complete the description of the task.

2. If you wish, put a name or initials in the Assigned To box.

3. Add a due date.

4. Click Add. PowerPoint places the action item in the lower box and activates the Export button, as shown here:

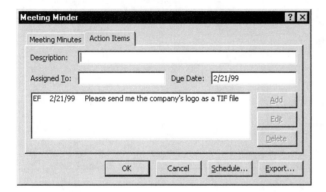

5. Choose Export. PowerPoint opens the Meeting Minder Export dialog box, shown here. If you only want to export the action item to Outlook, uncheck the second item.

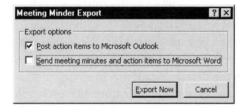

6. Click Export Now. The action item is posted to your task list in Outlook, as shown in Figure 12-1. You can then use Outlook's tools to reassign the task to someone else. (You need to use Outlook for e-mail for this technique to work.)

Let Non-PowerPoint Users View Your Presentation

You may need to send your presentation to someone who does not have PowerPoint. In order to collaborate with clients, managers, or colleagues who do not have PowerPoint, you need to send them PowerPoint Viewer, a free program for viewing PowerPoint presentations.

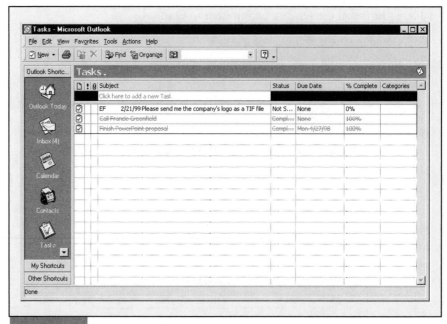

FIGURE 12-1 You can send action items from PowerPoint to Outlook

PowerPoint Viewer is contained in the file Ppview32.exe. You can find it in the Pfiles\MSOffice\Office\Xlators folder on the Office CD-ROM. If you installed the viewer when you installed PowerPoint, you can find it on your hard disk at Program Files\Microsoft Office\Office\Xlators—assuming you installed Microsoft Office in the default location.

Tip: You can include the PowerPoint viewer with your presentation when you use Pack and Go. See Chapter 15 for more on Pack and Go.

The viewer is also available from Microsoft's Web site. For example, you can also direct someone who doesn't have PowerPoint Viewer to this Web site. There is a special update site for PowerPoint at **http://officeupdate.microsoft.com/updates/updpowerpoint.htm** that lists updates. Click the Downloads button to download the viewer (as well as other downloadable updates).

Once installed, PowerPoint Viewer can easily be loaded, and any PowerPoint presentation viewed. Some advanced features may not be supported (such as picture bullets). The latest version of the viewer will view not only PowerPoint 2000 presentations but PowerPoint 97 and PowerPoint 95 presentations as well.

Cross-Reference: Chapter 16 covers PowerPoint Viewer in more detail.

Professional Skills Summary

In this chapter you learned the features that PowerPoint offers for collaborating with others on a presentation.

Collaboration is often as simple as e-mailing a presentation to others. However, if you have a supported e-mail program, you can also route the presentation in order to others and have it come back to you at the end of the cycle.

You can add comments to a presentation. If you send you presentation to others, they can add comments to your presentation. When you get the presentation back, you can incorporate the suggestions in the comments.

If you work on a network, you can use two other features: online meetings with NetMeeting (or another online meeting program) and discussions. Online meetings allow several people to view the PowerPoint presentation and communicate about it simultaneously. Discussions let you create newsgroup-type threaded discussions about a presentation. You can also send action items to Outlook and forward them to others as a means of collaborating on a presentation.

If you need to collaborate with someone who doesn't have PowerPoint, you can include PowerPoint Viewer along with the presentation. The viewer comes with PowerPoint and can also be downloaded free from Microsoft's Web site.

chapter 13

Displaying a Presentation on the World Wide Web

In this chapter, you:

- Create a presentation for a Web site

- Save in HTML format

- Run a presentation on a Web site, intranet, or FTP site

- Broadcast a presentation over the Internet

PowerPoint 2000 makes creating Web content easy. You can save a presentation in HTML format, the format used on the Web, and then open it in PowerPoint like any other presentation for further editing. PowerPoint 2000 has added new templates designed especially for the Web. Viewers can see your slide show on your Web site, in some cases with all the animation and special effects intact. You can actually present a slide show live on a Web site, using the new On-line Broadcast feature. This chapter describes these new features as well as some of their limitations.

Creating a Presentation for a Web Site

You can use PowerPoint to create Web pages. In this situation, you are not creating a presentation at all; rather, you are using PowerPoint's ability to create fully graphic slides as a tool to design a Web page. You must take into account the usual design features of a Web site, such as a title, links to other pages, more (and smaller) text, and so on.

You can add a presentation to an existing Web site. In this case, you want your audience to be able to run the slide show while browsing the Web site. You create a typical presentation, although you may add special design elements because it is shown on the Web site.

Professional Pointer

An application that specializes in creating Web sites (Microsoft FrontPage is just one example) is probably the best way to create a Web site. However, you can use your PowerPoint creations within these applications.

Using PowerPoint to Create Web Pages

When you use PowerPoint to create a Web page, you are using PowerPoint as your design tool. You then save the presentation in HTML format. HTML (HyperText Markup Language) is a format that browsers can read. However, when you save a presentation in HTML format, PowerPoint actually creates many supporting files, including separate files for each slide, for graphic files, and for the navigational tools your viewers use to browse through the presentation.

While designing Web pages is beyond the scope of this book, here are a few simple guidelines:

- *Format the page's text and graphics appropriately.* Most Web pages include graphics. However, too many large graphics make a Web page slow to download. Text for a Web site can be smaller than for an on-screen slide show. PowerPoint presentations saved as HTML make extensive use of graphics to preserve the "look and feel" of a PowerPoint presentation.

- *Provide links on each page to go to other pages.* Most pages should also have a link to your home (main) page. Figure 13-1 shows an example of a Web page for a human resources department Web site. To view this Web page in color, refer to number 128 in the Slide Gallery.

- *Create consistent navigational tools throughout the Web site pages using action buttons or AutoShapes.* Chapter 11 explains how to create hyperlinks in your presentation.

- *Make sure that each slide has a meaningful slide title.* On a Web site, these titles appear in a frame at the left listing each slide's title. Viewers can click any slide's title to go to that slide.

- *Add alternative text for graphics.* Browsers use this text while pictures are loading because some people use the Web with graphics turned off to speed the load time. Alternative text offers impact even without the graphics. Search engines also use this text. Select the object, right-click, and choose

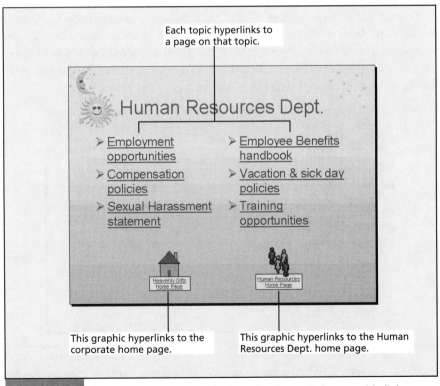

FIGURE 13-1 When you design a Web site using PowerPoint, provide links on each page to navigate to other pages

Format AutoShape (or Picture or Table). On the Web tab, type the text. (Text in a WordArt object is used by default for the alternative text.) Click OK.

- *Keep the colors simple.* The rich, dark colors appropriate for an on-screen presentation are often overwhelming on a Web site.

- *Don't use builds or other animation that requires a mouse click.* Your viewers have no way of knowing about this animation. If you want to use animation, set automatic timing. See Chapter 15 for details.)

- *Remember that, traditionally, a Web site includes a way to contact the Webmaster and the organization that created the Web site.* Add an e-mail link to the Webmaster on the first page. See Chapter 11 for instructions.

- *Before publishing your Web pages, open them in your browser and check out all the links and graphics.* Once you send the Web pages to your server or Web site host, check them out again.

You can include all the pages of the Web site in one presentation using each slide in the presentation as a Web page. You can also create a different presentation for each Web page; you may end up with a large number of files, but each file is smaller and loads faster.

PowerPoint's AutoContent Wizard includes a presentation for a corporate web site. In the AutoContent Wizard, choose the Corporate topic, then choose Corporate Home Page. To get a similar presentation, choose File | New | Presentations and choose the Group Home Page presentation, shown here, which is designed to be an intranet home page for a workgroup or project:

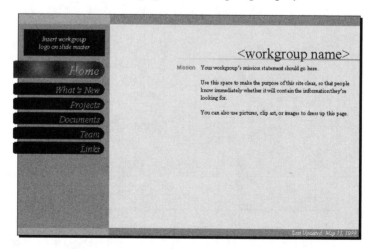

Of course, you can customize this presentation with your own background, logo, graphics, and text. This presentation includes hyperlinks, but be sure to create your own hyperlinks as you add pages to the presentation/Web site. Figure 13-2 shows the AutoContent's Corporate Home Page after some minor adjustments. To view this slide in color, refer to number 129 in the Slide Gallery.

Before saving your presentation in HTML format, you can preview it as a Web page. Choose File | Web Page Preview. PowerPoint opens your default Web browser and displays the first slide in the presentation. Figure 13-3 shows a slide viewed in Internet Explorer 5.0. To view this slide in color, refer to number 130 in the Slide Gallery.

Using this preview, you can test all the links that don't require Internet access, such as links within the presentation.

Publishing a Presentation to the Web

Once you have created and previewed your Web pages, you save them in HTML format and save them to their final location on the Internet—a process called *publishing* to the Web. In order to save a presentation to the Web, you need access to a server, ideally one with a direct connection to the Internet. You can also save a presentation to an intranet server within your company. You also need permission to save to this server. If you are saving to an intranet, your companys' system administrator has the information you need to save files to the intranet. If

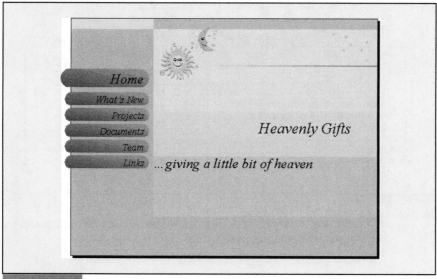

FIGURE 13-2 A corporate Web site based on PowerPoint's Corporate Home Page presentation

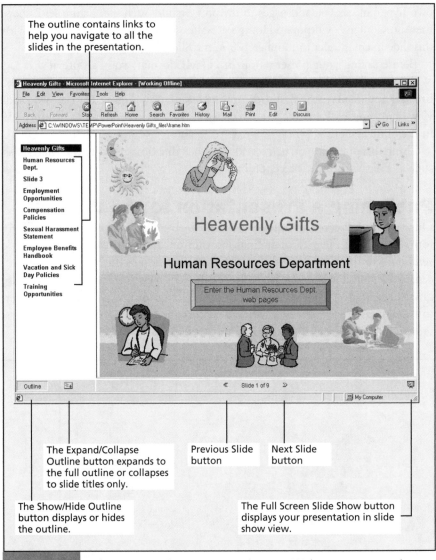

The outline contains links to help you navigate to all the slides in the presentation.

The Expand/Collapse Outline button expands to the full outline or collapses to slide titles only.

Previous Slide button

Next Slide button

The Show/Hide Outline button displays or hides the outline.

The Full Screen Slide Show button displays your presentation in slide show view.

FIGURE 13-3 When you preview a presentation as a Web page, you see the same navigational tools that PowerPoint adds when you publish a presentation on the Web

you are saving to the Internet, you usually do so via an Internet service provider (ISP) who can provide you with the information you need.

The following table lists Web sites that contain services you may find useful for checking out your Web site.

Web Site	Description
www.cast.org/bobby/	Analyzes Web pages for their accessibility to people with disabilities
www.htmlhelp.com/links/validators.htm	Offers a variety of validators and document checkers
http://validator.w3.org/	An easy-to-use HTML validation service

When you save a presentation in HTML format, PowerPoint creates a new folder and places all the new files in that folder. One presentation creates a bewildering array of GIF and HTM files. You may also have WAV, AVI, JPG, and other types of files.

The procedure for publishing to the Web is the same whether you are using PowerPoint to create a Web site or using the Web to present your slide show.

Before you publish to the Web, you need to consider which format you want to use. PowerPoint 2000 offers three choices for converting a presentation to HTML format. Each format has its advantages and disadvantages:

Professional Pointer

Use this format for intranets where you know that your viewers have Internet Explorer 4.0 or later. This format is ideal for situations where you want to present an entire slide show on an intranet and need to retain your special effects.

- **Microsoft Internet Explorer 4.0 or Later**, which PowerPoint calls "high fidelity," retains almost all of the features of a presentation, including transitions, animations (builds), sounds, and video clips. Viewers can view your presentation in full-screen mode, which makes it look like a real presentation rather than just a presentation inside a browser. When you save a presentation in this format, you can open and edit it in PowerPoint like a regular presentation. The disadvantage is that many viewers use Netscape or earlier versions of Internet Explorer—they will probably get an error message or lose many of the features of your presentation.

- **Microsoft Internet Explorer or Netscape Navigator 3.0 or Later** loses many of your special effects. You still get a good basic presentation, and more people can view it. You cannot open and edit this format in PowerPoint. Therefore, if you edit your presentation, you need to resave it using this HTML format. Use this format when you need to make your presentation available to a wide variety of people and don't need special effects—for example, when you are using PowerPoint to create a Web site.

- **All Browsers Listed Above** creates a presentation with the capabilities of both of the previous options. Viewers with Internet Explorer 4.0 or later can see your special effects, and others get the basic version of your presentation. The disadvantage of this format is that it creates more and larger files.

Now you're ready to publish your presentation to the Web. Follow these steps:

1. Choose File | Save as Web Page. PowerPoint opens the Save As dialog box with special Web publishing options, as shown in Figure 13-4.

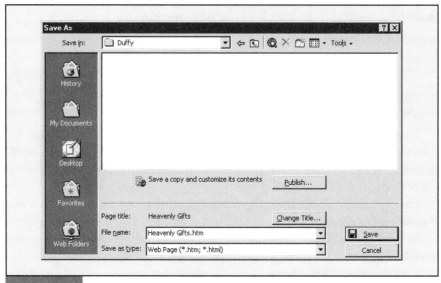

FIGURE 13-4   When you choose File | Save as Web Page, the Save As dialog box has options to let you save your presentation to the Internet

2. In the File Name text box, type a name for the Web page. By default, PowerPoint uses the name of the presentation. PowerPoint creates a master file with this name along with a folder containing all the other files that are associated with the presentation in Web format.

3. In the Save In drop-down box at the top of the dialog box, choose a location for the Web page. You should ask your Internet service provider or your company's network/Web administrator for this location, as well as how supporting files (such as graphics) should be organized. You can use the Search the Web button to open your browser to find a Web location, such as a recently used URL.

4. If you would like the Web page title to be different from the filename, click Change Title. The Web page title is the text that appears in the title bar of your Web browser. (The page title also appears in the browser's history and favorites lists.) Make this title descriptive because many search engines use this title as the primary method of searching the Web. In the Page Title box, type the new title and click OK.

5. Click Publish. PowerPoint opens the Publish as Web Page dialog box, shown in Figure 13-5.

6. In the Publish What? section, specify if you want to publish the entire presentation, certain slides, or a custom show (if available). Uncheck Display Speaker Notes if you don't want your viewers to see your notes. Leave this option checked if you are publishing the presentation for others to review or if you have used the notes pane to provide additional information that you want your viewers to see.

Tip: If you don't want to publish your presentation to the Web yet but want to save it in HTML format, click Save instead of Publish. Others can then preview your presentation in a browser, and you can make further changes before finally publishing the presentation to the Web.

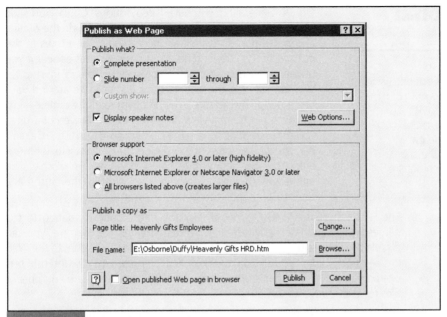

FIGURE 13-5   In the Publish as Web Page dialog box, you specify the options you want for publishing your presentation in HTML

7. Click Web Options to open the Web Options dialog box, shown in Figure 13-6.

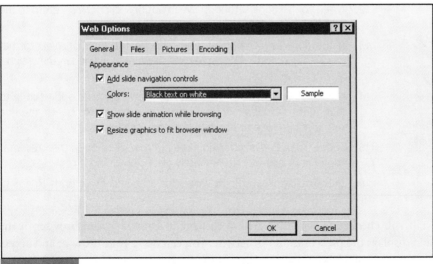

FIGURE 13-6   The General tab of the Web Options dialog box

Professional Pointer

Using one of the two presentation colors options (with either the text or accent color) provides the viewer with a unified appearance in the browser. The outline pane appears related to the slide show because the colors are the same.

8. On the General tab you have three options. Check Add Slide Navigation Controls (it's on by default) to include the outline and notes panes, as well as the navigational arrows at the bottom of the screen. (The notes pane will not appear if you unchecked Display Speaker Notes as explained in step 6.) Viewers can use the outline pane to navigate around your presentation by clicking on any slide listed in the outline—just as you do in normal view. In a nice touch, PowerPoint gives you some color options in the Color drop-down list. For example, you can use presentation colors, black on white, white on black, or your default browser colors. You can disable slide animation (builds). You can also disable the automatic resizing of graphics to fit the browser window.

9. The Files tab of the Web Options dialog box offers options relating to the names and location of the files that PowerPoint creates. For example, you can disable the feature that puts all the files of a presentation published to the Web in a separate folder. You should do this only if instructed by your Internet service provider or Web administrator, since PowerPoint creates a large number of files for each presentation.

10. Use the Pictures tab to fine-tune some options relating to graphics. On this tab, you can also specify the screen resolution. If you are publishing to an intranet and know the screen resolution of your viewers' monitors, you should set it here. If you are publishing to the Web for anyone to view, you should try different resolutions and view them with different browsers to see the results. The default is 800 × 600, which works fine for the majority of Web users.

11. The Encoding tab offers the option to save in various language versions of Windows, DOS, and other operating systems. Use this if text and symbols are not properly readable from your browser.

Tip: Be careful after changing any of these options because they persist into other presentations. Always check the Web Options dialog box before publishing to make sure the options are the way you want them to be.

12. When you're done setting the Web options, click OK to return to the Publish as Web Page dialog box.

13. In the Browser Support section, choose the type of Web format you want to create. The three options were explained in the list preceding these steps.

14. In the Publish a Copy As section, you have another opportunity to change the filename and text title. Click Change to change the title text. Click Browse to browse to a new location.

15. Check Open Published Web Page in Browser to open the presentation in your browser immediately after publishing it.

16. Click Publish. PowerPoint works for a couple of seconds to create the new files.

If you checked Open Published Web Page in Browser, your browser opens and displays the presentation. Otherwise, you can open your browser and access it as you normally would access files on the Web.

Saving a Presentation to an FTP Site

FTP stands for File Transfer Protocol. An FTP site offers the capability of sending and receiving files. When you go to a Web site and download a file, you are usually connected to an FTP site for the transfer. If your Web server or Internet service provider offers access to an FTP site, you can save a presentation to it. Others can then download your presentation from that site.

To save to an FTP site, you need to add the site to PowerPoint's list of Internet sites. Follow these steps:

1. Click Open on the Standard toolbar.
2. In the Look In drop-down list, choose Add/Modify FTP Locations.
3. In the Name of FTP Site box, type the URL of the site.
4. If the site allows anonymous access, choose Anonymous. (No password is required.) Otherwise, choose User and type your name. Type your password if you are prompted for it.
5. Click Add.

You can now save presentations to the FTP site. Choose File | Save As. In the Save In drop-down list, choose FTP Locations. From the list of FTP sites, double-click the site you want, then double-click the location within the site. In the File Name box, type the name of your presentation and click Save.

Testing Your Web Site

Once you have published your Web site, you should access it as your viewers would and test it out. Here are some things to test for:

- *Test any links that link to sites outside your Web site.* You may have forgotten to save supporting files to the Web, such as text files containing additional data that you have linked to.
- *Test any multimedia objects, such as sounds and video clips.* Are the means to open these objects clear to your viewer? If not, add instructions such as "Double-click to see the video."
- *Test any action buttons that you created.* These may have hyperlinks, may open programs, or may play a sound, for example.
- *If you added animated GIFs, make sure they work.*

If you can manage it, an extra precaution is to view your Web site using both browsers (Microsoft Internet Explorer and Netscape Navigator), at varying screen resolutions, and with varying numbers of screen colors. These factors can affect how your Web site appears.

Presenting a Slide Show on the Internet

You can publish a presentation to a Web site so that others can view the presentation. As explained earlier in this chapter, when you publish to the Web, the presentation appears in the browser with navigational tools so that users can view the presentation. You can also *broadcast* a presentation. When a presentation is broadcast, the presentation runs itself, and your viewers just watch.

Creating a Viewer-Controlled Presentation

Create a viewer-controlled presentation when you want to simply place your presentation on a Web site and let viewers decide when they will view it. A presentation can be part of a larger Web site. You may have seen Web sites that included PowerPoint presentations.

Creating a viewer-controlled presentation is easy. Publish the presentation to the Web as explained earlier in this chapter. PowerPoint automatically creates the navigational tools your viewers need. (You can turn off the navigational tools, but you shouldn't do so for a presentation designed to be controlled by your viewers.) The navigational tools are the same as those shown in Figure 13-2.

Figure 13-7 shows the first slide of a presentation as it appears in a browser. To view this slide in color, refer to number 131 in the Slide Gallery.

Remember that viewers may need instructions to get the most out of the presentation. The navigational controls are not large, and some viewers may miss them. One solution is to include instructions for using the controls on the first slide.

If you include an AVI file, it may need to be double-clicked to run. Viewers will not know this, so you should include a text box with instructions to this effect.

You need to pay special attention to designing a presentation that is viewed on a Web page. Animation (builds) appears automatically but may be confusing to viewers because they have no control over the timing. Dimming does not work well because viewers may not have finished reading a line of text before it dims.

Broadcasting a Slide Show

You can present a slide show in real time over the Internet. PowerPoint calls this *broadcasting*. You invite viewers to view the presentation at a specific time so they know when to go online. PowerPoint uses Advanced Streaming Format (ASF) technology to send the presentation to all your viewers at once. You need access to a server that can also be accessed by everyone in your intended audience.

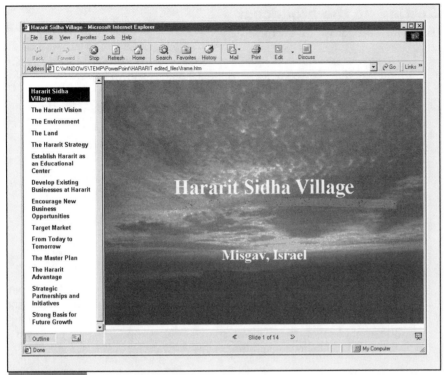

A presentation as it appears in a browser; viewers can use the navigational tools and the outline to view the presentation

New in 2000:   Broadcasting is new for PowerPoint 2000.

Although broadcasting is an exciting concept, it has some major limitations—viewers must have Internet Explorer 4.0 or later, and if you want to broadcast to more than 15 locations at once, you need a NetShow server, available from Microsoft. Broadcasting is most useful in an organization with an intranet, where you have access to a network administrator, have a means of contacting all the viewers, and know that all your viewers have Internet Explorer 4.0.

Broadcasting involves the following steps:

1. Set up server options. You only need to do this once.

2. Schedule the broadcast using Microsoft Outlook or your e-mail program.

3. Start the broadcast.

Setting up the broadcast

To set up a broadcast, follow these steps:

1. Open your presentation and choose Slide Show | Online Broadcast | Set Up and Schedule. PowerPoint opens the dialog box shown here:

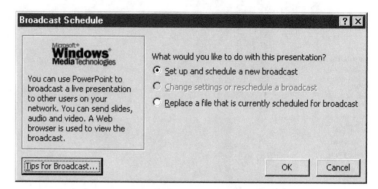

2. Choose Set Up and Schedule a New Broadcast, and then click OK. PowerPoint opens the Schedule a New Broadcast dialog box. Figure 13-8 shows the Description tab. The information on this tab appears later on the "lobby" page (the front page) of the broadcast, so that viewers know what the broadcast is about and can contact you if they want.

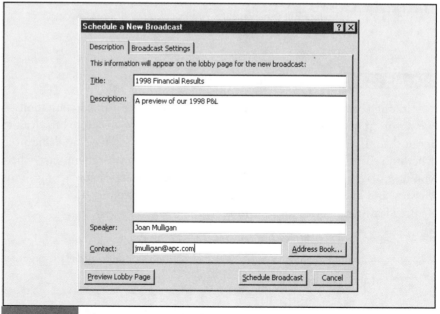

FIGURE 13-8   The Description tab of the Schedule a New Broadcast dialog box

3. Click the Broadcast Settings tab, shown in Figure 13-9.

- Choose Send Audio if you want to talk during the presentation, just as you would with a live presentation. You need to connect a microphone to your computer. You have the option of attaching the microphone to another computer.

- Choose Send Video if you want to send live video—perhaps of you speaking—from a video camera connected to your computer. Note that sending video consumes a great deal of computer resources.

- To broadcast to over 15 locations, you must use a NetShow server. Microsoft also recommends NetShow for broadcasting video. You can obtain more information on NetShow in the Microsoft Office 2000 Resource Kit, which is free at **www.microsoft.com/office/ork/2000/**.

- Click Preview Lobby Page to see how the first page of the presentation will look. This page contains the information from the Description tab, as shown in Figure 13-10.Click the close button of your browser to return to the dialog box.

- Click Server Options to open the Server Options dialog box. Use this box to specify the shared folder, generally on a server, that contains the presentation and to which all your recipients have access. The format is \\servername\sharename. You will probably need to ask your system administrator for this information.

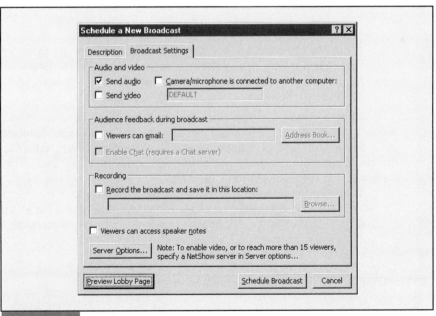

FIGURE 13-9 Use the Broadcast Settings tab to specify how you want to broadcast the presentation

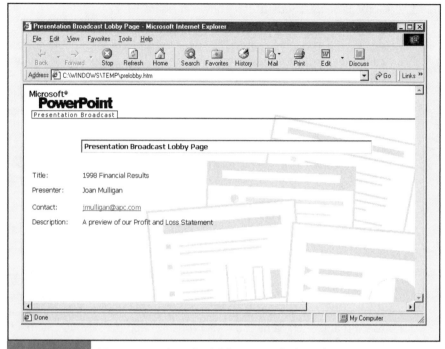

FIGURE 13-10   You can preview the lobby page of a broadcast

If you want to use a NetShow server, specify the server information in this dialog box as well. If your Internet service provider offers NetShow services, you can get directions from the provider. Click OK. PowerPoint returns you to the Schedule a New Broadcast dialog box.

4. Click Schedule Broadcast to schedule the broadcast. PowerPoint opens your e-mail program. If you use Outlook, you can use it to schedule the broadcast. You can even set Outlook to automatically start PowerPoint and prepare it for the broadcast. Your viewers receive notification of the broadcast time and location as they would of any other meeting.

Tip: You can schedule a broadcast to just yourself to test everything out in advance.

If you and your viewers do not use Outlook, just use your e-mail to notify them of the date and time of the broadcast. PowerPoint places the URL of the broadcast location that you specified in the e-mail message. If your e-mail supports hyperlinks, viewers just click the hyperlink to go to the location at the time of the broadcast.

PowerPoint saves the broadcast settings with your presentation.

Starting the broadcast

Once you have scheduled a broadcast, it's easy to start it:

1. Open the presentation and choose Slide Show | Online Broadcast | Begin Broadcast. PowerPoint goes through a checking process and saves the presentation in HTML format to the server you specified when setting up the broadcast.

2. If you want to display a last-minute message on the lobby page, click Audience Message, type the message, and click Update.

3. To start the broadcast, click Start.

Viewing the broadcast

As mentioned earlier, your audience needs Internet Explorer 4.0 or later to view the broadcast. Encourage viewers to go online early to view any last-minute message you have put on the lobby page or in case they need to download some ActiveX controls for Internet Explorer. Viewers can start viewing the broadcast in one of two ways:

- If they are using Outlook (and it is open), they should receive a reminder message. Viewers click the View This NetShow button to start viewing.

- If you notified viewers via e-mail, they open the e-mail message and click the URL for the broadcast. If the e-mail program doesn't support active hyperlinks, viewers can copy the URL from the message and paste it in their browser's Address box.

Viewers see the lobby page, including a countdown to the time of the broadcast, until the broadcast begins. If you chose e-mail and chat options during setup, viewers can chat with other viewers and send e-mail messages to you during the broadcast.

Professional Skills Summary

In this chapter you learned about creating a presentation for a Web site. You can use PowerPoint to create a Web site or place a presentation on a Web site so that browsers can view it. Once you have created the presentation, you publish it to the Web. PowerPoint creates the HTML and other files for you.

You can broadcast a presentation over the Internet. Viewers can view the presentation live if they have Internet Explorer 4.0 or later. In the next chapter, you learn about customizing PowerPoint.

Customizing PowerPoint

Most of the customization you do in PowerPoint is not visible in your final presentation; rather it helps you work more quickly and easily. Customizing a menu or a toolbar makes it easy for you to find the features you use most. If you create a macro, you can automate some of your editing and turn a long task into a short one. You can, however, create macros and Visual Basic for Applications (VBA) programs that change how your presentation appears or works—and the results are readily visible to your viewers.

Customization offers you great power to control PowerPoint. This chapter explains what you can accomplish without being a programmer and introduces you to all the advanced capabilities of customization.

Customizing Menus

You can create new menus or add to menus commands from toolbars. These commands could be macros that you have created or existing PowerPoint commands. You also have some control over how menus function.

Some toolbars have menus. The best example is the Drawing toolbar, which has Draw and AutoShapes menus. I discuss these toolbar menus later in this chapter.

Controlling How Your Menus Function

PowerPoint offers several ways to control the functioning of your menus. While these features do not actually customize the contents of a menu, they can certainly make your life easier.

Unteaching the old dog new tricks

As explained way back in Chapter 1, PowerPoint automatically adjusts menus and toolbars so that the commands you use most are available and those that you never use are not immediately visible, but still there when you need them. As you work and use commands that are not initially on a menu (by placing the cursor over the bottom of the menu to expand it), these additional commands are added to the menu. If you find that the commands you usually need are available most of the time, you can let PowerPoint's adjustable menus expand and collapse themselves without further input from you.

If you prefer the PowerPoint 97 menu behavior, you can have it. However, note that changing PowerPoint menu behavior affects all your other Office menus as well! Follow these steps:

1. Choose Tools | Customize.
2. Click the Options tab, shown in Figure 14-1.
3. Uncheck the Menus Show Recently Used Commands First check box.
4. Click Close.

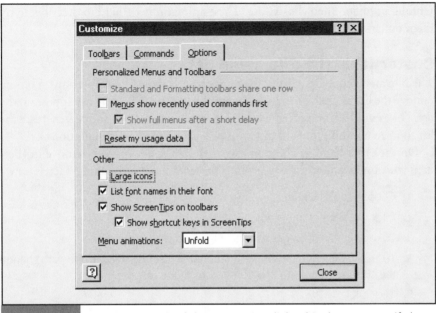

FIGURE 14-1   The Options tab of the Customize dialog box lets you specify how you want menus and toolbars to function

Retrieving your default menus

If you are fed up with your menu and toolbar changes, you can wipe out the data that Microsoft collects about your menu and toolbar usage and return to the default settings. Click the Reset My Usage Data button on the Options tab of the Customize dialog box, shown in Figure 14-1. This feature only affects PowerPoint.

If you have the Menus Show Recently Used Commands First check box checked—the default—clicking the Reset My Usage Data button starts you back from scratch, with the menu items PowerPoint showed when you first installed it. If you have added or deleted toolbar buttons, however, those buttons remain unchanged.

Animating your menus

It seems especially appropriate that you can animate menus in PowerPoint. You don't have many choices, and they affect all your Office programs. The animation is somewhat reminiscent of slide transitions; but in the end, you may find it more distracting than useful.

To animate a menu, choose Tools | Customize and click the Options tab. From the Menu Animation drop-down list, choose None (the default), Random,

Unfold, or Slide. Then click Close. These animations are hard to describe, so try them out and see what you think.

Customizing the File menu list

The File menu contains a list of the most recently opened presentations. You can remove the list entirely or change the number of presentations that appear on the list. For example, if you often work on several presentations at once, increase the list to its maximum, nine, to give you easy access to your presentations.

On the other hand, if you don't want the list at all, you can remove it. (Perhaps you don't want others to see which presentations you opened!) Here's how:

1. Choose Tools | Options.
2. Click the General tab, shown in Figure 14-2.
3. To remove the list, uncheck Recently Used File List.
4. To change the number of files that appear, use the arrow buttons to change the current number to any number from one to nine.
5. Click OK.

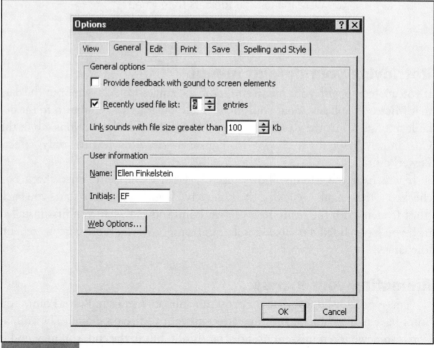

FIGURE 14-2 Use the General tab of the Options dialog box to customize the list of recently opened presentations at the bottom of the File menu

Making Menus Work Harder for You

You can add a new menu on the menu bar and populate it with any menu commands, including custom commands. You can even hide a built-in menu, although it remains available so that you can add it back again. You can also change a menu's name and add your own dividing lines on the menu bar.

You can add commands to a menu or delete commands that you never use. PowerPoint has a long list of appropriate commands that do not normally appear on even the expanded menus but might be just what you need. You can also create macros and add them to a menu.

Adding a menu

You can add a completely new menu to the menu bar. You might place some of your own macros there. Macros are covered later in this chapter. The advantage of adding a menu (over a toolbar) is that the menu is always displayed and doesn't take up space on your screen. Here's how:

1. Choose Tools | Customize.
2. Click the Commands tab, shown in Figure 14-3.
3. In the Categories list, scroll down and choose New Menu from the list of menus.

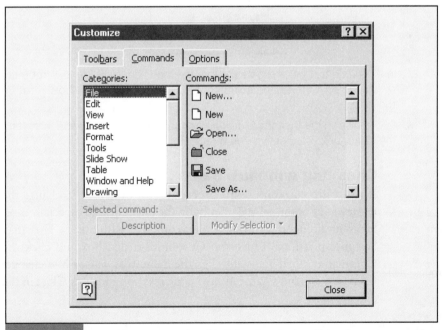

FIGURE 14-3 Use the Commands tab of the Customize dialog box to customize the commands that appear on menus

4. In the Commands window, select the New Menu item that appears there.

5. Drag this item to the menu bar. As you drag on the menu bar, PowerPoint places a vertical I-beam cursor to show you where the new menu item will appear.

6. With the Customize dialog box still open, right-click the new menu, which is now called New Menu to display the shortcut menu shown here:

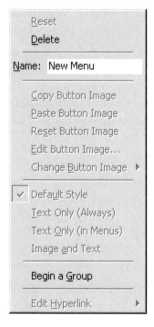

7. In the Name text box, rename the menu. (Somehow New Menu is not quite satisfactory.) A menu name should be only one word and should not be too long.

8. Click Close on the Customize dialog box to close both the shortcut menu and the dialog box. Your new menu is ready for commands.

Tip: To allow access to the menu by keyboard, place an ampersand (&) before any letter. The first letter is ideal, but make sure that the letter is not used by any existing menu item. PowerPoint places an underscore under that letter. You can then access that menu by pressing ALT along with that letter.

Changing a menu's name

If you wish, you can use the procedure just explained to change the name of one of the existing menus on the menu bar. Be especially careful about doing so if you share your computer with others. They may be quite mystified! Open the Customize dialog box and click the Commands tab. Then right-click the menu that you wish to change. Change the menu's name in the Name text box and click Close in the dialog box.

Opening the Customize dialog box may seem strange, since you don't actually use it; however, having this dialog box open activates all the menu and toolbar customization features.

Deleting a menu

You can also delete a menu. Again, I urge caution. Although you can retrieve any built-in menu that you delete, you may not remember how to do so. Anyone else using your computer may have a difficult time indeed! In general, you should delete only custom menus that you have added. However, a new word of caution: When you delete a custom menu, it's really gone!

Later in this chapter, I explain how to create and display toolbars.

Adding a menu item to a menu

Now that you have created a new menu, you need to add commands to it. You could move your most often used commands to one menu for convenience. A common use for a new menu is for macros that you have created. To the right you see a menu with two commands on it that format AutoShapes with a gradient using a company's special colors. You can select any AutoShape and format it exactly as you have specified in the macro by choosing one of the two items on this menu. Macros are covered later in this chapter.

You can also add commands to existing menus. PowerPoint offers a long list of available commands that don't normally appear on the menus. For example, you can add often-used AutoShapes to a menu. You can also add custom commands that you or someone else wrote using Visual Basic for Applications (VBA) or another programming language. Later in this chapter I discuss add-ins and VBA. To add a menu item to a menu, follow these steps:

> **Tip:** You can create a custom toolbar and use it for storing unused custom menus as well as unused custom toolbar buttons. Then, instead of deleting a custom menu, you can move it to the custom toolbar. You can hide this toolbar until you want to revive your custom menu or toolbar button. To revive a custom menu, open the Customize dialog box, display the toolbar you created, and drag the menu item onto the menu bar.

1. Choose Tools | Customize.

2. Click the Commands tab.

3. In the Categories box, choose a category. To add a macro, choose Macros.

4. Drag the command or macro you want from the Commands box to the menu you want to add it to. The menu opens. Drag to the desired location on the menu. PowerPoint places a horizontal I-beam cursor to show you where the menu item will appear.

5. Release the mouse.

Deleting a menu item from a menu

Deleting a menu item is easier than adding one. As usual, you need to open the Customize dialog box. Choose the menu with the menu item you want to delete.

It opens up. Drag the menu item anywhere off the menu and release the mouse button. Voilà—it's gone!

Customizing menus on toolbars

Oddly enough, you can place a menu on a toolbar. As I mentioned earlier, the Drawing toolbar contains menus. You can customize these menus in the same way that you customize menus on the menu bar. Here you see the same menu shown earlier but placed on the Drawing toolbar. If you usually keep the Drawing toolbar open, you might want to place a menu there that contains commands that relate to drawing.

Working with Shortcut Menus

A shortcut menu is the menu that appears when you right-click somewhere in PowerPoint. You can't add or delete a shortcut menu, but you can remove and add menu items to it. Many of these menus display both text and icons—you can customize how these menu items are displayed. You can rename a menu item on a shortcut menu just as you can for regular menus.

Before customizing a shortcut menu, try to figure out where you right-click on the screen, and in which view, when you display that menu. For example, here you see the menu that appears when you right-click the background of a slide in normal or slide view.

Let's say you often wish you could get to the slide master from this shortcut menu. Perhaps you sometimes open the menu to format the background of a slide and then realize that you should change the slide master instead of the individual slide. So you want to add the View | Slide Master menu item to the shortcut menu. Here's how:

1. Choose Tools | Customize.

2. Click the Toolbars tab of the Customize dialog box.

3. In the Toolbars list, check the Shortcut Menus check box. PowerPoint displays a toolbar with four items on it, as shown here. All the shortcut menus can be accessed from this toolbar.

4. Find the shortcut menu you want to change. You may have to search around a bit. For example, you can find the shortcut menu that appears when you right-click the background of a slide by choosing Draw | Slide Background. PowerPoint displays the shortcut menu.

5. To delete a menu item, drag it off the shortcut menu. Then go to step 9.

6. To add a menu item, click the Commands tab of the Customize dialog box.

7. Choose a category from the Categories list. For example, to add an item to go to the slide master, choose View because you get to the Slide Master menu item from the View menu.

8. Find the command in the Commands list and drag it to the desired location on the shortcut menu.

9. Click Close in the Customize dialog box.

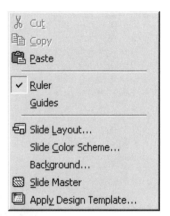

Here you see the new shortcut menu with its new item. This also appears on a slide in number 132 of the Slide Gallery.

A useful menu to customize is the Slide Show shortcut menu that appears when you right-click during a slide show. In the following example, First Slide and Last Slide commands have been added to the viewing options. You can also see this illustration as number 133 in the Slide Gallery. In addition to individual commands, you can add VBA macros to help you navigate during a slide show.

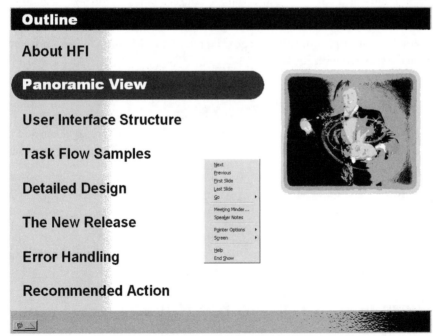

A shortcut menu can contain both text and icons. PowerPoint enables you to customize whether you see text, icons, or both. Having both available means you can put a command on either a menu or a toolbar (or both) for maximum flexibility.

To control the appearance of a menu, open the Customize dialog box. Click the menu to open it. For a shortcut menu, choose Shortcut Menus from the Toolbars list in the Toolbars tab, and navigate to the shortcut menu until PowerPoint displays it. Right-click the menu item you want to change. PowerPoint displays the menu shown to the left.

Most of the items pertain to button images, which I discuss in the next section on customizing toolbars. However, you have four options that are appropriate for menus:

- **Default Style**   Displays the button image and the text if the command is in a menu, but displays only the image if you move the command to a toolbar
- **Text Only (Always)**   Displays just the text
- **Text Only (In Menus)**   Displays just the text in a menu but the button image if the command is on a toolbar
- **Image and Text**   Displays both the button image and the text, whether on a menu or on a toolbar

You cannot display only an image on a menu. Some commands do not have images associated with them.

Customizing Toolbars

Toolbars are customizable in much the same way that menus are. You can add or delete items from a toolbar. You can create a new toolbar and add existing or custom commands to it.

Cross-Reference: Chapter 1 explains how to add or remove buttons from the standard choices of buttons as well as how to display and hide toolbars.

In addition, you can customize those little button images to your heart's content. If you create a new command, you can use any graphic image for the button, or you can edit an existing button image.

Keeping a Clean Toolbar House

Some simple display tactics can help keep your screen useful, yet uncluttered. For example, when you first install PowerPoint, both the Standard and the Formatting toolbars are on the same row, freeing up a row of screen real estate. The result is that a number of buttons are not displayed. PowerPoint displays the buttons that you have used most frequently. If you don't use many of the buttons, this arrangement may work for you. On the other hand, you may find it annoying to have to click the arrow at the end of the toolbars to find the missing buttons. (Once you use the button it appears on the toolbar.)

You move a toolbar, to place it either on a different row or on the same row as another toolbar, by dragging its move handle, a vertical bar at its left or top edge. If the toolbar is floating, it has a title bar that you can use to move it. When you drag a toolbar to the edge of the application window, PowerPoint docks it so that it cannot cover up any of your work.

You can resize and reshape a floating toolbar. Move the cursor over any edge until it changes to a double-headed arrow, and then drag the edge either inward or outward. For example, you can change a long, skinny toolbar into a compact box shape.

Of course, you can display any of PowerPoint's toolbars by right-clicking any toolbar and choosing it from the list of toolbars.

A great trick is to detach a submenu from a toolbar to create a floating palette. For example, if you want to work with fill colors on several objects, you might find it annoying to constantly have to open up the Fill Color submenu on the Drawing toolbar. If you could turn it into a floating toolbar, it would stay open on your screen, and you could access the buttons immediately. It's easy. Choose the submenu so it opens. PowerPoint displays the submenu with a small move bar at the top. Then drag the move bar to anywhere on your screen.

To remove the floating palette, click its Close button. The submenu remains available from its original toolbar.

Adding and Removing Toolbar Buttons

Adding and removing a toolbar button is similar to adding and removing a menu item. It's easy to add an existing button, but you can also create your own.

Removing buttons from a toolbar

If you never use a toolbar button, you can hide it. The button is still available if it is a built-in button—that is, if it came with PowerPoint. First, display the toolbar. Then display the Add or Remove Buttons menu in one of two ways:

- If the toolbar is docked, click More Buttons, then Add or Remove Buttons.
- If the toolbar is floating, click the down arrow at the upper-left corner of the toolbar's title bar and choose Add or Remove Buttons.

PowerPoint displays the list of buttons. Uncheck any button or buttons that you want to hide from the toolbar.

Tip: You can use the same method to redisplay a built-in button at any time.

Tip: Remember to look first for a button on the Add or Remove Buttons menu. Click the toolbar's down arrow, choose More Buttons (if it is docked), and then Add or Remove Buttons.

Adding buttons to a toolbar

You can add a toolbar button to a toolbar, either from another toolbar or from PowerPoint's long list of toolbar buttons. You can also create a custom button for a custom command and add it to a toolbar.

To add a button from another toolbar, display both toolbars and open the Customize dialog box. If necessary, move the dialog box out of the way. To move the button (remove it from one toolbar and add it to another), drag the button from one toolbar to the desired location on the other toolbar. To copy the button, press CTRL while you drag.

You can add a toolbar button to a menu, too. Just drag the button to the menu, wait until the menu opens, and continue to drag to the desired position on the menu. PowerPoint automatically adds the appropriate text to the button image.

As mentioned earlier, the opposite also holds—you can drag a menu item to a toolbar. You can even put one of the built-in menus (File, Edit, View, and so on) on a toolbar. Here's how:

1. Display the toolbar.
2. Choose Tools | Customize.
3. Click the Commands tab.
4. From the Categories box, choose Built-in Menus. You see a list of the built-in menus in the Commands box.
5. Drag the menu that you want to the toolbar.

If a button is not so easily found, you need to search for it. To add a button from PowerPoint's list of commands, follow these steps:

1. Display the toolbar you want to customize.
2. Choose Tools | Customize.
3. Click the Commands tab.
4. Choose a category from the Categories box.
5. In the Commands box, find the command you want and drag it to the toolbar.

It's worth the time to look through the available commands. You may find some useful ones!

Creating a New Toolbar

Adding and removing buttons on existing toolbars may not be enough for you. You may want to create your own toolbar from scratch. You can place existing buttons together there, for convenience, or you can add custom buttons containing custom macros. Follow these steps to create the toolbar.

1. Choose Tools | Customize.

2. Click the Toolbars tab, shown in Figure 14-4.

3. Click New.

4. In the New Toolbar dialog box, shown here, type a name for the toolbar and click OK. It can have spaces, but try to keep the name fairly short and meaningful.

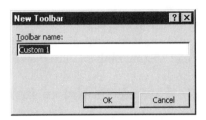

5. PowerPoint creates a tiny toolbar, all ready for some buttons, as shown here.

The procedure for adding buttons of existing commands to a custom menu is the same as described previously for adding buttons to existing menus.

If you have created a macro, as discussed later in this chapter, you can add it to a custom toolbar. With the Customize dialog box open, choose the Commands tab. From the Categories list, choose Macros. Then drag the macro you want from the Commands list to the toolbar. PowerPoint creates a toolbar button from the name of the macro.

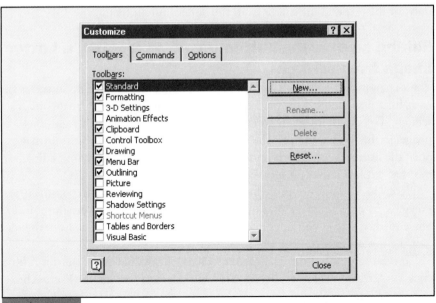

FIGURE 14-4   Use the Toolbars tab of the Customize dialog box to create, rename, and delete toolbars

One use for a custom toolbar is to hold custom buttons and menus that you don't want to display. If you remove a custom button or menu, it's gone forever. Instead, you can create a new toolbar. Instead of removing custom buttons or menus, move them to the holding toolbar. Then hide the toolbar. The toolbar stores them for you in case you ever need them again.

Getting Artistic

Once you start creating your own custom toolbars and custom commands (as with macros), you need to create your own buttons. Here's your chance to get artistic! You can even change existing built-in button icons to suit your whims.

Choosing from PowerPoint's list of buttons

You can avoid the artistic route by using one of PowerPoint's buttons, but they aren't suitable in most circumstances. Here's how:

1. Display the toolbar.
2. Choose Tools | Customize to open the Customize dialog box.
3. Right-click the toolbar button you want to change.
4. Choose Change Button Image from the shortcut menu.
5. Choose one of the button images from the submenu. PowerPoint uses that image for the toolbar button.

Remember that you can choose to display the button image only, the text only, or the text and the image from the same shortcut menu.

Editing an existing button image or creating a button image from scratch

You may want to slightly change a button image or use an existing image as the basis for a new one. It's easier to edit an existing image than to create one from scratch. To edit an image, with the Customize dialog box open, right-click the image on the toolbar to open the shortcut menu. Choose Edit Button Image to open the Button Editor, shown in Figure 14-5. Note that you cannot edit a button that displays a list or a submenu.

 Here you see a button image for a macro that reformats certain text to correct previous errors. The image of a medicine bottle came from an existing button. Since medicine fixes you up, only a "T" needed to be added to convey the idea that the button fixes up text.

To create a new button image from scratch, click Clear in the Button Editor, click a color, and then start clicking those little boxes. You can drag across boxes to create a line.

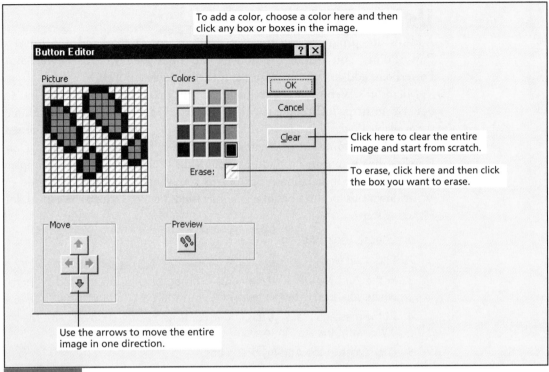

To add a color, choose a color here and then click any box or boxes in the image.

Click here to clear the entire image and start from scratch.

To erase, click here and then click the box you want to erase.

Use the arrows to move the entire image in one direction.

FIGURE 14-5 Use the Button Editor to edit button images, box by box

Using a graphic image

You can find an image you like and use it for your button. For example, many Web sites offer free graphic images that you can legally download and use. You can also use an image that you create in a graphic program. For best results, use an image that is 16 × 16 pixels, the size that PowerPoint normally uses. Larger images are scaled down and may become unclear or distorted.

The first step is to copy the graphic to the clipboard. If you have downloaded an image, you need to insert it into any program—PowerPoint is fine. Then select it and choose Copy on the Standard toolbar. If you have created the graphic in a program, you can select it and copy it to the clipboard directly from that program.

Display the toolbar and open the Customize dialog box. Right-click the toolbar button and choose Paste Button Image. PowerPoint replaces the current image with the image on the clipboard.

Don't forget that you can use button images for menus and shortcut menus as well. As explained earlier, you can customize whether the menu shows just text or text along with an image. For toolbar buttons, you can show just the image or text and the image.

Using Add-ins

Add-ins are programs (written by a programmer) that add a feature to PowerPoint. You install the add-in and then load it into PowerPoint. PowerPoint add-ins are files with the filename extension .ppa.

Microsoft's Web site has a couple of add-ins that you can download and try out. Go to **http://officeupdate.Microsoft.com** and click PowerPoint. Among the available PowerPoint downloads are the add-ins. If the add-in is compressed, you need to decompress it. Microsoft provides self-extracting .exe files. Double-click the file to install the add-in. Follow the simple instructions to complete installation. The installation program tells you where it is installing the add-in. Write down this location because you may need it later. To load the add-in, follow these steps:

1. Choose Tools | Add-ins.
2. Click Add New.
3. In the Add New PowerPoint Add-In dialog box, locate the add-in. Here's where you need to remember where you installed it. Choose it and click OK.
4. At the message that says the Add-In contains macros, choose Enable Macros if you want the Add-In to work.
5. Click Close in the Add-Ins dialog box.

Of course, how to use an add-in depends on the add-in. Most add-ins come with a text file or some other method to provide you with instructions. (You may see instructions at the Web site where you can print them.)

You can also unload an add-in when you are finished using it. Choose Tools | Add-Ins and select the add-in. Click Unload.

If you have some VBA code, you can save it as an add-in. Type the code in the Visual Basic Editor (discussed later in this chapter). You can use any presentation to do this. Then choose File | Save As. In the Save as Type drop-down list, choose PowerPoint Add-In (*.ppa). Type a name in the File Name text box and click Save.

Working with Macros

A macro is a series of PowerPoint commands that you save. You can then run the macro and execute all the commands in the macro. A macro can save you hours of time doing repetitive tasks. All macros are written in Visual Basic for Applications, or VBA.

There are two ways to create a macro. If you can execute the commands for the macro in PowerPoint to get the result you want, you can record the macro. For example, let's say you need to format fills in a certain way. You find yourself going through the same formatting steps over and over. Instead, you can select an object, start recording, and go through the same steps. When you stop recording, you have a macro. From now on, you can run the macro and let it do the work for you.

Other macros cannot be recorded. If you want a procedure to be executed only under certain conditions, you need to write the macro using VBA. Macros used in slide show view also need to be written, since slide show view doesn't have menus and toolbars to let you run through the macro's commands. In these cases, you need to learn how to program in VBA—or find someone who knows how.

In this chapter I explain how to record and run macros. I also provide an introduction to writing VBA macros with the assumption that you are not a programmer. If you are, this chapter will provide you with an introduction to the programming tools available in PowerPoint 2000.

Recording a Macro

If you want to record a macro, it often pays to practice the macro steps first. If the macro is long, you might even want to write down the steps you need to take. Otherwise, if you make a mistake, you may need to record the macro again. It's a little like rehearsing a presentation!

When you know what you need to do, set up the initial conditions first. For example, if you want to write a macro to format the fill of objects, you need to select an object first. It doesn't make any difference which object you select. If the macro will be run in slide sorter view, go into slide sorter view. Macros may not work if you try to run them in a different circumstance than the one you recorded them in.

The macro recorder is a wonderful tool, almost magical, but it cannot track where you move or click your mouse on the part of the screen that contains your presentation. Therefore, if you try to select an object while recording a macro, the results will not be what you expect. Sometimes this requires learning new ways of doing familiar tasks. However, you can record using the mouse to click a toolbar button or choose a menu item.

To record a macro, follow these steps:

1. Choose Tools | Macro | Record New Macro. PowerPoint opens the Record Macro dialog box, shown here:

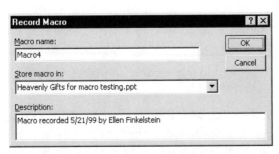

2. In the Macro Name text box, type a name for the macro. Macro names may not have spaces, and the first character must be a letter. You can use an underscore. Examples of macro names are FormatFill and Format_Fill.

3. If you wish, add a description of the macro in the Description box. You can describe exactly what the macro does.

4. Click OK. PowerPoint places the Stop Recording button, shown here, on your screen, both to remind you that you are recording and so that you can stop recording when you're done.

5. Execute each command that you want to record. If you make a little mistake, you can correct it. For example, if you choose the wrong color, you can go back and choose the correct color. PowerPoint records both the mistake and your correction, but the end result is okay, although the macro might take a couple of milliseconds longer to run.

6. When you are done, click the Stop Recording button.

If you make a big mistake while recording, stop recording and start over. Use the same macro name. PowerPoint asks if you want to replace the existing macro. Choose Yes and continue the process. You may also be able to edit the macro, as explained later in this chapter in the section "Managing Macros."

Using a Macro

Once you have recorded a macro, you should test it. If necessary, recreate the situation you want to start with first. Then follow these steps:

1. Choose Tools | Macro | Macros. PowerPoint opens the Macro dialog box, shown in Figure 14-6.

2. Choose the macro from the list.

3. Click Run.

Tip: Once you apply the macro to one object, you can press CTRL-Y to apply it to other objects.

If the macro does not work properly, try recording it again. If you get an error message, it may be because the environment has changed, as mentioned earlier.

For quick access to a macro, you may want to place it on a toolbar button or menu. You can also attach it to an object. For example, in slide show view, the only way to run a macro is to attach it to an object. Placing a macro on a toolbar button is discussed earlier in this chapter under "Adding a Menu Item to a Menu." Use the same procedure for both menus and toolbars.

Cross-Reference: For details on attaching a macro to an object, see the section "Using Action Settings to Run a Macro" in Chapter 11.

Figure 14-7 shows a slide with several shapes filled using a macro that creates a two-color gradient. This macro is described in detail in the next section. Refer to number 134 in the Slide Gallery to see the results in color.

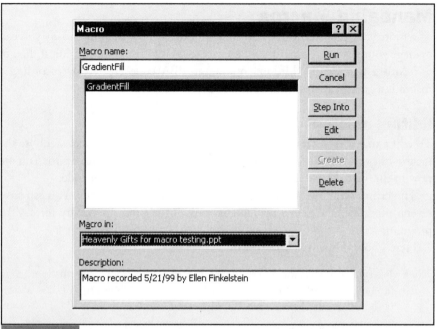

FIGURE 14-6   Run and manage macros from the Macro dialog box

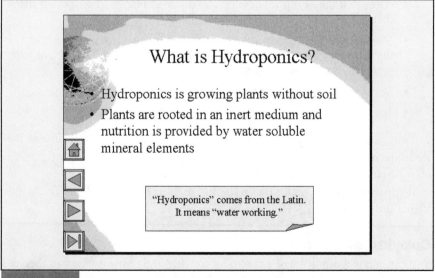

FIGURE 14-7   You can use a macro to speed up editing objects. Here a
two-color gradient in the AutoShapes was created with a macro

Managing Macros

The more you understand about how VBA code works, the more easily you can manage your macros. Sometimes it's easier to go into the code and edit it than to re-record a macro. In addition, looking at VBA code created by recording a macro is a great way to learn about VBA.

Editing macros

To edit a macro and view the code, choose Tools | Macro | Macros, choose the macro you want to edit, and click Edit. Figure 14-8 shows the macro. You are now in the Visual Basic Editor, where you can write your own code.

The Editor window contains a *module,* which stores VBA code. You can have several modules in a *project,* which contains all the pieces necessary for a VBA program.

Here's how this simple macro works:

- The first line starts the macro. A VBA macro always opens with the word *Sub.* (It stands for subroutine.) The name of the macro follows. The line always ends with a set of parentheses, in this case empty.
- The next three lines start with an apostrophe. The apostrophe tells VBA that what follows is a comment, not code. You can, and should, place comments in your code to explain what the code is doing. When you record a macro, PowerPoint automatically places a comment containing the date and your name.
- The next line starts a With function. Because a shape was selected, the code states that the next few lines apply to the ShapeRange (one or more shapes) that is selected in the active window.
- The next four lines specify the gradient, setting the fill to be visible, specifying the two colors, and creating the two-color gradient and its variant (repre-sented by the number 3 in this case).
- Now the code ends the With function.
- The last line ends the routine, with the expression *End Sub.*

You can see that you could easily fix the colors if you knew their Red-Green-Blue numbers. You could also change the variant—most gradients offer variants from one through four.

If you edit a macro, click Save on the Visual Basic Editors toolbar. To close the Visual Basic Editor, click its Close button.

Copying macros

You can create a duplicate of a macro by copying and pasting. You can then edit the new macro to create a new macro, instead of creating it from scratch. To create a duplicate, open the Visual Basic Editor to display the macro. Select all the text and copy it to the clipboard. Then choose Insert | Module to create a new module window. Paste the macro into the new window and edit it. You can also paste the text at the bottom of the same window to create a new macro.

You can use the Project Explorer to copy a macro module to another presentation. Open both presentations. In Figure 14-8, you can see two presentations open in the Project Explorer. If necessary, click the plus next to the presentation to display its modules. Then drag a module from one presentation to the other, all within the Project Explorer.

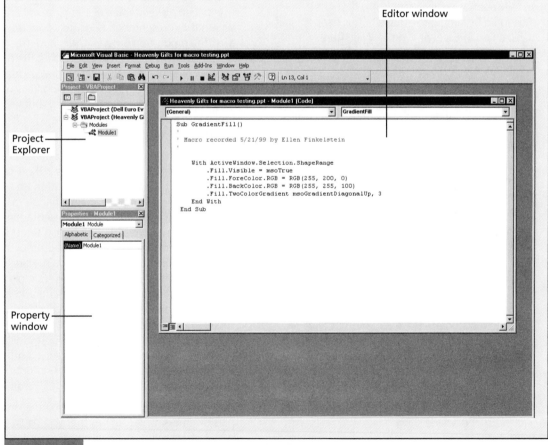

FIGURE 14-8   The Visual Basic Editor and the GradientFill macro

Programming with PowerPoint

by Brian Reilly

Programming in PowerPoint with VBA first appeared in PowerPoint 97. It was, and still is in PowerPoint 2000, a challenge for both PowerPoint experts and VBA programmers. Initially, both the PowerPoint experts, who generally are not programming types, and the VBA programmers, who generally are not skilled graphically, thought it would be simple to "make things happen, just like I do in Excel or Word." Well, frankly, that is not the case. But everyday we learn new things we can do with VBA in PowerPoint. It has taken a little while for many of us to understand what we can expect to do with VBA in PowerPoint. It has taken some further time to figure out just how to accomplish that.

This section covers three real-world examples of what can be accomplished with VBA in PowerPoint. You'll find sample VBA code at the end of the chapter that shows the actual code for two of these applications.

You can use VBA to accomplish three major types of functions in PowerPoint:

- Accelerate routine production tasks that are either very time-consuming or highly prone to human errors

- Automate the integration of tasks in other Office (or VBA-aware) programs when the task is better done in another program

- Add interactive data-gathering capability to PowerPoint from a person viewing a slide show

Accelerating Routine Production Tasks

Many routine production tasks (that is, tasks performed while creating a presentation) take a lot of time or are just not straightforward in PowerPoint. For example, in many production environments (that would be the folks who do lots of presentations—every day, every week), users need to keep track of the filename and where that presentation is located during and after the production process. Users have frequently requested a means of including the path and filename of a presentation on draft printouts of a presentation. Hey, the production folks want to find the presentation again quickly, but we all know that the audience doesn't care what it's called or where it came from.

So what is the problem here? Type the filename and the path into the footer. OK, it takes a few steps, but then that information isn't dynamic—it doesn't change if you change the filename or the location of the presentation. That's not so bad, but it certainly isn't good. A simple VBA routine can help you accomplish your goal quickly and dynamically. The first example at the end of this chapter is a simple macro that toggles between showing and not showing a complete path and filename in the footer. You can use just this kind of VBA macro to print presentations for draft purposes (with path and filename). You can then turn it off for either the real presentation or real printouts. One click turns it on if it's off or off if it's on.

You can probably think of many more examples of time-saving routines that you could run while you are editing a presentation and that could greatly shorten your production time. Time-consuming, repetitive, and error-prone operations can be vastly improved with a well-thought-out set of production tools that are VBA driven and customized to your own personal specifications.

Automating the Integration of Tasks in Other Programs

Let's face it, PowerPoint is a very good presentation and report assembly tool. But compared to Excel, it just doesn't have the horsepower to automate charts easily. The first problem is that the MSGraph datasheet can't add any better than I did before I went to prekindergarten. And MSGraph can't tell you the minimum or maximum values on a series of charts. So if you wanted a series of charts to all use the same scaling, you would have to manually change the scaling on each of those charts. And when the numbers that the charts are based on change at the last minute, each chart would have to be manually rescaled. If you use Excel to do your charts, with a little planning, you'd be able to let Excel recalculate your scales and automatically apply that to the appropriate charts for you.

But you also wouldn't want to copy and paste every chart back into PowerPoint. You can use VBA to automate the deletion of the old chart and the copying and pasting of the new charts back into PowerPoint. In some cases you could legitimately do this without VBA and use linking. But if you needed to add charts or change the scaling, you might be best off by automating the task and controlling Excel from PowerPoint.

Adding Interactive Data-Gathering Capability to PowerPoint

Suppose you are at a trade show and have set up a presentation to show in kiosk mode. Now suppose you'd also like to make it easy for someone to give you some information or request to be added to your mailing list.

Simply create the entry form on a PowerPoint slide and export the information from that page into an Excel workbook. This simple application is actually a combination of controlling Excel from within PowerPoint as well as using PowerPoint as a way to capture information and store it for you. This is a very simple example of taking the data from the user during a PowerPoint slide show and automatically placing it in a worksheet in Excel. The user never sees Excel. In this case, PowerPoint is opening Excel in the background, capturing the data supplied by the viewer of the slide show and telling Excel to place those values into an Excel worksheet. PowerPoint then tells Excel to save that file and wait for the next viewer's input. You can see the code for this example at the end of this chapter.

Brian Reilly is the owner of Reilly & Associates, a consulting firm that specializes in automating MS Office applications. He is also a Microsoft MVP and frequent contributor to the Microsoft PowerPoint newsgroup. He can be reached at 212-683-5969 or reilly_and_associates@compuserve.com.
*Note: You can find more VBA resources on Steve Rindsberg's Web site, **www.rdpslides.com**. Steve is another Microsoft PowerPoint MVP and coauthors a variety of PowerPoint production toolbar utilities with Brian.*

Programming with VBA

Learning how to program in VBA is quite a large project. Here I explain how you can get some basic information to get started.

Note that when you first try to use VBA help, you may see a message telling you that it is not installed. Click Yes to install it. You'll need your original program CD-ROM.

To start writing a macro, choose Tools | Macro | Macros. In the Macro dialog box, type a name for the macro in the Macro Name box and click Create. PowerPoint opens the Visual Basic Editor with a new module already started and the beginning (Sub) and the end (End Sub) of the macro in place. The cursor is between the two so that you can just start typing your code.

Understanding the Object Model

VBA uses a hierarchy of objects to enable you to specify where an object is. Each application has its own hierarchy. In this way, you can distinguish text in a text placeholder from shapes or pictures. To view the object model, follow these steps:

1. Choose Tools | Macros | Visual Basic Editor.

2. Click the Object Browser button on the toolbar, shown here, or press F2. The Visual Basic Editor opens the Object Browser.

3. From the Object Browser's Project/Library drop-down list, choose PowerPoint.

4. Click the Help button inside the Object Browser window to open the Object Model schematic shown in Figure 14-9.

The top of the hierarchy is always the application—in this case, PowerPoint. The most obvious object below the application is a presentation (or the collection of presentations). You can click on any object listed here to get further help on that object.

Another way to follow the line of a hierarchy is to use the Object Browser, shown in Figure 14-10. For example, if you want to find out about the ActiveWindow object used in the macro explained earlier, you can type **ActiveWindow** in the Search Text window (just under the Project/Library drop-

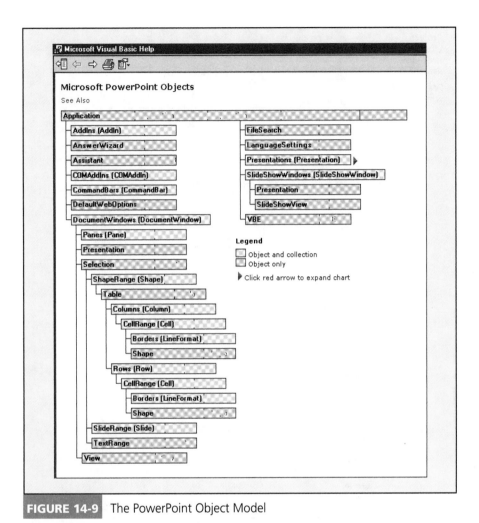

FIGURE 14-9 The PowerPoint Object Model

down list). You then see the text highlighted. With any text highlighted in the Object Browser, click Help to get information on that term. You can then find out more about the code snippet ActiveWindow.Selection.ShapeRange—that Selection is an object that belongs to ActiveWindow and ShapeRange is an object that belongs to Selection.

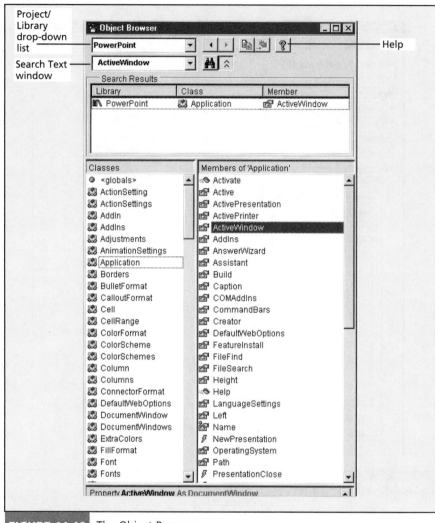

Project/
Library
drop-down
list

Search Text
window

Help

FIGURE 14-10 The Object Browser

Using Methods and Properties

It's not enough to specify objects—you need to do something with them. In VBA, objects have methods and properties. A method is an action that you perform on an object. A property is a property, such as the fill color of an object or the font of text. After looking up any object (type it in the Search Text window, highlight it and click Help), you can find its methods and properties. You usually also get some examples of code using that object. In Figure 14-11, you see the Help page for ShapeRange.

At the top of each object's Help page, you can click a link to its methods and properties. When you click Properties on the ShapeRange Help page, you get a list of ShapeRange's properties, including the Fill Property used in the example shown previously.

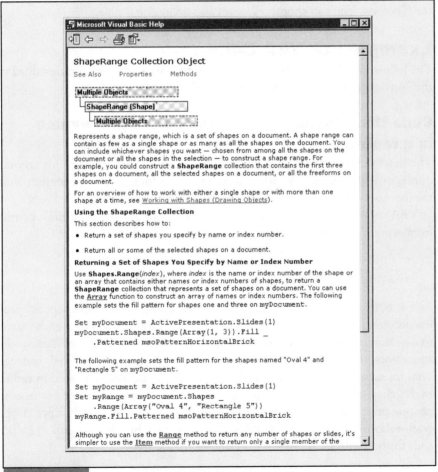

FIGURE 14-11 The ShapeRange Help page

All VBA code uses this structure of the object hierarchy and accomplishes tasks by means of methods and properties. You can also use built-in functions, such as If and For Each…Next.

You can create dialog boxes that appear when you run a macro. This is a more involved topic, but to start, choose Insert | UserForm from the Visual Basic for Applications menu. A UserForm is the raw material for a dialog box. The toolbox appears, letting you draw typical dialog box controls such as buttons and text boxes onto the dialog box. You can double-click any control to write code that specifies how the control functions. To create a form that viewers can use in slide show view, choose View | Toolbars from the PowerPoint menu and choose Control Toolbox. You can choose a control and drag it on a slide.

Examples of VBA Code

The following VBA code shows examples of two of the applications described in the "Advice from a Pro" section, earlier in this chapter.

Code that places presentation path and filename in a footnote

The first example creates a one-button toolbar. When you click it, PowerPoint displays the presentation's path and filename as a footnote. Click it again, and the footnote disappears.

VBA code that is meant to run while not in slide show view cannot be run from assigning a macro to an object. That means you have two choices:

- Choose Tools | Macro | Macros and choose the macro to run.
- Assign the macro to a custom toolbar button.

The best way to do this, especially if you are going to have many special production tools is to create an add-in with a custom toolbar and assign each macro to a button on that toolbar. The code that follows would reside in that add-in and automatically build the toolbar every time PowerPoint is started. Instructions for saving VBA code as an add-in are in the "Using Add-ins" section earlier in this chapter. You can type this code in the Visual Basic Editor of any new or existing presentation. You can also download "Join Our Mailing List.ppt" from **www.osborne.com/download/index.htm**. This presentation contains the VBA code for both this example and the example that follows.

```
Option Explicit

Sub auto_open()
'In PPT auto_open only runs automatically if in an add-in
'First declare the variables to be used
Dim oCmdBar As Object           'The commandbar object
Dim oAddFooters As Object        'The toolbar button object
On Error GoTo errorhandler       'Handles a possible error

BuildcmdBar:
'Build the command bar by first creating the commandbar

Set oCmdBar = _
CommandBars.Add(Name:="Reilly & Associates Toolbar", _
Position:=msoBarRight, Temporary:=True)
oCmdBar.Visible = True
Set oAddFooters = oCmdBar.Controls.Add_
(Type:=msoControlButton)
With oAddFooters
    .DescriptionText = "Toggle Path"
    .Caption = "Toggle Path"
    .OnAction = "Toggle_Path"
    .Style = msoButtonIcon
    .FaceId = 29
End With

Exit Sub
'''''''''''''''''''''''''''''''''''''''''''
errorhandler:
'Attempting to add toolbars that already exist causes an
'error. This error is captured here and the existing
'toolbar is deleted before it is then added.
Application.CommandBars("Reilly & Associates Toolbar").Delete
'The Resume statement takes the code back to the
'BuildcmdBar: line
Resume BuildcmdBar:
End Sub
'Add the code to be called from that toolbar button
Sub Toggle_Path()
    'This will only put the path on the Slide Master and
    'not on the Title Master
    'You would have to put it specifically on the Title
    'Master if you wanted it 'there.
    Dim strfullname As String
    strfullname = ActivePresentation.FullName
```

```
'will carry 'the value for the.sourcefullname
''''''This checks to see if the Footer is on or off
'and switches off or 'on''''''''''
    'Note: this only looks at the SlideMaster
'and not the TitleMaster
    With ActivePresentation.SlideMaster.HeadersFooters
        If .Footer.Visible = False Then
            With .Footer
                .Visible = msoTrue
            End With
        Else
            With .Footer
                .Text = strfullname
                .Visible = msoFalse
            End With
        End If
    End With
End Sub
```

Code that collects data from a slide show

The next code example does two different things: first it gets the values of the text boxes and a combo box on a PowerPoint page, and then it places those values into a workbook in Excel—completely in the background. The user never sees Excel open because it is invisible. The Excel file is saved, and Excel is closed. If you listen to your hard drive, you may hear the activity, but you won't see it on the screen.

To use this code, you need two files: "Join Our Mailing List.ppt" and "Submit to Mailing List.xls." They should both be in the same folder. Open the presentation and switch to slide show view. Click in the text boxes and type the requested information. Click the Submit for Mailing List button. You can try typing in several names and addresses. Then open the Excel worksheet, and voilà!—you see the data on the spreadsheet. Figure 14-12 shows both the presentation and the Excel worksheet. You can download these files from the Osborne Web site at **www.osborne.com/download/index.htm**. The presentation already contains the necessary VBA code for both this example and the previous one.

```
Private Sub btnSubmit_Click()
'This runs in a Private Sub so it is only available to this
'specific page in 'PowerPoint and it is attached to the
'btnSubmit_Click event.
    Dim oAppXL As Object 'Declare Excel application object
    Dim strName As String      'Holds the Name text string
    Dim strAddress As String   'Holds the Address text String
    Dim strCity As String        'Holds City
    Dim strState As String       'Holds State
```

```
    Dim strZip As String                'Holds Zip
    Dim strPath As String        'Lets the database location
    'be in same location as presentation
    'no matter what drive you are on

    strPath = ActivePresentation.Path
    Set oAppXL = CreateObject("Excel.application")
    'This next line sends the command to Excel to minimize
    'Each Excel command is preceded with "oAppXL."
    'The path is hard-coded here but wouldn't have to be
    oAppXL.Workbooks.Open _
    FileName:=strPath & "\Submit to Mailing List.xls"
    'We don't want to see Excel but it
    'doesn't have to be visible to run
    oAppXL.Visible = False

    'Now get the values from the text boxes
    'and combobox in PowerPoint
    strName = tbName.Text
    strAddress = tbAddress.Text
    strCity = tbCity.Text
    strState = cboState.Text
    strZip = tbZip

    'Now run Excel and place the values
    'oAppXL.Windows("McGraw example.xls").Activate
    'oAppXL.Sheets(1).Activate
    oAppXL.ActiveCell.Value = strName
    oAppXL.ActiveCell.Offset(0, 1).Value = strAddress
    oAppXL.ActiveCell.Offset(0, 2).Value = strCity
    oAppXL.ActiveCell.Offset(0, 3).Value = strState
    oAppXL.ActiveCell.Offset(0, 4).Value = strZip
    oAppXL.ActiveCell.Offset(1, 0).Activate

    'Turn off warnings in Excel since the file
    'is overwriting an existing file
    oAppXL.Application.DisplayAlerts = False
    oAppXL.ActiveWorkbook.Save
    'Wouldn't need to close or Quit if the
    'upfront code handled that differently
    'but it still all happens quickly, so
    'it might be a good idea anyway.
    oAppXL.ActiveWorkbook.Close (False)
    oAppXL.Application.Quit
End Sub
```

As you can see, VBA is an extremely powerful tool for customizing PowerPoint.

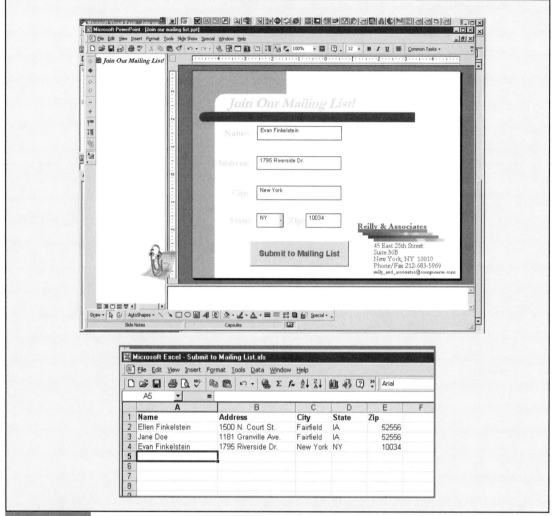

FIGURE 14-12 A slide containing a form for collecting names and addresses and the resulting Excel worksheet that collects the information

Professional Skills Summary

In this chapter you saw how to customize menus and toolbars. You can change the way menus and toolbars look and function. More importantly, you can add your own menus, menu items, toolbars, and toolbar buttons. This chapter also explained how to use add-ins. The second part of the chapter explained how to record and use a macro, and then introduced you to programming in Visual Basic for Applications (VBA).

In the next chapter, you prepare to present your slide show.

Preparing for the Perfect Presentation

You have completed your presentation. Now is not the time to run out and present it. Now is the time to prepare. You need to decide on some of the mechanical aspects of your presentation, such as which type of slide format and projector you will use. Will you manually forward each slide or let PowerPoint do it for you? Then it's time to rehearse until you are thoroughly familiar with your presentation. You may want to create custom shows so that you can vary your presentation based on your audience's reactions. Finally, if you will be traveling, you need to collect in one place all the files you need for your presentation.

Deciding on the Best Slide Format

Your first decision is how you will present your slide show. Your decision should be based on the equipment you have available, what type of impression you want to give, and the venue of the presentation.

Printing Handouts

If you want or need a low-tech method, you can print handouts from your presentation and give them to your audience. You don't need any equipment (or even any electricity). You should consider this method if you will present outdoors or in a country where you can't count on electricity. However, in all other situations, your audience probably expects you to take advantage of the electricity!

Of course, handouts are a great aid to your audience members, helping them remember what you said after they have gone home. In most cases, use handouts as an addition to your presentation. Research shows that handouts increase the effectiveness of a presentation in a sales situation.

Cross-Reference: In Chapter 16 I explain more about printing handouts and using them during your presentation.

Using 35mm Slides

You can send your presentation to a slide bureau to have 35mm slides made and show the slides from a slide projector. Using 35mm slides has two advantages:

- They generally provide the clearest, sharpest picture, with very bright colors.
- A 35mm slide projector is inexpensive and easy to use.

If you have only a 35mm slide projector available, you may want to go this route. Of course, remember that 35mm slides are static; you lose all your builds (animation) and transitions. You also lose any video, sounds, or music.

To create 35mm slides, choose File | Page Setup before starting the presentation to open the Page Setup dialog box, shown in Figure 15-1. In the Slides Sized

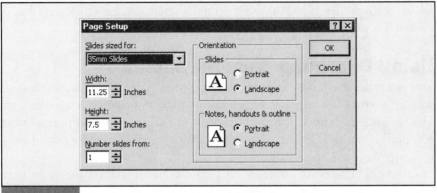

FIGURE 15-1 Use the Page Setup dialog box to choose the type of presentation you will use

For drop-down list, choose 35mm Slides. PowerPoint sizes your slides appropriately for 35mm slides.

Once you have completed your presentation, you send it to a service bureau that makes the actual slides. PowerPoint offers a direct connection to Genigraphics, a large service bureau. Genigraphics creates 35mm slides, posters, handouts, badges, transparencies, and other presentation materials. They also provide creative support and services. Choose File | Send To | Genigraphics. PowerPoint starts the Genigraphics Wizard (which you may need to install—PowerPoint automatically asks you if you want to install it). The wizard lets you order the materials you want. You can then send Genigraphics your presentation directly via modem connection or their Web site. Follow the wizard's instructions.

Of course, you can use any service bureau you want. Look in the Yellow Pages for Photographic Color Prints & Transparencies or Slides & Filmstrips. Otherwise, use any search engine for "35mm slides." Don't hesitate to ask your colleagues for referrals. You should check the following:

- Do they use Macs or PCs, and does what they use match what you use?
- Can you send them your PowerPoint 2000 presentation as is, or do you have to convert it? For example, if you have to convert it to a PowerPoint 97 presentation, you will lose features not included in PowerPoint 97 (such as picture bullets).
- Can you e-mail them your presentation?
- How quickly will they send your 35mm slides back to you? (Expect to pay more for rush service.)

New technology now enables you to make your slides in-house using a 35mm slide scanner. Some of these scanners sell for less than $1,000 and do an excellent job of making slides. If you make 35mm slides often, you can save a great deal of money this way.

Using Overhead Transparencies

You can make overhead transparencies from your slide show and project them with an overhead projector. Overhead projectors are much less expensive than LCD or DLP projectors. You are more likely to find an overhead projector in an educational setting. Overhead projectors usually need dimmed lights to work well, especially in larger groups.

Overheads are easy to create. Many printers can print directly onto a special transparency acetate that stops the ink from creating puddles. If you do not have this special transparency acetate, you can also print onto paper and use a copier to copy onto acetate. Of course, you would ideally use a color printer or copier to make the transparencies. Service bureaus can also create transparencies for you.

Generally, overhead backgrounds should be light. You can even create overheads with no background at all. Remember, all the color on the slide needs to be printed onto the acetate. To create a quick, inexpensive color background, you can buy colored acetate that acts as the background.

To create overheads, before starting your presentation, choose File | Page Setup. In the Slides Sized For drop-down list, choose Overhead. While 35mm slides and on-screen presentations almost always use a landscape orientation, overhead transparencies often use a portrait orientation. In the Page Setup dialog box, choose the orientation you want. PowerPoint then sizes your slides appropriately for overhead transparencies, as shown here. To view this slide in color, refer to number 135 in the Slide Gallery.

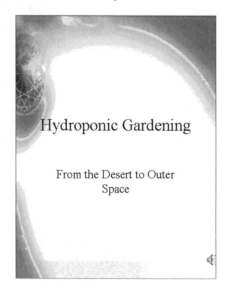

Hydroponic Gardening

From the Desert to Outer Space

Overheads are a great backup for an on-screen presentation; you can use them if your projector or computer dies. Of course, as with 35mm slides, you lose any animation, video, or sound when you print to overheads.

Presenting Directly from a Computer

Nowadays, most presenters show presentations directly from a computer using an LCD or DLP projector. The general term is a *data projector* because it transmits data from your computer onto a screen. You could possibly use an LCD panel over an overhead projector, but LCD panels are rarely used any more—they are not bright enough for most situations.

For very small groups (1–5), you can present directly from a laptop with no projector. If you use a large monitor, you can show a presentation to a group of 15 or so. You could do a new employee orientation like this. You can also buy very large display systems, such as 80-inch televisions and plasma screens, that will present to larger groups—but they are quite expensive. For larger groups, you need a projector and a screen. For more information on choosing a projector, see the next section and the upcoming, "Advice from a Pro" box, "Ten Questions to Ask Before You Buy a Projector."

Choosing Equipment for Presentations Without Problems

LCD and DLP projectors are quite complex. To buy one, look under Projection Apparatus in the Yellow Pages. Projectors are rarely sold in computer stores.

Before going into any more detail, you need to understand the terminology involved. Table 15-1 explains terms related to projectors.

Using a projector is generally simple—you connect its cable to the external display port of a laptop or computer. You may need to read your computer's documentation for details. Almost all projectors come with a remote controller so that you can move around the room as you control the presentation.

Projectors have a *native* resolution, a resolution that is built into the projector. If your computer screen uses the same resolution, no adjustments are necessary. Many projectors automatically adjust for differences in resolution.

New in 2000: PowerPoint has a Projector Wizard that helps you test and adjust your projector before using it. To use the wizard, choose Slide Show | Set Up Show. Then click Projector Wizard. The screen shown next appears. Follow the instructions to test the picture and sound and adjust for any resolution differentials.

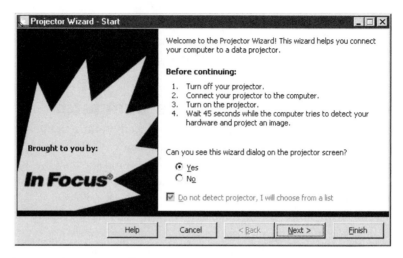

The wizard automatically restores your original resolution settings after the presentation is over.

Term	Definition
LCD projector	LCD stands for Liquid Crystal Display. An LCD projector electronically takes the data from your presentation and displays it on a screen.
DLP projector	DLP stands for Digital Light Processing. Developed by Texas Instruments, a DLP projector uses a technology involving over a million micro-mirrors, each attached to a micro-motor. The motors move the mirrors to help focus the image. DLP projectors generally produce a brighter, smoother image and are especially valued for video and photographs, where accurate color fidelity is most important.
LCD panel	An LCD panel fits on top of an overhead projector. The overhead projector provides the light, optics, and focus, and the LCD panel reads the data from your computer. LCD panels are less expensive than projectors.
Projector	A projector includes a light source and lens, and the ability to read data from your computer. Most include speakers.
Overhead projector	Overheads are mostly used for transparencies, with no computer involved. You can combine an LCD panel with an overhead projector to project a PowerPoint presentation.
Passive LCD	Passive LCD is the oldest technology for projectors. It is lower in cost, but the color contrast is unsuitable for video clips.
Active LCD	This is the current technology for LCD projectors, providing higher color contrast. Suitable for video.
Resolution	The number of horizontal × vertical pixels displayable on a screen. There are four major types: VGA (480 × 640), SVGA (800 × 600), XGA (1,024 × 768), SXGA (1,280 × 1,024).
Lumens	A measure of the brightness of light.

TABLE 15-1   Presentation Equipment Terminology

Ten Questions to Ask Before You Buy a Projector

by W.K. Bohannon

1. **How much can I afford?** Even Bill Gates sometimes asks how much; well, so do I. In order to determine the ideal price range for your projector, you need to find out your budget—and then stick to it.

   Of course, having a realistic budget helps. You will be able to find plenty of SVGA projectors in the $4,000 price range and XGA projectors in the $7,000 price range. The newest lightweight ultraportables cost a little more; but they, too, will drop in price if you're willing to wait. It goes without saying that you'll have to pay more if you want more performance, features, or brightness.

   Regardless of your budget, there is probably a projector out there that's just right for you; so explore all the possibilities. Even if your budget is shockingly low, you can often find refurbished rental-return units and close-out models at a significant discount. Some of these projects come with respectable warranties.

2. **How will I use the projector?** While this probably sounds like an obvious question, you'd be surprised how many people consult me for advice on buying a projector who haven't thought about it yet.

   Do you expect to carry it around every day? If the answer is yes, the weight of the projector is a very important issue. But if you're not going to lug it around very often, the weight isn't as crucial. A sturdier, heavier projector with more features will work perfectly well—and you can get it for the same price or less. Once you start taking a careful look at projectors, you'll be amazed how many features you can get by adding just a few more pounds.

   You also need to determine where you will put the projector and the size of the screen that you will use. These are important because no universal standard for projector placement and image size exist. This means that if you line up several, similarly priced projectors and turn them on, the projectors will give you a variety of image sizes (and elevations), even though they are at the same distance and height from the screen. Some projectors are designed to be used close to the screen, and others come with a wide-ranging zoom lens so that you have the option of being either close to the screen or farther away.

   Then there's the matter of keystoning. *Keystoning* is the image distortion caused by projecting at an angle that the projector wasn't designed for—you see an image that is wider on the top than on the bottom. While some projectors offer "keystone correction" so that you can adjust the image to compensate for the distortion, others don't have this feature.

3. **How bright should my projector be?** Like everyone, you want to have the brightest image possible. However,

there's a catch—the size of the image a projector is projecting greatly affects your perception of its brightness. A 600-lumen projector looks great on a 60-inch screen (measured diagonally), but the same projector looks quite dim when you need to fill a 120-inch screen, because it has quadruple the area.

While projector manufacturers may brag that you can use even their smallest projectors to fill a 300-inch screen, in practice you need closer to 6,000 lumens of brightness to do that effectively, which is ten times the light output of the average ultraportable.

In general, ultraportable projectors deliver from 400 to 1,000 ANSI lumens, heavier conference-room projectors from 1,000 to 2,000 lumens, and large-venue projectors from 2,500 to 10,000 lumens.

In my experience, manufacturers can fib about projector brightness, the way most people fib about their weight or annual salary. You may find hundreds of lumens of difference between the claims of the manufacturer for the model line and the actual brightness of individual projectors in that model line. Try to find a reputable, trustworthy salesperson who is honest with you about these discrepancies.

4. **How long will the lamp last and how much does it cost?** While you're asking questions, also ask about the projector's lamp. Except in the case of a CRT projector, the lamp is your projector's light source—and it will burn out just like any lightbulb. Replacement bulbs can be expensive and are a hidden cost of owning a projector. Find out how often you'll need to replace them and consider that answer in your buying decision.

You may find that buying a more expensive projector with a longer lamp life is less expensive in the long run than buying a cheaper projector that burns bulbs faster. If you need to light up a large screen under harsh ambient lighting, for instance, then you need your projector to operate at the peak of its capabilities; otherwise, you may find yourself buying lots of replacement lamps so that your projector always operates at its optimal level.

As an education for yourself, ask three questions about the lamp—how many hours of use can you expect to get from the lamp, how bright will the projector be after the lamp has been run for several hundred hours (it often dims dramatically), and how bright will it be near the end of its life?

Don't forget to ask about the lamp's rated power in watts. Let's say you're trying to decide between two projectors with similar lumens of brightness, but one uses a 500-watt lamp to produce its light and the other uses only a 100-watt lamp. In that case, you should choose the 100-watt lamp projector—it will stay bright longer, produce less heat, and require a less noisy cooling fan. Also, it will use less energy and last longer because it is inherently more efficient.

5. **What is the projector's resolution?** As explained earlier, a projector's resolution is a key factor in a projector's price. There are four options: VGA (480 × 640), SVGA (800 × 600), XGA (1,024 × 768), and SXGA (1,280 × 1,024 or higher). Before you start shopping, know which resolution you need.

You probably don't need the highest resolution if you're going to use your projector just for simple, bulleted-text PowerPoint slides. SVGA or even VGA (if you can find it any more) may be fine. On the other hand, you'll need the highest resolution possible—SXGA or better— if you will be presenting a circuit design you created on a workstation. Find out from your salesperson the projector's native resolution. Most new projectors can shrink or expand a computer's image to fill the fixed matrix of pixels of the projector. With most images, when this resizing is accomplished skillfully, you will have a hard time discerning the projector's exact native resolution. There are some SVGA projectors that can make an XGA or even an SXGA signal look decent. But if you try to project a detailed CAD drawing on that same SVGA projector in full SXGA resolution, some of the lines will be missing and other lines will be blurry. These resizing problems will not occur if you project the same image with a projector that has a native SXGA resolution.

6. **What are the lens specifications?** Besides knowing whether you need a motorized zoom lens (only a few projectors are zoomless these days), what else is there to know? Plenty. Anyone who has ever shopped for an SLR camera knows the importance of an f-stop or f-number—the smaller the number, the more light transmitted (the brighter the image).

   Besides the zoom range (the amount of change you can get in image size), look for a lens with all-glass elements. To save weight, many projector lenses are made of plastic or of a plastic composite, but the on-screen image from a good glass lens cannot be beaten; it will be sharp and in focus, even in the corners.

   If you are buying a projector for a conference room, an optional projection lens is important to consider. In order to allow projectors much greater flexibility to "throw" images farther and wider, many manufacturers are starting to offer a range of lens options. If conference room flexibility is important, definitely ask about optional lenses. If the projector's manufacturer doesn't provide them, a third-party lens company such as Buhl Optical probably will.

7. **What contrast and color saturation do I need?** Like Mom and apple pie, everybody loves color and contrast— but few people can say exactly why.

   Most projectors have more than enough contrast for the vast majority of situations. Contrast shouldn't be much of an issue unless you're very picky about video quality, which looks better with lower black levels.

   For some strange reason, color—or more specifically, color saturation—is rarely defined in any precise manner by those in the projector industry. However, if what you want is great color, it's not hard to provide a few useful pointers.

   For today's projectors, a three-panel LCD projector or a three-chip DLP projector provides the best color saturation. One-panel LCD and one-chip DLP projectors usually provide less color saturation, and sometimes they display weak reds and blues. CRT projectors deliver a level of color saturation somewhere between the three-panel and one-panel projectors. The big light-valve projectors are close behind the LCD and DLP units but show more color variation across their images.

As mentioned earlier, most projectors produce acceptable colors for most situations. Why complain if you like what you see? Nevertheless, don't forget to check color intensity under various lighting conditions to get an idea of the projector's performance in the real world.

8. **How is the projector's weight, and what are its other features?** Projectors today offer such a wide range of features that I usually have to make a chart to compare two projectors' features. To start with, find out how many inputs, outputs, and onboard speakers the projector has. Other capabilities, such as a motorized zoom, focus, and lens shift, should be added to the list.

Additional features I like to see are related to ease of use: easily operated elevator feet, handles that are comfortable and sturdy, easy-to-use on-screen menus, and a lightweight carrying case for portables and ultraportables.

If weight is important, it's not enough to find out how much the projector itself weighs—you also need to consider the total carrying weight of the unit, case, and accessories. When you add in all the required cables and accessories, you'd be surprised how much different projectors' carrying weights are equalized. Besides the weight of the carrying case, the signal cables and remote-control unit usually add about two pounds to a projector's overall heft.

9. **What should I expect from the warranty and service?** Let's say you've already handed over the cash for that new projector. Now, you're out in the field and the thing suddenly quits on you. Perhaps the lamp blows up or some circuitry fries. What now? Now's when your warranty kicks in—and you'd better make sure you have one.

The good news is that, because the overall quality of projectors is now so good, many manufacturers are competing to offer the best warranty and service options. Some manufacturers now even offer free overnight replacement of a dead unit, no questions asked. If you're a road warrior, that's the kind of service you need.

Otherwise, warranties of one, two, or three years are the rule. Still, you should read the fine print carefully, since there are a wide range of service plans to choose from, depending on the manufacturer and dealer. In particular, check out how long the lamp is covered under the warranty; it may be for only a few months.

As always, get everything in writing, and keep a file with your warranty and other projector-related materials in it. When you need to use that warranty, you'll know where it is.

10. **May I see a demonstration?** The best way to learn about a projector is to see it perform. So ask for a demo—or better yet, a number of demos.

To make sure that I can judge a full range of image-quality parameters, I usually bring to a demo a disk of professional test patterns and images. One of my favorites is Sonera Technologies'

DisplayMate (**www.sonera.com**), but there are a number of others on the market. If you don't have a professional test pattern available, just use a disk of your favorite images and see what that new projector can do.

A great way to decide between two competing models is to ask your salesperson to arrange a "shoot-out," so you can view both projectors with the same image at the same time. In my experience, practically every projector looks good by itself; but make a direct comparison and all its warts appear.

William Bohannon, chief scientist at Escondido, California–based Manx Research (760-735-9678), has more than 25 years of experience in the computer and projector industry. As chief scientist for Display Products at Proxima Corporation from 1989 to 1994, he developed important business relationships with several Japanese laboratories and companies. His career also includes positions at TRW, Hughes Aircraft, and Kappa Systems. In addition, he is currently the Projector Review columnist for Presentations magazine.

Timing a Presentation

When giving a presentation, you can manually control the timing of each slide by clicking the mouse, or you can set timing and let PowerPoint forward each slide for you. Usually, timed slides are used when your presentation will run unattended at a conference or kiosk, for example. However, if you are presenting, you can always pause a presentation that has timed slides to maintain full control. Timing was more important before the days of ubiquitous remote controllers. In that case, automatic timing freed the presenter from being tied to the computer. Nowadays, with a remote mouse, you can control the computer and still walk around the room without restriction.

Timing slides can be used as a technique for rehearsal. When you rehearse timings, PowerPoint lets you know the length of the entire presentation, which is extremely useful information. You also learn how long you are spending on each slide. From this data, you might decide to divide a slide into two, in order to break up the message into smaller bites. On the other hand, you might realize that two slides should be combined.

Setting the Timing

There are two ways to set timing for a presentation. When you use the first method, you run through your presentation as a rehearsal and time the slides based on your rehearsal. In the second method, you directly assign a number of seconds to each slide. If your presentation is designed to run unattended, you can still use the rehearsal method to get an idea of how many seconds to assign to each slide. Then you can assign timings directly.

Rehearsing timings

Before rehearsing timings, especially if you will be presenting your slide show, gather together any notes you might need so that you are ready to present. You are about to rehearse your entire presentation for the first time! Follow these steps:

1. Open your presentation and make sure that the first slide is displayed.

2. Then choose Slide Show | Rehearse Timings. (The Rehearse Timings item is on the extended menu and may not appear immediately.) If you are in slide sorter view, choose Rehearse Timings from the Slide Sorter toolbar. PowerPoint switches you to slide show view and opens the Rehearsal dialog box, shown next.

Next   Slide time   Total time

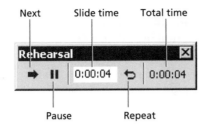

Pause   Repeat

3. Start talking! Present your slide show as you plan to when you are actually presenting.

4. When you are finished with the first slide, click Next in the Rehearsal dialog box (or just click as usual).

5. Continue until you have finished the last slide, clicking Next after each slide.

6. After the last slide, PowerPoint displays the time of the entire presentation and asks if you want to record the timing and use it when you view the slide show, as shown here. Click Yes unless you made a mistake and want to start over. PowerPoint switches you to slide show view and ends the rehearsal.

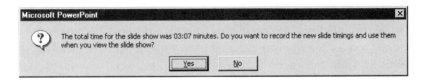

While timing a presentation, you have two other options in the Rehearsal dialog box. To pause the timing process, click Pause. Click Pause again to continue timing the slide. If you make a mistake and want to start a slide over, click Repeat.

After you have recorded the timings, you can see them as timing icons in slide show view, as shown here. This slide show appears in color as number 136 in the Slide Gallery.

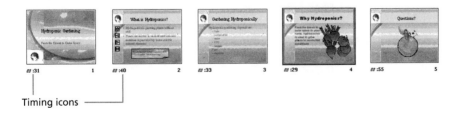

Timing icons

Assigning timing to slides

You can directly assign timing to slides without going through the rehearsal process just described. You can also rehearse the presentation and then use the timings you obtain as a guideline for assigning your own timings. To assign timing to the slides in your presentation, follow these steps:

L▶ Tip: To select a contiguous group of slides, click the first slide in the group, press SHIFT, and click the last slide in the group. To select additional noncontiguous slides, press CTRL and click each slide you want to add to the group.

1. Switch to slide sorter view.

2. Select the first slide. If you want other slides to have the same timing, select them as well.

3. Choose Slide Transition from the Slide Sorter toolbar (or choose Slide Show | Slide Transition). PowerPoint opens the Slide Transition dialog box, shown in Figure 15-2.

4. In the Advance section of the dialog box, check Automatically After. Then use the textbox or the arrows to set the number of seconds you want the slide or slides displayed.

5. Click Apply to apply the slide timing to the selected slide or slides. To apply the slide timing to all the slides in the presentation, click Apply to All.

PowerPoint closes the dialog box, and you will see the timing icon on all the slides if you clicked Apply to All, as shown in Figure 15-3 (or on all the slides you selected). Continue to set timing for other slides as necessary, using the same

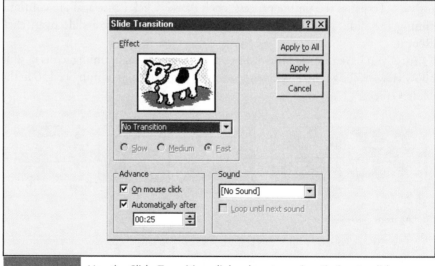

FIGURE 15-2 Use the Slide Transition dialog box to assign timing to slides

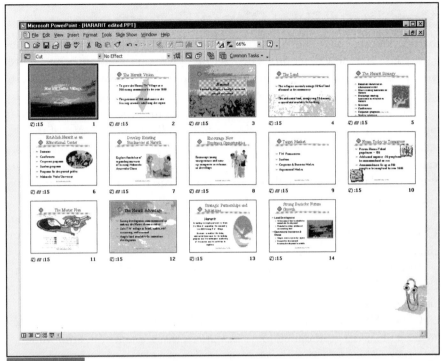

FIGURE 15-3 You can quickly set a time for all the slides using the Apply to All button in the Slide Transition dialog box

procedure just outlined. Look for number 137 in the Slide Gallery to see this presentation in color.

Using Timing When You Present

To use the timing you set, you need to activate it. PowerPoint's default is manual advancing of slides, so you need to specifically tell PowerPoint to use your timing. Here's how:

1. Choose Slide Show | Set Up Show.
2. In the Advance Slides section of the Set Up Show dialog box, click Using Timings, If Present.
3. Click OK.

Now, when you run your presentation in slide show view, PowerPoint uses your timings. You can go back and choose Manually in the same section of the dialog box if you decide not to use the timings you have set.

Setting Slide Show Parameters

Before running a slide show, you can set a number of parameters that determine how your slide show functions. These settings give you last-minute control over your presentation. To set these parameters, choose Slide Show | Set Up Show to open the Set Up Show dialog box, shown in Figure 15-4.

The main section of the dialog box determines the type of show you want to present. By default, your presentation is shown full screen. However, if the presentation will be browsed by an individual at a kiosk or computer station, you can choose Browsed by an Individual (Window) to have the presentation run in a window and include a menu that users can use to run through the presentation at their own pace.

For self-running presentations at trade shows and conferences, choose Loop Continuously Until 'Esc'. As soon as the presentation ends, PowerPoint starts the presentation from the beginning again.

If you chose Browse at a Kiosk, you must create a timed presentation because the Manually option does not work, and the Loop Continuously Until 'Esc' option is unavailable.

Choose Show Without Narration if you have recorded narration but don't want to use it. This is a great option for presentations that are sometimes run without a presenter and sometimes with one. You can also record narration for practice purposes and then check this box when you are ready to give the presentation.

Choose Show Without Animation to show the presentation at the end point of any animation on each slide. Use this option when you want to allow individuals to browse the presentation themselves. Since they are not familiar with the

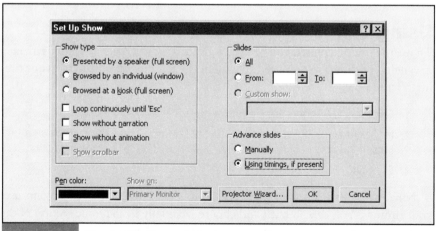

FIGURE 15-4   The Set Up Show dialog box contains parameters that determine how your presentation will run in slide show view

animation, they could find it confusing to have to click several times before going to the next slide.

If you select the Browsed by an Individual option, you can also choose Show Scrollbar. The scrollbar is a mechanism for individuals to browse your presentation by themselves. In Figure 15-5, you see a slide displayed in a window with a scrollbar. To view this slide in color, refer to number 138 in the Slide Gallery.

In the Slides section you can choose to display all the slides or only a group of slides. Specify which slides you want to display. If you have created a custom show (covered later in this chapter), you can choose it here. Click OK when you are done.

Preparing Your Notes

It's now time to think about what you will say when you stand up in front of your audience. If you haven't already done so, before going any further, research your audience. How much do they know about the topic? What do they want to get

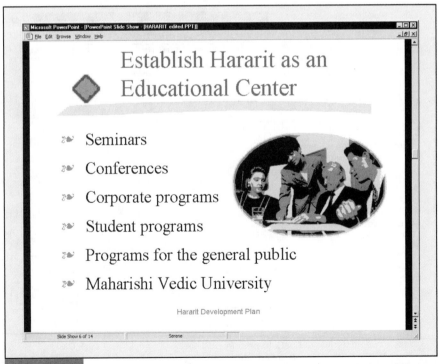

FIGURE 15-5 You can set up a slide show to be displayed in a window with a scrollbar so that individuals can browse through the slide show on their own

Professional Pointer

One secret is to record narration for your entire presentation as if you were presenting. Then run your presentation, and sit back and listen. You get an entirely different perspective when you pretend to be the audience. Listening to your presentation enables you to pick up awkward moments, unclear passages, and boring spots much more easily.

from your presentation? Even if the slides are the same, your explanation of the slides will change for varying audiences. Always get as much information as you can in advance.

As a last resort, if you can't get any information in advance, you may be able to ask questions of your audience just before you start presenting. You may need to make some quick changes to your planned talk based on the answers you receive.

If you will work from notes, print them out and use them when you rehearse. If you haven't been creating notes as you worked, now is the time to go back and add presentation notes for each slide. To print notes from the notes pane in your presentation, choose File | Print to open the Print dialog box, shown in Figure 15-6.

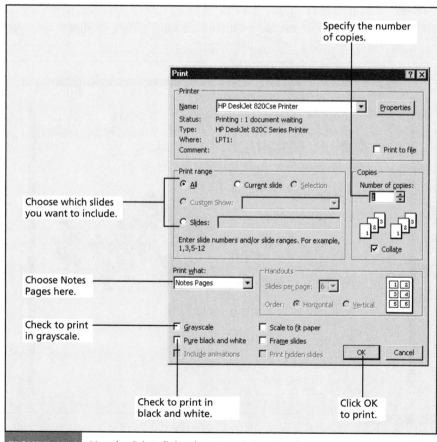

FIGURE 15-6   Use the Print dialog box to print notes that you can use to guide you when you present

Practice in front of a live person, preferably not one of your parents or children. Others can pick up potential problems more easily than you can. A useful technique is to leave out your overview and summary slides and see what the person remembers as your main points. Ask your audience of one what was interesting, appealing, or confusing.

Rehearsing: The Professionals' Secret

Running through your presentation one time to set timings is not enough. Before you present, you need to rehearse your presentation until you are thoroughly familiar with it. The goal is three-quarters of the way between reading and memorizing. In other words, you should know your presentation so well that it is almost memorized, but not well enough that you can repeat it by rote.

Run through your presentation in the actual physical environment you plan to use, if possible, or somewhere that closely resembles it. If you will use a projector and screen, set them up and use them. Where will you put the projector and screen? Where will you stand? Practicing includes not only speaking out your text but also using your equipment and moving your body in the same way you will when you are actually in front of your audience.

Have a backup plan. Every presenter has experienced, or heard stories about, equipment catastrophes. Practicing with your equipment not only benefits you, it tests your equipment. Then think what you would do if your computer died, your projector conked out, or your remote controller stopped working. Practice your backup plan, too. Here are some musts:

- Always have printed handouts or overhead transparencies for the worst-case scenario—no electricity, a dead computer, and so on.
- Make sure you have a regular mouse if your remote controller doesn't work or gets lost.
- Always carry at least one spare bulb for your projector.
- If you are traveling, call ahead to see what equipment is available locally.

Creating Slide Show Variations

Sometimes you want to vary a presentation. If you present a slide show more than once for different audiences, you can hide a slide in your presentation that isn't suitable for a specific situation. You hide the slide in advance, so you need to think ahead.

To hide a slide, select the slide you want to hide (for example, in normal view) and choose Slide Show | Hide Slide. In slide sorter view, select the slide and choose the Hide Slide button.

Creating a Custom Show

You can create a presentation that includes slides for more than one situation. You can then specify which slides you will use for one situation and which for another. These variations are called *custom shows*. Let's say you are giving a presentation on a new employee benefit package but the packages vary slightly for two different groups of employees. You can create slides appropriate for each group and include them all in the presentation. Then you create custom shows that show only the slides you need.

Often you start with a set of slides that are common to both groups. When the presentation must diverge, you jump to the custom show.

Another use for a custom show is to allow for more than one possible response from your audience. You could include some slides with more details if you find out at the last minute that your audience is more sophisticated that you expected.

L▶ Tip: The best place to put the group of slides that you may or may not use is at the end of the presentation.

To create a custom show, you must first create all the possible slides you will need. The variations should be together in a group so you can do as little jumping around as possible.

Choose Slide Show | Custom Shows | New to open the Define Custom Show dialog box, shown in Figure 15-7.

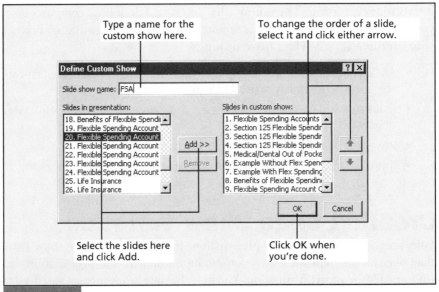

FIGURE 15-7   Use the Define Custom Show dialog box to create a new custom show

To select a contiguous group of slides, click the first slide in the group, press SHIFT, and click the last group. To select a noncontiguous group of slides, press CTRL, and then select each additional slide.

Once you have created your custom show and clicked OK, PowerPoint displays the Custom Shows dialog box with your new custom show listed. To preview the custom show, select it from the list and click Show. Figure 15-8 is a custom show consisting of one slide. You could use this slide when you are in a situation appropriate for taking questions from the audience. To view this slide in color, refer to number 139 in the Slide Gallery.

Editing a Custom Show

To make modifications to a custom show, choose Slide Show | Custom Shows and select the show you want to edit. Click Edit. PowerPoint opens the same Define Custom Show dialog box you used to create the custom show originally. Use the same tools to add or remove slides or to move them around in the custom show.

To delete a custom show entirely, choose Slide Show | Custom Shows and select the show you want to delete. Click Remove. Note that the slides are not deleted from the presentation.

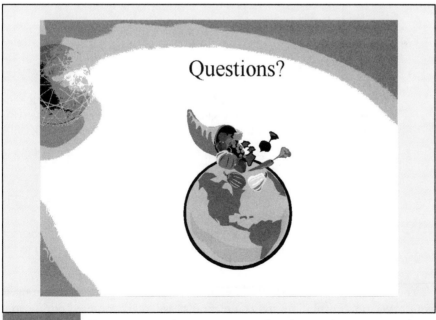

FIGURE 15-8 You can customize your presentations by creating a custom show, which consists of one or more slides that you display only when you choose to

Using a Custom Show

To set up your presentation so that PowerPoint displays only the slides in the custom show, choose Slide Show | Set Up Show. In the Set Up Show dialog box, choose Custom Show in the Slides section. This item is available only if the presentation includes a custom show. Then click OK. Now, when you start your presentation in slide show view, only the slides in the custom show are displayed. To display all the slides of the presentation again, open the Set Up Show dialog box again and choose All in the Slides section. In most cases, you want to display slides not in the custom show with the option of using the custom show slides when you choose to. Using a custom show is like hyperlinking. There are three ways to jump to a custom show during a presentation:

- Select an object on the slide where you want to create the option to jump to the custom show. Choose Slide Show | Action Settings. On either tab, choose Hyperlink To. From the drop-down list, choose Custom Show. PowerPoint opens the Link To Custom Show dialog box, shown here:

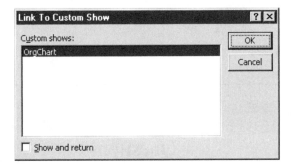

Choose the custom show you want. If you want to return to the same slide after displaying the custom show slides, click Show and Return. (Otherwise, PowerPoint displays the custom show and ends the presentation.) Click OK.

- Select an object on the slide where you want to create the option to jump to the custom show. Choose Insert | Hyperlink. Click Place in This Document. Under Custom Shows, choose the custom chart you want. If you want to return to the same slide after displaying the custom show slides, click Show and Return. Click OK.

- During a presentation, right-click, choose Go | Custom Show and choose the custom show you want. When you use this method, you can't return to the current slide.

You can create several custom shows if you wish, but be careful not to make your navigation possibilities too complex. It's easy to get confused during your presentation!

Using the Road Warrior's Tools—Pack and Go

Many presentations are shown on the road. When you travel, you first need to check and double-check that you have all the equipment you need and that it's working properly. You also need to make sure that you have any supporting files that your presentation might require. Examples are custom fonts and video and music files that are not embedded.

Pack and Go analyzes your presentation and copies all the files you need for a presentation onto a diskette or other removable storage medium. To start Pack and Go, follow these steps:

1. Choose File | Pack and Go. It's on the extended menu, and you may have to install it the first time you use it. (PowerPoint automatically offers to do so.) PowerPoint opens the Pack and Go Wizard, shown here:

2. Choose Next.

3. On the next screen, choose the presentation you want to pack. Click Next.

4. On the next screen, choose the destination. The wizard automatically reads available locations, but you can choose another location. For example, you may have a writable CD drive. Choose Next.

5. On the next screen, check if you want to include linked files. You can also choose to embed TrueType fonts. Click Next.

6. On the next screen, choose if you want to include PowerPoint Viewer. Include the viewer if you will present from a computer that doesn't have PowerPoint installed. Click Next.

7. On the last screen, the wizard summarizes where it will save your presentation and gives some final instructions. Click Finish. PowerPoint copies the presentation and any other necessary files.

Professional Skills Summary

In this chapter, you reviewed all the steps you need to take to prepare for a presentation. You need to decide what medium you will use: handouts, 35mm slides, overhead transparencies, or on-screen projection. The chapter covered information about choosing and using a projector.

You can rehearse timing for your presentation or directly assign timing. You can choose whether or not to use your timing at the time you actually present.

Before you start to rehearse, you should prepare notes that you will use. Then rehearse, rehearse, rehearse!

You can create a custom show to let you easily create variations on a presentation. Finally, if you are traveling, you can use Pack and Go to collect all the files you need for your presentation.

The next chapter covers the actual process of presenting a slide show.

chapter 16

Presenting Your Slide Show

In this chapter, you:

- Print and use handouts
- Send your presentation to Microsoft Word
- Use the PowerPoint viewer
- Learn professional presentation skills
- Control your slide show
- Use the Meeting Minder
- Let your slide show run itself

The time is at hand! You have completed your presentation, practiced and timed it, and now you're finally ready to present it to an audience. You need to decide if you want to print handouts. You may want to work on your presenting skills. Think about what will happen during the presentation—will you need to take minutes or write down action steps? This chapter discusses these issues and more.

Printing and Using Handouts

Of course, handouts are a great memory aid for your audience members, helping them remember what you said after they have gone home. In most cases, use handouts as an addition to your presentation, not as a substitute.

If you are going to make your presentation using only printed handouts, you don't need any equipment except a printer, which you almost certainly already have. You should invest in a color printer if you don't already have one. It's a shame to create color slides in PowerPoint and then print them in black and white.

Professional Pointer

Don't give handouts to your audience during your presentation, unless necessary (perhaps you're giving a new employee orientation, and you need them to fill out forms). Most audiences tend to read the handouts instead of listening to you.

Even if you want to give handouts to your audience members only as take-home material, make them look as professional as possible. Your handouts will be sitting on their desks long after your voice has faded. Don't forget to package the handouts. No stapled pages, please! Provide a pocket or binder folder at the very least.

PowerPoint lets you print your presentation to use as handouts. When you print handouts for your audience, you are simply giving them a copy of your presentation, minus the animation and transition effects. You may also want to print handouts simply to show your colleagues and supervisors. To format your handouts, use the handout master. Don't forget that you can add a logo or other graphics to the handout master.

Cross-Reference: See Chapter 7 for an explanation of the handout master.

Once you have formatted your handouts, click the Close button on the Master toolbar. You are now ready to print. Follow these steps:

1. If you wish to change the orientation of the page for printing, choose File | Page Setup. Under Notes, Handouts & Outline, choose Landscape or Portrait. Click OK.

2. Choose File | Print.

3. In the Print What drop-down list, choose Handouts.

New in 2000: You now have more options for formatting the number of slides per page and can choose a horizontal or vertical order for your slides.

4. If you created a handout master, PowerPoint sets the Slides per Page drop-down box accordingly, but if you change your mind, you can change the setting here.

5. If you choose four or more slides per page, choose Horizontal or Vertical to specify the order that PowerPoint places the slides on the page. The dialog box provides a diagram to show you the results of your choice.

6. If you don't have a color printer, choose grayscale to optimize the look of your color slides for your printer.

7. If you wish, uncheck Frame slides to remove the border around the slides. (The dialog box diagram does not display the result of this choice.)

8. Click OK.

Sending the Presentation to Microsoft Word

You may feel that printing handouts does not provide you with enough options. Perhaps you want to provide more information than you can fit using the handout master. For example, you may want to add supporting documentation or include references to the sources of your material. Perhaps you want your audience to take home only the text outline. For whatever reason, you should consider sending the presentation to Microsoft Word. In Word, you can make changes, additions, or deletions. You can also format the text differently. PowerPoint offers a number of options for sending your presentation to Word. Here's how:

1. Choose File | Send To | Microsoft Word. PowerPoint opens the Write-Up dialog box, shown in Figure 16-1.

2. Choose one of the options. The options that include notes with the slides print the contents of your notes pane. Most of your notes may be for your eyes only. However, remember that you can change the contents of these notes once you have sent them to Word. For example, you could replace your notes with supporting information you would like your audience to take home.

3. At the bottom of the dialog box, choose to either paste or paste link the slides. If you paste link the slides, the Word document is updated whenever you make changes in your presentation and then open the Word document. If you are sending your presentation to Word to print handouts for a one-time presentation, you don't need to link the slides.

4. Click OK.

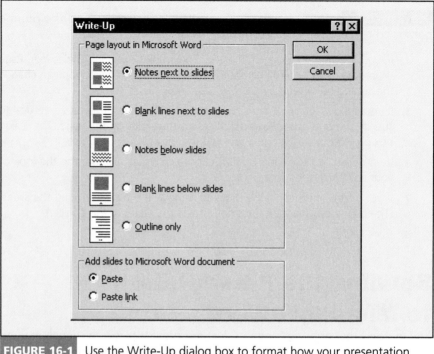

FIGURE 16-1 Use the Write-Up dialog box to format how your presentation appears in Microsoft Word

Microsoft Word opens with your presentation in the format you specified. It's a good idea to save the document before making further changes.

Once you have created your file in Word, you can use Word's features to edit the text as you wish. Here are some ideas for additions to your handouts:

Professional Pointer

Use handouts as you would a follow-up call—to make sure that your audience understands and remembers your message.

- Thank your audience for attending.
- Tell your audience where they can contact you if they have any questions or want further information.
- Offer access information for Web sites and other resources where audience members can obtain further information.
- Add supporting data such as a price list, delivery schedule, your resume, your company's history and accomplishments, and so on.
- Offer your audience a means of providing feedback on your presentation.

Using PowerPoint Viewer

PowerPoint Viewer is a program that can run a slide show on a computer that doesn't have PowerPoint. PowerPoint Viewer is an essential part of the road warrior's equipment. While you are on the road, your computer's hard drive may crash. If you have your presentation and PowerPoint Viewer on a removable storage medium (such as a ZIP drive), you can still show your presentation on any available computer. In another scenario, your client might tell you that there is no time for a presentation or you may not be planning to show a slide show at all. However, if you have Viewer and a presentation with you, you can still show your presentation if the opportunity arises.

The Pack and Go Wizard includes a step to pack PowerPoint Viewer along with your presentation.

If you installed PowerPoint Viewer when you installed Microsoft Office, you should find it in the Program Files\Microsoft Office\Office\Xlators folder. The filename is ppview32.exe, but Viewer requires several DLL files as well. If you can't find Viewer, you can add it using Setup or copy the files in the PFiles\MSOffice\Office\Xlators folder on the Microsoft Office CD-ROM to the folder previously mentioned on your hard drive. PowerPoint Viewer is free and can be distributed with no license required. For example, you can send it to a client along with a presentation. You can also download Viewer from the PowerPoint Web site at **www.microsoft.com/office/powerpoint/default.htm**. You can view not only PowerPoint 2000 presentations but PowerPoint 97 and 95 presentations with Viewer. It also works with presentations created on a Macintosh. However, PowerPoint Viewer does not yet support some PowerPoint 2000 features, such as picture bullets and automatic numbers.

Tip: If you use Viewer often, create a shortcut on your desktop. Right-click the file and choose Create Shortcut. Then drag the shortcut to your desktop and rename it.

Presenting a Slide Show with PowerPoint Viewer

To start PowerPoint Viewer, locate ppview32.exe in the Program Files\Microsoft Office\Office\Xlators folder. Double-click the folder to start Viewer, shown in Figure 16-2.

While PowerPoint Viewer doesn't offer as many controls as PowerPoint, you can click Options to open the Options dialog box shown here. You have the following options:

- By default, Viewer uses the settings saved with the presentation, but you can choose to override those settings.

- If you override the presentation settings, you can loop continuously until you press ESC, show the presentation without narrations, and show the presentation without animation.

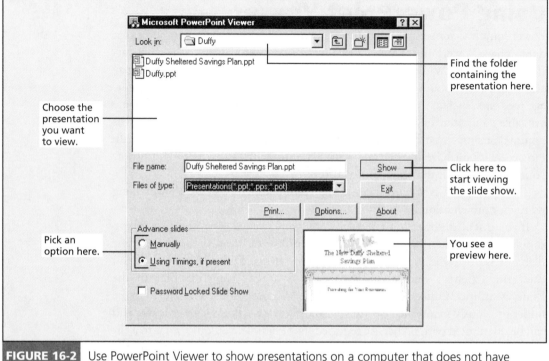

Choose the presentation you want to view.

Find the folder containing the presentation here.

Click here to start viewing the slide show.

Pick an option here.

You see a preview here.

FIGURE 16-2 Use PowerPoint Viewer to show presentations on a computer that does not have PowerPoint installed

- You can disable the menu that appears when you right-click during a slide show. (You might want to do this for a slide show that is controlled by your viewers at a kiosk or employee information center.) You can also disable the menu button that you click to display the menu.

- You can end with a black slide—to avoid returning to Viewer's dialog box and your Windows desktop by accident and showing your audience the mess you have there.

When you have finished your settings, click OK.

If you think you may show your presentation using PowerPoint Viewer, practice presenting using PowerPoint Viewer. Make sure you can easily open Viewer—you don't want to have to fuss to find it in front of your audience. Check that the closing of your slide show is smooth and professional so that your audience doesn't see the mechanics behind the magic.

Presenting Slide Shows from a Play List

You may sometimes be in a situation where you want to show several presentations at a time. You might create a presentation for each product you sell and want to put several together end-to-end. If you are an educator, you might have a presentation for each topic you want to cover so that you can easily mix and match them to suit the time available and the current curriculum.

PowerPoint Viewer can display presentations from a play list, which is a simple text file that lists the presentations you want to show. Using a play list is extremely simple:

1. Open Notepad or a new document in any word processing application. To open Notepad, choose Start | Run and type **Notepad**. Click OK.

2. Type the filenames of the presentations you want to show with each presentation on a separate line. Include the filename extensions. If the filenames have spaces, enclose the entire filename in quotation marks. If the presentations are not all in the same folder, include the entire path to the presentation. Here you see a sample play list:

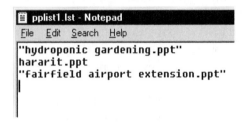

3. Save the file as a text file with a filename extension of .lst. If you use a word processing application instead of Notepad, make sure to change the file type to Text Only using the Save as Type drop-down list. If all your presentations are in the same folder and you did not include complete paths, save the file in the same folder as your presentations.

4. Close Notepad or your word processing application.

5. Start PowerPoint Viewer.

6. From the Files of Type drop-down list, choose Playlists (*.lst).

7. Navigate to your play list and choose it.

8. Click Show.

You can continue to show the entire list over and over by choosing Options, choosing Override saved settings, and checking the Loop Continuously Until 'Esc' check box.

Learning Professional Presentation Skills

Most of the skills required for an effective presentation apply whether you use PowerPoint, paper handouts, or no visual aids at all. These skills are based on the relationship you create with your audience. A successful presentation includes the following characteristics:

- The audience has a need—for information, for a product, for training, and so on.
- Your presentation meets the audience's need.
- The audience understands and appreciates how your presentation meets its need.

As you can see, in order to create an effective presentation, you need to know what your audience needs. You also need to meet that need in a way that your audience can understand and appreciate.

Sometimes, you are the one who determines your audience's needs. If you are a sales manager presenting your company's latest products to your sales representatives, you have decided that your audience needs to know your company's latest products. All you need to do is present in a way that your sales representatives can understand and appreciate. The information you present in a clear manner provides the understanding. The excitement you generate helps your audience appreciate your message.

In many instances, however, you need to do some research to determine your audience's needs and level of understanding. If you are speaking to a large group, you should try to find out from the group's organizers something about the audience members. How much do they already know about the topic? What is their level of education and expertise? Why are they attending? The answers to these questions can help you avoid a presentation that is either too simplistic or too advanced for your audience, or one that misses the mark entirely.

Setting Up the Room and Checking Your Equipment

One of the best ways to prepare for a presentation is to get a good night's sleep the night before. Feeling fresh and rested makes you appear brighter, happier, and more enthusiastic.

If you're nervous, settle down just before your presentation. If you know how to meditate, do so. If not, sit quietly for a few minutes with your eyes closed. Get up slowly and then start moving about and making preparations to gear up for the presentation.

Professional speakers generally plan to arrive about two hours early to check out the room and their equipment, make any necessary adjustments, and do a dry-run of their presentation. If you find that the room doesn't have enough chairs, how long will it take to get them? Will you have to help carry them in and set them up yourself? If so, will that leave you enough time to check out your equipment? (This is the stuff that nightmares are born of.) Don't be afraid to ask others for help setting up. Often this allows others to feel part of the event, and it can allow you more time to focus on the presentation as a whole.

Sometimes, you have no control over a room. If you are presenting in a potential client's office, you are probably not at liberty to move the furniture. When you are presenting in a larger group situation, such as in a classroom, convention center, or auditorium, you may have more leeway.

Here are some ideas for checking out a room:

- Do you feel too hot or too cold? Find the thermostat or the windows. Cooler is better than hotter.

- Does the air smell stuffy? (Or does it just smell?) Open the windows. Leave the doors open until your presentation starts.

- Do you have enough chairs? Are they comfortable? If necessary, get more chairs or move existing chairs farther apart. Hopefully, you won't have to replace all of the chairs, but an uncomfortable audience has a hard time appreciating anything.

- Can people get to the chairs? Perhaps the rows are too close together. A center aisle can help if the rows are too long.

- Does everyone have an unobstructed view of your screen? If the room has columns, move the chairs that are behind them.

- Will latecomers have to pass between you and your audience? Perhaps you can create an aisle going toward the back of the room.

- If you will use a microphone, is it working? How do you turn it on and off? Can you remove it from the podium or its stand if you want to walk around? Try it out before the audience arrives to make sure it doesn't squeal. If you have a pin-on mike, make sure you can put it on and take it off easily.

- Where are the lights? If you need to turn down the lights to start your slide show, can you do so without walking to the back of the room or asking an audience member to do it for you? (A well-designed presentation room should have light controls at the podium, but you might not be in a well-designed presentation room.)

> ## Professional Pointer
>
> When you arrive, find out quickly who is available and has the knowledge to help you with room and equipment problems. In a hotel, it is usually easy to get help, especially if you're willing to offer a tip. Try to avoid having to run around for half an hour looking for the right person later on.

Once you have checked out the room, set up your equipment. Set up your slide show as you want it to appear when your audience walks in. If you want to speak a while before turning on the slide show, open the presentation and simply turn off the projector or toggle off its image. Then you can start your slide show with one simple motion.

Now, with the slide show displayed, walk to the back of the room and see if you can read the text. Make sure the slide looks straight and centered on the screen. Where is the room's natural focus of attention? Based on that analysis, decide where you will stand and where you will walk. If there is a podium and you want to use it, make sure it doesn't hide you too much. Otherwise, ask to have it removed. Practice using your remote mouse or laser pointer so you can stand in front of the audience and still see your slide show from your computer screen.

Finally, practice using every piece of equipment you have, in every possible circumstance. Practice going back one slide. Practice using your hyperlinks and action buttons. If you are using equipment provided by the facility, find out where the spare bulbs and batteries are kept, who can replace them, and how you can contact that person at a moment's notice.

When you are done, you can heave a sigh of relief. While the unexpected can always happen, at least you did everything you could to ensure a problem-free presentation.

Speaking in Front of a Group

Many people are afraid of speaking in front of a group. While being 150 percent prepared helps, the truth is that once you strike up a relationship with your audience, much of your fear will dissipate. An actor cannot create a relationship with his or her audience in advance because the requirement of acting is to stay in character, but you have a lot more control over the situation when you present. Here are some tips:

- *Chat with audience members as they come in to the room.* Smile and introduce yourself. If they traveled, ask them how their trip was. Say anything to start up a brief conversation. You may even be able to use this opportunity to find out more about your audience.

- *Start your presentation with some humor, a quotation, or a personal experience.* This personal touch creates a pleasant relationship between you and your audience immediately (unless your jokes aren't funny or are in bad taste).

- *Dress conservatively.* You can never go wrong and will feel more comfortable.

- *Don't hide behind a podium or your computer.* Face your audience. If you are going to turn down the lights, start talking before you do so to let the audience see your face and get to know you.

- *Look at one or two individuals in more detail.* Pick a person to talk to, then another, and so on, so that you can focus on something. You will also get some feedback during your presentation—such as someone sleeping! You should be able to give your presentation with only occasional glances at your slides or notes.

- *Don't mumble.* Express your enthusiasm for your topic. It's infectious.

Remember, your audience members are just people, like you. They probably empathize with you. They want you to succeed, since they want to learn something. So they're with you, not against you. Just start!

Coping with Disasters

Sometimes a disaster occurs. Your computer crashes or the projector dies. You leave your projector on the plane. You rip your sleeve. Well, anything *can* happen.

For technological mishaps, always come with an alternative—overhead transparencies if you will have an overhead projector available, or simple paper handouts. Bring a change of clothes. Make sure you have a comb with you and any other personal articles that you might need.

Oh, and always use the bathroom before you start your presentation.

The Internet offers a number of useful Web sites for presenters. These sites offer tips and advice for everything from organizing your presentation text to standing up in front of an audience. Table 16-1 lists some Internet resources for presenters.

Name	URL and Comments
Presenting Solutions	This site includes information on LCD projectors and other equipment, tips on the art of communicating effectively, a glossary, and more at **www.presentingsolutions.com**.
Presentations magazine	*Presentations* magazine offers lots of resources, including articles from past issues. From the home page, click Delivering for a list of articles on delivering presentations. At **www.presentations.com**.
Presenters Online	This Web site is all about presenting and offers loads of articles and tips for presenters at **www.presentersonline.com**.
3M Meeting Network	Although run by 3M, there's lots of general information here. Click on Presentations, then Delivering Presentations, for a list of articles. At **www.3m.com/meetingnetwork**.
TrainingSuperSite	For training and human resources professionals, this huge Web site offers publications, training materials; a superstore where you can buy books, tapes, and other training products, and connections to listservs and discussion groups. At **www.trainingsupersite.com**.
IAPP (International Association of Presentation Professionals)	You can read past newsletters and joint forums and bulletin boards, as well as find out about their next conference, at **www.iapp.org**.
Training Forum	This Web site offers information on training courses, a speaker's database, a huge list of seminars, conferences, and events, as well as a products listing for trainers at **www.trainingforum.com**.

TABLE 16-1   Internet Resources for Presenters

Go 10 Extra Steps When Using Computer Projection

by George Torok

LCD and DLP projectors paired with laptop computers have undeniably changed the way presentations are delivered. They encourage the use of color, photography, animation, and even three-dimensional effects. The portable and ultra portable models have led on-the-go presenters to take along their own equipment for assurance that proper equipment will be available and for ease of familiarity no matter what far-flung outpost they are visiting.

If you've recently adopted such technology, you're likely to read at least part of the user's manual to learn how to configure and adjust the system. Once you've mastered the physical connections and the software, remember to go these extra 10 steps to make presenting with computer projection smooth and comfortable for both you and your viewing audience.

1. **Check colors for accuracy.** Be aware that colors will vary among the desktop on which you design the presentation, the laptop screen, and the projection screen. If an exact color is important (for example, in a company logo), test and adjust the color in its final projection form ahead of time.

2. **Keep the colors and special effects simple.** Use no more than six colors on each side. Use slide transitions and builds to entertain without detracting from your message. A partial build, for instance, will reveal one point at a time, allowing your audience to stay right with you.

3. **Test your slides for size and readability.** Stand 6 feet away from your computer monitor. If you can read the monitor, your audience will likely be able to read the screen.

4. **Turn off all screen savers.** Remember to disable the screen savers on your computer—any that are part of the computer software, plus the one that comes with the laptop. You would be embarrassed if you were talking about important points on the screen only to realize your audience is staring at flying toasters. It is even worse should your energy saver kick in and shut down the whole presentation.

5. **Learn how to use the toggle switch.** Find the switch that shows the image on both the computer and projection screens. Often the toggle is a function key; it controls whether your laptop or your projector or both are on (showing an image). You want both to be on so you can look at the laptop while the audience watches the same image behind you on the screen.

6. **Arrive early and test everything.** Reread this line—again!

7. **Stand on the left as the audience sees you.** Because in English we read from left to right, if you stand on the right side, attendees' eyes will have to make too many movements to read your slides and watch you. If you stand to the audience members' left, however, they can look at you, following your gestures to the screen—reading left to right—then they return their eyes to you. If you present using Hebrew or other languages that are read right to left, reverse the approach, and stand to the audience's right side of the screen.

8. **You are the show.** Be heard and be seen. Too many people hide in the dark behind the laptop. You should stand away from the computer and in the light. Use a remote mouse so you can walk away from the computer. Arrange the lightning in the room so you are in the light while the screen is dark. To do this well, you might even need to unscrew some of the lightbulbs.

9. **Motion attracts people's eyes.** Gesture to the screen when you want audience members to look there. Use moving text to grab their attention. Stand still when you want them to focus on the screen. Then move when you want to capture their attention again.

10. **Murphy loves applying his law to technology.** Any little thing might go wrong, so be ready to give your presentation *without* the hardware. If your presentation absolutely must be given by computer projection, have a backup system. Be prepared with backup files, a power source for the laptop and projector, and batteries for your remote mouse.

George Torok is licensed by Peter urs Bender to deliver keynotes and seminars on power presentations. He specializes in helping sales and marketing people present themselves effectively. He is based in Burlington, Ontario, Canada and can be reached at 905-335-1997. He also hosts a weekly radio show, "Business in Motion."

Controlling Your Slide Show

As mentioned earlier, you should display the first slide on the screen in slide show view before your audience arrives. You can turn off the projector or the switch that projects to the screen before you start, if you wish. If you cannot set up in advance, as when you present in someone else's office, you can open the presentation and switch to slide show view before turning the monitor around for others to see. The general guideline is to create a clean start.

Once you start, simply click the remote mouse to move from slide to slide.

For more controls, you use the slide show view menu. As you move the mouse around, the menu button shown here appears at the lower-left corner of the screen. Click this button to open the slide show shortcut menu shown here:

If you don't see the menu button, right-click anywhere on the screen to open the same menu. You should be very familiar with this menu so that you can quickly navigate anywhere in your slide show. Here are your options on this menu:

- **Next**   Moves you to the next slide. Of course, you can also click the mouse to move to the same slide unless you have a complex build, in which case you might need several clicks.

- **Previous**   Moves you to the previous slide.

- **Go**   Opens a submenu with its own submenus. You have four options. Choose Slide Navigator to open the Slide Navigator dialog box, shown in Figure 16-3. You can navigate to any slide. If your presentation has a custom show, you can choose that show and then navigate to any slide in that custom show. Choose By Title to open a menu listing every slide by number and title. You can display any slide in your presentation most quickly using this option. If you have a custom show, choose Custom Show to choose from a list

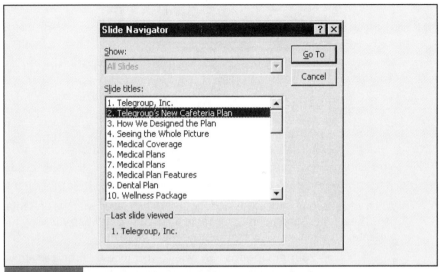

The Slide Navigator lets you display any slide in the current presentation as well as any slide in a custom show

of custom shows you have defined, as shown here. Choose Previously Viewed to view the last viewed slide.

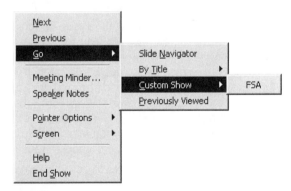

Cross-Reference: See Chapter 15 for details on creating a custom show.

- **Meeting Minder**   Takes you to the Meeting Minder, discussed later in this chapter.
- **Speaker Notes**   Opens the Speaker Notes dialog box, shown next, enabling you to add notes during the presentation.

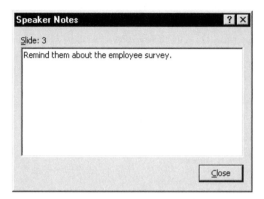

When you are done, click Close, and these notes are saved with the presentation. These notes subsequently appear in the notes pane when you view the presentation using any view that displays the notes pane.

Professional Pointer

You can use the Speaker Notes box to add speaker notes that occur to you while you are rehearsing your presentation.

- **Pointer Options**   By default, your mouse cursor is an arrow. However, you can change your cursor to a pen and temporarily annotate your slides, as explained later in this chapter. You can also hide the arrow by choosing Hidden from the Pointer Options submenu. Hiding the arrow removes any distraction for your audience. All they see is your slide show. To use the slide show shortcut menu with the pointer hidden, you need to right-click. (The cursor reappears on the menu so you can choose menu items.) You can also change the pen color.

- **Screen**   Offers three suboptions. Use the Pause option to pause a slide show that uses timings that you have set. You can then take questions, for example. When you want to resume, choose Resume from the Screen submenu. Choose Black Screen to display a black screen. If you don't want to leave the last slide on the screen at the end of your slide show, a black screen is an alternative to returning to the PowerPoint screen. Returning to your application looks unprofessional because your audience sees the nuts and bolts behind the presentation. If you have annotated a slide and want to continue discussing the slide without all those marks, choose Erase Pen.

Tip: If your mouse dies, you won't be able to use it to open the Help screen. Press F1 instead to get the same screen.

- **Help**   Hopefully, you don't need to use this option during a slide show. After all, you are supposed to come across as knowledgeable about PowerPoint during a slide show. However, this option can be a lifesaver if your remote mouse dies. PowerPoint displays a list of keyboard shortcuts (see Table 16-2) that you can use to navigate through your presentation. Click OK to close the Help screen.

- **End Show**   Choose this option to immediately end the show. You can also press ESC.

Table 16-2 lists the many keyboard shortcuts that you can use if your mouse fails or if you like to use the keyboard. In general, these shortcuts should be used only in an emergency, since they require you to take your attention away from your audience.

Professional Pointer

Copy this chart and always carry it with you in case of an equipment failure.

Marking Slides as You Present

As a presenter, you have several techniques for focusing the audience on a specific item. The simplest is to use words, for example, "Look at the sales in the

Shortcut	Result
N, ENTER, PAGE DOWN, RIGHT ARROW, DOWN ARROW, or SPACEBAR	Advance to the next slide or perform the next animation build
P, PAGE UP, LEFT ARROW, UP ARROW, or BACKSPACE	Return to the previous slide or perform the previous animation build
Any slide number-ENTER	Go to that slide number
B or .	Display a black screen or return to the slide show from a black screen
W or ,	Display a white screen or return to the slide show from a white screen
S or +	Pause or restart an automatic slide show
ESC, CTRL-BREAK, or -	End a slide show
E	Erase existing annotations
H	Go to the next hidden slide
T	Set new timings (use while rehearsing)
O	Use original timings (use while rehearsing)
Both mouse buttons for two seconds	Return to the first slide (unfortunately hearing an error bell at the same time)
CTRL-P	Redisplay hidden pointer; change the pointer to a pen
CTRL-A	Redisplay hidden pointer; change the pointer to an arrow
CTRL-H	Hide the pointer and menu icon immediately
CTRL-U	Hide the pointer and menu icon in 15 seconds (or less)
SHIFT-F10 (or right-click)	Display the shortcut menu
TAB	Go to the first or next hyperlink on a slide
SHIFT-TAB	Go to the last or previous hyperlink on a slide
ENTER while a hyperlink is selected	Perform the "mouse click" action of the hyperlink
SHIFT-ENTER while a hyperlink is selected	Perform the "mouse over" action of the hyperlink

TABLE 16-2 Slide Show View Keyboard Shortcuts

Tip: Practice using your laser pointer. Don't move the laser too quickly; use a support such as the podium to steady your hand; after illustrating a point, turn the laser off; and do not flash the laser around the room, because your audience will follow the movement.

Professional Pointer

Use annotation in a more informal situation, or when you are getting feedback from the audience. Annotation is great for brainstorming sessions. With a buttoned-down audience or in a formal presentation, use a laser pointer.

Northeast Division for last year." However, can you be sure that everyone in your audience has found the correct bar in your chart?

Many presenters use a pointer—either the old-fashioned wooden kind or an up-to-date laser one. A laser pointer is a necessity, of course, if you can't reach the screen.

PowerPoint offers the ability to annotate a slide directly. For example, you can circle a word or draw an arrow to that bar on your chart. The advantage of using annotation is that the audience can't miss it. The results are striking and immediate. The disadvantage is that annotation sometimes looks messy; with a mouse, you don't have much control over your circles and arrows.

Figure 16-4 shows how you can use annotation effectively—and ineffectively. To view these slides in color, refer to numbers 140 and 141 in the Slide Gallery.

To annotate a slide, you need to change the pointer from its default arrow to a pen. If you are close enough to the keyboard, press CTRL-P because it is less distracting to your audience. Otherwise, right-click to open the slide show menu and choose Pointer Options | Pen. The cursor now looks like a pen. To draw, move the cursor to where you want to start and hold down the mouse button as you move the mouse. Release the mouse button to stop drawing.

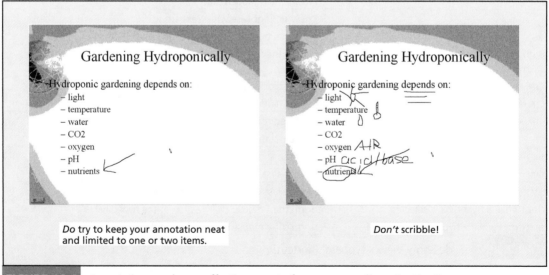

Do try to keep your annotation neat and limited to one or two items.

Don't scribble!

FIGURE 16-4   Annotation can be an effective way to focus your audience's attention on part of a slide

You can't leave the mouse cursor as a pen if you want to use the mouse to navigate through your slide show. If you try to click the mouse button, you just keep getting little dots on your screen! To change the cursor back to an arrow, choose Pointer Options | Arrow or CTRL-A. If you want to keep the pen and can use the keyboard, you can use N, ENTER, PAGE DOWN, RIGHT ARROW, DOWN ARROW, or SPACEBAR to navigate through your slide show.

Tip: If you present using an online meeting, participants can also use the pen. The annotations are visible to all participants. See Chapter 12 for more information.

As mentioned earlier, you can hide the mouse cursor, whether it is an arrow or a pen. From the slide show menu, choose Pointer Options | Hidden.

Use the slide show menu to control the annotation color. Often the default black color doesn't contrast clearly against your slide. Choose Pointer Options | Pen Color, as shown here:

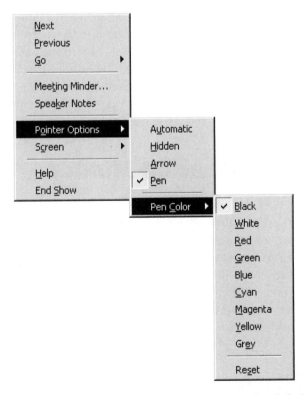

Choose Pointer Options | Pen Color | Reset to return to the default pen color.

You can also preset the pen color before starting your slide show. Choose Slide Show | Set Up Show. From the Pen color drop-down box, choose the color you want to use. Choose More Colors to open the Colors dialog box for a wider range of color choices.

Using Hyperlinks and Action Buttons

If you have created hyperlinks and action buttons to help you navigate through a presentation, now is the time you get to use them. While most hyperlinks and action buttons work with a mouse click, some may be set to work when you pass the mouse cursor over them. Watch out that you don't end up somewhere else by mistake!

You also need to be careful that you don't get lost! It can be embarrassing if you travel all over the place and forget where you left off.

What you need is a compass. As discussed in Chapter 11, each hyperlink and action button should provide a return trip mechanism, but you need to make sure you know what it is, because not all hyperlinks and action buttons are obvious. In addition, you can forget that an object on your screen is a hyperlink or action button, especially if you have camouflaged it.

Create a list of hyperlinks to help you out or include the information in your speaker notes. List the location of the hyperlink or action button, what it looks like (if necessary), where it goes to, and how to get back. If you have action buttons that use a mouse over effect, be sure to note it. Make sure to take the list with you when you present, but just as important, become very familiar with the list so that you don't need to refer to it except in a rare lapse of memory. The more complex your slide show, the more you need to know its myriad paths.

Using the Meeting Minder for Expert Follow-Up

The Meeting Minder is a PowerPoint feature to help you take minutes and create a list of action steps during a presentation. Obviously, the Meeting Minder is not suitable for a formal presentation environment where you are standing up and presenting before a large audience. However, it is ideal for a meeting or brainstorming situation. You may even want to use it when presenting to clients—your clients may appreciate seeing that you took note of their comments.

To open the Meeting Minder, use the slide show menu and choose Meeting Minder.

Taking Minutes

The Meeting Minder has two tabs. Use the Meeting Minutes tab, shown in Figure 16-5, to take minutes or any type of notes you wish. These notes are not associated with any individual slide but with the presentation as a whole. Therefore, you see the same minutes wherever you open the Meeting Minder. You can add some notes during slide 1 and then add to them on slide 5. You can also

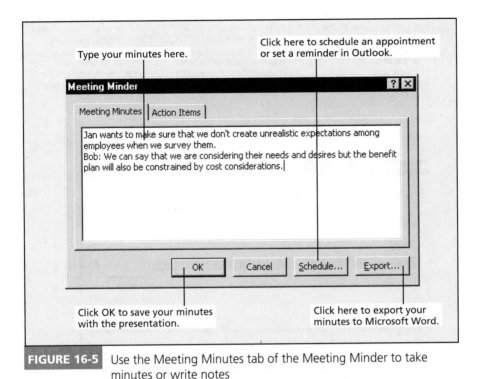

Type your minutes here.

Click here to schedule an appointment or set a reminder in Outlook.

Meeting Minder   ? ☒

Meeting Minutes | Action Items

Jan wants to make sure that we don't create unrealistic expectations among employees when we survey them.
Bob: We can say that we are considering their needs and desires but the benefit plan will also be constrained by cost considerations.|

OK   Cancel   Schedule...   Export...

Click OK to save your minutes with the presentation.

Click here to export your minutes to Microsoft Word.

FIGURE 16-5   Use the Meeting Minutes tab of the Meeting Minder to take minutes or write notes

schedule an appointment in Outlook or export your notes to either Outlook or Word.

If you simply click OK and don't export your minutes, you can view them later by entering slide show view and opening the Meeting Minder. Look for number 142 in the Slide Gallery to see how the Meeting Minder looks on a slide during a presentation.

When you export your minutes to Word, the Meeting Minder immediately opens a Word document and places your minutes in the document. This document is temporary, so you must save it if you want to keep it.

Creating an Action List

If you would like to structure your notes into action steps, you can use the Action Items tab, shown in Figure 16-6. Number 143 in the Slide Gallery shows how the Action Items tab looks on a slide during a presentation. As you can with minutes, you can start an action list at any time during a slide show and add to it while you display any slide. You can export these action steps to your task list in Microsoft Outlook. When you use the Action Items tab, PowerPoint automatically creates a new slide at the end of your presentation containing your action steps plus any minutes you have written.

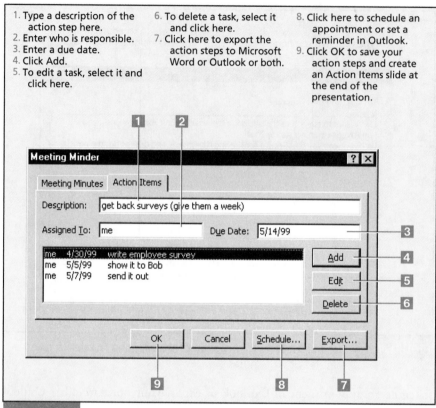

1. Type a description of the action step here.
2. Enter who is responsible.
3. Enter a due date.
4. Click Add.
5. To edit a task, select it and click here.
6. To delete a task, select it and click here.
7. Click here to export the action steps to Microsoft Word or Outlook or both.
8. Click here to schedule an appointment or set a reminder in Outlook.
9. Click OK to save your action steps and create an Action Items slide at the end of the presentation.

FIGURE 16-6 The Action Items tab lets you create action steps based on your presentation

Tasks exported to Outlook are added to the Outlook task list. Task exported to Word are handled as just previously explained for minutes. After your presentation, you can format and save this Word document for later reference. Figure 16-7 shows an action items slide created using the Meeting Minder. Don't expect great formatting. Use this slide for informal, in-house meetings or for your own use. To view it in color, refer to number 144 in the Slide Gallery.

Cross-Reference: For details on setting up a presentation to run unattended, see Chapter 15.

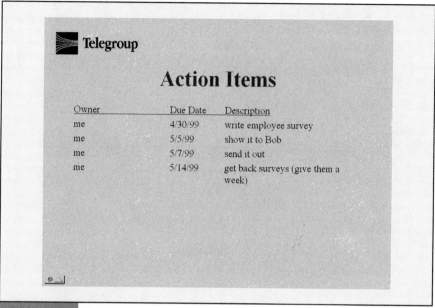

The Action Items tab of the Meeting Minder automatically adds a slide to the end of your presentation listing the action steps you have created

Professional Skills Summary

In this chapter, you saw how to create and use handouts for maximum effect with your presentation. This chapter also explained how to present a slide show using PowerPoint Viewer. A good part of this chapter covered the basics of professional presentation skills—these are skills that you can use whether or not you are showing a PowerPoint presentation.

Once you start presenting, PowerPoint offers a number of controls that let you navigate wherever your presentation might lead—even if off the beaten, linear track. You can also use any hyperlinks or action buttons that you have created.

To keep track of remarks and ideas that arise during a presentation, use the Meeting Minder to take minutes and create an action list.

You now have the knowledge you need to create and give professional presentations. I wish you all success. Enjoy!

Index

NOTE: Boldfaced references to slides (for example, **slide 1**) indicate color slides in the Slide Gallery sections.